Sunset
California
TRAVEL GUIDE

RICHARD ROWAN

Colorful poppies brighten Carmel Mission courtyard

By the Editors of Sunset Books and Sunset Magazine

LANE PUBLISHING CO.
Menlo Park, California

Mickey leads Disneyland parade down Main Street

DISNEYLAND

Discover the world of California

From sun-drenched beaches to snow-clad mountains, California encompasses a wealth of scenic beauty and man-made attractions. To offer visitors a complete look at this year-round vacationland, Sunset Books has combined its guides to the state's northern and southern regions into one comprehensive volume.

Front cover: *California meets the Pacific along the Big Sur coastline. Photography by Jeff Gnass.* ***Back cover:*** *Photography by Craig Aurness (top) and Sea World (bottom).*

Sunset Books
Editor: David E. Clark
Managing Editor: Elizabeth L. Hogan

Second printing April 1987

C O N T E N T S

Northern California Travel Guide

A complete tour of the state's northern
reaches, from towering redwoods
and scenic shoreline to lush vineyards,
captivating ghost towns, and
majestic mountains. Sample the history of
Monterey, the charm of Carmel, and the magic of
San Francisco.

Southern California Travel Guide

A close look at the Southland's
myriad attractions—entertainment
meccas, historic cities, palm-
filled desert resorts, and pine-clad
mountain retreats. Special features focus on
studio tours, spa vacations,
boat cruises, and golfing trips.

Sunset

Northern California
TRAVEL GUIDE

By the Editors of
Sunset Books and Sunset Magazine

Lane Publishing Co. • Menlo Park, California

Hours, admission fees, prices, telephone numbers, and highway designations in this book are accurate as of the time this edition went to press.

Maps have been provided in each chapter for the special purpose of highlighting significant regions, routes, or attractions in the area. Check automobile clubs, insurance agencies, chambers of commerce, or visitors bureaus in major cities for detailed maps of Northern California.

Book Editors: Barbara J. Braasch
Julie Anne Gold

Design: Cynthia Hanson

Cartography: Ted Martine

Illustrations: Susan Jaekel

Cover: Mendocino's graceful Victorian architecture faces grassy headlands, steep bluffs, and secluded coves at mouth of Big River. Photographed by Ells Marugg.

Thanks . . .
to the many people and organizations who assisted in the preparation of this travel guide. Special appreciation goes to city and county visitors bureaus and chambers of commerce, as well as other visitor service agencies throughout the Northern California area.

Photographers

Craig Aurness: 3. **Barbara J. Braasch:** 94 top left. **Ron Botier:** 34, 63, 67 top, 78, 83 bottom. **William Carter:** 94 top right, 99 bottom. **Glenn Christiansen:** 22 bottom, 42 bottom. **Ed Cooper:** 91 bottom. **Lee Foster:** 39 top, 107. **Gerald R. Fredrick:** 22 top, 30 bottom, 39 bottom, 47 top left, 102 top, 118. **Gerald L. French:** 55 bottom right, 91 top right. **Peter Fronk:** 27 bottom. **Bruce Hayes:** 19 top, 70 top left. **René Klein:** 102 bottom left. **Russell Lamb:** 75 bottom left. **Hal Lauritzen:** 6 top right, 19 bottom right. **Luther Linkhart:** 30 top, 115 top left. **Jack McDowell:** 14 bottom right, 47 bottom, 70 top right, 94 bottom, 99 top, 115 top right. **Ells Marugg:** 70 bottom, 75 top. **Chuck O'Rear:** 126 all. **Norman Plate:** 55 top. **John Reginato:** 115 bottom. **Dick Rowan:** 50, 58 bottom, 102 bottom right. **Carol Simowitz:** 14 bottom left, 67 bottom. **Ted Streshinsky:** 6 bottom, 19 bottom left, 42 top, 55 bottom left, 58 top, 83 top, 86, 91 top left, 110, 123. **Tom Tracy:** 11, 14 top, 27 top, 47 top right, 75 bottom right. **Phillip Wallick:** 6 top left.

Sunset Books
Editor, David E. Clark
Managing Editor, Elizabeth L. Hogan

Sixth printing April 1987
(Updated 1986)

Contents

*SHIP SLIPS into San Francisco Bay under
fog-draped Golden Gate Bridge.*

Special Features

Crescent City

REDWOOD NATIONAL PARK

Yreka

To Portland

97

OREGON
CALIFORNIA

Lava Beds National Monument

To Klamath Falls

Goose Lake

To Burns

Weed

CASCADE RANGE

Mt. Shasta

89

139

Alturas

Clair Engle Lake

5

299

139

Eureka

Lake Shasta

395

COAST RANGE

Redding

44

44

Eagle Lake

101

Red Bluff

36

LASSEN VOLCANIC NATIONAL PARK

36

Susanville

Sacramento River

Lake Almanor

89

Fort Bragg

Oroville Reservoir

Mendocino

49

SIERRA

89

Reno

1

80

Truckee

Ukiah

175

Clear Lake

5

Lake Tahoe

89

Placerville

50

South Lake Tahoe

101

29

Lake Berryessa

NEVADA

395

Santa Rosa

Napa

80

Sacramento

88

49

Pt. Reyes National Seashore

1

San Francisco

Oakland

580

Stockton

108

Sonora

YOSEMITE NATIONAL PARK

Mono Lake

17

108

120

49

San Jose

Modesto

Santa Cruz

101

COAST

Merced

140

Monterey Bay

Salinas

41

Monterey

Fresno

Pinnacles National Monument

RANGE

1

San Simeon

101

99

To Santa Barbara

To Los Angeles

To Bakersfield

PACIFIC OCEAN

N

Northern California

Scale in Miles

0   20   40   60

Scale in Kilometers

0   20   40   60

Northern California

Areas of Interest

Redwood National Park—Cathedral-like coast redwoods *(Sequoia sempervirens)* blanket 46-mile stretch of Northern California coast. Three state parks fall within the national park boundary, offering camping, recreational facilities.

Mount Shasta—Mountain's sheer size dominates landscape in California's far north. Glaciers, pristine lakes, wide valleys, and vibrant wildflowers lure ambitious climbers.

Lassen Volcanic National Park—Steaming streams, bubbling mudholes, sulphur smells, and hissing vents against the backdrop of forested slopes, clear lakes, and steep peaks make Lassen one of country's showiest thermal areas.

Mendocino—New England architecture characterizes this former lumbering port along the coast north of San Francisco; at grassy headlands, enjoy walking, fishing, wave-watching.

Lake Tahoe—Second highest lake in the world straddles California-Nevada border; area provides year-round playground, with California's finest winter skiing and summer boating.

Sacramento—California's capital city, once known for lusty gold rush life, dominates agriculturally rich valley. Tour State Capitol, Capitol Park, historic Old Sacramento; or leisurely cruise the Delta on a houseboat. Sacramento is a gateway to Sierra Nevada, Lake Tahoe, and Gold Country.

Napa Valley—Best known of wine country valleys north of San Francisco. Tour and taste at wineries dotting State Highway 29 near St. Helena. Picturesque country roads, quaint towns and missions, historic

museums, and mineral health spas attract teetotaling travelers as well as wine enthusiasts.

Point Reyes National Seashore—Marin County's long, lonely, windswept beaches contrast with grassy, forested slopes; at the visitor center, explore Morgan horse ranch, blacksmith shop, and earthquake trail.

San Francisco—Sparkling city by the bay fulfills every visitor's fantasy. Ride cable cars, stroll through Fisherman's Wharf and Ghirardelli Square, relax in Golden Gate Park, explore mysterious Chinatown, cruise bay to Alcatraz or Angel Island, or just drink in breathtaking views from city's famous hills and bridges.

Yosemite National Park—Here nature's spectacular magic shows off on a grand scale; park boasts cascading waterfalls, ice-carved granite cliffs, far-reaching meadows, and groves of massive sequoias.

Monterey Peninsula—State Highway 1 dips, twists, climbs, and falls between Santa Lucia Mountains and pounding Pacific Ocean on its way to Big Sur. Explore Monterey's Cannery Row and Fisherman's Wharf; sample 17-Mile Drive's spectacular scenery and golf courses; tour Carmel's delightful shops.

Pinnacles National Monument—Spires and crags stretch 1,200 feet above canyon floors at Pinnacles, southeast of Monterey. Duck, crawl, and squeeze through dark caves when you explore these fascinating remnants of California volcanic activity.

San Simeon—William Randolph Hearst's "castle on the hill" dominates spur of surrounding mountains. La Casa Grande tours lead you through an eclectic collection of mansions and gardens that now form a state historic monument.

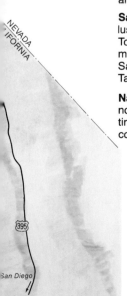

HORSE BRAKES SHARPLY
as roper settles lasso over calf's head
(below). Summer rodeo at Taylorsville
is one of Northern California's
western events, culminating in
prestigious Grand National
in San Francisco Bay Area.

BRIGHTLY COLORED SAIL (right)
catches bay breeze. In background,
San Francisco's distinctive skyline
rises dramatically from waterfront
Golden Gate National Recreation
Area to cone-shaped Transamerica
Pyramid Building.

BIKERS TOUR valley
floor (left) at Yosemite
National Park. Half
Dome, in background,
is one of park's
glacier-carved pinnacles.

"Kaleidoscopic" is the best word to describe Northern California. Vacationers can choose from a wide range of activities: hiking, camping, and fishing in the high mountains or recapturing the past at a ghost town in the Sierra foothills; beachcombing along the coast or strolling through stately redwood groves; savoring San Francisco's big-city pleasures.

This *Travel Guide to Northern California* contains information on exploring both the well-established, well-known attractions and the lesser-known but equally appealing spots.

San Francisco—famous for its bay, bridges, hills, views, waterfront, and fine food—is Northern California's biggest tourist attraction. Along with the surrounding Bay Area, this is also Northern California's largest cultural, business, and industrial center.

The state capital, Sacramento, is the main city in the agriculturally important Central Valley. Sacramento has recently renovated its downtown area, including a stellar re-creation of the Gold Rush era in Old Sacramento. To the east of the valley rises the mighty Sierra Nevada, whose western foothills hold remnants of days when gold ruled the lives of Californians.

Other popular destinations in Northern California are Sonoma, with its Spanish landmarks; the Napa Valley, with its vineyards and wineries; Monterey, with its historical buildings and waterfront; Carmel, with its quaint shops; and Mendocino, with its dramatic coast and arts and crafts atmosphere. Those who prefer to get away head for the Northern Wonderland, above Redding, where lonesome roads lead to small villages in which time seems to have stood still. The most visited spots for outdoor recreation are Lake Tahoe, Yosemite National Park, Lake Shasta, and Redwood National Park.

Land of contrast

The area covered in this book differs from the southern part of the state in climate, history, topography, and temperament. For this reason, separate books are devoted to exploring Northern California and Southern California.

The boundary line that we have used to divide the state begins at the ocean near San Simeon, continues across the Coast Range and the southern tip of the Central Valley, and then turns northward across the Sierra Nevada south of Yosemite National Park. The area south of this arbitrary dividing line is described in our companion book *Southern California Travel Guide*.

Climate & terrain

Northern California has three distinct climate zones. Coastal temperatures are mild the year around; rarely will there be extremes in temperature. Fog frequently blankets the coast during the summer, especially in the morning and evening, and in winter it rains.

As you move inland, the seasons become more pro-

Discover in these pages the diverse attractions and experiences that are uniquely Northern California. From high mountains to ghost towns, redwoods to big city life, this area offers something for everyone, any time of year. The area map on pages 4 and 5 points out boundaries and special interests of this northern part of the Golden State.

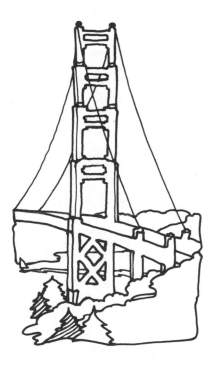

nounced. Summers become hotter (with relatively little humidity), winters colder (with an occasional snow). The Sierra Nevada has the most dramatic seasonal changes. Summer days are warm, ideal for outdoor recreation; autumn brings a crispness to the air and dramatic fall colors; heavy snowfalls during winter make the mountains a mecca for skiers.

Getting around

Major highways carry a heavy flow of traffic, especially near large cities and especially during the morning and evening commute hours. California's roads are exceptionally well maintained and well signed—most thoroughfares are divided, four-lane express highways.

For scenic beauty, the best north-south route through Northern California is State Highway 1. It's a winding coastal route, overlooking the ocean most of the way; plan to drive it leisurely. If you're in a hurry, take the inland routes. U.S. Highway 101, Interstate Highway 5, and State Highway 99 are the faster routes. The most heavily traveled east-west routes are Interstate highways 580 (U.S. 50) and 80, which connect San Francisco and Lake Tahoe.

Public transportation. Greyhound Bus Lines provides efficient and convenient coach service throughout Northern California from major western cities.

California Parlor Car Tours covers some of Northern California's most scenic highlights on jaunts from San Francisco. Especially popular are 3- to 7-day trips to Yosemite, the Monterey Peninsula, Hearst Castle, and Lake Tahoe. Overnight trips to Yosemite are offered from May through October. For more information, contact California Parlor Car Tours, 1101 Van Ness Avenue, San Francisco, CA 94109.

Amtrak runs daily trains from San Diego and Los Angeles through Northern California, then on to Oregon, Washington, and British Columbia. The California Zephyr still traces the original transcontinental rail line from Reno to Sacramento, crossing the Sierra Nevada above Donner Lake with a stop at Truckee. West Coast trains offer lounge cars with beverages, snacks, and card tables; some cars have sleeping accommodations. Amtrak also offers tours to major Northern California attractions. For schedule and price information, write Amtrak Public Affairs, One California Street, Suite 1250, San Francisco, CA 94111-5466.

Where to get information

The San Francisco Visitor Information Center, Hallidie Plaza, Powell and Market streets (lower level), should be a city visitor's first stop. Here you can get city maps and information on hotels, restaurants, and attractions. For information in advance, write to the San Francisco Convention & Visitors Bureau, P.O. Box 6977, San Francisco, CA 94101. In the city, dial 391-2001 for a 2-minute summary of daily events, as well as numbers to call for foreign language summaries.

The Redwood Empire Association publishes a free Visitors' Guide for San Francisco, Marin, Sonoma, Napa, Lake, Mendocino, Humboldt, and Del Norte counties. For a copy of this booklet, write to the association at One Market Plaza, Spear Street Tower, Suite 1001, San Francisco, CA 94105. Send $1 for postage.

For a list of Northern California wineries and their visiting hours, including descriptions of tasting rooms and picnic facilities, write the Wine Institute, 165 Post Street, San Francisco, CA 94108. Enclose a stamped (39 cents), self-addressed #10 envelope.

For travel information on the Monterey Peninsula, stop by the Chamber of Commerce and Visitors and Convention Bureau at 380 Alvarado Street, Monterey. Or write in advance to P.O. Box 1770, Monterey, CA 93940.

Accommodations

Though you'll find plenty of hotels and motels in major cities and resort areas, it's best to make reservations for summer and weekend travel. Write to the California Office of Tourist and Visitor Services (1121 L Street, Suite 103, Sacramento, CA 95814) for a listing of accommodations throughout the state.

Camping

For a guide to California's state parks, send $2 to the Publications Office, Department of Parks & Recreation, P.O. Box 2390, Sacramento, CA 95811. In some state parks, a 7- to 14-day camping limit is in effect during summer's heavy-use period. Fees are based on the type of campsite.

Although reservations are not required for camping in most state parks, it's wise to make them for the summer months, holidays, and weekends. Reservations may be made in person at any of the state's Ticketron offices (closed Sunday) or by writing Ticketron, P.O. Box 2715, San Francisco, CA 94126. You pay the campsite fee plus a small reservation charge.

National park and forest campsites are available on a first come, first served basis except during the summer months, when Yosemite National Park (see page 88) and many national forest campgrounds are available on a reservation-only basis through Ticketron outlets. Reservations may be made in person or by mail only to Ticketron. For information on national park campgrounds, write to the National Park Service, Fort Mason, Building 201, San Francisco, CA 94123, or call (415) 556-0560. For information on specific forest campgrounds or to get a California National Forest Map List, call the U.S. Forest Service Regional Office in San Francisco, (415) 556-0122. The U.S. Bureau of Land Management (2800 Cottage Way, Sacramento, CA 95825) also provides camping information.

Hunting & fishing

Every May the Department of Fish & Game (1416 9th Street, Sacramento, CA 95814) publishes a pamphlet outlining current hunting and fresh-water and salt-water fishing regulations for the coming year.

Vacation headquarters

Though this book is aimed primarily at the visitor and new resident, it includes information on possible discoveries for "back yard" vacations for those who call Northern California home. Even natives who haven't investigated surrounding regions lately are sure to find new attractions.

New to Northern California or not, you'll be energized by its variety of offerings—San Francisco, the Northland's charismatic city; burgeoning Bay Area attractions; historic Monterey and charming Carmel; towering redwoods and the scenic north coast seashore; wine touring and tasting; majestic mountains; foothill villages founded by gold.

Each time we update this guide we add new destinations like a ski bowl at Shasta, Vallejo's acquisition of Marine World/Africa USA, Monterey's handsome aquarium along old Cannery Row, Old Town Sacramento's expanded railroad museum, and a charming bed and breakfast inn at McCloud.

Outdoor activities are as varied as the area. The athletically inclined have choices from parcourse or golf course. Tennis buffs can get in a few sets at public parks or private resorts. Water enthusiasts are in their element, as boats dot San Francisco Bay, ply the Delta, or tow water-skiers on large lakes.

In the Sierra Nevada—the main winter sports area in Northern California—most major ski resorts cluster around Lake Tahoe. Other skiing centers are in the Donner Summit area, along State Highway 88, U.S. 50, and Interstate 80, and at Yosemite National Park.

FESTIVALS & FESTIVITIES

Here is a sampling of annual events and festivities of interest to Northern California visitors. Dates often change—so check with the chambers of commerce of individual cities and counties, or contact the San Francisco Convention & Visitors Bureau, P.O. Box 6977, San Francisco, CA 94101; or the Redwood Empire Association, One Market Plaza, San Francisco, CA 94105.

January
Año Nuevo Beach—Elephant Seal Watching
    (San Mateo Coast State Beaches)
Pebble Beach—AT&T/Pro-Am Golf Tournament
Stanford—East-West Shrine All-Star Football
    Game

February
Cloverdale—Citrus Fair
San Francisco—Chinese New Year (Chinatown)

March
Bodega Bay—Bodega Bay Fisherman's Festival
Pebble Beach—Victorian House Tour
San Francisco—Daffodil Festival (Maiden Lane)

April
Eureka—Rhododendron Festival
Monterey—Adobe House Tour
San Francisco—Cherry Blossom Festival
    (Japantown and Golden Gate Park)

May
Mendocino—Spring Art Fair
Angels Camp—Jumping Frog Contest
Sacramento—Dixieland Jazz Jubilee
Ukiah—Hometown Festival

June
Boonville—Buck-A-Roo Days and Rodeo
Gold Country—Melodrama at Coloma,
    Drytown, Columbia, and Oakhurst
Klamath—Klamath Salmon Festival

July
Carmel—Carmel Bach Festival
Ferndale—Humboldt County Fair
Folsom—Annual Championship Rodeo
Pebble Beach—Feast of the Lanterns

August
Blue Lake—Annie-Mary Day
Marin County—Renaissance Pleasure Faire
Sacramento—California State Fair
Santa Rosa—Scottish Gathering and Games

September
Monterey—Monterey Jazz Festival
Sonoma—Vintage Festival
Weaverville—Bigfoot Daze

October
Half Moon Bay—Half Moon Bay Art and
    Pumpkin Festival
San Francisco—Grand National Livestock
    Exposition, Rodeo, and Horse Show
Vallejo—Whaleboat Regatta and Marine
    Festival

November
Mendocino—Thanksgiving Art Fair

December
Amador City—Calico Christmas
San Juan Bautista—Las Posadas Fiesta
San Rafael—Festival of the Trees

San Francisco

The West's most enchanting city, San Francisco, is a cornucopia of sights, sounds, and excitement. Climb on a cable car to dizzying heights atop the city's famous hills; stroll or skate through Golden Gate Park; splurge in Union Square shops; take in one of the country's finest operas; enjoy impromptu performances of street artists; and drink in the awesome meeting of land and sea at the Golden Gate.

What makes San Francisco so compelling? This is a question often asked by people who have never visited "The City," and it's hard for even a native to answer. Much of its charm lies in its location, its climate, its topography—and its people.

Surrounded on three sides by water, San Francisco still harbors the flavor of its early day remoteness. And because of its setting, the weather is tempered to perpetual spring.

It's a city of hills. Someone once said that if you get tired of climbing them, you can always lean against them. But it's from the tops of these hills that you get the well-touted views—watching the fog roll in from the ocean across the Golden Gate Bridge, gazing east along the meandering span of the San Francisco-Oakland Bay Bridge, or peering north across the bay, past the islands anchored in the channel, to the bluffs of Marin County.

San Francisco was a city from the first cry of "Gold!" Few miners found anything here worth shouting about, but the Gold Rush transformed the town into a booming metropolis where literally anything went, provided you could pay for it. The wide assortment of nationalities who settled here gave the city its aura of cosmopolitan sophistication—an urban world center quite out of proportion to its actual size.

San Francisco is a big city without being big. Even with a total geographical area of only 47 square miles and a population of less than 735,000, it has the qualities common to all of the world's great cities—a rich historical background, a diversity of activities, cultural depth, hustle and bustle, pervasive charm—and more.

"The City" (as it is called by aficionados; *never* call it "Frisco") is noted for its many and various-size hills and spectacular sweeping views. Its skyline is jagged with skyscrapers dwarfing once-tall buildings; a closer look shows crowded row houses and apartments marching endlessly up and down the hills, roof-to-roof.

One of the world's most visited cities, San Francisco welcomes its guests. Whether the visit is your first or your fifth, you will enjoy seeing old landmarks as well as discovering the new ones.

Maps in this section include the downtown area, a scenic drive, Golden Gate Park, and the Golden Gate National Recreation Area.

Tales of the city

Though founded in 1776 by the Spanish as a mission post, San Francisco hardly existed until the discovery of gold in 1848. The peninsula village was transformed from a drowsy Spanish pueblo to an instant city as "49ers" came rushing to California from every point of the compass. These immigrants—a unique blend of

GOLDEN GATE BRIDGE veils view of "The City" from Marin Headlands across bay. Historic Fort Point huddles beneath bridge's southern tip.

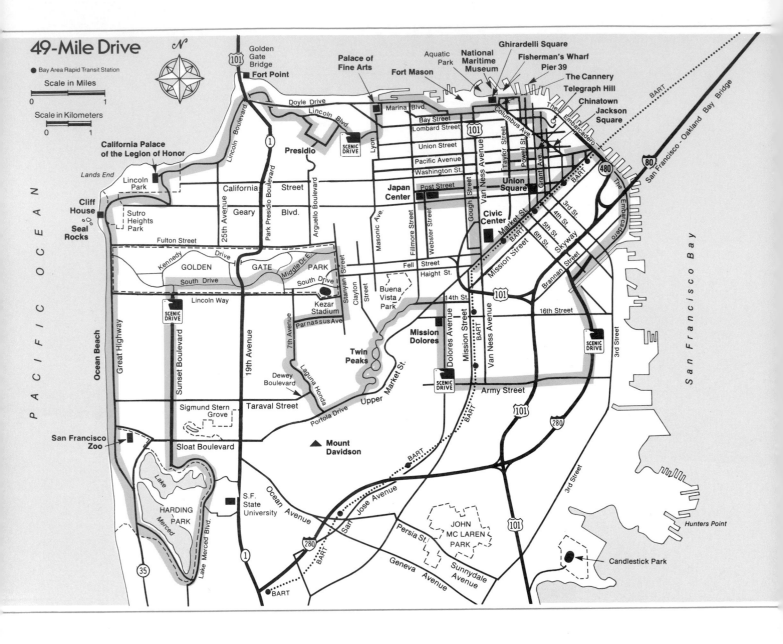

49-Mile Drive

● Bay Area Rapid Transit Station

Scale in Miles
0 _____ 1

Scale in Kilometers
0 _____ 1

PACIFIC OCEAN

SAN FRANCISCO BAY

Golden Gate Bridge
Fort Point
Palace of Fine Arts
Aquatic Park
National Maritime Museum
Fort Mason
Ghirardelli Square
Fisherman's Wharf
Pier 39
The Cannery
Telegraph Hill
Chinatown
Jackson Square
Doyle Drive
Lincoln Blvd.
Marina Blvd.
Bay Street
Lombard Street
Union Street
Pacific Avenue
Washington St.
Post Street
California Palace of the Legion of Honor
Presidio
SCENIC DRIVE
Lincoln Boulevard
Park Presidio Boulevard
Arguello Boulevard
25th Avenue
Lands End
Lincoln Park
Cliff House
Sutro Heights Park
Seal Rocks
Fulton Street
California Street
Geary Blvd.
Japan Center
Union Square
Civic Center
Masonic Ave.
Fillmore Street
Webster Street
Gough Street
Van Ness Avenue
Taylor Street
Powell St.
Grant Ave.
Columbus Ave.
The Embarcadero
San Francisco – Oakland Bay Bridge
GOLDEN GATE PARK
Kennedy Drive
South Drive
Middle Dr. E.
Lincoln Way
Stanyan Street
Kezar Stadium
Clayton Street
Fell Street
Haight St.
Buena Vista Park
Parnassus Ave.
Mission Street
Market St.
Mission Dolores
14th St.
16th Street
Dolores Avenue
Van Ness Avenue
4th St.
5th St.
6th St.
Skyway
Brannan Street
3rd St.
Great Highway
Sunset Boulevard
19th Avenue
7th Avenue
Twin Peaks
Dewey Boulevard
Laguna Honda
Portola Drive
Upper Market St.
SCENIC DRIVE
SCENIC DRIVE
Army Street
3rd Street
Ocean Beach
Sigmund Stern Grove
Taraval Street
Mount Davidson
San Francisco Zoo
Sloat Boulevard
HARDING PARK
Lake Merced
Lake Merced Blvd.
S.F. State University
Ocean Avenue
San Jose Avenue
JOHN McLAREN PARK
Persia St.
Geneva Avenue
Sunnydale Avenue
Hunters Point
Candlestick Park

---

races, customs, and nationalities—set the pattern for the city's future personality. An adage of the era was, "The weak never made it to California and the timid never tried." Certainly, early-day San Franciscans were a good illustration of the saying.

Growth accelerated with the discovery of Nevada's Comstock silver lode and the completion of the first transcontinental railroad to San Francisco in 1869.

In the earthquake of April 18, 1906, and the 3-day fire that followed, 28,000 buildings were destroyed and about 500 people died. But San Franciscans rebuilt, showing off their "new" city at the Panama-Pacific International Exposition in 1915. Later, Treasure Island, dredged up in the mid-bay, became a stage for the Golden Gate International Exposition in 1939 and 1940.

Today, the city is still changing: ultramodern skyscrapers jostle venerable Victorians; old factories become unique shopping areas; fountains splash where warehouses once stood; and part of the formerly raucous Barbary Coast (Jackson Square) now provides handsome quarters for a number of antique dealers, attorneys, and architects.

The city's culture has been enriched by the traditions and life styles of countless ethnic groups. Three distinct "cities" exist within San Francisco: Chinatown, the largest Asian settlement outside of the Far East; North Beach, magnet for nearly 150,000 San Franciscans of Italian descent; and Japantown, landmarked by the $15 million Japan Center. You'll find some 50 foreign language publications throughout the city, and its lauded cuisine offers choices of food from all parts of the globe.

The connecting links

Whether you drive on the bridges or merely glimpse the spans across the water from one of many observation spots, you'll notice the dramatic relationship between San Francisco and the water.

The bridges link the city to the rest of the world, to the east and to the north.

Most glamorous of San Francisco's bridges is the Golden Gate, designated the country's most popular manmade attraction. One of the best things about this suspended structure is that you can walk and bike across it. As a pedestrian or bicyclist, you can enjoy gull's-eye views (220 feet down) denied the automobile traveler. Park your car at the toll plaza and walk out to the middle and back for some magnificent views of the San Francisco skyline. The Marin County lookout at the north end of the bridge gives an exceptional wide-angle view of the city. You pay to cross the Golden Gate Bridge only when coming south into San Francisco; northbound you don't stop. Golden Gate Transit provides bus service to the toll plaza. For schedule information, call (415) 332-6600.

San Francisco's main bridge connection to the east is across the San Francisco-Oakland Bay Bridge. From San Francisco, two spans are joined at a central anchorage. The roadway follows a tunnel through Yerba Buena Island, coming out on a 1,400-foot cantilever span followed by a series of truss bridges. The bridge has two levels (east bound traffic uses the lower deck; westbound, the upper deck) and altogether extends 8¼ miles.

Two bridges connect East Bay towns and cities to the peninsula communities that stretch from San Francisco to San Jose. They are the San Mateo Bridge, from San Mateo to Hayward, and the Dumbarton Bridge, from Menlo Park to Fremont; another crosses north of San Francisco between Richmond and San Rafael. One-way toll collections (westbound) help the flow of traffic.

The water around San Francisco keeps the city airconditioned all year. The average high is 65°F/18°C, the low 45°F/7°C. Fog is frequent in early morning and evening, especially during the summer. Usually the rains begin in November and last into April. September is normally San Francisco's warmest month.

The city's continual mild temperatures call for lightweight wools at any time of the year, and it's a good idea to bring a coat. Residents tend to shy away from casual clothes, preferring to dress conservatively and elegantly, especially downtown.

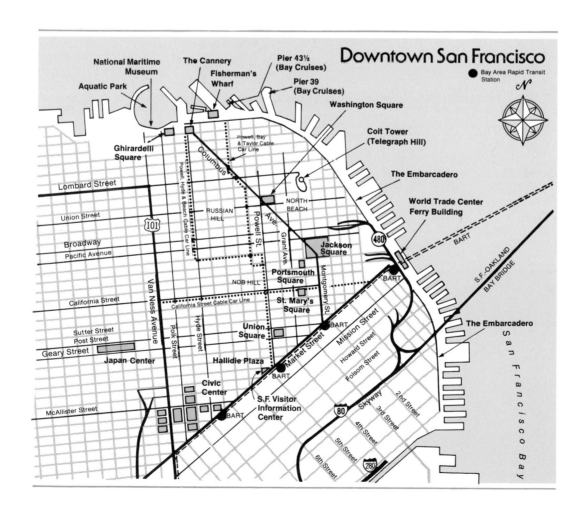

CABLE CAR CLIMBS
California Street (left) on its way up Nob Hill. At top, riders catch glimpse of Bay Bridge.

TREES FORM shady nave (below), secluding young couple from skyscrapered and shopper-thronged Market Street. Attractive benches, lights, and brick-paved mall provide refreshing oases in bustling downtown area.

A FINE HOW-DO-YOU-DO greets visitor to Maiden Lane's Daffodil Festival (below). Each spring the 2-block alley closes to traffic as mimes, musicians, and minstrels revel among blossoms.

How to see San Francisco

San Francisco is a compact city. Part of its charm lies in the ease with which a visitor can move from attraction to attraction. You can park your car if you wish and get around on foot, by cable car, streetcar, bus, and BART (the modern transbay subway). If you're a first-time visitor, we suggest following the 49-Mile Drive (see page 12), a marked route leading throughout the city.

The first stop for any newcomer to San Francisco should be the San Francisco Visitor Information Center at Hallidie Plaza (Powell and Market streets). Here you'll find information on transportation, lodging, and what's happening where. By dialing (415) 391-2001, you'll get an around-the-clock daily rundown of special events, cultural happenings, and sports news.

Ever ride a national landmark?

A cable car ride is a must for every visitor. An excellent means of transportation in the most heavily congested part of the city, the cable cars also provide thrills and good views.

You'll find three cable car lines—two that run on Powell Street and one on California Street. Cars from the line on Powell leave the turntable at Powell and Market (Hallidie Plaza) and are spectacular hill climbers. They take you up steep Powell Street, then down and around several sharp turns to arrive in 15 or 20 minutes at their respective turntables at the north waterfront. Cars marked "Powell and Market/Bay and Taylor" clang through the edge of Chinatown and along a section of North Beach, coming to the end of their line at Bay and Taylor at Fisherman's Wharf. The cars marked "Powell and Market/Hyde and Beach" bypass most of Chinatown and North Beach. But they take you down Hyde for a magnificent view of the bay and a hang-on-tight ride to your destination below Hyde and Beach at Aquatic Park.

The cars of the California Street line leave from California and Market and take you through the financial district and Chinatown, up steep Nob Hill, and finally down a gentler grade to the end of the line at Van Ness Avenue.

San Francisco's "municipal roller coaster" currently costs $1.50 for adults, 75 cents for ages 5 to 17, and 15 cents for seniors and the handicapped. A transfer good on any MUNI vehicle (cable car, bus, or streetcar) is given upon request. Riders should purchase tickets before boarding; look for self-service ticket machines at all terminals and major stops.

There's no easy way to get on or off a cable car. Usually there are more people waiting to ride than there is room. When the car stops, step right up to find a place. If you're on the outside, hang on tight. Don't ring the bell when you want off—just tell the conductor or gripman.

You can take a free tour of the Cable Car Barn and Powerhouse at Washington and Mason streets every day from 10 A.M. to 5 P.M. The museum is a treasure house of photos, original cars, and scale models. From the mezzanine gallery you'll get a good look at the cable and winding gear; below decks, you watch from a glass-enclosed room as the cable passes to the street through large, saucerlike casings.

Other ways to get around

Wherever you are in the Bay Area, public transportation departs frequently for San Francisco's downtown Transbay, train, or Greyhound terminals. There is also ferry service from Sausalito, Tiburon, and Larkspur to the city.

Whether you ride above ground or below, take a cab, or join a tour, San Francisco is one of the easiest big cities in which to get around.

Buses and streetcars run frequently on an efficient schedule from morning through early evening. You will find a route map and a description of routes at the front of the classified section of the San Francisco telephone directory.

A complete city map showing all streets, transit routes, and points of interest is printed by the San Francisco Municipal Railway. It's available at stores throughout the city.

If you call 673-MUNI, information center personnel will tell you which line reaches your destination. Take note: Express buses, making limited stops, may not stop at your destination. Local buses and streetcars currently charge 75 cents a ride (25 cents for children, 15 cents for seniors and disabled riders). Since drivers do not carry change, you must have the exact fare ready. Special price all-day tickets offer unlimited daily rides over the entire system. You can buy these tickets at the end of the cable car lines.

Regularly scheduled Airporter Bus service is available between the San Francisco Airport and downtown city hotels or the Downtown Air Terminal at Taylor and Ellis streets. Buses run every 15 minutes during the day, less frequently after 10 P.M.

Taxicabs are more numerous than in most western cities. Because distances are short between most of San Francisco's main points of interest, taxis are popular.

BART (Bay Area Rapid Transit), a modern, direct, and comfortable subway system, operates in the East Bay and in San Francisco, connecting the two areas by a tube under the bay. In downtown San Francisco, you'll find four stations (see map on page 13). Phone BART's Information Center—(415) 465-BART—toll free from San Francisco for schedule information.

Guided sightseeing tours are popular—particularly with first-time visitors. Gray Line offers several different ones. You can make arrangements to be picked up at major hotels, or you can board a shuttle bus at Union Square (opposite the St. Francis Hotel) which will take you to the depot. Buses leave from First and Mission streets at the East Bay Bus Terminal.

Several sightseeing companies offer limousine tours for small groups. Heritage Walks explores the city's architectural character on Sunday strolls. Make arrangements for any tour through your hotel or check the classified section of the telephone directory.

The 49-Mile Drive

San Francisco's excellent public transportation system, convenient touring schedules, and compact size allow you to explore without ever getting into a car.

If you do drive, one way to grasp the city as a whole is to follow the scenic 49-Mile Drive; later you can return to explore on foot the places that interest you most. Well marked by blue, white, and orange seagull signs, the 49-Mile Drive is easy to follow, though it does take you through the most congested streets of the downtown area. You should allow about a half-day to fully enjoy the sights along the route.

You can start anywhere, but here are some highlights, beginning at the Civic Center on Van Ness Avenue and McAllister Street:

Van Ness Avenue. Former automobile row, now becoming a center for hotels and trendy restaurants.

Union Square. Heart of the shopping district downtown; bordered by Geary, Post, Powell, and Stockton streets.

Chinatown. Grant Avenue leads through this exotic, bustling community. (See page 18.)

North Beach. San Francisco's Italian community, its Bohemia—a region of good restaurants and a lively center of night life. Where Columbus Avenue crosses Grant and north to the Wharf. (See page 21.)

Telegraph Hill. Coit Tower crowns this site of spectacular bay and bridge views. (See page 28.)

Marina. Beautiful residences look out to the Yacht Harbor across Marina Green—favorite place for flying kites, walking dogs, jogging, sunbathing. (See page 24.)

Palace of Fine Arts. "Temporary" structure for 1915 Panama-Pacific International Exposition, now restored and housing a museum of science. (See page 24.)

Presidio. Active military post established by the Spanish in 1776, now U.S. Sixth Army headquarters. Its 1,500 acres of parklike hills, cliffs, and beaches are open to the public. The oldest building houses the Army Museum (Lincoln Boulevard and Funston Avenue).

Lincoln Park. Home of the California Palace of the Legion of Honor, a city museum. (See page 28.)

Great Highway. Successor to the original Cliff House Restaurant stands at the north end, with Seal Rocks behind it. Up the hill is Sutro Heights Park, once the grand estate of Adolph Sutro, Comstock Lode millionaire.

San Francisco Zoo. One of the country's leading zoos borders western end of Golden Gate National Recreation Area. (See page 28.)

Golden Gate Park. Probably the finest city park in the country; includes museums and Japanese Tea Garden among its attractions. (See page 25.)

Mission Dolores. Sixth mission in the California chain, it was established in 1776. (See page 31.)

Ferry Building. Headquarters for San Francisco's Port and World Trade Center, it's the terminal for ferries to Sausalito and Larkspur (south end) and Tiburon (to the north). Vaillancourt Fountain is across the street.

Major city areas

Once you take an overall look at San Francisco, you will want a closer view of some of the city's areas. Because of its compact size, the major points of interest are easy to reach. Bring comfortable shoes and plan to do some walking; it's the best way to make your own discoveries.

Civic center—dynamic heart of the city

A monumental group of federal, state, and city structures, San Francisco's Civic Center stretches from Franklin Street to the intersection of Market Street at the United Nations Plaza. Ornate City Hall, a model of French Renaissance grandeur, crowned by a lofty dome rising 300 feet above the ground, dominates Civic Center Park. The War Memorial Veterans' Building houses the San Francisco Museum of Modern Art and the 911-seat Herbst Theater, setting for intimate chamber music concerts and other recitals. Its companion building, the War Memorial Opera House, site of the United Nations Charter signing in 1945, is now home to the San Francisco Opera and the San Francisco Ballet.

Breathing new life into the Civic Center is the bold Performing Arts Center, constructed at a cost of $38.5 million. Most of this money—about $27.5 million—was used in building the handsome Louise M. Davies Symphony Hall. Situated opposite the Opera House at Grove and Van Ness streets, the 3,000-seat concert hall is home to the San Francisco Symphony; it also provides an expanded space for visiting performers. Known in the trade as a "wrap-around," the hall is designed to make the audience feel close to the action—right at the conductor's elbow.

When the Zellerbach Rehearsal Hall was completed in 1981, the Performing Arts Center (Opera House, Louise M. Davies Symphony Hall, and Herbst Theater) became the country's second largest such center, just behind New York's Lincoln Center.

Also part of the Civic Center is the Civic Auditorium. Seating more than 8,000, it is the scene of conventions, as well as sporting and cultural events. Subterranean Brooks Exhibit Hall, underneath the Civic Center Plaza, was added in 1958. The Main Public Library, another handsome neo-Classical building, is open Monday through Thursday from 9 A.M. to 9 P.M., Friday and Saturday until 6. Nearby are the Federal Building, the Federal Office Building, and the State Office Building.

Union Square—for shoppers

For browsing and shopping in the downtown area, Union Square makes an ideal starting point. You can park your car in the cavernous garage beneath the square—it goes down four floors and provides places for over 1,000 automobiles.

Stop first at the square itself. On a nice day, its benches will be lined with people relaxing in the sun or feeding the hundreds of pigeons that swirl about and congregate around the feet of anyone offering a handout. On the sidewalks, street artists will be displaying their wares.

Union Square is a hub of activity, hosting fashion shows, rallies, and concerts. In spring, Rhododendron Days are celebrated—huge tubs of colorful plants are placed throughout the square. A summer highlight is the Cable Car Bell Ringing Contest. In the center of the square stands a 97-foot granite monument commemorating Admiral Dewey's victory at Manila Bay during the Spanish-American War.

The fashionable Westin St. Francis Hotel, on the west side of the square across Powell Street, is only one of the hostelries in the area. Many visiting dignitaries stop here—if you see a foreign flag displayed above the entrance, you can assume it is honoring a very important guest from that country. You'll enjoy browsing through some of the hotel shops. For good skyline views, ride the tower elevators to the top.

Post, Stockton, and Geary streets also border the square. The Children's Fountain in the plaza of the Hyatt on Union Square deserves a stop. Designed by Ruth Asawa, who also designed the fountains in Ghirardelli Square and Buchanan Mall in Japantown, it takes a whimsical look at the city's history.

Around Union Square and spreading south toward Market and east toward Kearny Street are some of San Francisco's fashionable shops. I. Magnin, Neiman-Marcus, Saks Fifth Avenue, and Macy's are among the largest stores surrounding the square.

A major attraction in the Union Square area is Gump's at 250 Post near Stockton. Worthy of special attention is the Jade Room, where you'll find a unique collection in a multitude of shades. Other rooms contain rare imports and unusual locally made items.

More large department stores and tempting shops are located along Grant, Geary, Post, and Stockton. The Galleria at Crocker Center (a three-level complex housing 65 stores and restaurants) takes up the block bounded by Post, Kearny, Sutter, and Montgomery streets. Modeled after Milan's vast Galleria Vittorio Emmanuelle, the pavilion features elegant boutiques offering the best of American and European designers.

You can't miss the colorful sidewalk flower stands, a kind of streetside almanac: sprigs of daphne and violets in spring, tiny Pinocchio roses in summer, chrysanthemums in fall, and holly in winter.

On the east side of the square across Stockton is Maiden Lane, a 2-block tree-lined alley transformed from its bawdy past to a street of intriguing shops. Of particular interest is a building designed by Frank Lloyd Wright, with an unusual yellow brick front and an interior circular ramp; it houses an art gallery.

In late March or early April, Maiden Lane welcomes spring with the annual Daffodil Festival. The lane is then closed to traffic; local dignitaries, bands, and troubadours celebrate among the blossoms.

The financial district

North of Market Street, impressive office buildings shade the narrow slot that is Montgomery Street, heart of San Francisco's business and financial district. Here, and spreading into the nearby streets, are the banking, brokerage, and insurance firms that are a part of the Wall Street of the West. Here also are the general offices of many of the West's largest business organizations.

The heart of the financial district is the Pacific Coast Stock Exchange (Pine and Sansome streets), where business begins at 6 A.M. to coincide with the hours of the New York Stock Exchange. One block west of the stock exchange is the Bank of America Building, headquarters for the world's second largest bank. The 779-foot-high, 52-story structure, with its bronze-tinted, bay-windowed façade, covers most of the California, Pine, Kearny, and Montgomery block. From the Carnelian Room on the 52nd floor, you'll get a magnificent view of the city.

The 853-foot-high Transamerica Pyramid at Montgomery, Washington, and Clay streets projects its unique shape on the ever-changing San Francisco skyline.

Another skyscraper, the Wells Fargo Building at 44 Montgomery Street, rises 43 stories—561 feet. On the 16th floor of this unusual glass and steel structure is Montgomery Lane, where a collection of diverse shops cater to employees. Visitors are welcome during the day. Just below the main lobby level is a restaurant displaying early California artifacts from the Wells Fargo History Room. The History Room, at 420 Montgomery Street, highlights photographs, documents, and mementos from Gold Rush days to the 1906 earthquake. The collection includes a circa-1860 stagecoach that ran from San Francisco to the Santa Cruz Mountains. Visiting hours on banking days are from 10 A.M. to 3 P.M.

The Bank of California's Collection of Money of the American West, finest of its kind in the country, features pioneer gold quartz, gold and silver ingots, privately minted gold coins, and currency from the West. Open during banking hours (10 A.M. to 3 P.M.), it's located on the lower level at 400 California Street.

Along the Embarcadero

How do you change decaying waterfront property into a revitalized urban landscape? Take 51 acres of land, add $150 million, and come up with the Golden Gateway Center. In the late 1950s the San Francisco Redevelopment Agency did just that. Bounded by Clay, Battery, and Jackson streets, this former produce marketplace blossomed into a slick urban center of apartments, townhouses, offices, and parks.

From the heart of the center, the dark-glassed, diagonally braced Alcoa Building rises dramatically. The 2-block-square Maritime Plaza, an elevated park, provides a place to stroll and relax. Here pedestrian bridges serve as elevated passageways to all sections of the center.

South of the Golden Gateway is architect John C. Portman's ambitious Embarcadero Center. Hailed by one critic to be "superbly conceived, fine in taste, and full of life," the center is a stunning success of multi-use urban development.

Truly a "city within a city," Embarcadero Center comprises four major towers (two 32-story, two 45-story) and the grand 850-room Hyatt Regency Hotel. Each thin, elegant tower springs from a common three-level pedestal of plazas, promenades, and shopping arcades. Public art treasures stud the 8½ bayside acres on which the towers and hotel stand. On the north, pedestrian bridges link the Embarcadero Center to the Golden Gateway Center, site of the Alcoa Building.

The architecturally innovative Hyatt Regency is a favorite San Francisco attraction. Charles Perry's 40-foot sculpture *Eclipse* graces the 16-story atrium lobby, from which glass elevators speed you up 20 stories to a revolving restaurant offering 360-degree views of the city.

Elevated pedestrian bridges connect the various parts of Embarcadero Center, separating visitors and shoppers from the traffic below.

Adjacent to and north of the Hyatt Regency is the Justin Herman Plaza, adding a green oasis to this financial district. At noontime, artists and brown baggers congregate around the controversial Vaillancourt Fountain.

Across Market Street, south from the Hyatt Regency, One Market Plaza creates yet another "people place." A soaring skylight connects the old Southern Pacific Building's façade to two new office towers, creating a block-long airy atrium. Sunlight pours in over the tree and flower-lined concourse of shops and restaurants.

Across the street on Mission and Spear, at the Rincon Annex Post Office, the colorful WPA historic murals are worth a look. You'll get speedy mail service here—pickup every hour on the hour until midnight.

Though the cavernous 2,000-car Embarcadero garage offers plenty of parking space, public transportation efficiently serves all the centers along the Embarcadero. BART's Embarcadero station meets the California Street cable car across from the Hyatt on Market Street. MUNI's streetcars, buses, and cable cars also take you within walking distance of the centers. Ferry service to and from the Marin County towns of Sausalito, Tiburon, and Larkspur leaves from the pier of the Ferry Building across the street from the Hyatt Hotel.

Jackson Square

Once San Francisco's rowdy Barbary Coast, this part of the city became a dismal warehouse area when the city rebuilt in other directions following the 1906 fire. The old buildings were eventually boarded up and deserted and remained so until, in 1951, an enterprising group began extensive restoration, converting the district's old structures into showplaces for architectural and interior design. In 1972, the area bounded by Columbus Avenue on the west, a line midway between Broadway and Pacific on the north, Sansome on the east, and Washington on the south was designated an Historic District.

By 1982, the success of the restoration began to displace the people largely responsible for it. As rents rose, the decorating community diminished, many members moving to new design complexes around Potrero Hill. Their old premises were snapped up by attorneys, architects, ad agencies, and land developers.

The good news is that not all of the square's elegant façades frame mundane offices. Many antique dealers have moved in, with more to come. A stroll through this storied precinct still offers extensive enticements for browsers.

Restored buildings include such old structures as the A. P. Hotaling Co. liquor warehouse at 451 Jackson; built in 1866, it still retains the iron shutters with which it was originally fitted. The hulls of two ships abandoned in the Gold Rush form the foundation of 441 Jackson. At 472 Jackson, built between 1850 and 1852 and home to the French Consulate from 1865 to 1876, ship masts serve as interior supporting columns.

Lawyer Melvin Belli owns the Barbary Coast landmark building at 728 Montgomery which houses a courtyard and his purposely peekaboo office.

Chinatown

The largest Asian community outside the Orient, San Francisco's Chinatown covers about 24 blocks and is roughly bordered by Kearny, Mason, and Bush streets and Broadway. It's best to arrive in Chinatown on foot or by public transportation, for the area is heavily congested with traffic.

Grant Avenue is the main street, where for 8 blocks, between Bush and Columbus, visitors are guaranteed a delightfully unusual walk. You can get there from either the financial district, Union Square, or Nob Hill. Remember that if you are atop a hill, your walk will be down several steep blocks. The California Street cable car will put you in the heart of Chinatown.

One of the most colorful approaches to Chinatown is a walk down Sacramento to Grant. You will see peaked pagoda-style rooftops and bright-colored balconies in the foreground and the bay and bridge beyond. Along Grant Avenue is the tourists' Chinatown—curio shops, import shops, restaurants.

To get a glimpse of the "inside," prowl up and down some of the cross streets and explore the side alleys that parallel Grant. Scattered among gift shops and restaurants are stores and markets with exotic smells and sounds. The language here is still mostly Cantonese.

In the early morning, Friday through Sunday, Stockton Street, between Washington and Broadway, becomes a throbbing open-air market. Truck farmers in sidewalk stalls sell anything from live turtles to squawking chickens and ducks. Each weekend over 10,000 Chinese gather to shop and socialize.

Between California and Pine is St. Mary's Square, a quiet little park with Beniamino Bufano's striking marble and stainless steel statue of China's one-time president, Sun Yat-sen. Beneath the park is an underground garage; entrances are on Kearny, Pine, and California.

Old St. Mary's Church, a San Francisco landmark since 1854, stands at Grant and California. The Gothic structure was built of granite from China and brick brought around Cape Horn from New England.

Waverly Place, paralleling Grant Avenue to the west, reveals some of Chinatown's few remaining temples. Of special interest is the Tin How Temple, 125 Waverly (top floor), dating back to Gold Rush days. The main shrine is dedicated to T'ien Hou, protectress of travelers. The temple is open from 10 A.M. to 4 P.M. daily. Also on Waverly is the Chinese Culture and Arts Center. On weekends instructors teach classes in caligraphy, *tai chi chuan*, Chinese violin, and butterfly harp.

(Continued on page 21)

CROWNING TELEGRAPH HILL, Coit Tower (above), offers grand clear-day views of bay, Alcatraz, distant Marin hills.

"IT REALLY IS CROOKED!" squeal motorists (left). Lombard Street, snaking between Hyde and Leavenworth, reveals blossoming hydrangeas and breathtaking views.

UNDULATING LINE of Embarcadero Freeway (below) dramatically sweeps above noontime lunchers enjoying verdant park in Golden Gateway Center.

19

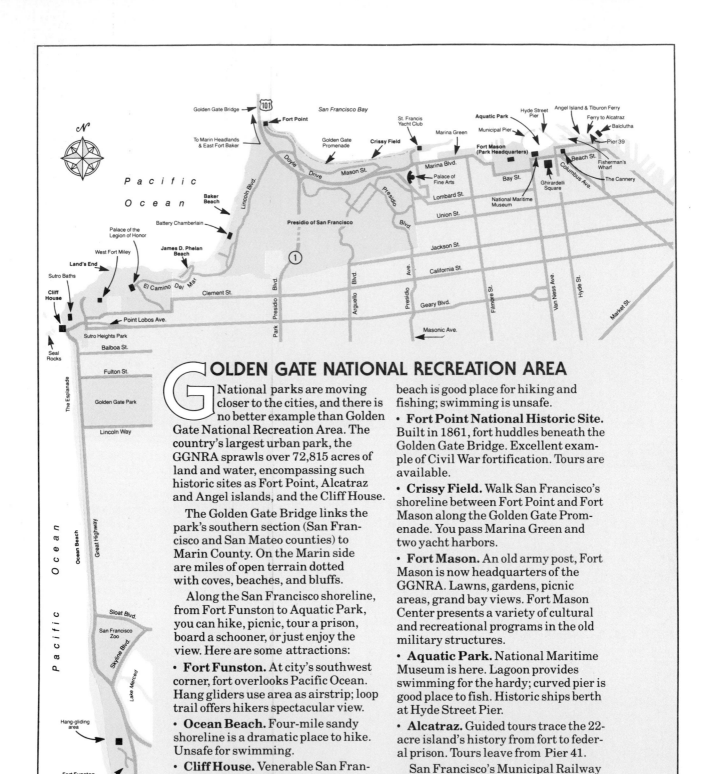

GOLDEN GATE NATIONAL RECREATION AREA

National parks are moving closer to the cities, and there is no better example than Golden Gate National Recreation Area. The country's largest urban park, the GGNRA sprawls over 72,815 acres of land and water, encompassing such historic sites as Fort Point, Alcatraz and Angel islands, and the Cliff House.

The Golden Gate Bridge links the park's southern section (San Francisco and San Mateo counties) to Marin County. On the Marin side are miles of open terrain dotted with coves, beaches, and bluffs.

Along the San Francisco shoreline, from Fort Funston to Aquatic Park, you can hike, picnic, tour a prison, board a schooner, or just enjoy the view. Here are some attractions:

• **Fort Funston.** At city's southwest corner, fort overlooks Pacific Ocean. Hang gliders use area as airstrip; loop trail offers hikers spectacular view.

• **Ocean Beach.** Four-mile sandy shoreline is a dramatic place to hike. Unsafe for swimming.

• **Cliff House.** Venerable San Francisco landmark offers sweeping view of Marin coast. Offshore, view Seal Rocks, home of sea lions and birds.

• **Baker Beach.** At northwest shore of Presidio facing the Golden Gate, beach is good place for hiking and fishing; swimming is unsafe.

• **Fort Point National Historic Site.** Built in 1861, fort huddles beneath the Golden Gate Bridge. Excellent example of Civil War fortification. Tours are available.

• **Crissy Field.** Walk San Francisco's shoreline between Fort Point and Fort Mason along the Golden Gate Promenade. You pass Marina Green and two yacht harbors.

• **Fort Mason.** An old army post, Fort Mason is now headquarters of the GGNRA. Lawns, gardens, picnic areas, grand bay views. Fort Mason Center presents a variety of cultural and recreational programs in the old military structures.

• **Aquatic Park.** National Maritime Museum is here. Lagoon provides swimming for the hardy; curved pier is good place to fish. Historic ships berth at Hyde Street Pier.

• **Alcatraz.** Guided tours trace the 22-acre island's history from fort to federal prison. Tours leave from Pier 41.

San Francisco's Municipal Railway (MUNI) makes getting to the park fun. Board the Hyde Street or Mason Street cable car to reach Aquatic Park. For information on other GGNRA destinations, call (415) 673-MUNI.

. . . Continued from page 18

Walking tours offer keys to many of Chinatown's mysteries. Since little English is spoken in some of the more intriguing places, you may want to arrange for a guided tour. The Chinese Culture Center and Ding How Tours offer guided walks covering cultural, culinary, and social aspects of Chinatown. All require reservations; some include dinner.

Portsmouth Square, just east of Grant Avenue, at Kearny and Clay, is where San Francisco began. Here Captain John B. Montgomery raised the American flag in 1846, proclaiming the Mexican village to be a possession of the United States. Portsmouth Square (named for Montgomery's ship, the USS *Portsmouth*) today is a landscaped park atop a parking garage.

Though Portsmouth Square doesn't have a Chinese name, it is Chinatown's village plaza. In the early morning students practice *tai chi chuan,* exercises perfected by Chinese monks centuries ago. By afternoon, elders gather for chess and conversation while youngsters romp in the nearby playground.

From Portsmouth Square you can cross a footbridge east over Kearny Street to the dramatic 27-story Holiday Inn housing the Chinese Culture Center on the third floor. Open Tuesday through Saturday from 11 A.M. to 5 P.M., the center presents films, exhibits, lectures, and tours.

The Chinese Telephone Exchange at 743 Washington (now the Bank of Canton) is a Chinatown landmark. From 1909 to 1949 the building held the main switchboard for the "China" exchange, when Chinese operators memorized as many as 2,400 names and numbers of Chinatown subscribers. You can see photographs of these exceptional women at the Chinese Historical Museum on Adler Place, an alley one-half block south of Broadway off Grant Avenue. On display are memorabilia covering a century of Chinese life in America. The free museum is open Tuesday through Saturday from 1 to 5 P.M.

North Beach

Where Grant Avenue crosses Broadway and Columbus, it takes on a new personality. Though not as solidly Italian as it once was, the North Beach area is still an enticing mosaic of cappuccino houses, cabarets, and gelato parlors. Not really a beach at all, this district acquired its name in the 1850s, when a finger of the bay extended inland and the neighborhood was a sunny shore between Telegraph and Russian hills.

Here, in the center of the Italian community, are Italian bakeries, pastry shops, delicatessens, and kitchen specialty stores. In the pastry shops you'll find rum babas, marzipan, and cylindrical *cannolis* filled with sweetened ricotta cheese and glacéed fruits.

The bakeries, or bread shops, offer long loaves of sweet and sourdough French breads and *panettone,* a round, sweet, Italian bread filled with raisins and fruits.

Kitchen specialty shops sell noodle machines, cheese graters, *caffè espresso* machines, ravioli rolling sticks, baking irons for *pizzelle* and *cialdi* cookies, copper *polenta* pots, and round-bottomed pans for *zabaglione.*

Excellent meals are served in the restaurants of North Beach. Beside the well-known establishments, look for modest, unassuming little ones serving savory specialties.

For many years, a flourishing colony of writers, painters, and craftspeople has had headquarters in the North Beach area; you'll find a number of galleries, studios, and shops along Grant and adjacent streets. Once annually, usually in June, the artists display their crafts in a street bazaar.

Parking in the district is at a premium at all times, but the Taylor and Bay cable car runs along Mason between Vallejo and Union. From there it's only a 3-block walk east to shops on upper Grant Avenue.

Broadway, San Francisco's Bohemia in the heart of North Beach, comes alive at night. Fanning out from the intersection of Broadway and Columbus, North Beach presents some lively entertainment in a collection of cabarets, small theaters, and bistros. Here, the flavor of Italy mixes with some wild nightlife—tourist style.

Washington Square, at Columbus and Union, is a perfect spot for a picnic lunch in the sun. The Church of Saints Peter and Paul is across Filbert Street from the square. Its two tall towers, illuminated at night, are visible from many sections of the city. The two statues in the square honor San Francisco's firemen and Benjamin Franklin—a typically unusual San Francisco combination.

The north waterfront

Once run-down and neglected, San Francisco's north waterfront is now pulling and pleasing tremendous crowds. Today, this 22-block district facing the water is a mélange of restaurants, unusual museums, art galleries, excellent shops, small theaters, even a national recreation area.

Here are the turn-around points for two of the city's cable car lines and the piers for the bay tour boats.

In the north waterfront district, you'll see items ranging from painted seashells and postcards sold near Fisherman's Wharf to bronze turnbuckles at a ship chandlery, from zebra skins in an import shop to a choice of 200 cheeses on sale at The Cannery.

The biggest and most famous retailer is Cost Plus Imports, a rambling bazaar of housewares, antiques, foods, jewelry, and garden supplies. At the east end of the district is the Northpoint Shopping Center. Its street floor has a candymaker, a market, an ice cream parlor, and several restaurants.

At the west end of the district are Ghirardelli Square, The Cannery, and The Anchorage (newest of the area's shopping complexes); a majority of shops are open 7 days a week.

Fisherman's Wharf (Jones and Jefferson streets) is a world-famous combination of tourist attractions, sidewalk seafood stalls, steaming cauldrons, and seafood restaurants.

Jefferson Street is one vast open air fish market where you'll see oceans of steaming crabs and mountains of sourdough French bread. Try a "walkaway" seafood

NEON SHROUDS the night in San Francisco's Chinatown (right). After dark, dragon-laced latterns illuminate a labyrinth of restaurants, shops, and specialty stores along Grant Avenue.

EAST MEETS WEST as Taiwan expert teaches American enthusiast the timeless grace of tai chi chuan (left). Early morning workouts enliven Chinatown's Portsmouth Square; by afternoon, square becomes gathering place for Chinese of all ages.

cocktail, sold in a disposable container. Beyond the seafood counters, activity centers around the fishing boats coming in with their catch. At the foot of Jones and Leavenworth, fishermen hoist crates of fish to the pier.

For thousands who come to the city, a San Francisco visit calls for a meal at Fisherman's Wharf. The view is the big reason to go. If you get a window table, below you are the bobbing fishing boats. In the distance loom the tall orange red towers of the Golden Gate Bridge and beyond them the purple Marin hills.

At the seafood restaurants, specialties include fresh crab (during the season, early November to mid-June or July), cracked and served cold with lemon and mayonnaise; crab Louis, the classic wharf salad, served with San Francisco's sourdough bread; abalone; and *cioppino,* the heroic shellfish stew you eat with your fingers.

Restaurants elsewhere along the north waterfront are not easily categorized—however, if you're looking for Italian, Japanese, Mexican, or American food, you can find it here.

About 2 blocks east along the wharf is the berth of the *Balclutha,* a regal old three-masted sailing ship. Refurbished and restored, she looks like what she was: a Scottish-built, square-rigged ship that plied the seas between the 1880s and the 1920s and logged 17 Cape Horn doublings. Though presently berthed at Pier 43, the *Balclutha* is part of the fleet of the National Maritime Museum at the foot of Polk Street in Aquatic Park. She is open from 10 A.M. to 10 P.M.; there is a fee.

Aquatic Park is now part of the Golden Gate National Recreation Area (see page 20). Its ship-shaped National Maritime Museum houses an extensive collection of ship models, nautical artifacts, photographs, and paintings. The most pleasant way to reach the museum is by the Powell and Hyde Street cable car; the turntable is just south of the museum.

Most of the National Maritime Museum's historic ships are located at the Hyde Street Pier. The ships include three-masted schooner *C.A. Thayer,* river tug *Eppleton Hall,* ferry boat *Eureka,* scow schooner *Alma,* and steam tug *Hercules.* The S.S. *Jeremiah O'Brien,* last of WWII Liberty Ships, is tied up at Pier 3 East, Fort Mason. You can board most of the ships; audio earphones are provided for a self-guided tour.

Boat tours offer striking views of San Francisco from the water. For a sightseeing tour of the bay, go aboard one of the trim ships of the Red and White Fleet, leaving Pier 43½ near Fisherman's Wharf, or the Blue and Gold Fleet, leaving from Pier 39's west marina. Their routes extend to the Golden Gate Bridge, past "the rock" (Alcatraz) and Treasure Island, under the Bay Bridge, and along the waterfront. From shipboard you'll see the city of San Francisco as a dramatic rim around the bay. North lie the gentle hills of Marin County, and to the east Oakland and Berkeley spread out along the shore and up into the hills. It gets chilly on the bay so take along warm clothing.

Boats for the 1¼-hour excursions leave frequently, beginning at 10 A.M. daily all year (weather permitting). Prices are moderate, and you can get snacks on board.

You can also take guided excursions to Alcatraz, now part of the Golden Gate National Recreation Area. A federal prison until it was abandoned in 1963, Alcatraz is now visited by more than 400,000 people each year. Tours leave Pier 41 every 45 minutes from 9 A.M. to 3 P.M. (longer hours in summer) and are so popular that the boats are usually filled. Tickets for each day go on sale at 8:30 A.M. at the ticket booth on the pier; reservations are suggested. For information and reservations, call (415) 546-2805.

In summer and on winter weekends, excursion boats take passengers from Pier 43½ to quaint Tiburon or for a day's outing on Angel Island (see page 37). For information, call (415) 546-2815.

Ghirardelli Square, just south and west of the National Maritime Museum, covers the block bounded by Beach, Larkin, North Point, and Polk streets. First a woolen works and later the Ghirardelli Chocolate Factory, this red-brick building complex has been remodeled and restored to contain an enticing miscellany of shops, art galleries, restaurants, and a theater.

Ghirardelli Square includes a number of buildings (with names such as Mustard, Cocoa, and Chocolate), all of which are situated around an inviting plaza. The brick tower that marks the square was copied from one at the Chateau Blois in France. If you wish to rest, select one of the benches near the splashing fountain or one that affords a view of the bay and boats. In the plaza, entertainment may range from an impromptu concert to a brief ballet.

Shops in the square contain imports from such places as Africa, Holland, Ireland, the Orient, Finland, and Greece. Stores feature wearing apparel, toys, cutlery, flowers, kites, jewelry, and leather goods.

Part of Ghirardelli's charm lies in the outdoor cafés and in the variety of food available here. For instance, you can watch thin crêpes being made, and sample them, as well as Mexican, Chinese, Hungarian, Indian, or Italian food. And you can enjoy a Twin Peaks sundae or a Golden Gate banana split at an old-time ice cream parlor. At the Ghirardelli Chocolate Manufactory you can watch chocolate being made.

The Cannery is similar to Ghirardelli Square in some ways. Bounded by Beach, Leavenworth, and Jefferson streets, it was originally constructed in 1894 to house the Del Monte Fruit and Vegetable Cannery. Today, the old brick building with its concrete walkways and arched windows has been restored and refurbished.

The Cannery contains three levels of shopping and eating pleasures. You can buy an assortment of goods, from contemporary household furnishings to primitive art objects. Other shops feature such items as candles, fine foods and wines, apparel, flowers, linens, and books. Relax in the flower-filled courtyard where jugglers, mimes, and magicians perform under century-old olive trees. Outside escalators and stairs lead to different levels; you can also take a glass-enclosed elevator from the ground floor to the top.

The Anchorage occupies the block bounded by Jones, Leavenworth, Beach, and Jefferson. Its contemporary design re-creates the feeling of being on board ship; stairways and outdoor promenades lead to shops, boutiques, restaurants, and a hotel. Musicians and street artists perform in the open-air courtyard.

(Continued on next page)

Across Leavenworth Street a parking lot provides an hour of free parking with your validated ticket from either the Cannery or The Anchorage.

Pier 39, once an abandoned shipping cargo pier, is the newest of the restaurant-shopping meccas along San Francisco's northern waterfront. Just east of Fisherman's Wharf, this pier—the length of three football fields—embraces 14 restaurants, over 100 specialty shops, and two marinas, as well as a bayside park. Adding to the authenticity of the complex is a two-level arcade built from weathered wood salvaged from the demolition of other piers.

One of the nicest features of Pier 39 is its 5-acre waterfront park. Step away from the bustling shopping arcades to enjoy serene views of the surrounding bay. The park stretches along the southwestern edge of Pier 39 to about the middle of Pier 41. When completed, it will extend to Pier 35.

Marinas flank Pier 39, offering 350 berths to fishing boats, pleasure craft, and guest boats. The Blue and Gold Fleet runs bay tour excursions; instructions in windsurfing, sailing, and sportfishing are also offered.

There's no lack of entertainment at Pier 39. Musicians, street artists, jugglers, even a high-dive stunt team perform on the pier's three main stages, adding a carnival dimension to the nautical atmosphere.

A covered pedestrian bridge over Beach Street leads from a parking garage to the second level of the complex. Mini-buses provide free transportation along the pier.

The Marina

This lovely residential area with a Mediterranean flair now offers most of the bayside walking in San Francisco. Though the Marina Green is still a city park, it is now within the boundaries of the Golden Gate National Recreation Area—a preserve encompassing over 72,000 acres of land and water in San Francisco, Marin, and San Mateo counties (see page 20). In the Marina, this urban recreation area runs along the shoreline from Aquatic Park and Fort Mason to Fort Point, huddled beneath the Golden Gate Bridge.

The Golden Gate Promenade is a 3½-mile shoreline walk between Aquatic Park and Fort Point. Since its incorporation into the GGNRA, the promenade has changed on its eastern end. From Aquatic Park you walk west to Fort Mason. Once army land, off limits to civilians, Fort Mason now houses the headquarters and visitors center of the GGNRA. You can wander around the historic buildings and enjoy grand bay vistas. The area around Fort Mason is a vast, grassy park where visitors may rest and picnic.

Along Fort Mason's waterside portion are the piers and buildings of the old Port of Embarcations, now the Fort Mason Center. A unique cultural complex, the center houses museums, galleries, theaters, and a restaurant. Classes are offered in everything from ballroom dancing to fitness conditioning. For information and a schedule of events, call (415) 441-5705.

A paved path leads to the Marina Green. A favorite of both residents and visitors, the Marina Green is the perfect spot for flying kites or sunbathing—and it's a jogger's paradise. Try the parcourse exercises on the way to Crissy Field.

Crissy Field is a quiet stretch of shoreline skirting the water's edge for about a mile. With its great views, driftwood, and windblown sand, this is a quiet retreat from the urban jostle.

To reach the end of the promenade, head west past a U.S. Coast Guard station to Long Avenue. Long Avenue leads you to Fort Point and the Golden Gate. Walking enthusiasts can retrace their steps to the Marina; the less hardy can climb the hill to the Golden Gate Bridge toll plaza and catch an inbound Golden Gate Transit bus back to the downtown area.

The Palace of Fine Arts (Marina Boulevard and Baker Street) was a centerpiece for the 1915 Panama-Pacific International Exposition. Set in a natural lagoon in the city's Marina district, the Greco-Romanesque rotunda was restored at a cost of $8 million in 1967. It now houses the Exploratorium and a 1,000-seat theater.

The Exploratorium, an internationally acclaimed museum of science, technology, and human perception, features over 600 exhibits to be manipulated, tinkered with, or activated by the push of a button. Easy-to-follow instructions aid in understanding the exhibits. Admission to the museum, set inside the Palace of Fine Arts, is moderate (free on first Wednesday of each month and every Wednesday after 6 P.M.). For reservations to the Tactile Gallery, call (415) 563-7272 (there will be an additional charge). The Exploratorium is open from 10 A.M. to 5 P.M. weekends, 1 to 9:30 P.M. Wednesday, and 1 to 5 P.M. Thursday and Friday. It's closed Monday and Tuesday.

Japantown—Japan without a passport

Today over 12,000 people of Japanese descent live in San Francisco. Though the first Japanese arrived here in the 1860s, it was not until after the 1906 earthquake that many Japanese chose to rebuild their homes in this part of San Francisco. Houses, businesses, churches, shops, and restaurants were often patterned after traditional Japanese architecture. It was not long before the area took on a Japanese character and became known as *Nihonmachi,* or Japantown.

In 1968, the dedication of the multimillion-dollar Japan Center complex supplied the community with a much needed ethnic focal point. Designed by architect Minoru Yamasaki, the 3-square-block center exudes the serenity and dignity characteristic of Japanese architecture. A string of handsome white buildings between Geary Expressway and Post, the center begins on the east at Laguna Street, boldly leaps Webster Street with a curved bridgeway of shops, and ends on the west at Fillmore Street. Street signs are in both Japanese and English.

Tenants include the Japanese Consulate, manufacturers' showrooms, and retail stores with goods ranging from bonsai to jade and pearls. The 5-acre complex houses shops, restaurants, a theater, teahouses, sushi bars, the Miyako Hotel, and Japanese baths.

The Peace Plaza, containing a five-tiered, 35-foot Peace Pagoda with reflecting pool, is the hub of the

Japan Center. A graceful wooden drum tower stands at the entrance to the plaza, and a copper-roofed walkway at the north end of the plaza connects the East and Kintetsu buildings.

Colorful festivals take place in the plaza. Most popular is the annual Spring Cherry Blossom Festival (*Sakura Matsuri*) held in April. This 7-day event spans two weekends, offering traditional Japanese music, dance, art, and tea ceremonies. *Aki Matsuri,* the annual fall festival, is a 3-day fête held sometime in September. *Tanabato,* or Star Festival, marks the weekend closest to July 7. One of the oldest and most romantic of Japanese festivals, it celebrates the yearly reunion of the mythical heavenly lovers, Vega and Altair. The celebration is joyously filled with colorful decorations, traditional songs, and graceful dance.

Inspired by the center and other urban renewal programs, residents of Japantown continue to revitalize this section of the city. In 1975, the Kyoto hotel opened at Sutter and Buchanan streets. The Buchanan Mall leading to the center's main entrance was completed shortly afterward. Dotted with flowering trees and unique fountains, the block-long mall is lined with an assortment of Japanese shops, restaurants, and businesses.

Only a mile from Union Square, Japantown and the Japan Center are easy to reach. From downtown, take MUNI No. 38 bus on Geary or No. 1, 2, or 3 and get off at Buchanan or Laguna. If you have a car, drive west on Geary to the center's garage entrance.

Golden Gate Park—a park for all seasons

San Francisco owes a great debt of gratitude to the late John McLaren, whose vision and perseverance in San Francisco's early years turned more than 1,000 acres of rolling sand dunes into a park. Today, Golden Gate Park is one of the most beautiful metropolitan parks in the world.

Park visitors benefit from an enlightened policy of operation; the park is meant to be used. You can walk, play, or picnic on the grass anywhere except the small plot of lawn surrounding McLaren's statue in Rhododendron Dell. The bridle paths, equestrian field, and bicycle trails are for public use; you can rent horses at the stables at Kennedy Drive and 34th Avenue and bicycles just outside the park in the 600 and 800 blocks of Stanyan Street.

The M. H. de Young and Asian Art museums, the Academy of Science, the concessions, the Arboretum, and the Conservatory close at night; otherwise the park is open 24 hours.

John F. Kennedy Drive takes you by many of the park's attractions; it's the entrance from the northwest corner. The nine-hole pitch-and-putt golf course located a short distance inside the park is open every day. To get to the clubhouse, turn left at the first intersection of Kennedy Drive after you leave the Great Highway.

The Chain of Lakes, a series of three artificial lakes, runs from north to south across the park near its western end. Largest of the three is North Lake (north of Kennedy Drive), dotted with several landcaped islands. The banks of Middle Lake (south of Kennedy Drive) are

planted with camellias and Japanese cherry trees. South Lake, smallest in the chain, hosts large numbers of wild ducks.

North of Kennedy Drive and just east of the Chain of Lakes, the fences of the Buffalo Paddock are so carefully concealed by artful landscaping that buffaloes within the enclosure seem to be roaming at large.

Anglers will find an ideal practicing spot at the Flycasting Pool south of the drive. The cement-lined pool is divided into three sections—one for distance casting, another for accuracy, and a third for practicing difficult overhead casts.

As you approach Spreckels Lake, you'll pass some of the largest and oldest rhododendrons in the park. Planted on an island in the center of Kennedy Drive, they're at their best in May.

The lake itself is north of the drive. Its waters are usually freckled with wildfowl, and during summer the lake is used for sailing model boats. The San Francisco Model Yacht Club has its headquarters in the building just west of the lake.

Continuing east on Kennedy Drive, you pass 25-acre Lindley Meadow and tiny Lloyd Lake. A gravel path encircles the lake, leading to the "Portals of the Past" on its shore. The six white marble pillars that form the portals were the entrance to the A. N. Towne residence on Nob Hill. All that remained of the house after the 1906 fire, the pillars were later presented by Mrs. Towne to the park.

Stow Lake, largest of the park's manmade lakes, is the central reservoir for the irrigation system and also a popular recreation spot. Tree-lined walks border the lake, a road goes around it, and there's a snack bar near the dock where boats can be rented. Two footbridges lead to Strawberry Hill, a wooded island in the center of the lake. Here you'll see the Golden Pavilion, a gift from Taipei. A 5-minute walk up a fairly steep slope brings you to Huntington Falls, at the crown of the hill. From the summit you view not only the park—a wide green swath through the city's west end—but also the towers of the Golden Gate and Bay bridges and, on clear days, the Farallon Islands, 30 miles out into the Pacific.

The Rose Garden, just east of Stow Lake Drive on the north side of Kennedy Drive, contains about 75 varieties of roses, including recent award winners.

The M. H. de Young Memorial Museum opened in 1895 after Michael de Young, publisher of the San Francisco *Chronicle,* proposed that the profits of the California Midwinter International Exposition of 1894 be used to house a permanent collection of art. The original museum buildings were torn down in 1926, and today's museum consists of two wings extending from either side of a 134-foot tower that faces a landscaped court. Both the Pool of Enchantment at the entrance and the bronze sun dial at the building's southeast corner are the work of sculptor M. Earl Cummings.

A special wing overlooking the Japanese Tea Garden was added in 1966 to house the Avery Brundage Collection of Oriental Art (now called the Asian Art Museum). On display are nearly 6,000 treasures covering 60 centuries of Asian civilization.

The museum houses extensive and varied art collections displayed in spacious galleries enclosing the court. Paintings include works by famous American and European artists. Though the Asian Art Museum is open daily from 10 A.M. to 5 P.M., the de Young is closed Monday and Tuesday; there is an admission charge.

The Japanese Tea Garden just west of the museum is open daily. Created for the 1894 Midwinter International Exposition, this 5-acre display of Oriental landscaping includes a moon bridge, temple, Oriental gateways (recently replaced) and lanterns, a large bronze Buddha, and a teahouse where Japanese women serve tea and cookies. In spring, blooming cherry trees make the garden an enchanting fairyland. The blossoms are at their peak around April 1. There is a modest admission fee.

The California Academy of Sciences grouping includes the Steinhart Aquarium, Morrison Planetarium, and a respected history museum—all under one roof. Steinhart's 14,000-member family includes, among others, 16 tuxedoed penguins (they queue up for meals every day at 11:30 A.M. and 4 P.M.), dolphins, seals, crocodiles, and that rarity of rarities—an Australian lungfish.

Steinhart's latest creation is the Fish Roundabout. A dizzying array of sharks, tuna, and open-ocean fish flash through the giant, ring-shaped, 100,000-gallon tank; observers stand on a platform in the center. At the nearby Touching Tidepool, children splash happily while docents pluck out a starfish or hermit crab for examination.

In the Wattis Hall of Man you view lifelike habitats ranging from the icy environs of the Arctic Eskimo to the parched desert home of the Australian Aborigine. In the new Earth and Space Hall the Safe-Quake simulates the movement of an earthquake up to 6.0 on the Richter scale.

The academy and the aquarium, open daily from 10 A.M. to 5 P.M. (later in summer), charges a small admission fee. There's an added charge for the Theater of the Stars planetarium's spectacular shows.

The Music Concourse, situated between the de Young Museum and the Academy of Sciences, is the setting for band concerts at 2 P.M. on Sundays and holidays (weather permitting). You can sit on terraces around the concourse or on benches.

Strybing Arboretum is a "must" for anyone interested in plants. Here in this self-contained, 60-acre world are about 5,000 species and varieties of plants from all over the globe, conveniently arranged according to geographical origin and carefully labeled.

The Arboretum, located along South Drive, is open from 8 A.M. to 4:30 P.M. on weekdays and from 10 A.M. to 5 P.M. on Saturday and Sunday; admission is free.

Conservatory of Flowers (open 8 A.M. to 4:50 P.M. daily) shelters another world. The atmosphere is warm and humid, the plants lush and tropical.

The conservatory houses many fascinating collections—bright crotons, large-flowered hibiscus, rare cycads, graceful ferns, exotic orchids. Along the path, among tall palms, are some of the largest and oldest philodendron plants under cultivation.

Be sure to look at the greenhouse itself. A replica of the conservatory at Kew Gardens, England, it was bought by James Lick, a San Francisco philanthropist. Its sections were transported from England around the Horn on a sailing ship. After the owner's death, the greenhouse was purchased by the city and erected in Golden Gate Park in 1878. The framework is wood, but the beams, unlike those of most greenhouses, are laminated. If you look closely, you can see how short pieces have been fitted together to form the dome.

Children's Playground and Zoo, in the southeast corner of the park adjacent to the Sharon Building (arts and crafts lessons), is popular with visitors of all ages. Kids from the small animal farm nuzzle other "kids" for handouts. Nearby, a newly restored 1912 Hershel-Spillman Carousel offers rides.

Kezar Stadium, a municipal field, is used principally by local high school football teams. Through 1970, Kezar was the home of San Francisco's professional football team, the '49ers. Kezar Pavilion, the indoor stadium, is used for sporting events, including professional boxing and roller derbies.

Public transportation makes getting to the park easy. Just take the No. 38 Geary bus west on Geary Street to 10th Avenue, then transfer to No. 10 Monterey bus and get off at the de Young Museum complex.

Cars can park along most of the drives—there are few "No Parking" signs. On Sundays, auto traffic is restricted along Kennedy Drive.

The city's western perimeter

Fortunately for all of us, the Golden Gate National Recreation Area saved the existing greenbelts on both sides of the bay (see page 20). On the San Francisco side of the bay, a coastal fortification plan, developed in 1854, coincidentally protected much of the city's western edge from development by establishing a natural greenbelt from Fort Mason to Fort Funston.

Because of the dangerous undertow, most of San Francisco's waterfront is not safe for swimming. However, James D. Phelan Beach offers one of the few safe swimming areas in the city. At Baker Beach you'll find one of the huge coastal guns remounted in the Battery Chamberlain, and a small museum depicting the seashore defense system. For a look at Mile Rock Lighthouse, the Golden Gate Bridge, and the Pacific Ocean, take the northern turnoff from Point Lobos Avenue to Land's End. Besides a view, you'll see the shelled bridge of the USS *San Francisco,* torpedoed in 1942 at Guadalcanal.

Several other recreational activities are available, you can sun or fish from the beaches; golf among cypress trees; visit an art museum or a zoo; or stroll through historic Fort Point.

Fort Point National Historic Site, huddling under the southern end of the Golden Gate Bridge, is reached from Lincoln Boulevard. Here Colonel Juan Bautista de Anza planted a cross in 1775. In 1853 the Americans, on the site of an old Spanish fort, started work on this massive brick, iron, and granite structure built roughly along the lines of Fort Sumter in South Carolina. The fort, which never fired a defensive shot, has been abandoned since 1914.

(Continued on page 28)

Ghirardelli

WARM GLOW of nighttime Ghirardelli Square (above) invites visitors to explore delightful mélange of shops and restaurants now sprinkled throughout former chocolate factory.

PROUD VENDER (left) displays still-wriggling catch of the day. Fisherman's Wharf, spiced with old salts, sounds, and smells of the sea, still lures visitors and residents alike, seeking a walk-away crab cocktail, steamed clams, or a taste of its famous sourdough bread.

27

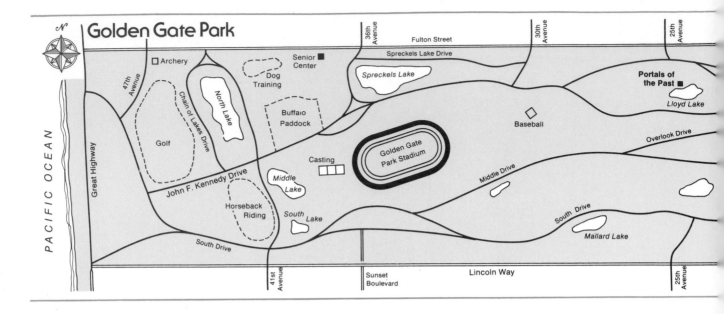

Golden Gate Park

Fulton Street · Spreckels Lake Drive · 36th Avenue · 30th Avenue · 25th Avenue · Archery · Senior Center · Dog Training · Spreckels Lake · Portals of the Past · Lloyd Lake · 47th Avenue · Chain of Lakes Drive · North Lake · Buffalo Paddock · Baseball · Overlook Drive · Golf · Casting · Golden Gate Park Stadium · PACIFIC OCEAN · Great Highway · Middle Drive · John F. Kennedy Drive · Middle Lake · Horseback Riding · South Lake · South Drive · Mallard Lake · South Drive · 41st Avenue · Sunset Boulevard · Lincoln Way · 25th Avenue

. . . Continued from page 26

Its most serious adversary proved to be the weather. Wind-driven salt water and fog have rusted out iron balustrades and spiral staircases and have eaten into the mortar. If the Golden Gate Bridge's imaginative chief engineer, Joseph Strauss, had not ordered construction of a special arch over the fort, it would have been torn down to make way for the bridge in the mid-1930s.

Part of the Golden Gate National Recreation Area, the fort is open daily from 10 A.M. to 5 P.M. Guided tours reward visitors with unusual views of the bridge and the bay's shifting tides. For information call the National Park Service, (415) 556-0560.

Fort Funston, the western boundary of the Golden Gate National Recreation Area, offers a wheelchair-accessible loop trail with beautiful views and occasional picnic areas. You can watch hang gliders soar in the strong winds above the area's high cliffs. The fort is open from 7 A.M. to dusk.

The California Palace of the Legion of Honor commands a heady view of the city from its hilltop in Lincoln Park at the end of El Camino del Mar, an extension of Lincoln Boulevard in the Presidio. Modeled after the Palais de la Legion d'Honneur in Paris, the art museum was given to the city in 1924 by the Spreckels family. Auguste Rodin's *The Thinker* graces the entrance to the collection of 16th to 20th century artworks. The museum is open daily from 10 A.M. to 5 P.M.

San Francisco Zoo ranks among the top six city zoos in the U.S. It's out at the edge of Ocean Beach (turn off the Great Highway at either Sloat Boulevard or Park Road). Open daily from 10 A.M. to 5:30 P.M., the collection boasts over 1,000 animals and birds.

Among some of the newer exhibits: A colony of koalas in a habitat patterned after an Australian outback station; an innovative Primate Discovery Center; and Gorilla World, a $2 million playground for the boisterous gorilla family.

Sigmund Stern Grove is an open-air wooded amphitheater just east of the San Francisco Zoo at 19th Avenue and Sloat Boulevard. The grove's annual Midsummer Music Festival features ten consecutive Sundays of free musical entertainment, from classical offerings to Gilbert and Sullivan. Concerts begin around 2 P.M., but come early to picnic.

The city's hills

San Francisco is famous for its many hills and the views that each affords. Some hills are more accessible than others (only a footpath reaches the summit of Mount Davidson, for instance), some are more interesting physically, and some provide exceptional views. Nob, Telegraph, and Russian hills, along with Twin Peaks, are probably San Francisco's best-known heights.

Telegraph Hill

At Lombard and Columbus streets, you pick up the road that climbs up Telegraph Hill to Coit Tower. Parking space at the top of the hill is limited, but with patience you can usually get a place. Or you can leave your car at a garage and board a MUNI bus. It will take you to the top and, if you prefer, you can walk down the footpath on the east slope of the hill.

Telegraph Hill gives good views of San Francisco's waterfront, Russian Hill, Nob Hill, the Bay and Golden Gate bridges, Alcatraz Island, Angel Island, Treasure Island and, on a clear day, some East Bay landmarks.

For an even loftier view, take the elevator (slight charge) to the top of Coit Tower (210 feet). Elevator operates from 11 A.M. to 5 P.M.

Coit Tower, dramatically lighted at night, is an easily recognized landmark against the city's skyline. It was

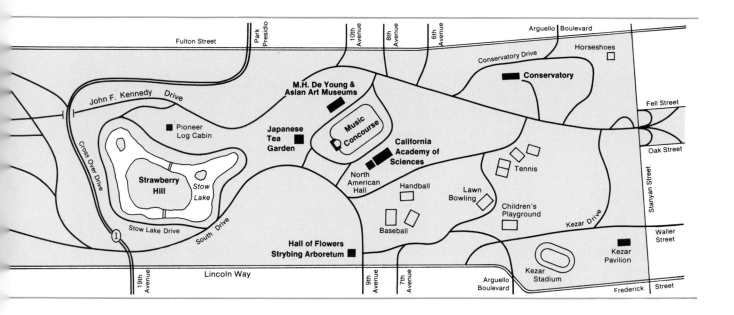

built in 1934 as a memorial to the city's volunteer fire-men from funds left to the city by Lillie Hitchcock Coit, a great fire buff. The shape of the tower is often said to resemble a fire hose nozzle. Inside the fluted cylindrical column are murals done by artists in 1934 under the Work Projects Administration.

If you choose to walk down from Telegraph Hill, take the pathway that curves down the eastern slope. You will come to two sets of steps, one leading to Filbert and the other to Greenwich Street. Either stairway takes you down to Montgomery, a short distance below, and then drops down a long, steep flight to Sansome at the foot of the hill.

Russian Hill

Located west of Telegraph Hill, roughly between Hyde, Taylor, Vallejo, and Greenwich streets, is Russian Hill. In the immediate area you'll find small green parks, quaint cottages, and skyscraper apartment buildings. Here you can drive on two of San Francisco's most interesting streets. Filbert between Hyde and Leavenworth is one of the city's steepest streets; Lombard between Hyde and Leavenworth is the crookedest—the brick road coils down in snakelike fashion amidst bright hydrangea gardens.

Nob Hill

To reach the top of this hill, take the California or Powell Street cable car. If you prefer to drive, you'll find several parking garages on California, close to Mason.

The very top of the hill covers about three square blocks. Before the earthquake and fire of 1906, this small hilltop was the site of the city's grandest mansions. Only one survives: the imposing brownstone built by James C. Flood. Now the Pacific Union Club, it faces California, just west of Mason.

Two of San Francisco's most famous hotels, the Fairmont and the Mark Hopkins, stand atop Nob Hill at California and Mason. The luxurious Fairmont, the tallest building on the hill, has several restaurants, a spacious lobby, and a cocktail lounge at the top. You can reach the Crown Room in an outside glass-walled elevator or, if you prefer, in an inside elevator.

Across California is the Mark Hopkins Hotel, long known for the elegant Top of the Mark cocktail lounge. Panoramic views unfold from both the Crown Room and the Top of the Mark.

Next to the Mark Hopkins Hotel, at the corner of California and Powell, is the elegant Stanford Court Hotel, on the site of the Stanford mansion. Rebuilt and refurbished in turn-of-the-century decor, the hotel has a dramatic circular driveway entrance, accented with a round fountain and topped by an opulent stained-glass dome. The lobby, with its potted palms, reminds you of an early 1900s photo. A glass-enclosed restaurant and cocktail lounge look out on the city skyline.

Up the hill, at 1075 California Street, are the chic Huntington Hotel and a renowned restaurant.

Grace Cathedral, a study in Gothic architecture, stands at California and Taylor. The country's third largest Episcopal cathedral, it was built in 1910. Of particular interest are the interior murals, stained-glass windows, and the Ghiberti doors—gilded bronze replicas of those at the Florence Baptistry.

Across from the cathedral is the Masonic Temple, a spacious auditorium used for fine arts and musical productions. It is open to visitors Monday through Friday.

Twin Peaks

Situated in the center of the city, Twin Peaks are noted for their panoramic views of the Bay Area. Now a 65-acre park, their crests are popular lookouts. To get there, take Upper Market Street to Twin Peaks Boulevard.

CITY LIFE seems far away when you're fishing near Fort Point (above), along Golden Gate National Recreation Area. Country's largest urban park, GGNRA stretches along city's waterfront from Fort Funston to Aquatic Park.

COUPLE STOPS a moment to savor serene surroundings of Golden Gate Park's Japanese Tea Garden (left). Graceful tiered pagoda highlights 3 acres of Oriental landscaping, with delicate blossoms, wandering pathways, cool pools.

Streets that unlock the city

You'll make your own discoveries of some of San Francisco's most interesting byways. Here are a few of its famous (and some not-so-famous) streets, with an idea of what you'll find along them.

Market Street. San Francisco's best-known thoroughfare runs diagonally across the city from Twin Peaks to the Ferry Building. The strip of Market south of Union Square is a continuation of the downtown shopping area. Underneath Market runs BART, giving the street a new look—less traffic, wider sidewalks, new landscaping, and old-fashioned street lamps.

At the foot of Market is the Ferry Building, partially obscured by the double-decked Embarcadero Freeway. Across the street lies Justin Herman Plaza with its monumental Vaillancourt Fountain, a walk-through design of 101 concrete boxes. Extending from the Ferry Building to the base of the Oakland Bay Bridge, the Waterfront Promenade is an ideal spot for jogging, sunning, picnicking, and fishing. Tidal stairs bring strollers right to the water's edge.

High-rise buildings accent Market Street's rejuvenation. The Crown-Zellerbach building, an impressive, 20-story green monolith, rises above a pleasantly landscaped park (popular with noon "brown baggers") at the corner of Market and Bush. At 555 Market Street you can stroll through colorful gardens at the Standard Oil Company Plaza; on weekdays you can go inside the 43-story building to view an exhibit on the history of petroleum. The Crocker Building (Post, Montgomery, and Market) towers 38 stories above its green mall.

At Market and New Montgomery streets stands a San Francisco landmark—the Sheraton-Palace Hotel. The reputation of this magnificent 8-story structure began with its opening in 1875. Built by silver king William Ralston, the building was severely damaged in the 1906 earthquake-fire; restoration was completed in 1909. The glass-roofed Garden Court dining room (a historical landmark) is a fine example of old San Francisco elegance—and a popular place for lunch or Sunday brunch.

Geary Street. A street of many faces, Geary runs west from Market, ending at Sutro Park near the ocean. On its way through town it passes by some of San Francisco's smartest shops, Union Square, the theater district, stunning St. Mary's Cathedral, and the Japan Center.

Mission Street. Running roughly parallel to Market through downtown, Mission takes an abrupt turn south after crossing Van Ness en route to Daly City. This area and other "South of Market" streets are gradually acquiring a renewed luster with the opening of new hotels, restaurants, galleries, and cabarets.

A block south of Mission between Third and Fourth streets stands the $126 million Moscone Convention Center, location of the 1984 Democratic National Convention. Its huge exhibit hall is the largest column-free structure of its kind in the U.S.

The Old Mint at Fifth and Mission, now a free museum, is considered one of the finest examples of Federal classical revival architecture in the West. You'll see restored rooms, western art, and a collection of pioneer gold coins. A pyramid of gold bars valued at $4 million is dramatically displayed in a circular vault. In the rear, a special coins and medals division provides treasures. The mint is open weekdays 10 A.M. to 4 P.M.

Se habla Espanol signs appear around the Mission District, with Duboce, Castro, Harrison, and 28th streets forming the perimeter. Walking around near Mission Dolores, you'll feel the strong Spanish influence. Mission Street once linked the village of Yerba Buena to this Franciscan outpost; now BART tunnels beneath it.

Mission Dolores, established in 1776, was the sixth of the California mission (Franciscan) chain. Its ceilings are decorated with Indian art, and the original bell and altar from Mexico remain. Be sure to walk through the garden cemetery, final resting place of many San Francisco pioneers. An impressive statue of Father Junipero Serra stands in the courtyard.

California Street. Taking off from Market at the Justin Herman Plaza, California extends all the way through town, avoiding much of the business traffic and ending at Lincoln Park. Along the way, you'll climb from the canyons of Montgomery's "Wall Street" through colorful Chinatown to the heights of Nob Hill, passing some of San Francisco's famous hotels, the Masonic Temple, and Grace Cathedral.

Union Street. Passing by the North Beach and upper Grant Avenue areas, Union becomes better known and less residential after crossing Van Ness. In pre-Gold Rush days, the district was known as Cow Hollow—it was, in fact, the city's dairyland. But its renaissance began in the late 1950s when ingenious merchants began reclaiming its vintage dwellings, cow barns, and carriage houses and converting them to a flourishing shopping area with galleries, boutiques, and restaurants.

Clement Street. A melting pot of ethnic life, Clement is trying hard to maintain its identity. This shopping area, not really frequented by tourists, has a little bit of everything—almost all authentic. Long known as a Russian neighborhood, it now harbors so many Asians it's called Chinatown II.

Polk Street. In an afternoon you can explore on foot much of the 10-block length of Polk between Union Street on the north and Pine Street on the south. Sandwiched between the odds and ends emporiums are intriguing specialty shops, antique stores, galleries, and restaurants that give the street a reputation for both good eating and good shopping.

Sutter Street. Its name appropriate for today's shopping prospector, this 1.8-mile street runs from the financial district to the residential uplands and includes a rich lode of treasure in 8 blocks. Lined with grand and small hotels, specialty houses and boutiques, serious art galleries and import emporiums, fashionable restaurants and small cafés.

Outer Sacramento Street. This part of Sacramento has blossomed into a shopping sector reminiscent of Union Street. What was formerly a service area for Pacific and Presidio Heights residents is now a browsable, 7-block cluster of shops, galleries, and boutiques, many of them occupying turn-of-the-century clapboards. Most shopping is between Broderick and Spruce streets.

The city's cultural side

San Francisco's cultural life began simultaneously with its financial history—in the 1850s. It is reported that the city's first classical concert was a trombone solo in 1850. From the beginning, local audiences were warm to actors and musicians; concert halls and theaters abounded, and performers were handsomely rewarded with gold. The city has never lost its zest for the arts.

The performing arts

Music and theater are not limited to legitimate stages. Sunday afternoon outdoor concerts are held in Golden Gate Park and, in summer, in the Sigmund Stern Grove (along Sloat Boulevard near 19th Avenue; see page 28).

American Conservatory Theatre is internationally acclaimed as North America's finest resident theater company. ACT presents classical and modern drama in its season from early October into May. Curtain time for the performances at the Geary Theatre (415 Geary Street) is 8 P.M. Monday through Saturday and also 2 P.M. on Saturday and some Wednesdays.

San Francisco Ballet performs at the Opera House in the Civic Center. The present repertory season extends from January into May; in addition, the company performs *The Nutcracker* at the Opera House during Christmas time. The American Ballet Theatre also dances at the Opera House from late winter to early spring.

San Francisco Chamber Orchestra music can be heard at Herbst Theater and the California Palace of the Legion of Honor from mid-December through April.

San Francisco Opera's 11-week season begins in mid-September. Performances are usually held on Tuesday, Wednesday, Friday, and Saturday nights as well as on Sunday afternoons. In March or April, "Spring Opera" performances showcase young stars who have progressed through the Opera Center's training program. Spring "Pocket Opera" is presented at a downtown theater.

San Francisco Symphony's regular season starts in December and extends through May. The Louise M. Davies Symphony Hall (opposite the Opera House in the Performing Arts Center) is the symphony's permanent home. Performances take place Wednesday through Saturday nights and Thursday afternoons. The symphony often plays pops concerts during the summer.

Touring companies perform at the Opera House, Herbst Theater, Curran Theater, Masonic Memorial Auditorium, Grace Cathedral, the Legion of Honor, and the Cow Palace (south of the city). Check the Sunday newspaper's "Datebook" for listings and ticket information.

Beach Blanket Babylon at Club Fugazi (678 Green Street) is a musical paean to San Francisco. Cabaret-style entertainment takes place Wednesday through Sunday nights; there's also a Sunday matinee. Advance reservations are necessary for both preferred and general admission. Children are admitted only for the matinee. For reservations, call (415) 421-4222.

A mélange of museums

Museum subjects range from history and culture to oil and economics; take your pick. Here's a sampling.

African-American Historical Society exhibits, at Fort Mason, Building C, deal with Black California and Black Civil War history. Exhibits are open noon to 5 P.M. Tuesday through Saturday.

California Historical Society's opulent Whittier Mansion seems an appropriate setting for exhibits tracing California's development in art and literature. The museum, located at 2090 Jackson Street, is open 1 to 5 P.M. Wednesday, Saturday, and Sunday afternoons.

Chinese Culture Center, at 750 Kearny Street (third floor of the Holiday Inn), is both a meeting place for the community and a free museum for the display of Chinese arts and culture. The center is open 10 A.M. to 4 P.M. Tuesday through Saturday, plus Sunday afternoon.

Chinese Historical Society of America has displays of early California mining activity and the building of the transcontinental railroad, as well as personal memorabilia. It's open 1 to 5 P.M. Tuesday through Saturday, except Christmas and New Year's Day; admission is free. The museum is in Chinatown at 17 Adler Place, just off Grant Avenue.

The Mexican Museum displays art from pre-Hispanic to the contemporary Mexican period. The museum is open noon to 5 P.M. Wednesday through Sunday. A small admission fee gets you into the museum at Fort Mason, Building D.

Museoitalo Americano is dedicated to the preservation and display of Italian and Italian-American art, culture, and history. Located at Fort Mason, Building C, the free museum is open Wednesday through Sunday, afternoons only.

San Francisco Fire Department Pioneer Memorial Museum (655 Presidio Avenue at Bush) houses a unique collection of equipment, photos, and memorabilia of the city's fire companies since their 1849 volunteer days. Hand pumpers, elegant coaches, and the city's first fire engine are on view from 1 to 4 P.M. Thursday through Sunday.

Special exhibits include Chevron's "World of Oil" in the lobby of 555 Market Street. Working models, moving displays, actual equipment, and a film (shown at noon) tell the complete story of oil. The free museum is open daily Monday through Friday. On the lobby level of the Federal Reserve Bank (101 Market Street) the "World of Economics" is explained in a hands-on fashion.

Vintage houses include the 1861 Octagon House—an elegant home of unusual design, owned by the National Society of Colonial Dames. The completely restored house features authentic furnishings. Located at Gough and Union, it's open from 12 to 3 P.M. on the second and fourth Thursday and second Sunday of each month.

The Haas-Lilienthal House (2007 Franklin Street) occupies nearly an entire block. With its gables, intricate gingerbread trim, and four-story "witch hat" tower, it's a Victorian classic. A small admission fee includes the price of a tour; guides will escort you through the house from 12 to 4 P.M. Wednesday and 11 A.M. to 4:30 P.M. Sunday. The lower level contains a bookshop.

Looking at art

You'll find art galleries scattered throughout the city, but there are four main museums.

San Francisco Museum of Modern Art, on the third and fourth floors of the Veterans Building in the Civic Center, is the nucleus of modern art in the Bay Area. Traveling exhibitions add depth to the collection. Permanent acquisitions include works by Henri Matisse, Paul Klee, Alexander Calder, Jackson Pollock, and other noted artists. The museum is open from 10 A.M. to 6 P.M. on Tuesday, Wednesday, and Friday; 10 to 5 on Saturday and Sunday; and 10 to 10 on Thursday; it is closed on Monday. There is a fee.

Asian Art Museum's collection of treasures spanning 60 centuries is internationally acclaimed. You'll see bronze Hindu deities, sandstone Khmer figures, whimsical ivory and jade figures, fine porcelains, and silken scrolls. The museum (open 10 A.M. to 5 P.M. Tuesday through Sunday) charges admission. It's located in the de Young Memorial Museum at Golden Gate Park.

California Palace of the Legion of Honor is one of San Francisco's most splendid museums and sites. This neo-Classical edifice, set among green lawns, dominates the height of Land's End in Lincoln Park, in the city's northwest corner. Paintings span the 16th to the 20th centuries, with emphasis on 18th and 19th century French artists. The collection of Rodin sculpture is one of America's finest. Check the schedule for free docent tours of permanent collections. The museum is open from 10 A.M. to 5 P.M. Wednesday through Sunday; admission fee.

M. H. de Young Memorial Museum houses such treasures as Rembrandt portraits, El Greco paintings, Flemish tapestries, and many works by other major artists. The gallery of American art is a recent addition. Besides paintings and sculpture, you'll see displays of period furniture, porcelain, and silver. Exhibits include artifacts from Africa and Oceania.

Located in Golden Gate Park, the museum is open Wednesday through Sunday from 10 A.M. to 5 P.M.; admission fee. Guided tours are given daily.

GOURMET TIPS FOR CITY DINING

San Francisco menus are as international as the United Nations. With restaurants ranging from modest to expensive, the city has more than 2,600 places to dine. The quality and variety of cuisines—from Basque, Moroccan, or Hungarian delicacies to gold field creations—have made eating San Francisco's number one attraction.

San Franciscans take food seriously. Many arguments rage over the relative merits of a favorite restaurant. Proper atmosphere is almost as important to enjoyable dining as good food, and San Francisco establishments have met the challenge. You'll find elegant restaurants in grand hotels, cozy corners in family-run eateries, and salty atmosphere at Fisherman's Wharf.

The sea provides many traditional San Francisco delicacies—Dungeness crab, abalone, and Hang Town Fry (an oyster and egg dish favored by the 49ers). Other local favorites are the crusty sourdough French bread, green goddess salad, artichoke specialties, cheeses from neighboring counties, and California wines.

Because of the prominent international influence, you can expect to find Spanish and Mexican cuisines (they are different) competing for diners' attention with Chinese, French, and German food. You'll also discover Russian, Indian, Vietnamese, Italian, Korean, Filipino, Japanese, Greek, and Scandinavian menus.

Chinese cooking is in a class of its own; selection is the problem. Most is Cantonese, predominantly steamed and stir-fried foods, lightly seasoned.

You'll notice the crisp vegetables. Sauces are light and delicate. Mandarin and Szechwan dishes are more highly spiced (sometimes volcanically) and usually stir-fried. Wine is often used in cooking.

Don't go to a Japanese restaurant with a hole in your sock, for you may be asked to remove your shoes. You may find yourself seated on the floor in order to eat from a traditionally low Japanese table, and your food might be cooked at the table. Your waitress will probably wear the traditional Japanese kimono.

Plunge right in and try *sushi* (a combination of rice with an endless variety of fillings). *Sukiyaki* is best known, but try *sashimi, tempura,* or *teriyaki*. *Saki* (the Japanese wine) is served warm.

Italian food is a never-ending series of courses. Go easy on each dish—otherwise, after antipasto, soup, salad, and pasta, you may find it difficult to eat your entrée.

French cooking needs little introduction. It's done imaginatively in San Francisco, where some of the most elegant restaurants feature French cuisine. Ask your waiter for house specialties.

Basque food centers around lamb. You'll probably eat boarding-house style with community serving dishes. A bottle of wine is served for every four people, and a bowl of fruit is your dessert.

Armenian, Jewish, Swiss, and Indian fare are only a sampling of the additional around-the-world discoveries in the city. Finally, you might want to end a meal at a coffee house, sipping an Italian *cappuccino* or an Irish coffee—both popular in San Francisco.

Many visitors to the San Francisco Bay area find Marin County the surprise treat of their visit. Marin's bay side is one of the most photogenic shorelines in California. Two ridges project like stubby fingers, forming a narrow horseshoe that encloses shallow Richardson Bay. The main Marin peninsula, with Mount Tamalpais in the background, faces across this small bay to the Tiburon peninsula and the low, offshore pyramid of Angel Island. Sausalito and Tiburon offer unusual shops, good restaurants, and lots of bay and boat watching. These two waterside centers have long been known as gathering places for artists, sailors, anglers, commuters, and visitors.

Across the Bay Bridge, crowded into a narrow strip between the water of San Francisco Bay and the low hills that rise to the east, the East Bay communities parallel the shoreline.

East Bay's attractions are plentiful. Discover Lake Merritt (in the heart of Oakland), handsome Oakland Museum, fine waterfront restaurants, California's largest university, and some of the state's finest parks.

The narrow belt of land south of San Francisco is divided into two distinctly different regions by a forested ridge of mountains that runs down its length. The bay side of the mountains is crowded with cities; the ocean side is sprinkled with peaceful farms, unspoiled beaches, and lightly traveled country roads.

Marin-on-the-bay

Sausalito is a hill town; Tiburon includes 10 square miles of salt water; Belvedere was once an island. But you catch only tantalizing glimpses of these bayside areas from U.S. Highway 101. For a real look, you must follow the slow roads along the shore east of the freeway. To absorb the special flavor of the Marin County communities, you'll want to browse through charming shops, stop at a seaside café, or stroll past harbors and nearby chandleries.

Sausalito's Mediterranean pleasures

Sausalito's setting has the quality of a southern European seacoast village. Its harbors are full of small vessels of varied sizes and shapes; its hillside-hung homes recall those of the Italian Riviera. Shops and restaurants are concentrated at the water's edge.

Before the time of the Golden Gate Bridge, Sausalito was the transfer point for Marin commuters. They came this far south by train and went on to San Francisco by ferry. These services stopped in 1937 with the completion of the bridge; however, commuter service has been revived. Modern ferries operate from the foot of Anchor Street.

Across the Golden Gate, North Bay seaside villages lure artists, sailors, and visitors. Windswept cliffs, virgin redwoods, stately mountains, and deer-dotted islands invite outdoor enthusiasts. East Bay discoveries include Oakland's downtown lake, a handsome museum, and next-door parks. Berkeley boasts California's largest university. South, along the peninsula, you'll find the way to San Jose, Stanford, an amusement park, and delightful foothill communities. Santa Cruz is ringed by mountains and a string of sparkling state beaches.

SEASIDE SAUSALITO hugs Richardson Bay at southern end of Marin County. Bridgeway, town's waterfront street, leads past shops and restaurants.

The Bay Area

A short distance north of the Golden Gate Bridge, the road to Sausalito (Alexander exit) branches to the east. As you descend you have superb views of Raccoon Straits and Angel Island. Then the road drops, with abrupt turns, to Bridgeway, the waterfront main street of Sausalito. Along the way you'll get your first good look at the stair-stepped hill houses rising above you.

You can get a good view of the Sausalito terrain and the bay from the dining deck of the historic Alta Mira Hotel on Bulkley Avenue.

Sausalito is a town of small shops. The most complicated (and varied) shopping place is The Village Fair on Bridgeway not far from Plaza Viña del Mar. On its various levels, 40 small specialty shops contain intriguing handcrafted goods and imports from all over the world. In the past, Village Fair has served as an opium and gambling den, a hideout for gangsters, and a distillery (during Prohibition).

Walking south from Village Fair along either side of Bridgeway, you'll encounter one small shop after another; most are housed in refurbished, colorfully painted buildings. At the south end of the beach, a pier supports several restaurants.

At 2900 Bridgeway, the Army Corps of Engineers operates an impressive hydraulic model of the San Francisco Bay and Delta. From 9 A.M. to 4 P.M. Tuesday through Saturday, you can watch the movement of the tides, the flow and current of water, and other forces affecting the sea.

Turn to Tiburon

Perched on the shore of Richardson Bay directly opposite Sausalito, Tiburon epitomizes the good life. Day-trippers, locals, and yachtsmen sip their fizzes on its sunny docks, while across San Francisco Bay the city slips beneath the fog. The century-old Main Street remains so intact that the city founders would feel right at home. Outside of town, a wealth of bayside beauty invites leisurely exploration.

Trails at the 11-acre Richardson Bay Audubon Center, at 376 Greenwood Beach Road, meander to fresh-water ponds, salt-water habitats, and a mud flat. Birdlife abounds, especially in winter, on more than 900 acres of tidelands supervised by the center. Free guided walks leave Sunday at 9 A.M. and 1 P.M. The center also has a natural history bookstore, interpretive displays, films, and lectures. Hours are 9 A.M. to 5 P.M. Wednesday through Sunday; admission is free of charge. Tours of the center's 1876 Lyford House are conducted from 1 to 4 P.M. most Sundays.

Nearby Richardson Bay Park offers bike and running paths, a playing field, and a fitness course. It's a busy place on weekends.

On a steep hillside overlooking town, splendid Old St. Hilary's Church and adjoining wildflower preserve is open for visits on Wednesday and Sunday afternoons. The redwood carpenter's Gothic church was built in 1886. Paths lead among 217 species of ferns and seed-bearing plants, many native to the area.

Beach Road will take you over Belvedere Lagoon past the yacht club and the 1866 China Cabin, formerly the social saloon of a clipper ship and now a museum. Most tourists head toward Main Street to shop, eat, or look at the yachts. Ark Row's floating summer homes (circa 1890) now rest on land and house an array of shops. At Tiburon Vintners, there's wine tasting daily, starting from 10 A.M.

Commuters ferry between Tiburon and San Francisco during the working week; tourists fill boats on weekends. Ferries also connect Tiburon and Angel Island. For information, call the Red & White Fleet at (415) 546-2815.

Roaming through Marin

Small towns are grouped near Marin County's main north-south thoroughfare—U.S. 101. Many lodge in canyons west of the highway. San Rafael extends down to the bay, and you can take a bridge across the bay to Richmond, on its east side.

Mill Valley got its name from a historic saw mill which still stands in skeleton form. The charming public square in the center of town evokes memories of England. From here you can see the meandering streets and the steeply gabled roofs of lovely homes tucked in the hills surrounding the town. At the botanical gardens on Edgewood Avenue, you walk among native California plants in a natural environment.

Marin's most traveled east-west road is Sir Francis Drake Boulevard. Starting from its junction with State Highway 17 just west of the Richmond-San Rafael Bridge, it threads its way from U.S. 101 west to the Point Reyes Peninsula. Along its route you'll pass the towns of Ross, a treasury of stately homes with an Art and Garden Center, and San Anselmo, once the junction for railroad lines throughout Marin. Like a medieval French castle, the San Francisco Theological Seminary dominates the southern hillside. Near Fairfax, to the west, are the lovely lakes of Bon Tempe, Lagunitas, Alpine, and Phoenix—ideal for picnicking, hiking, and horseback riding.

In San Rafael you'll find a replica of Mission San Rafael Archangel, founded in 1817; Boyd Park and Museum; the Marin Historical Society Museum; and to the east, on San Pablo Bay, a fishing village and swimming beach.

Nestled in a group of hills just north of San Rafael is the imaginative, domed Marin County Civic Center, designed by Frank Lloyd Wright. It's open daily and there's no charge to look around. Here, also, stands the Veterans' Memorial Auditorium-Theater, a center for performing arts.

Situated in the rolling hills of northern Marin County, Novato's residential areas belie its early Spanish settlers. Nine miles west of Novato is the Marin French Cheese Company, a good place to watch cheese being made on weekday mornings, when the factory is busiest. Tours are given daily; call (707) 762-6001 for information.

Each fall the Renaissance Pleasure Faire, an Elizabethan festival, is held on the meadows south of State Highway 37. At this replica of an English country fair, you'll find food, drink, crafts, and entertainment—both on stage and off. (For information, write to Renaissance Pleasure Faire, P.O. Box B, Novato, CA 94947.)

High to low: Marin's parks

Ranging from an island in the bay to one of the bay area's tallest peaks, Marin's parks are a varied lot. Marin, curiously, has greater extremes of climate than the counties farther north, principally because Mount Tamalpais and the high ridges leading up to it form a sharp barrier against sea fogs.

Marin Headlands—a bay view

Minutes north of San Francisco lie the Marin Headlands, now part of the Golden Gate National Recreation Area. Plummeting from bare-crested hills into deep water all along its length, the westerly section of Marin Headlands stretches from the Golden Gate Bridge to Point Bonita. Here you'll find protected coastal valleys, windswept beaches, former army forts, abandoned artillery bunkers, and magnificent views of San Francisco, the Golden Gate Bridge, and the Pacific Ocean.

If you seek solitude—take a hike. The Miwok, Coast, and Tennessee Valley trails begin in the headlands and traverse the coastal hills. Rodeo Beach and Kirby Cove offer fine grounds for a group outing or family picnic. These beaches afford sweeping ocean views, but their waters are not safe for swimming. A hostel at Fort Barry offers day and overnight facilities for a slight fee; call (415) 331-2777 for information.

Point Bonita Light Station perches on the eroding tip of the Golden Gate's north side. A prime weather station and warning point for the bay, it's a reliable gauge of the comings and goings of the summer fog bank. The first sounding device installed here in 1856 to help befogged mariners was an army sergeant, charged with firing a muzzle-loading cannon at half-hour intervals whenever the weather demanded. At the end of 2 months, he was exhausted and had to petition for relief. The station is open on winter weekends for a 2-hour tour at 1 P.M.; guided sunset walks take place the first and third Wednesday of each month. Call (415) 331-1540 for information.

Fort Cronkhite is the outermost of three sentinel forts on the north side of San Francisco Bay. Reasons for visiting are several: rockhounds roam Cronkhite's gravelly shore in search of jadeite and jasper, especially in winter; the summer crowd comes to bask in the lee of bluffs that offer some protection from the prevailing westerlies; and people who like to watch seabirds fly have a superior arena.

To reach the headlands from San Francisco, take the Alexander Avenue exit off U.S. 101. There are two entrances; one follows Conzelman Road along the coastal cliffs, the other heads through the tunnel into Rodeo Valley. From the north, take the last exit to your right before crossing the bridge.

Angel Island State Park

Part of the fun of going to Angel Island is the way you get there. A tour boat of the Red & White Fleet (pier 43½) at San Francisco's Fisherman's Wharf or ferry service from Tiburon delivers you to this woodsy, mountainous island in the morning and picks you up in the afternoon. At Ayala Cove, you'll find picnic facilities and beaches for sunning. Bike rentals are available in summer; you can also take along your own. You'll find posted hiking trail maps. A small museum and partially restored immigration station contain relics of the island's past.

Mount Tamalpais—for the view

"Mount Tam" is the keystone of four park units that have common boundaries. A finger reaches down to sea level at Muir Beach, but the main body of the park drapes across the upper slopes of the 2,571-foot mountain. Here you'll find a labyrinth of hiking and riding trails.

Picnic grounds are at the Bootjack area on Panoramic Highway leading up from Mill Valley, near the park headquarters; campsites are at Pan Toll and still higher at East Peak. The large parking area at East Peak is as far as cars can go.

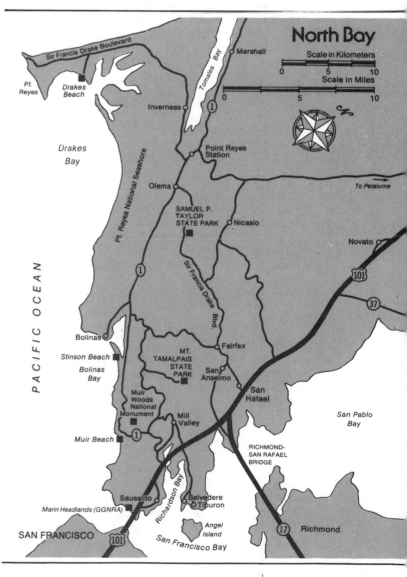

Muir Woods: Closest redwoods to San Francisco

Always cool and green, the 502-acre national monument named for naturalist John Muir preserves a stand of virgin coast redwoods (*Sequoia sempervirens*) at the foot of Mount Tamalpais.

For a leisurely walk, follow the ½-mile, sign-guided Bootjack Trail. Redwoods and Douglas fir tower above the forest floor. You will also find tanoak, alder, buckeye, and California laurel, from which one type of bay leaf finds its way into spice jars.

The central part of the park and most of its paths are on a relatively level stretch of forest floor. If you want to do some exploring off the main trail, consider the two trails that climb high up the canyon wall to lookout points and a panoramic view to either side of the Golden Gate.

Muir Woods, part of the Golden Gate National Recreation Area, is open daily during daylight hours. No camping or picnicking is allowed.

You can reach the woods by way of State 1 and the Panoramic Highway. The road into the park, like all those flanking Mount Tamalpais, is narrow and winds tortuously up the long grade from sea level.

Oakland: East Bay's major city

Though Oakland's "big city" reputation may not equal San Francisco's, some Oakland attractions can match, or even exceed, those of its fabled sister.

The third largest city in Northern California, Oakland is an important industrial center with the second largest Pacific Coast shipping port. The city prides itself on its recreation areas, international airport, impressive sports complex, and exceptional museum. Here, too, is the headquarters of BART—the Bay Area Rapid Transit system. Berkeley, also on this side of the bay, contains California's largest university, plus some of the Bay Area's finest parks.

Oakland was incorporated in 1852. In the early days of the city's development, its economic life was clustered close to the waterfront in the area known today as Jack London Square. Oakland's main artery was Broadway; business activity expanded to the north along this street, now the center of urban renewal.

Knowledgeable volunteers offer free walking tours through Oakland's landmark areas Wednesday and Saturday afternoons. Call (415) 273-3234 or 273-3831 for information.

For additional information, write to the Oakland Convention and Visitors Bureau, 1000 Broadway, Suite 200, Oakland, CA 94607; or call (415) 839-9000.

Riding BART is an experience for everyone. Moving from underground stations to elevated tracks, shining BART cars streak from Richmond and Concord on the north to Fremont on the south, and underneath the bay through San Francisco to Daly City. Visit BART Headquarters (800 Madison Street) for a route map.

Oakland's International Airport, within minutes of downtown, is served by interstate and major U.S. carriers. Limousine and bus service is available to Berkeley, downtown Oakland, and San Francisco.

The Port of Oakland, Northern California's leading shipping center, is the country's largest container port. It's fun to drive through and watch cargo from all over the world being unloaded. Six well-maintained parks dot the industrial waterfront. You can enjoy a dockside meal at Jack London Square while watching ships pass in and out of the Oakland Estuary, or view the action from the 140-acre Seventh Street Terminal (it's easy to reach).

From May through August, the Port of Oakland offers harbor boat tours. Leaving from Jack London Square twice each Thursday, the 1½-hour tours are free; for reservations, call (415) 839-7493.

Downtown Oakland

Oakland has undergone a face lift. Overlooking some beautifully restored old buildings is the 20-story Hyatt Regency Hotel. From its top-floor restaurant you'll enjoy sweeping views of the entire Bay Area. Adjoining the Hyatt is the huge Oakland Convention Center. Between the two structures are landscaped pedestrian malls and the most beautiful BART station in the system (14th and Broadway).

A favorite recreation spot for Oakland and other East Bay residents, Lake Merritt is a 155-acre body of salt water right in the heart of the city. The Y-shaped lake is encircled by a 122-acre park strip and a main thoroughfare. Green lawns and cool shade greet you as you turn off Grand Avenue and enter Lakeside Park to sample its variety of activities.

The oldest waterfowl refuge in the country is an area on the northeast arm of the lake. The refuge was set aside in 1870 for the protection of the ducks and other waterfowl that flock to the lake. Between November and April, the bird count here may climb as high as 5,000. You can buy a bag of grain and feed the birds, or watch them any day at 3:30 P.M. being fed by park naturalists.

The Camron-Stanford House, an Oakland landmark at 1418 Lakeside Drive, is the last Victorian on the shore of Lake Merritt. Built in 1876 for $15,000, it later served as the Oakland Public Museum for 57 years. When the new museum opened, the stately Victorian was painstakingly restored as an example of ornate Victorian design and lifestyle. You can tour the building Sunday from 1 to 5 P.M., and Wednesday from 11 A.M. to 4 P.M. Docents provide detailed descriptions.

Other activities around the lake include a children's fairyland, gardens, lawn bowling and putting greens, summer band concerts, and boating facilities. The sailboat clubhouse near the wildlife refuge has launching ramps for sailboats and motorboats. On the west shore of Lake Merritt is the main boathouse, where you can rent canoes, rowboats, and sailboats. Launch trips around the lake on the *Merritt Queen,* a replica of an old Mississippi riverboat, are offered on weekends.

QUEEN QUAFFS *goblet of mead (right) at Renaissance Pleasure Faire. Each year costumed "royalty" and visitors imbibe Elizabethan music and merriment in Marin countryside.*

WINDSWEPT HILLS, *plummeting cliffs, steel blue waters welcome day hikers to wildly beautiful Marin Headlands (below). Just north of Golden Gate and cosmopolitan San Francisco, these open, rugged lands are a protected part of Golden Gate National Recreation Area.*

For excitement, try Oakland's museum

Oakland's handsome museum covers four square blocks alongside and beneath an evergreen park. The three-tiered complex is constructed so that the roof of each level becomes a garden and terrace for the one above. To enter the museum at 10th and Fallon streets, on the south shore of Lake Merritt, you walk down, not up.

The basic concept of the museum is not only intriguing but, in many ways, unique. Three different disciplines—history, natural science, and art—are combined in one museum displaying its treasures as environments. In the Cowell Hall of California History, you'll see actual rooms—kitchens, parlors, offices out of the past—or vivid displays suggesting a historical period, such as the time of an election campaign, the Gold Rush era, or the 1906 earthquake. Visitors to the Natural Sciences gallery take a simulated walk across California's eight biotic zones re-created through imaginative life-like exhibits.

The museum is located at 10th and Oak streets, a block from the Lake Merritt BART station. It's open Wednesday through Sunday; admission is free. There's parking beneath the building. For recorded information, call (415) 834-2413.

Pause for history at Jack London Square

Oakland's waterfront, the birthplace of the city, begins at historic Jack London Square, a 10-block area located on the Oakland Estuary at the foot of Broadway. Here, around landscaped malls, are shipping wharves, marina docks, restaurants, and shops.

Of special interest is the First and Last Chance Saloon, a weathered and rustic old building located on the edge of the square at 50 Webster Street. Built in 1880 from the remains of a whaling ship, the building was first a bunkhouse for oystermen and later a saloon. A favorite boyhood hangout of California author Jack London, the saloon is filled with photos and mementos of the era. It's open from 1 P.M. to 2 A.M. daily except Sunday. Ask the bartender about its history.

Oakland sports complex

The Oakland-Alameda County Coliseum complex is two separate circular structures—an outdoor stadium and an indoor arena. At the outdoor stadium you can watch professional baseball; in the arena, ice hockey, basketball, stage shows, and civic and cultural activities take place. The coliseum complex is well designed—every seat is comfortable and provides a good view. Adjacent to the arena floor is an exhibit hall for trade, boat, home, and car shows.

The coliseum is just east of the Nimitz Freeway. Take the Hegenberger or 66th Avenue exit to the spacious parking lot, or take BART to the Coliseum station.

Knowland Park: home of the zoo

Animals—real ones and sculptured ones—welcome visitors to the Oakland Zoo, located in Knowland Park. One observation point allows you to look a Bengal tiger right in the eye. From across a narrow moat, you can toss peanuts to Malaysian sun bears. Children are welcome to pick up goat kids and piglets and to pet a baby llama.

To reach the zoo, take the Golf Links Road turnoff from MacArthur Freeway (Interstate Highway 580).

A look at Victorians

Many of the Oakland area's old homes are dilapidated, and many have been torn down, but a few choice examples of Victoriana remain.

Dunsmuir House, in southern Oakland, is a notable product of Victorian wealth and taste. The 37-room estate cost a cool $350,000 in 1899. The house and its 48-acre grounds are open to the public on Sundays from noon to 4 P.M. Golden Gate Park designer John McLaren did the landscaping; that alone is worth a visit. The house is located at 2960 Peralta Oaks Court; there's a nominal admission charge.

The McConaghy Estate, just south of Oakland in Hayward, looks much as it did in 1886. The 93-year-old farmhouse estate, authentically renovated and refurbished, is now open for touring Thursday through Sunday from 1 to 4 P.M. for a slight admission fee. The McConaghy Estate is about ½-mile west of State 17 at 18701 Hesperian Boulevard (next to J. F. Kennedy Park); it is also served by the A.C. Transit bus service.

More visual treats around town

A few other buildings deserve at least a "pass-by." The Paramount Theatre of the Arts (2025 Broadway) was an opulent movie palace in the 1930s. Carefully restored, it is now a center for concerts, as well as symphony and ballet performances. On the 4700 block of Lincoln Avenue are two architectural treasures: the Mormon Temple and the Greek Orthodox Church. For a parkside stop, visit the Morcom Rose Garden at Jean Street off Grand Avenue. And for stargazing, ascend Mountain Boulevard to the Chabot Science Center on Friday or Saturday evening for a 7:30 show (small admission charge).

Berkeley backs up to a university

Dating back to the 1800s, Berkeley achieves its fame and notoriety from one of the world's largest educational institutions—the University of California. It's an inviting place to park your car and walk around. Telegraph Avenue, just south of the campus, has a 4-block stretch (between Bancroft and Dwight ways) where street artists and skilled artisans display their wares.

The city is also popular for its fine restaurants, distinctive Maybeck-inspired architecture, and bay-oriented recreation development. In addition to 90-acre Shoreline Park, the Berkeley Marina includes a well-used fishing pier that extends 3,000 feet out over the bay. Waterfront treats include popular restaurants and a hotel.

University of California—Bear country

The University of California's Berkeley campus—some 1,232 acres of it—spreads up into the hills and surrounds sections of the town. University buildings, especially Sather Tower (the Campanile), punctuate the landscape.

For a magnificent view of the campus, the whole East Bay area, and San Francisco across the water, take the elevator 175 feet up the 307-foot Campanile, then climb 25 feet to the observation tower. Open daily between 10 A.M. and 4:15 P.M., the ride costs 10 cents—just as it did in 1923.

To take a walking tour of the campus, pick up a self-guided tour map outlining the nearly 2-mile walk (about 1½ hours) at the Visitor Center in the Student Union at the end of Telegraph Avenue. Escorted tours leave there at 1 P.M. on weekdays.

You'll want to see the California Memorial Stadium (seating capacity: over 76,000) where the Golden Bear football team plays out its fall schedule; pace across the 133-foot stage of the Greek Theatre, a beautiful amphitheater presented to the university by Phoebe Appersen Hearst in 1903; linger on the footbridges that cross Strawberry Creek, a thin stream that becomes fairly boisterous after the first rains; and visit the Botanical Garden (located near the stadium in Strawberry Canyon), a 30-acre tract of more than 8,000 different plants, including rare rhododendrons, cacti, and succulents.

One architectural highlight is the university's art museum: a sculpture in itself with its jutting balconies, staggered levels, interesting angles, open galleries, and ramps—all arranged around an open central gallery. Museum hours are 11 A.M. to 5 P.M. Wednesday through Sunday (closed Monday and Tuesday); admission is free. Three floors of prehistoric animals and fossils fill the Museum of Paleontology; the Lowie Museum of Anthropology rotates exhibits depicting the life of man; and the Bancroft Library displays paintings of 18th and 19th century California life.

Lawrence Hall of Science, built as a research facility for science education, has exhibit areas housing dozens of colorful, do-it-yourself displays demonstrating scientific principles on a child's level. Youngsters operate complex electronic equipment and control preprogrammed experiments. Open daily, the complex is on North Canyon Road, reached from Gayley Road on the east side of the campus or from Grizzly Peak Boulevard, a scenic route that follows the crest of the East Bay hills. There's a moderate admission charge.

Berkeley's performing arts

If you're an avid theatergoer, you'll enjoy the intimate atmosphere and the professional excellence of the Berkeley Repertory Theatre. Performances take place in a 400-seat house at 2025 Addison Street off Shattuck; for information, call (415) 845-4700. From early July to late September, enjoy Shakespeare under the stars in John Hinkel Park on Southampton Road off Arlington Avenue. For schedule information, call (415) 845-0303.

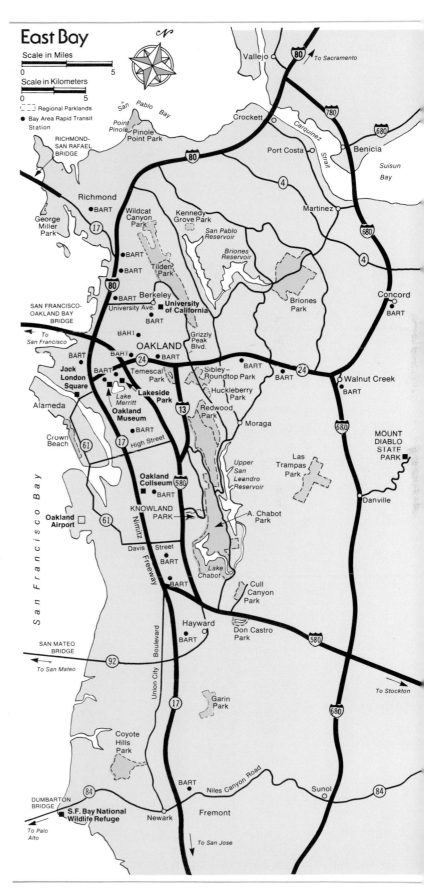

East Bay

Scale in Miles
0 ————— 5

Scale in Kilometers
0 ————— 5

☐ Regional Parklands
● Bay Area Rapid Transit Station

STUDENTS FLOOD SPROUL PLAZA on
noontime break at U.C. Berkeley (above). Sather
Gate and Campanile are familiar landmarks
at California's largest university campus.

OVER OAKLAND MUSEUM ROOF spills
a terraced hillside park (left), open to three
gallery levels and linked by wide stairway
to courtyard below.

East Bay parks

In the low hills that rise behind the East Bay cities, 51,600 acres of beautiful countryside have been set aside for recreational use. About 4,600 acres of San Francisco Bay beach and swampland in Alameda and Contra Costa counties have also been incorporated into the East Bay Regional Park System. Some of the parks are small, some large; some are highly developed, some relatively untouched and primitive. Many miles of hiking and bridle trails lead through unspoiled woods and fields. Picnicking, swimming, fishing, boating, and archery are offered at most of the parks, which are primarily designed for daytime use. Three areas allow overnight camping.

Interconnecting trails link several parks. You can hike some 21 miles along the Mission Peak Trail in Fremont to Del Valle Regional Park near Livermore. Hikers and horseback riders also enjoy the 31-mile trail from Wildcat Canyon Regional Park southeast through Tilden, Sibley, Huckleberry, Redwood, and Chabot parks; some of the trail is paved for bikes.

Parks of particular interest are Tilden (Environmental Education Center, model railway, Little Farm, merry-go-round, golf course), Temescal (one of seven East Bay parks that offers swimming, picnicking, hiking, fishing), Redwood (redwood groves, heated outdoor swimming pool at Roberts Area), Chabot (marina, horse rental, overnight camping), Crown (beachcombing, annual sandcastle contest), Point Pinole (bicycling, hiking, fishing from 1,225-foot pier in San Pablo Bay), Shadow Cliffs (swimming), Coyote Hills (ancient Indian shellmounds, nature programs, bicycling), and Black Diamond Mines (historical area).

For detailed information and a free brochure on all the parks in the region, write to the East Bay Regional Park District, 11500 Skyline Boulevard, Oakland, CA 94619.

A wildlife refuge on the bay

Fringing the levees that stretch along the south end of San Francisco Bay is the recently established 23,000-acre San Francisco Bay National Wildlife Refuge.

Refuge headquarters is located atop a hill in Fremont near the Dumbarton Bridge toll plaza; a visitor center here is open 7 days a week from 10 A.M. to 5 P.M. A trail overlooking the salt marsh encircles the headquarters. For schedule information on nature walks, film programs, and slide presentations, call (415) 792-0222.

Up Mount Diablo

Mount Diablo's summit provides exceptionally fine views. On a clear day you can see the Sierra, Mount Lassen, San Francisco, and the inland waterways of the Central Valley. Because such an expanse of California is visible, Mount Diablo has been the surveying point for Northern and Central California since 1851.

Diablo's main peak is only 3,849 feet in elevation; however, it seems higher because it rises so abruptly.

Occasionally during the winter the conical peak gets a coating of snow.

A state park covers a portion of the area with 80 campsites, group camping facilities, and about 250 picnic sites. You'll find a number of good hiking trails. The park is open all year; day-use hours are 8 A.M. until dark. You can reach Mount Diablo from Interstate 680 at Danville.

Carquinez Straits

Fresh and salt water mingle in the swift tidal flow that ebbs and floods through Carquinez Straits. Mare Island Ferry Service lets you venture out into the waters that link San Pablo and Suisun bays. Located at Vallejo's Georgia Street Wharf, the ferries have been operating since 1854. The hour-long tours require reservations; call (707) 643-7542 for information.

Port Costa, seen from Carquinez Straits, is just a tuck in the rolling Contra Costa hills. Yet from the late 19th century to the early 1930s, this town of 300 people was one of the West's busiest grain-shipping ports. To save the town from encroaching decay, a community redevelopment effort began in the 1960s. No longer a gallimaufry of deserted docks and abandoned structures, Port Costa now offers a charming new face. Around Main Street you'll find an ornately refurbished hotel, antique shops in restored shipping docks, and boutiques and restaurants in converted warehouses.

To reach Port Costa take the Crockett exit off Interstate 80. It's a 3-mile drive south of Carquinez Bridge.

At Martinez, east of Port Costa, is the John Muir Historic Site. You can follow Pomona Street from Port Costa or take Interstate 80 to State Highway 4. Follow State 4 to Alhambra Avenue and turn left under the overpass. The John Muir home is about 100 yards beyond the overpass to the left.

Tours of the house start every hour from 1 to 4 P.M., Wednesday through Sunday. There's a small admission charge for visitors over 15 years of age.

Benicia, across the strait, was California's state capital in 1853 and 1854. Once a thriving port, it's a quiet town today. Many of its weathered buildings house antique shops; most are along First Street from G to C streets. The two-story State Capitol Building at First and G streets is open for daily touring (small admission fee), as is the adjacent Fischer-Hanlon House.

When you finish exploring downtown, drive out Military East to the former Benicia Arsenal for lunch at historic Commandant's Residence, once the home of poet Stephen Vincent Benét. Also on the arsenal grounds are a number of artist's studios. Stop by the Chamber of Commerce offices at 831 First Street for further information and a city walking map; or call (707) 745-2120.

Vallejo was originally part of a Mexican land grant. Although it became the California Legislature's first meeting place in 1851, the town owes most of its development to the U.S. Navy, which established Mare Island Naval Shipyard there in 1852.

(Continued on next page)

...Continued from page 43

Today, Vallejo's marine facilities and attractive waterfront make it a favorite among sailors, fishers, and joggers. The Napa River marshes at the city's northern and western edges offer good bird-watching. At the Vallejo Naval and Historical Museum (734 Marin Street) in Old Town, you get a good look at the city's marine background. The museum is open the year around; hours are 10 A.M. to 4:30 P.M. Tuesday through Friday, plus Saturday and Sunday afternoon. There's a slight charge.

Marine World Africa USA recently moved its facility to Vallejo from Redwood City. Located at 1000 Fairgrounds Drive, the 165-acre wildlife complex features over 1,000 animals in theme shows, most in outdoor settings. Among the attractions—performing killer whales, dolphins, sea lions, tigers, elephants, chimpanzees, and exotic birds. A ski and boat show, children's playground, and hands-on animal experiences add to the fun. Open daily through the summer and on weekends all year round, Marine World charges a daily admission fee. Phone (707) 644-4000 for specific information.

The Peninsula

Geographically, Palo Alto lies at the end of the San Francisco Peninsula, but the cities of Mountain View, Los Altos, Sunnyvale, Santa Clara, and San Jose—though farther south—are generally considered part of this south-peninsula region. At the southern tip of the bay, this area is the scene of heavy industry. Moffett Naval Air Station is located here, along with many electronics firms and allied industries that have given the area the name of Silicon Valley.

Several main routes run down the peninsula from San Francisco, so you can actually drive to the southern tip of the bay without encountering a single stop light. State Highway 1 skirts the ocean, Skyline Boulevard (State Highway 35) follows the ridge of the mountains, and Junipero Serra Freeway (Interstate 280) runs along the east side of the mountain spine. The Bayshore Freeway (U.S. 101) and El Camino Real (State Highway 82) pass through population centers that edge the bay.

Traveling the Bayshore

There are many highlights on the peninsula and the Bayshore Freeway provides rapid access to them.

Candlestick Park is a stadium that huddles along the edge of Candlestick Point, on the bay side of the freeway, 8 miles south of San Francisco. The stadium is in use almost all year: the San Francisco Giants play baseball from mid-April to late September, and the San Francisco '49ers play football from September to December.

The Rod McLellan Company, the world's largest hybrid orchid grower, offers daily tours at 10:30 A.M. and 1:30 P.M. You'll see scientific labs and lush tropical grounds at the headquarters at 1450 El Camino Real in South San Francisco.

The Cow Palace, a huge, strangely named sports arena, is on Geneva Avenue in Daly City. This is the site of the Grand National livestock exposition, horse show, and rodeo—an event that draws large crowds every fall. You can also attend basketball games, circuses, prize fights, big conventions, and concerts in its vast arena.

San Francisco International Airport spreads along the edge of the bay east of the highway near San Bruno. Three terminals accommodate passengers arriving and departing on the more than 1,200 flights daily.

Bay Meadows Race Track, next to Bayshore Freeway in San Mateo, is where horses compete 200 racing days a year. Times and admission vary according to type of racing. Call (415) 574-7223 for information.

Allied Arts Guild, at Arbor Road and Creek Drive in Menlo Park, offers a glimpse of the early, more leisurely Spanish California. The 3½-acre site is part of the once-vast Spanish land grant, El Rancho de las Pulgas (Ranch of the Fleas). The barn and sheep sheds of the old ranch still stand but now house crafts shops. Buildings containing a variety of shops preserve the Spanish Colonial theme of the original ranch. The dining room opens at noon for luncheon; tea is served from 3 until 4:30 P.M. Reservations are advised; call (415) 324-2588.

Sunset Magazine and Books (Lane Publishing Company), in Menlo Park, welcomes visitors to its editorial and business offices. The two buildings are located at Willow and Middlefield roads (between Bayshore Freeway and El Camino Real). Hostesses offer conducted tours Monday through Friday at 10:30 and 11:30 A.M. and 1, 2, and 3 P.M. You will see the kitchen where recipes are tested before they are published, and you can stroll through the extensive demonstration gardens of outstanding trees, shrubs, and flowers native to sections of the Pacific Coast.

Ames Research Center, in Mountain View, gives fascinating tours through its large wind tunnel, flight simulation facilities, and flight operations hangar at Moffett Field. Tours are offered by reservation only; phone (415) 694-6497 for information.

Stanford University—the elegant "Farm"

University Avenue, Palo Alto's main street, crosses El Camino Real on an overpass southeast of Menlo Park. West of El Camino Real, University becomes Palm Drive, the approach to Stanford.

At the entrance of the Quadrangle at the end of Palm Drive, the Stanford Guide Service Information Center has an assortment of maps (one outlines a tour of the campus) and descriptive material. The center is open daily from 10 A.M. to 4 P.M. Guided tours leave daily at 11 A.M. and 2 P.M. from the center.

An easily visible campus landmark is the 285-foot tower of the Hoover Institution of War, Revolution, and Peace. An elevator goes to the top where you get a visual orientation of the campus. Call (415) 723-2053 for hours.

You'll want to see the Memorial Church, dedicated in 1903 and completely rebuilt after the 1906 earthquake. The large, ornate church is decorated with Venetian mosaics, most striking of which are reproductions of "The Sermon on the Mount" on the front façade and Rosselli's "Last Supper" in the chancel. Unless services are in progress, the church is open to visitors from 10 A.M. to 5 P.M. daily.

Located on Lomita Drive and Museum Way, northeast of the Medical Center, is the Stanford University Museum of Art. Among the museum's permanent exhibits are galleries of ancient Oriental, Egyptian, and primitive art, baroque paintings, and early Californiana. Of particular interest are an extensive Rodin collection, and the Stanford Collection, with exhibits of family photographs and paintings, Leland Stanford Jr.'s boyhood collection of toys and artifacts, and other memorabilia. Hours are weekdays (except Mondays) from 10 A.M. to 4:45 P.M., weekends from 1 to 4:45 P.M. Admission is free.

San Jose: A growing city on the bay

One of the nation's fastest-growing cities, San Jose was founded in 1777 with a population of 66. It remained a small town, taking a back seat to San Francisco, until the early 1950s when industry moved in.

For a recorded message on what to do and see in the San Jose area call (408) 293-4678, or write to the San Jose Visitors Bureau, 1 Paseo de San Antonio, San Jose, CA 95113. Another good source of information is the Santa Clara Chamber of Commerce, 1414 El Camino Real, Santa Clara, CA 95052; phone (408) 296-7111.

Downtown San Jose—a changing scene

If you have not been to San Jose recently, you're in for a surprise. With the help of a major urban renewal program, this city—more than 200 years old—is blossoming into a pleasant mélange of old and new. An exciting center of performing arts and a new convention center serve as the cultural anchor for the downtown renaissance. Park Center Financial Plaza, Paseo de San Antonio mall, and nearby San Jose State University attest to continuing commitment to downtown development.

The new engenders a growing respect for the old. The Chamber of Commerce offers a self-guided, history walk past some of downtown's architectural treasures. Included are the Peralta Adobe (San Jose's oldest building), a handsome Romanesque-revival building now housing the city's art museum; the site where A.P. Giannini, Bank of America founder, was born; and the multidomed St. Joseph's Catholic Church, now over 100 years old.

The Center of Performing Arts, designed by Frank Lloyd Wright's Taliesen West Foundation, brings theater, music, and dance into the heart of San Jose. The 2700-seat theater with its bold stucco façade is home of the San Jose Symphony, the San Jose Civic Light Opera, and the stage for visiting performing arts companies. The center is located at 225 Alamaden Boulevard between San Carlos Street and Park Avenue.

Paseo de San Antonio offers a green space for walkers, sitters, and picnickers. A stroll along the 3-block, brick-paved pedestrian mall (between Market and 3rd streets) reveals grassy knolls, fountains, sculpture, and outdoor cafés.

Parks and gardens are sprinkled throughout the San Jose area. Visitors can smell the roses, peer at animals, meditate in a temple, or hike through a rugged canyon. Children enjoy Kelley Park with 150 acres of grassy hills and tree-shaded picnic sites. In the park's 2-acre Happy Hollow and Baby Zoo, youngsters can pet and feed small animals and watch bear, tiger, and leopard cubs at play. Also located in the park are the Japanese Friendship Gardens, featuring a teahouse, picturesque footbridges, miniature maple groves, and a pagoda. To reach Kelley Park, take the Story Road exit off U.S. 101 and continue 4 blocks south.

San Jose's museums—from the Old West to Egyptian art

To catch a glimpse of turn-of-the-century San Jose, visit the historical museum. Not a typical museum, this city-run complex consists of ten full-size structures reconstructing the San Jose of the 1890s. Stroll through the restored lobby of the Pacific Hotel, gaze at a 115-foot electric light tower, or stop at Dashaway Stables, where a blacksmith shoes horses. The museum is located at 635 Phelan Avenue near Senter Road.

The San Jose Museum of Art, housed in a state historic landmark at Market and San Fernando streets, is best known for its exhibits of post-War modernists and contemporary American art. Hours are 10 A.M. to 4:30 P.M. Tuesday through Saturday, noon to 4 P.M. on Sunday; admission is free.

The Rosicrucian Egyptian Museum (with an art gallery, library, and planetarium) displays authentic artifacts from Egypt, Babylon, and Assyria. Here you can examine mummies and jewelry, walk through a replica of a pharaoh's tomb, and enjoy the gardens highlighted by an obelisk, a sphinx, and murals. Admission to the museum at 1342 Naglee Avenue is free; there is a charge for planetarium shows.

Around San Jose

A potpourri of attractions in the Santa Clara Valley includes everything from a theme park (see below) and a mystery house to a prestigious observatory, an historic mission, fine wineries, and a bevy of appealing shopping centers.

Across from Santa Clara's City Hall, the Triton Museum (free) showcases contemporary, traditional, and international folk art and fine art. Also on the grounds at 1505 Warburton is an historic Victorian mansion, the Jamison-Brown House.

The Winchester Mystery House, 4 miles west of the city at the Winchester Road exit off Interstate 280, is a state historic landmark. Sarah Winchester, heir to her father-in-law's gun fortune, was an eccentric who believed that if she stopped adding rooms onto her house, she would die. The 160-room house, now refurnished, is a memorial to her obsession. Tours cover 6 acres of Victorian splendor—the house, museum, and extensive gardens—daily from 9 A.M. for a moderate charge.

University of California's Lick Observatory, 20 miles southeast of San Jose, is reached by a winding narrow road that climbs to the summit of 4,209-foot Mount Hamilton. Visitors are welcome every Saturday and Sunday (except national and university holidays) from 1 to 5 P.M. Guide service is provided at no charge. Of particular interest is the 120-inch reflector telescope, the second largest in the world.

Mission Santa Clara de Asis, eighth in the chain of California missions, was founded in 1777 along the banks of the Guadalupe River. After several locations and structures, the present site was selected and the church constructed in 1825. One hundred years later, fire practically destroyed the mission; however, in 1929 a concrete replica was completed.

You'll see a few original remnants: a cross, dating back to the founding, stands in a protective covering of redwood in front of the church; a bell, given by the king of Spain in 1778, still tolls in the tower; and a magnificent crucifix hangs above a side altar. Now part of the campus of the University of Santa Clara (on the Alameda), the mission is open daily.

Wineries are not new to the Santa Clara Valley. Settlers have planted grapes here since the 1800s. Now, of the more than 50 "hidden" wineries in the area, 27 offer tours. You can see how wine is made, question vintners about their wines, and, best of all, test the wines yourself in open tasting rooms. For detailed information on wineries in the area, see the *Sunset* book *Guide to California's Wine Country.*

Shopping is a San Jose pastime. The Santa Clara Valley offers abundant shopping centers ranging from boutiques and specialty shops in settings of early California to a well-patronized flea market.

Over 2 million visitors yearly find their way to The Flea Market at 12000 Berryessa Road off U.S. 101. With its labyrinth of over 1,800 booths, it's a weekend bargain hunter's paradise. The Pruneyard makes shopping easy, with its fountains and open plazas set amidst early California architecture. If you cannot find that "special" gift, try the Eastridge Shopping Center with over 160 stores—the largest enclosed shopping mall in the western United States.

Great America

Just 3 miles north of the San Jose airport, Great America has drawn millions of visitors to its gates since opening in 1976. Once inside the 100-acre park, you'll first encounter Carousel Plaza, featuring the world's largest two-level merry-go-round. The plaza opens onto five Americana theme areas: Hometown Square, County Fair, Yukon Territory, Yankee Harbor, and Orleans Place. Each area's rides, shows, shops, and restaurants are keyed to its particular theme.

Tiny tots enjoy their own particular "world" in Fort Fun and Smurf Woods. In these areas, all the rides (including a roller coaster) are kiddie-sized.

Live entertainment and visitor participation reign. Each year the park adds new shows and events, including live entertainment by popular musicians. A new

amphitheater in the park is the setting for summer concerts. Spirited musical revues appear in the Great America theaters, and special films flicker on the world's largest motion picture screen—seven stories tall and 96 feet wide.

If you're a thrill seeker, brave some of the park's 125-plus rides. New this year is The Grizzly, Northern California's largest wooden roller coaster. You'll drop 90 feet at the first swoop. Among other popular rides are The Edge, a 131-foot tower with a straight drop at 55 miles per hour; The Demon, a twin-looped, subterranean, corkscrew roller coaster; and The Tidal Wave, a 360-degree-loop roller coaster which attains a speed of 55 miles per hour in 3 seconds.

To reach Great America, take the Great America exit from either U.S. 101 or State Highway 237. The park is open daily during the summer, on weekends in spring and fall. A single moderate admission fee includes all attractions; children under 4 are admitted free.

Los Gatos and Saratoga—two foothill charmers

Nestled in the foothills of the Santa Cruz Mountains, the neighboring towns of Los Gatos and Saratoga have a country village charm. Here you'll find good shopping in a variety of tiny boutiques and restaurants, parks for picnics, rambling old houses, and wineries to tour. To reach these attractive towns, take the State 17 turnoff southwest from U.S. 101 in San Jose. Saratoga is 4 miles northwest of Los Gatos.

Old Town Los Gatos is a lively collection of shops, studios, restaurants, and theaters housed in a converted elementary school. Most stores are open Tuesday through Sunday; most restaurants serve lunch and dinner daily. Other galleries and antique stores are scattered around the town's main streets.

Hakone Gardens, tucked into the hills just behind Saratoga, is an unexpected bit of the Orient. Formerly a private garden established in 1917, it is now a city park. The 15½-acre hillside gardens are widely considered the most authentic Japanese gardens in this country. Two tea houses and several fish ponds are scattered along the curving pathways. Hakone is open daily from 11 A.M. to 5 P.M. To reach the gardens, follow Big Basin Way west about a mile.

Through the mountains

Skyline Boulevard (State 35) will take you along the mountain spine of the peninsula. Interstate 280 runs just east of the mountains. The Santa Cruz Mountains, a spur of the Coast Range, stretch from the Crystal Springs area to just below Santa Cruz, east of Monterey Bay. Standing 2,000 to 3,000 feet high, these mountains receive heavy rains in the winter, which help to produce the forests of Douglas fir, pine, madrone, maple, alder, bay, and the towering, shadowy redwoods that make this a shady retreat.

TWIST, TURN, LOOP, AND GLIDE on
roller coaster (above) at Great America,
just north of San Jose.

SANTA CRUZ waterfront (above) attracts Bay
Area residents in summertime. Fish from the
long pier, try deep-sea trolling, or enjoy the beach.

FRAMED BY ROLLING HILLS, Stanford University's
Memorial Church (below) exudes scholarly calm.
Church dominates 17-acre quadrangle of sandstone
buildings that forms heart of campus.

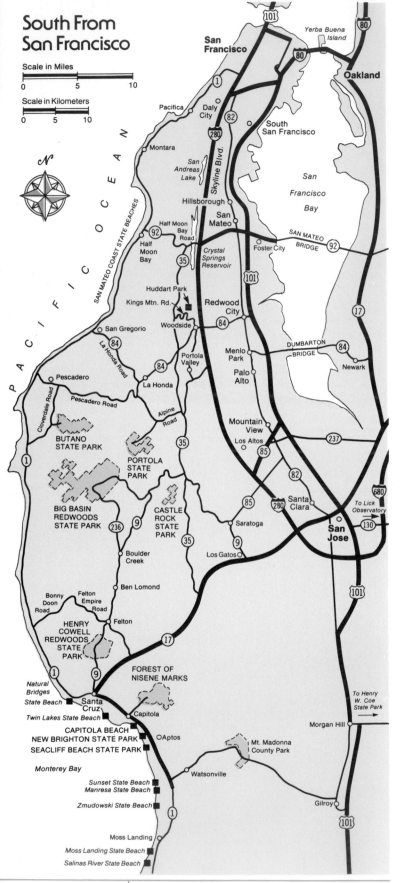

South From San Francisco

Scale in Miles
0   5   10

Scale in Kilometers
0   5   10

Off Interstate 280

The Junipero Serra Freeway (Interstate 280) is billed as the most beautiful in the country. You may agree when you drive through the rolling countryside between San Francisco and San Jose. Access to several attractions is from this highway.

You'll pass by Crystal Springs Reservoir, which holds the water supply for San Francisco. Toward the southern end of the reservoir, Interstate 280 intersects Cañada Road. If you take Cañada north, you'll see the Pulgas Water Temple at the southern tip of the reservoir. The temple marks the end of the Hetch Hetchy aqueduct, a 162-mile pipeline that begins at an impoundment on the Tuolumne River in the northern section of Yosemite National Park. It's a good place for picnicking, strolling, and just watching the waters surge past.

Filoli is better known to television viewers as the Carrington mansion on the TV show *Dynasty*. This elegant Woodside residence was built in 1916 by William Bowers Bourn II, who pulled millions in gold out of his Empire Mine in Grass Valley. The 43-room mansion's name is a contraction of Bourn's code—Fight, Love, Live.

In the 1970s, the house and its extensive grounds and beautiful gardens were given to the National Trust for Historic Preservation. Docents lead tours Tuesday through Saturday from mid-February to mid-November. Call (415) 364-2880 for tour reservations. Admission is moderate. Filoli is on the west side of Cañada road, north of its intersection with Edgewood Road.

Stanford Linear Accelerator Center in Menlo Park (Sand Hill Road exit) is open for touring with advance reservations; call (415) 854-3300, ext. 2204, for information. The 2-mile-long linear accelerator delivers electron and positron beams for use in studying elementary constituents of matter. Research at the center resulted in a 1976 Nobel Prize.

Foothill College's Electronic Museum (El Monte exit) also offers touring possibilities; call (415) 960-4383 for information. Here you'll see an array of early vacuum tubes and learn something about the principles of electricity and the history of the silicon chip.

Skyline Boulevard

South of San Francisco, Skyline Boulevard leads to some of the area's most-used parks: Huddart, Sam McDonald, San Mateo County Memorial, and Portola State Park. All lie to the west of Skyline. Some have campsites.

Where Skyline Boulevard meets Saratoga Gap, a left turn on State 9 will take you to Saratoga, or you can turn right and take State 9 through the San Lorenzo Valley to the coast, where it meets the Coast Highway (State 1) at Santa Cruz. State 9 is the valley's Main Street.

Big Basin Redwoods State Park, the first preserve of redwoods ever set aside as a state park, is today one of the most visited forest parks in California. The Big Basin junction is about 6 miles down State 9 from Skyline; it's 8 miles from the junction to the park.

A trail connects Big Basin with the newer Castle Rock State Park, just south of the junction of state highways 35 and 9.

Roaring Camp & Big Trees Railroad

One-half mile south of Felton, you can board a steam train at a quaint old depot for a 6-mile-loop trip through thick redwood groves. You may want to stop over at Bear Mountain for picnicking and hiking, then return on a later train.

Steam passenger trains leave Felton daily at 11 A.M., 12:15, 1:30, 2:45, and 4 P.M., June through Labor Day. Trains run daily the rest of the year, except Christmas, on a reduced-run schedule. Fares are moderate.

Roaring Camp trains run right alongside Henry Cowell Redwoods State Park, their whistles the only disquieting note in the cathedral-like stillness of a mature grove of redwoods and Ponderosa pines. The 4,000-acre park has two streams, good for winter steelhead fishing and inviting for summer swimming and wading.

The scenic coast highway

The most picturesque route down the peninsula is State 1. The Coast Highway follows the shoreline closely, staying away from large cities. You won't make good time on this road, but if you enjoy the ocean, beaches, hills, and windswept bluffs, this will be the most enjoyable route.

The San Mateo Coast State Beaches, with headquarters at Half Moon Bay, are a collection of nine beaches scattered along 50 miles of the San Mateo County coast and administered as a single park unit. Often foggy in summer, these narrow beaches, lying below low coastal bluffs or steep cliffs, are popular for strolling, picnicking, sunbathing, shallow wading, and surf and rock fishing. The currents are too dangerous for safe swimming though.

North to south the beaches are Thornton, Gray Whale Cove, Montara, Half Moon Bay, San Gregorio, Pomponio, Pescadero, Bean Hollow, and Año Nuevo (an elephant seal and sea lion reserve). All beaches except Thornton are accessible from State 1.

Butano State Park is 7 miles from Pescadero Beach. Here, you can hike, picnic, or camp. Easiest access is from State 1. In addition to dense forests of Douglas fir and redwood, you'll find a creek and a small fern canyon. Three major trails traverse the park's 2,186 acres; from Outlook Trail you get a good view of Año Nuevo Island just off the coast.

Santa Cruz retains its Victorian style

The town of Santa Cruz, at the north end of Monterey Bay and at the mouth of the San Lorenzo River, has undergone some real cultural ferment since the Santa Cruz campus of the University of California was established here in 1965. The city, known for its stunning Victorian architecture, is also a good base for exploring nearby beaches.

At the waterfront, you can fish off the long municipal pier, go deep-sea fishing, enjoy the ocean beach, or try the attractions and rides of a vintage boardwalk.

Pacific Avenue, the main street of the downtown area, is a shopping delight. Now a tree-shaded mall, it's full of crafts shops and interesting restaurants. A star attraction is Cooper House, the former County Courthouse that is now a restaurant-shopping complex.

Tree-Sea Tour, a 29-mile sightseeing route, has blue and white signs marking principal points of interest. To guide you, the Santa Cruz County Convention and Visitors Bureau provides a pamphlet, with map, many interesting facts about way points, and motel and restaurant listings. Copies are available from the bureau's office at Church and Center streets. Here, too, you can get your own walking guide of the city's Victorians.

Mission Hill—site of California's 12th mission, founded in 1791—is where the city began and where you'll find the largest concentration of "gingerbread" architecture. At the Reliquary (a small museum) attached to the replica of the mission, you can get a pamphlet on the history of Mission Santa Cruz and the surrounding buildings. The oldest building in town is across School Street from the mission.

Visit the University of California at Santa Cruz (on High Street in the sloping hills above the city), and take a walk through this innovative campus in the woods. There's a visitor kiosk just inside the entrance where campus activities are listed. You can pick up free, detailed campus maps and directions for guide-yourself tours through the forested campus.

Southeast of Santa Cruz, Capitola was one of California's first beach resorts, dating back to the late 1880s. Today it sparkles with new shops, galleries, and attractive restaurants. You'll find most of the new spirit along Capitola Avenue. Shops sell arts and crafts, antiques, books, coffee, tea, and imported goods.

At 2545 Capitola Road, the Antonelli Brothers' Begonia Gardens feature a begonia show from June through October, and a large, year-round selection of ferns and house plants.

To reach Capitola, take State 1 southbound to the Capitola exit. Northbound on State 1, take the Capitola/Soquel exit.

The beach parks

The coast in the Santa Cruz-Capitola area is dotted with excellent beach parks. Most of them have clean, wide beaches and are popular with swimmers, surfers, and surf fishermen. The water is warmer here than along the coast farther north, and the surf is usually gentle.

Within the Santa Cruz city limits, Natural Bridges Beach State Park is an excellent surf fishing, swimming, and picnicking park.

Twin Lakes Beach State Park, also within the city limits, is a favorite with local residents. Camping is not permitted, but there are firepits for day-use picnicking. One lagoon in the park is a wildfowl refuge; a second is an 850-berth small craft harbor.

Campsites are available at New Brighton and Sunset state beaches. Seacliff State Beach offers trailer hookups, as well fishing from an unusual pier—a 435-foot cement ship, *Palo Alto*. Zmudowski, Moss Landing, Salinas River, and Manresa beaches are day-use parks.

SANTA CRUZ **49**

Characterized by white beaches, craggy rocks, pounding surf, and twisted cypresses, the Monterey Peninsula juts into the Pacific Ocean south of Monterey Bay. Here you can view one of the most spectacular shorelines along the Pacific coast, explore carefully preserved historic Monterey, browse through the shops of charming Carmel, and drive through the densely wooded Del Monte Forest.

The peninsula's ocean setting conditions its weather. Summer months are likely to be overcast; you can expect morning or late evening fog. In autumn, the days are warm and the sky crystal clear. Rain is frequent from December to March; but even in January, the wettest month, there will be crisp, sunny days.

On the peninsula you'll find numerous accommodations, ranging from old hotels to modern motels. For a list of places to stay, write to the Monterey Peninsula Chamber of Commerce and Visitors and Convention Bureau, P.O. Box 1770, Monterey, CA 93940, or call (408) 649-1770.

State Highway 1, from north or south, runs directly through the heart of the Monterey Peninsula. If you want to follow the coastline, exit from the highway and follow the 17-Mile Drive (see page 54).

South of the peninsula, on State 1, the area is sparsely populated. On your way to San Simeon, site of Hearst Castle, you'll pass through Big Sur country, with the ocean on one side and the Santa Lucia Range on the other. Inland, U.S. Highway 101 will take you to Soledad, Pinnacles National Monument, Salinas, San Juan Bautista, and up to Gilroy and Morgan Hill—developing areas for the winegrowing industry.

Monterey: Mexico's last bastion

Juan Rodriguez Cabrillo, a Portuguese explorer sailing for Spain, discovered Monterey Bay in 1542, and Sebastian Vizcáino visited the bay in 1602. But it was not until 1770 that the area was settled. On the south shore of the bay, Gaspar de Portolá and Father Junipero Serra established the first of Spain's four California presidios and the second of the Franciscans' 21 Alta California missions. One year later Father Serra moved the mission to its present site on the Carmel River.

Until the middle of the 19th century, Monterey was California's liveliest and most important settlement. Beginning the century as the Spanish capital of Alta California, it became the Mexican capital in 1822 and the American capital in 1846. After the discovery of gold in 1848, San Francisco took over as California's number one city. Monterey's 20th century role centers around its tourist and waterfront attractions.

A historic past, a scenic setting, intriguing shopping at Cannery Row and Carmel, cypress-lined 17-Mile Drive, and renown as "the world's golf capital" attract visitors to the Monterey Peninsula. Cliff-hugging Highway 1 sweeps south along dramatic Big Sur coastline to castle at San Simeon. Inland, side trips lead to missions and monuments; Salinas, birthplace of John Steinbeck; and a cluster of wineries.

Monterey Peninsula

BIG SUR'S DRAMATIC COASTLINE rises almost vertically from ocean into Santa Lucia Mountains. Bixby Creek Bridge on State Highway 1 crosses inlet 260 feet above water.

The old Spanish and Mexican village of Monterey echoes in today's modern town of 29,000. Many buildings constructed before 1850 still stand, most in good repair. Over ten of these buildings and sites are preserved in Monterey's State Historic Park, near the downtown and wharf area. Stop first at the old Custom House near Fisherman's Wharf for a map that guides you past many of these venerable structures (see page 56).

The annual spring Adobe Tour includes a number of these buildings, but the tour focuses special attention on buildings not normally open to the public. Check with the chamber of commerce for schedule and ticket information.

Along the waterfront

The Municipal Wharf stretches into Monterey Bay from the foot of Figueroa Street. Here you can watch commercial fishing boats unload anchovies, cod, kingfish, herring, salmon, sole, and tuna. Seven fish-processing plants share space at the end of this wharf. If you don't mind getting your feet damp, you can watch from doorways as workers clean and pack fish. Municipal Wharf is the best place for pier fishing (the catch ranges from sunfish to tomcod) and for viewing Monterey spread along the crescent-shaped bay.

Fisherman's Wharf, around the Monterey Marina, 4 blocks west of Municipal Wharf, has novelty shops, an art gallery, excursion boats, several restaurants, and a broad expansive plaza reminiscent of old Monterey. You can join an early-morning sport fishing expedition, take a bay tour, or go whale-watching (winter).

Near Fisherman's Wharf, at One Portola Plaza, is the handsome Monterey Convention Center. This three-level complex complete with meeting rooms, ballrooms, and the 500-seat Steinbeck Forum lecture hall, can accommodate over 2,500 people. Its spacious art-filled lobbies, landscaped plazas, and expansive bay views make it worth a visit. Flanked by two resort hotels and a shopping plaza, the center brings new vitality to old Monterey.

Cannery Row's old canneries are still there, monuments to the sardines that mysteriously vanished from Monterey Bay near the end of the 1940s. But the row is not the same street Steinbeck described in *Cannery Row* as "a poem, a stink, a grating noise."

Today as you enter Cannery Row, you drive under the covered conveyor belts that once carried the canned fish from the canneries to the warehouse. Many of the old buildings have been renovated. You can browse through art galleries, antique shops, and boutiques, or eat at one of several restaurants. Some reminders of Steinbeck's novel remain—at 800 Cannery Row are the weathered clapboards of Doc Rickett's Western Biological Laboratory; across the street is Wing Chong's, the "Lee Chong's Grocery" of the book; and down the block is the Bear Flag Inn.

Around the corner from Cannery Row, at 101 Ocean View Boulevard, is the American Tin Cannery. Once the site of a large tin can factory, the refurbished building houses boutiques, antique shops, restaurants, and specialty stores in an airy, skylit indoor mall.

Monterey Bay Aquarium

Perched on the edge of the bay, the country's largest exhibit aquarium is dramatically housed in a rambling complex at the west end of Cannery Row. With its sprawling roofs, boiler stacks, and corrugated walls, the aquarium preserves the waterfront feeling that inspired John Steinbeck. Over 20 major indoor and outdoor galleries and exhibits focus on Monterey Bay habitats; many tanks are bigger than most swimming pools.

Among the most popular attractions are an above-and below-water sea otter habitat; a 3-story kelp forest tank; and an hourglass-shaped, 336,000-gallon tank displaying creatures living in Monterey Bay. Several species of large sharks cruise here along with bay fish.

The far end of the building is devoted to touchable displays such as bat ray petting and feeding, tidepools, and rocky shores explorations. Behind this area, a stunning walk-through aviary is occupied by a cross-section of the birds inhabiting the salt marsh and sandy shore. From here, you can look down on Stanford University's Hopkins Marine Station.

The Monterey Bay Aquarium is open daily (closed Christmas) from 10 A.M. to 6 P.M. Admission is moderate. A public parking lot lies nearby.

Two military retreats

Founded in 1770 by Gaspar de Portolá, the Monterey Presidio is a subpost for the 22,000-acre Fort Ord Area; the site of the Defense Language Institute, West Coast Branch (where 24 languages are taught); and the Training Center Human Research Unit. The main gate is at Pacific and Artillery streets, near where Sebastian Vizcaíno landed in 1602 and Father Junipero Serra and Captain Portolá founded Monterey in 1770.

Just east of downtown Monterey, alongside State 1, are the grounds of the old Del Monte Hotel, once one of the most elegant resorts in California. The hotel was purchased by the U.S. Navy in 1947; in 1951, it became the Naval Postgraduate School. Visitors may stroll through the campus daily between 9 A.M. and 4 P.M. The grounds contain more than 1,200 exotic trees, Del Monte Lake, and landscaped gardens. To reach the school, turn onto Aguajito Road from State 1; then turn right on 3rd Street to the main entrance.

Music in Monterey

One of the musical highlights on the Monterey Peninsula is the yearly Jazz Festival. Since it began in 1958, the September festival has followed the same highly successful formula: two afternoon and three evening concerts, along with such appealing fringe benefits as preconcert rehearsals and the chance not only to hear but also to see at close range quite a few of America's best-known jazz musicians.

Despite the lighthearted informality that prevails at the Monterey County Fairgrounds, the audience becomes serious and attentive when the performance starts. Everyone comes to listen.

Admission to the fairgrounds (located about 2 miles east of Monterey, just off State highways 1 and 68) is limited to ticketholders for the day's concerts. Because the festival is so popular, it's advisable to order tickets in advance. For information on dates and ticket prices, write to Monterey Jazz Festival, P.O. Box JAZZ, Monterey, CA 93940. Season tickets are sold April 1 to May 31. Single performance ticket sales start in August.

Pacific Grove— a butterfly town

The Methodists founded Pacific Grove in 1875 when they held the first of many seashore camp meetings here. Incorporated in 1889, the town was corseted with ordinances strictly regulating dancing, drinking, and public bathing. Today's Pacific Grove is more relaxed. Three annual events draw crowds to Pacific Grove: the Victorian House Tour in April, the Feast of Lanterns in July, and the Butterfly Parade in October.

The Monarch butterfly (*Danaus plexippus*) is the Pacific Grove symbol. Starting in October, thousands of Monarchs arrive to winter in a 6-acre grove of "Butterfly Trees" (follow the signs at the end of Lighthouse Avenue).

Point Pinos Lighthouse, just north of the intersection of Lighthouse and Asilomar avenues, has stood at the entrance to Monterey Harbor since 1855. The oldest continuously operating lighthouse on the West Coast, this Cape Cod-style structure has been run by women keepers for 40 years. Its tower rises over a cozy, redwood-roofed masonry house. The working third-order lens is still used, although the lighthouse is now a museum. It's open to the public from 1 to 4 P.M. Saturday and Sunday. Behind the building, deer roam protected and anglers fish from the rocky shoreline; there's also a golf course.

The Museum of Natural History, at Forest and Central avenues, displays animal, vegetable, and mineral life of the Monterey Peninsula. Of particular interest is the relief map of the peninsula and bay. You can see the great chasm of Monterey Bay, which plummets 8,400 feet, deeper than the Grand Canyon. The free museum is open Tuesday through Sunday.

FORE!

Few places in the world have as many beautiful golf courses as the Monterey Peninsula. No wonder it's called the "golf capital of the world."

Some of the courses are by the shore, some in the valleys; each has individual challenges, and all offer great adventure for player or spectator. The 16th hole at Cypress Point (private course) is one of the most talked about in the world; golfers must drive over 220 yards of undulating ocean to reach the green.

Peninsula hotels and motels often offer golf packages. Check with your travel agent for details. Below is a listing of courses:

Carmel Valley Golf & Country Club, 8,000 Valley Greens Drive, Carmel, CA 93923; (408) 624-5323; 18 holes; 6,756 yards (championship), 6,401 yards (regular); reciprocal arrangements with members of other private clubs.

Corral de Tierra Country Club, Corral de Tierra Rd., Salinas, CA 93908; (408) 484-1112; 18 holes; 6,532 yards; reciprocal arrangements with members of other private clubs.

Fort Ord Golf Course, North-South Rd., Fort Ord, CA 93941; (408) 242-5651; two 18-hole courses; 6,966 yards (bayonet), 6,239 yards (blackhorse); military and guests only.

Laguna Seca Golf Club, York Rd., Monterey, CA 93940; (408) 373-3701; 18 holes; 6,310 yards; public.

Monterey Peninsula Country Club, Box 2090, Pebble Beach, CA 93953; (408) 373-1046; 36 holes; 6,400 yards (shore course), 6,450 yards (dunes course); reciprocal arrangements with members of other private clubs.

Naval Postgrad School Golf Course, Box 665, NPS, Monterey, CA 93940; (408) 646-2167; 18 holes; 5,680 yards; military and guests only.

Old Del Monte Golf Course, 1300 Sylvan Rd., Monterey, CA 93940; (408) 373-2436; 18 holes; 6,175 yards; public.

Pacific Grove Municipal Golf Course, 77 Asilomar Blvd., Pacific Grove, CA 93950; (408) 375-3456; 18 holes; 5,493 yards; public.

Pebble Beach Golf Course, The Lodge at Pebble Beach, Pebble Beach, CA 93953; (408) 624-3811; 18 holes; 6,806 yards (championship), 6,389 yards (regular); semiprivate (reservation required at least 4 weeks ahead for busy periods).

Peter Hay Par 3 at Pebble Beach, The Lodge at Pebble Beach, Pebble Beach, CA 93953; (408) 624-3811; 9 holes; public.

Rancho Cañada Golf Club, Box 22590, Carmel, CA 93922; (408) 624-0111; 36 holes; 6,613 yards (west course), 6,401 yards (east course); public.

Spyglass Hill Golf Course, Box 787, Pebble Beach, CA 93953; (408) 624-3811; 18 holes; 6,810 yards (championship), 6,277 yards (regular); semiprivate.

Pacific Grove Marine Gardens Park, winding along the length of Ocean View Boulevard, features a delightful walking/jogging path with benches for enjoying rocky coastal and bay views. A white sand "pocket" beach offers good tidepooling (living tidepool creatures cannot be collected). Lover's Point is a good place for picnicking, enjoying bird life, and watching scuba divers explore the underwater world. Good boat fishing lies beyond the kelp; shore fishing is only so-so.

Asilomar State Beach fronts the ocean side of the Monterey Peninsula. The adjoining conference grounds are often used for large group meetings. If you cannot find hotel space on the peninsula, rustic and comfortable rooms are sometimes available at Asilomar. The beach here is perfect for hiking.

17-Mile Drive

Contained within 4,280-acre Del Monte Forest, the 17-Mile Drive is an exceptionally scenic route. For 17 miles you drive through thickly wooded areas and see spectacular views of Monterey Bay's breathtaking, rocky shoreline. At any of the four entrance gates (fee is currently $5 per car) you'll be given a map of the route showing points of interest. It's easy to drive this 17-mile route—just follow the yellow line. Bicyclists enter free but must sign a liability release; they're permitted all along the road weekdays except during special events.

Along the drive stand weathered Monterey cypresses, whose branches and foliage have been dramatically distorted by the sea winds. At Seal and Bird Rocks are black cormorants, sea ducks, sea gulls, and leopard or harbor seals. Between the shore and the rocks, sea lions roar.

Though overnight camping is not allowed within the Del Monte Forest, you can picnic in specified areas. Fishing is permitted from Fanshell Beach north; hunting is not allowed.

Along the peninsula's south shore is Pebble Beach. Here is the famous Pebble Beach Golf Course (one of six courses within the forest), The Lodge at Pebble Beach (a resort hotel), and exclusive homes.

If golf is not your game, note that the Pebble Beach Equestrian Center offers more than 34 miles of beautiful bridle paths. Or, as a spectator, you can watch polo and rugby matches, championship tennis, the Concours d'Elegance (a rally of vintage cars), the famous AT&T/Pebble Beach National Pro-Am Golf Tournament, or any of the other public events scheduled at Pebble Beach each year.

Carmel-by-the-Sea

Since its first settlement, Carmel has prided itself on remaining a simple village by the ocean, Even today, houses have no street numbers and mail delivery is nonexistent—everyone goes to the post office. Down-town there are no billboards, no large retail signs, and at night no flood lighting and almost no street lighting. On the side streets you see no curbs, no sidewalks.

But this lack of commercialism attracts tourists. The sidewalks are crowded on weekends, and the main street is jammed with cars. Now Carmel's motto seems to be, "If you can't beat 'em, join 'em."

Shopping. This is a village of shops—more than 150 of them, mostly small. And the shopping is good. Specialties are casual clothing for both men and women, often from Scotland, England, Ireland, or Italy; art and crafts work of all kinds, much of it created locally; decorative imports from Mexico, Sweden, France, Italy; basketry, pottery, furniture from Japan and Hong Kong. Shopping is a pastime in Carmel.

Carmel has always respected its artists, writers, and craftspeople. Many serious artists who live here display their works in downtown galleries. The Carmel Art Association maintains a sales gallery on Dolores Street.

Festivals. One of the yearly attractions here is the Bach Festival, held each July in Sunset Center. Entering its 49th season, the 3-week festival brings some of the world's finest musicians to the Monterey Peninsula.

Throughout the year, the Sunset Center coordinates other music, dance, drama, and film festivals. Here, too, the Friends of Photography's Sunset Gallery exhibits the work of contemporary American photographers. The center is located on San Carlos Avenue between 8th and 10th avenues.

Lodging. Carmel has several hotels and a large number of motels, inns, and guest cottages; yet advance room reservations are advisable, especially during such events as the Bach Festival.

Architecture. In exploring Carmel, you'll see a variety of architectural styles. Early rough summer cabins have given way to Hansel and Gretel-type structures and Monterey-style adobes. Fronting the ocean are some modern homes, including one designed by Frank Lloyd Wright.

Carmel's beaches were made for walking

Carmel's classically beautiful beach is ideal for walkers and, in good weather, sunbathers. The beach is unsafe for swimming, but most bathers find the water too cold anyway. On Scenic Drive, which runs along the water, you will see dark, gnarled cypresses, sparkling white sand, and crashing surf. At the southern end of the beach, the shoreline becomes rocky and pocked with tidepools.

South of the village limits, at the end of Scenic Drive, the beach becomes Carmel River State Beach. Here you can picnic around a beach fire or splash in the lagoon of Carmel River.

Carmel Mission Basilica

South of the town, just off State 1 at Rio Road (or follow Junipero Avenue south), is Basilica San Carlos Borromeo del Rio Carmelo. Fully restored through the efforts of craftsmen, benefactors, and clergy, the mission

(Continued on page 57)

MONTEREY BAY AQUARIUM (above) reflects a Cannery Row heritage in the strong industrial lines of its architecture. Inside, dramatic habitats get you close to marine life.

LONE CYPRESS (right) clings precariously to craggy outcrop at lookout point along exclusive 17-Mile Drive. Tourists enjoy unobstructed views of rocky shoreline and crashing waves.

CHAMPIONSHIP GOLF COURSES (below) designed to fit in between land and sea make Monterey Peninsula a golfer's paradise.

MONTEREY'S PATH OF HISTORY

Many Spanish-style adobes were constructed during the early 1800s to accommodate the 2,000 residents of Monterey. When New England seamen arrived, they modified the Spanish colonial design and created the "Monterey style"—two-story adobes with a balcony. Although many of the old buildings have disappeared, some buildings have been preserved and are maintained as the Monterey State Historic Park; most of them are open daily.

These historical structures are close to the downtown area and the harbor. A good place to start is at the Custom House near Fisherman's Wharf.

The Custom House, at 1 Custom Plaza, is the oldest government building on the Pacific Coast. Here the United States flag was officially raised for the first time by Commodore John Sloat in 1846. This building was the collection center for revenue from foreign shipping until 1867, when it was abandoned. Today, the interior has been restored; inside is a display of early ships' cargo. The plaza with its adobe walls and benches is reminiscent of early California.

The Pacific House, at 8 Custom House Plaza, dates back to 1847. This building was first used by the U.S. Quartermaster for military offices and storage; later it housed a tavern; now it's a museum. The first floor contains exhibits of California history and the second floor a collection of American Indian artifacts.

Casa del Oro is so named because of the unverified story that the building was once used as a gold depository. A general merchandise store in the 1850s, Casa del Oro stands at the corner of Scott and Oliver streets and displays trade items from early Monterey days.

California's First Theater, built in 1846-47, at the corner of Scott and Pacific streets, is open daily except Monday. Each week a theater group presents 19th century plays. The old bench seats are still there, and walls of the barroom are lined with old theatrical mementos.

Casa Soberanes, at 336 Pacific, is a private residence not open to the public. But it is an excellent example of "Monterey-style" architecture.

Colton Hall, on Pacific Street, was built in 1847-49 and is the largest and most impressive of the old buildings. A museum on the second floor displays early government documents.

The Larkin House, which dates back to 1835, is an excellent example of "Monterey-style" architecture. The two-story adobe, surrounded on three sides by a balcony, was built by Thomas Larkin, U.S. Consul. Many of the furnishings are original pieces. This home, at the corner of Jefferson Street and Calle Principal, is open to the public. Visitors are taken on a 35-minute guided tour daily except Tuesday.

Casa Gutierrez, at Calle Principal near Madison, is a typical adobe home of the Mexican period. Now it's a Mexican restaurant.

The Cooper House, at the corner of Polk and Murray, is the former home of Captain John Cooper, a trader and half brother to Thomas Larkin. The house is open for guided tours on Wednesday and Saturday.

The Stevenson House, named for Robert Louis Stevenson, who lived in this building during his short sojourn in Monterey in 1879, dates back to the late 1830s. At 530 Houston Street, the restored building devotes several rooms to Stevenson's personal mementos. The house is open for guided tours.

The Royal Presidio Chapel of San Carlos de Borromeo was founded in 1770 by Father Junipero Serra. The original, hastily constructed mud structure was rebuilt with a baroque façade by Father Serra's successor in 1794. A simple wooden cross sits atop the chapel. Inside are several statues and Stations of the Cross dating from the founding of the chapel. The chapel, on Church Street, is still in use; visitors are welcome.

The U.S. Army Museum, in the Presidio of Monterey, exhibits military items from early Spanish days to the present. The museum is open Thursday through Monday.

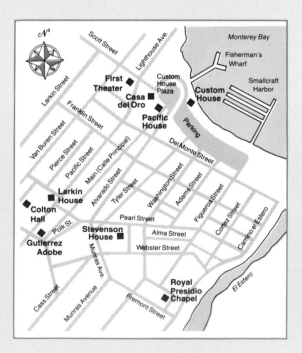

. . . Continued from page 54

provides one of the most authentic and picturesque links to early California history. The mission is open to visitors Monday through Saturday from 9:30 A.M. to 4:30 P.M., Sunday from 10:30 A.M. to 4:30 P.M.

In the mission museum are the original silver altar pieces brought by Father Junipero Serra from Baja California and the restored refectory of Father Serra. Behind the mission is a cemetery where 3,000 Indians are buried. Inside the mission is Father Serra's final resting place.

Point Lobos State Reserve

On State 1 just south of Carmel stands 1,500-acre Point Lobos State Reserve, one of the most beautiful spots on the California coast. Its broken coastline encompasses 6 miles. At this magnificent meeting of land and sea you can hike, picnic, explore tidepools, sun on the beach, or fish.

Around the headland and shoreline, low tides expose rocky pools teeming with marine creatures. Colonies of sea urchins, sea anemones, starfish, and hermit crabs are a few of the more conspicuous inhabitants. Remember that Point Lobos is a nature reserve; tidepools are for looking only. On prominent rocks you will see sea gulls and, on Bird Island, cormorants and brown pelicans.

If you visit Point Lobos in November, you might see the California gray whale, which travels close to shore here on its annual 12,000-mile migration to Baja California.

Only 150 vehicles are admitted to this day-use park (small fee), so plan to arrive before 11 A.M. on weekends. You can also park outside and walk or bike in.

Carmel Valley

South of Carmel, the Carmel Valley Road turns east from State 1 and heads inland along the Carmel River. Driving through the valley, you'll pass artichoke fields, fruit orchards, strawberry patches, rolling hills, and grazing cattle. Right off State 1, on Carmel Valley Road, is The Barnyard—a shopping complex built around the popular Thunderbird Bookshop. The collection of shops, boutiques, galleries, and restaurants housed in eight rustic barns attracts many visitors.

Carmel Valley is a vacationland. Its weather is sunny, warm, and clear—ideal for such outdoor sports as fishing, hunting, horseback riding, tennis, and swimming. Near the mouth of the Carmel Valley, spanning both sides of the Carmel River, are two championship golf courses—available for public play. The Carmel River holds an abundance of trout, and, during the annual spawning season, steelhead fishing is excellent. In the nearby Santa Lucia Mountains, you can hunt wild boar and deer.

At the Carmel Valley Begonia Gardens, 15,000 begonias form a massive wheel of color in the summer. The Korean Buddhist Temple also welcomes visitors. It lies west of the Farm Center off Robinson Canyon Road.

The Hidden Valley Opera's 300-seat theater is just off Carmel Valley Road about 10 miles inland from State 1 (just west of the Carmel Valley Village shopping area). For information and reservations write to the Hidden Valley Opera, Box 116, Carmel Valley, CA 93924, or call (408) 659-3115.

Hikers, joggers, and horseback riders enjoy the 540-acre Garland Regional Park, about 8 miles inland from State 1 along Carmel Valley Road. More than 7 miles of park trails amble over forested hills and riverside meadows. Maps of the area are available at the park ranger's office. You can camp at Riverside Park and Saddle Mountain Recreation Park.

Hotels and motels are more than places to spend the night; all offer a variety of interesting activities. For a list of accommodations and facilities available, write to the Carmel Valley Chamber of Commerce, Box 288, Carmel Valley, CA 93921.

South along the coast

The dramatic 30-mile drive along State 1 to the Big Sur area takes about an hour from Monterey and Carmel. The road south dips and rises, clinging precariously to the seaward face of the Santa Lucia Mountains as it follows the rugged coastline.

As you drive south from Carmel, you cross the dramatic Bixby Creek Bridge, 260 feet above the creek bed. Park your car and walk out to observation alcoves for a

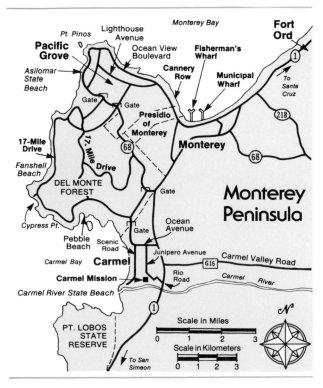

DOLL HOUSE architecture of Carmel restaurant (above) provides whimsical setting for intimate afternoon lunch or tea. Tourists throng Ocean Avenue, town's main street, on weekends the year around.

GLOWING POPPIES accent classic grace of Carmel Mission Basilica (left). Churchgoers and visitors alike delight in leisurely walk through mission's courtyard.

view of the surf, beach, and headlands. You'll pass a cliff-perched eating place—Rocky Point Restaurant—and Point Sur Lighthouse, rising on a headland of rock. Every 15 seconds a warning flashes that can be seen 25 miles out to sea.

Though the road is two lanes with narrow shoulders, vista turnouts are numerous. You can stop for a roadside picnic (Big Sur has a few small grocery stores) or a leisurely lunch at one of Big Sur's restaurants, take a stroll in the redwoods or a walk on the beach, do some shopping or gallery browsing. The Coast Gallery (center for local artisans) maintains two showrooms inside redwood water tanks. You can dine at Ventana Restaurant, a resort with rental condominiums and a gift shop.

Enjoy Nepenthe, 3 miles south of Pfeiffer-Big Sur State Park. The restaurant's redwood pavilion, designed by a student of Frank Lloyd Wright, sits 800 feet above the sea and affords a superb view of southern Big Sur. The original core building was the honeymoon "cottage" built in the 1940s for Rita Hayworth by Orson Welles. Nepenthe opens every day at noon. Besides being a restaurant, it has become an informal social-cultural center for the Big Sur region.

For more information on Big Sur's establishments and facilities, write to the Chamber of Commerce, Big Sur, CA 93920.

State parks along the way

Some of the finest meetings of land and water occur in three state parks along the coast. Two of the parks offer camping, but you have to walk in to one.

Andrew Molera State Park has 2,088 acres encompassing the lower section of the Big Sur River. Because it's closed to motorized vehicles, park your car off the highway and walk in to a designated camping area. Here you'll find somewhat primitive arrangements for about 50 campers. A network of fire-control roads makes it easy to get around in this preserve of redwoods, rocky bluffs, meadow land, and beach.

Pfeiffer-Big Sur State Park is one of the most popular of the state's nonbeach parks. Though the park isn't large, its trails give access to 300,000 acres of back country in Los Padres National Forest and the Ventana Wilderness. (Permits to enter the wilderness should be requested at least 2 weeks in advance from the District Ranger, Los Padres National Forest, 406 S. Mildred, King City, CA 93930.)

The park's campgrounds are likely to be crowded, especially in summer or on weekends. You can picnic, hike, swim, or fish upstream in the river. Hotel-type rooms and housekeeping cabins are available at Big Sur Lodge, Big Sur, CA 93920.

Pfeiffer Beach, south of the park entrance, is reached via narrow Sycamore Canyon Road from State 1. A scenic gem, the beach is open daily from 9 A.M. to 6 P.M.

Julia Pfeiffer Burns State Park's attractions include a dramatic waterfall, redwood groves, and vantage points for viewing gray whale migration. You'll also find 2 miles of scenic coastline and high country extending up canyons laced with trickling creeks. There's no camp-

ing, but you can picnic, hike, or stroll along the cliffs. The park is open in summer and during spring and fall weekends.

San Simeon: A castle fit for kings

The Hearst San Simeon State Historic Monument, a collection of mansions, terraced gardens, pools, sculpture, and exotic trees, occupies 123 acres atop a spur of the Santa Lucia Mountains. The focal point, designed by Julia Morgan, is *La Casa Grande,* a 137-foot-high structure resembling a Spanish cathedral. Its imposing ridge-top position gives it the aspect of a castle when viewed from afar.

In 1922, construction began on *La Casa Grande,* William Randolph Hearst's private residence. Hearst called the estate *La Cuesta Encantada*—The Enchanted Hill. Money was no object—Hearst imported furniture, antiques, Gothic and Renaissance tapestries, fine wood carvings, French and Italian mantels, carved ceilings, silver, Persian rugs, and Roman mosaics.

San Simeon is located on State 1, about 96 miles south of Monterey. Getting there has never been easy, entailing a long trip on the twisting highway. Bus tours leave for the historic monument from Monterey. For schedule information call or write the Monterey Peninsula Chamber of Commerce (see page 51). Four separate tours, each about 2 hours long, are conducted through the estate. Reservations (always required during the busy season) are available at Ticketron outlets. Tour prices are moderate, but there's a separate charge for each tour. All tours begin at the foot of Enchanted Hill; you board a bus for the ride up the hill.

Inland side trips

Two inland routes parallel the coastal highway and offer sights well worth seeing. U.S. 101 heads south through the valley of the Salinas River; State Highway 25 crosses the San Benito River in the coastal range.

Pinnacles National Monument

At Pinnacles National Monument, spires and crags—remains of a volcanic mountain—rise to 1,200 feet above the canyon floors and present a sharp contrast to the surrounding smooth countryside.

The best way to appreciate fully the extraordinary features here is to hike some of the trails. On the east side, short, easy trips lead through the cave area around Bear Gulch, near the visitor center and picnic area. The High Peaks Trail is strenuous; Juniper Canyon Trail makes it easier to reach High Peaks from Soledad.

On the Soledad side of the monument, you walk into the narrow defile between the overhangs of Machete Ridge and The Balconies. Huge boulders close the caves to natural light (be sure to carry a flashlight). You will have to crawl, stretch, duck, and squeeze along for a few hundred feet until you come to daylight and the other end of the cave. Children should not go in the caves alone—slippery places, low ceilings and dropoffs are hazardous in the dark.

Pinnacles National Monument is just off State 25, 32 miles south of Hollister. You can also reach the Pinnacles along U.S. 101 by turning onto State Highway 146 at Soledad and following the narrow, winding road 14 miles to the camping and picnic area. Fall through spring are the best months to visit the monument; the summer months are hot.

Campgrounds are at Chalone Creek and Chaparrel, with group camping at Chalone Annex.

Soledad mission ruins

A turn westward off U.S. 101 just south of Soledad will take you past a frame and adobe building on your right. This is Los Coches, former headquarters of a large ranch, part of the lands of Mission Nuestra Señora de la Soledad.

A half-mile drive west of Los Coches, and a turn to the north, will lead you to the mission ruins. Here, the thirteenth mission in the California chain was founded by Father Fermin Lasuen in 1791. With the nearby Salinas River to irrigate the dry fields, crops flourished and lush pastures amply fed horses and cattle.

But this same river would be the mission's nemesis. Recurring floods destroyed adobe walls, and epidemics killed Indians and missionaries. By the 1830s, the mission personified its name—"loneliness"—with only a handful of faithful remaining within its desolate walls. When resident friar Father Sarría died in 1835, the mission was officially closed. Winds, rains, and sun reduced "Our Lady of Solitude" to its present state of crumbling walls on windswept beet fields. A modern chapel stands in its place.

From the mission ruins, you can backtrack to U.S. 101 or take the back roads to Carmel and Monterey. Drive south up the steep Arroyo Seco Road, following its turn in a westerly direction to Paloma Creek Road. This is a dirt road—unsatisfactory for traffic for 24 hours after rain. Wind 18 miles through range land dotted with oaks, eucalyptus, sycamores, and pines, and you'll be back on the paved Carmel Valley Road.

Mission San Antonio de Padua

Named for Saint Anthony, Mission San Antonio de Padua was founded in 1771 by Father Junípero Serra. Though somewhat isolated in the middle of a military reservation, the mission rewards the persistent traveler who takes the time to find it. Almost completely restored, it unfolds in grand style amid an oak-studded valley. Take U.S. 101 south and turn off at the Jolon Road exit (near King City); it's about 18 miles.

Mission San Antonio de Padua is reminiscent of missions during the days of the padres. In place of the crumbling adobe walls you might expect, you'll see replicas of buildings that existed in the prosperous years between 1771 and 1830. Some of the original tiles still cover the roof.

Besides the mission itself, you'll see a water-powered grist mill, a tannery, the original wine vat, early mission art, and replicas of mission equipment.

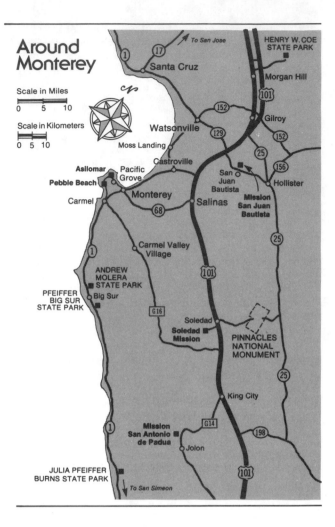

Around Monterey

Scale in Miles
0 5 10

Scale in Kilometers
0 5 10

In & around Salinas

Salinas, the heart of the "salad bowl of the world," is the birthplace of Nobel and Pulitzer prize-winning novelist John Steinbeck (1902–1968). His home, a two-story Victorian on Central and Stone streets, has been restored and opened as a restaurant. Downstairs is the Best Cellar gift shop offering local crafts and a selection of the author's works.

Salinas and the surrounding valley provided much of the local color of Steinbeck's novels. Visit the John Steinbeck Library at 110 W. San Luis Street to see exhibits of original manuscripts, photographs, letters, and tapes having to do with the author's life and works.

One of the oldest buildings in town, the Boronda Adobe at West Laurel Drive and Boronda Road, preserves the authentic mood of an early California rancho.

Built in 1848 by José Eusebio Boronda, the adobe graces the meadows above Alisal Slough. Now a state historic landmark, the estate is open to the public. The façade typifies the detailing of the Monterey colonial style, and the house is architecturally linked with the

Larkin House in Monterey. Inside you'll find a wealth of original furnishings, photographs, and artifacts depicting California's Mexican period. Admission is free. For additional information, call Monterey County Historical Society, (408) 757-8085.

The wild West is alive and well in Salinas when the rodeo comes to town. Held each third weekend in July, the Salinas California Rodeo is the main event in a week-long celebration of parades, barbecues, and hoedowns. Over 700 competitors round up for accolades and prizes in California's largest rodeo. You'll see the best men and women of modern rodeo buck wild broncos and bulls, rope wily calves, wrestle steers, and race around barrels. The action never stops—there is also thoroughbred racing, trick riding, and even gunfights. When you've eaten enough sawdust, settle down to the cheerful strains of bluegrass fiddling at Salt Flats Hoe-down. For ticket and schedule information, contact the California Rodeo Office, P.O. Box 1648, Salinas, CA 93902.

From Salinas it's only a few miles to the Monterey Peninsula or to Castroville (the artichoke capital) and Watsonville on State 1.

Mission San Juan Bautista

About 21 miles north of Salinas, 3½ miles off U.S. 101, lies Mission San Juan Bautista. After its founding in 1797 by Father Lasuen, the mission grew spiritually and financially. The mission's success reflected its founding friars' energy and zeal. Father Felipe del Arroyo, a linguistic whiz, preached to the Indians in seven dialects, teaching them everything from the simplest ways of the white man to the writings of Plato and Cicero. His counterpart, Father Estevan Tapis, was an ebullient music man. By depicting different musical parts in brightly colored notes, he taught choral music to the Indians and formed choirs that continued his legacy for forty years.

Now a state historic park, San Juan Bautista presents a carefully restored chapter of early California history. Once a crossroads of stagecoach travel, the old mission village declined after the railroad pushed south from San Francisco. But in 1933 San Juan Bautista was named a state historic park, and the flavor of old San Juan was preserved. Construction of the present mission building began in 1803 and reached completion in 1814. The carefully restored buildings still overlook the valley much as they did. Down in the town, though, new shops, galleries, and other attractions are moving into the old frame buildings that stand shoulder-to-shoulder along Third Street. Power lines have been laid underground and turn-of-the-century lighting installed.

In addition to the mission church, historic buildings open for touring include the Castro House (furnished in the style of the 1870s), Plaza Hotel (built in 1858), two-story Plaza Hall (combination residence and dance hall), and the Plaza Stable (blacksmith's shop, carriages, and wagons on display).

Camping choices

Among the nearby camping spots are Fremont Peak State Park, a rich historic and botanical area 11 miles south of San Juan Bautista on the San Juan Canyon-State Park Road; and Henry W. Coe State Park, 14 miles east of Morgan Hill on East Dunne Avenue.

Once a working ranch, Coe is little known and usually uncrowded. The park's headquarters occupy the old ranch buildings, perched high at 2,600 feet. When wildflowers bloom, scores of would-be Monets flock to the park's rolling, grassy hills, paints and canvases in hand. You'll find picnic tables and a few campsites. A fee is charged.

In the hills to the west lies Mount Madonna County Park at the Hecker Pass summit. Like Coe, this area developed from a one-time working ranch. Its last owner was cattleman Henry Miller, who bequeathed its formal gardens to posterity. At the park's upper elevations, roads meander through hillsides spotted with oak trees; you may spy a few shy albino deer. The entrance to the park is off State 152; a day-use charge is requested.

Try the Hecker Pass wineries

Stretching along U.S. 101 from Morgan Hill to Gilroy, then west along State Highway 152 toward Hecker Pass, is a group of wineries clustering like so many grapes on a vine. Once known almost solely for their robust jug wines, these wineries are rapidly expanding their bill of fare to include a wide selection of varietals.

Wine tasting is leisurely paced in the Hecker Pass region of vine-filled bottomlands, golden hills, oak knolls, and meandering creeks. Not all wineries are open to the public, but some offer informal tasting, others more formal tours ending in elegant tasting rooms. If you go in October, you'll have a good chance of seeing the picking and crushing. Here is just a sampling of what you'll find.

A. Conrotto Winery, 2 miles west on State 152, has tastings on summer weekends from 10 A.M. to 6 P.M. During the winter, stop by in the afternoon before 5 P.M.

Fortino Winery, along State 152, has a spacious tasting room and gift shop—a good place to pick up a red, white, or rosé for a picnic in the country.

Hecker Pass Winery, 5 miles west of Gilroy along State 152, is open daily for tasting and picnicking. Tours are offered only by appointment.

Thomas Kruse Winery, Hecker Pass Highway, offers informal tours, tasting rooms, and picnic grounds. Set in a classic wooden barn, the winery offers an uncommon list of wines—sparkling whites from Zinfandel, dry rosés from Cabernet Sauvignon, Pinot Noirs, and Grignolinos.

Kirigin Cellars sits on one of the oldest properties in Hecker Pass but has one of the newest wineries. North of State 152 and west of U.S. 101, the winery offers group tours, pleasant tasting rooms, and pine-shaded picnic grounds. Try a sample of their Chablis, French Colombard, Cabernet Sauvignon, and a dessert specialty, Vino de Mocca.

For a more complete listing of the area's wineries see the *Sunset* book *Guide to California's Wine Country.* To reach the wineries, leave U.S. 101 at Morgan Hill; just south of town, take Watsonville Road roughly 7 miles to the junction with Hecker Pass Highway (State 152). Besides wineries you'll find picturesque towns, parks, and picnicking spots in this area.

The North Coast

Sheer cliffs, pounding waves, rocky headlands, and offshore rocks characterize much of the northern shoreline. A national seashore, pocket beaches, and coastal inlets invite hikers, backpackers, and anglers. The oceanside highway passes by Fort Ross (former Russian fur trading outpost), old fishing ports, weathered farms and fences, and forested campgrounds. Mendocino, an artists' mecca, is a center for old inns; Eureka, a Victorian lumber town, lies among redwood groves. Just north is the stillness of the Redwood National Park.

Stretching almost 400 miles from San Francisco Bay to the southern border of Oregon, the virtually unspoiled Northern California coastline delights visitors. Photographers record the beauty of whitecapped waves pounding against rugged shores; anglers contest with fighting steelhead in mighty rivers emptying into the sea; campers choose between parks ranging from sandy dunes to dense forest; and crowds of urbanites flock to unique rural festivals.

Heading north across the Golden Gate Bridge, you can reach the coast either by way of U.S. Highway 101, an inland route until meeting the ocean at Humboldt Bay, or by the slower, scenic route—two-lane State Highway 1. Numerous back country roads connect these two major highways before they join at Leggett, just south of the redwood-lined Avenue of the Giants.

It would be impossible to list the chief attractions of this section of Northern California; everyone makes a personal discovery. Hikers may want to roam the vast open spaces of Point Reyes National Seashore. California's history takes on a new dimension when you view the wooden outpost of the Russian fur traders—Fort Ross. The charms of artistic Mendocino and its bustling fishing and lumbering neighbor, Fort Bragg, rank high among coast attractions. To the north, the mighty coast redwood makes spectacular daytime viewing as herds of Roosevelt elk munch in meadows fringed by titans.

Weather is usually foggy and cold along the coast during the summer; winter brings clear, warm days. Old-fashioned inns with modern accouterments dot the coastline and complement the often stark climate with a warm, intimate atmosphere. In any month, the North Coast provides a dramatic meeting of land and sea.

The Marin beaches

As far as mariners are concerned, the Marin County shore from Point Reyes to the Golden Gate has very little to recommend it. For them it is a treacherous obstacle to San Francisco, composed of sea fogs, howling winds, reefs, and shoals. But for those who are shorebound, it is something else: good rock fishing, good wave-watching, good rock-hounding and good clamming. In its shallow bays, the hardy enjoy good swimming.

Only one remote beach is more than an hour from San Francisco. Some of the shore is hardly 15 minutes away. In spite of its proximity to the city, Marin's coast has not been subjected to any permanent overcrowding, mainly because the terrain slopes skyward in many places. Lack of further development has been somewhat assured by the recent creation of parks along all but a handful of miles of shoreline.

SILHOUETTED STROLLERS, dwarfed by massive cliffs, make tracks along stark Sonoma coastline. Low tide's gentle waves scallop beach's shimmering sands.

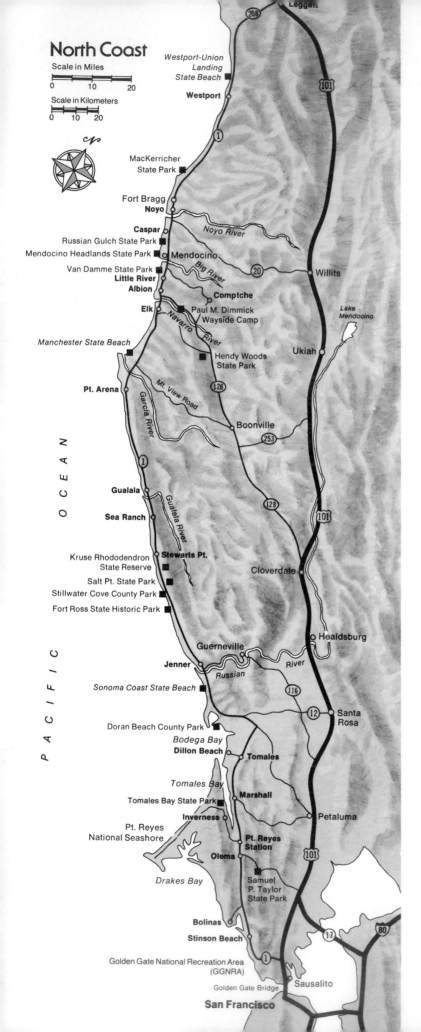

North Coast

Scale in Miles
0   10   20

Scale in Kilometers
0   10   20

Marin's shores from the north end of the Golden Gate Bridge are practically all open to the public as part of the Golden Gate National Recreation Area (which extends as far north as Olema). The land is a mixture of former army forts, ruggedly undeveloped open areas, and once-private ranch lands.

Stinson Beach is not only the name of a small town, but also a day-use park now part of the Golden Gate National Recreation Area. The park runs mostly south of town. Fishermen do well with ling cod, cabezone, and blenny at several rocky points toward the park's south boundary. Just opposite the town entrance is a 4,500-foot ocean swimming beach, its waters warmed by the shoal of Bolinas Bay. Swimming is permitted from late May to mid-September when lifeguards are on duty and the weather most temperate. The park, which attracts over a million visitors annually, is open from 9 A.M. to one hour after sunset; admission and parking are free. For weather and traffic conditions call (415) 868-1922.

Audubon Canyon Ranch, 3 miles north of Stinson Beach, is a good place to watch the courtship rituals of the great blue herons who rendezvous here every March. Bring binoculars or use the ranch telescopes to watch these, along with graceful white egrets. Most birds are gone by August.

Bolinas, sitting just across the mouth of a small lagoon from Stinson Beach, is a tiny town that doesn't try very hard to attract visitors but gets them anyway. Duxbury Reef, a principal cause of Bolinas's popularity, sets up the proper conditions for surfing, tidepooling, clamming, and rock fishing. Striped bass feed at the mouth of the lagoon. Each end of the town's east-west main street dips down to a beach access. The one nearest Stinson Beach serves bass fishermen and surfers; the westerly end is closest to the foot of Duxbury Reef.

Point Reyes National Seashore

U.S. Weather Bureau statistics cite Point Reyes as the foggiest and windiest station, bar none, between Canada and Mexico. Summer weather is often foggy and windy—so bring warm clothing.

The Point Reyes peninsula is an ideal place for an August, September, or October outing. The peninsula reaches another peak from February to late July when wildflowers bloom in the moist and mild climate. Limited lodging restricts the area as a vacation spot. Bear Valley has a few campgrounds, or you can camp at Samuel P. Taylor State Park (about 6 miles southeast of Point Reyes Station) or at a private campground near Olema.

Point Reyes is an island recently separated (geologically speaking) from the mainland by the San Andreas Fault, running northwest-southeast for about 600 miles. As a result of earthquakes, the land on the west side of the fault at Point Reyes has moved northward as much as 20 feet.

Though his log is lost, most historians believe Sir Francis Drake arrived in 1579 aboard his ship, the *Golden Hinde,* in the area just below Point Reyes—now Drakes Bay. His was the first landing on this continent by an English explorer.

In 1962, Congress declared the 64,000-acre Point Reyes area a national seashore because of its dramatic natural and historic significance.

Just 50 miles up the coast from San Francisco, Point Reyes can be easily reached from U.S. 101 and Sir Francis Drake Boulevard or State 1. It's divided into two distinct areas. You reach major beaches and dairylands through Inverness to the north; the Bear Valley trails and hilly forest of Inverness Ridge through park headquarters near Olema off State 1.

Drakes Bay: Home for the *Golden Hinde*?

A long and gentle curve facing almost due south, this bay has a wide, flat, sandy beach abutting steep sandstone bluffs all the way from Point Reyes on the west to a point next to Bolinas on the east. The one break in the arc is the mouth of Drakes Estero, a clutching hand of water that cups oyster beds in its palm.

Although some historians believe Drake brought his ship into Bodega Bay, Bolinas Bay, Tomales Bay, or San Francisco Bay, the prestigious Drake Navigators Guild claims a stronger case for Drakes Bay. Whether or not the argument is ever resolved by some dramatic new turn (like the discovery in Bolinas Lagoon of what might have been Drake's fort), the bay is a pleasant place to stroll the beach, hike, fish, or watch whales.

The Kenneth C. Patrick Visitor Center adjoins the parking lot. Sheltered picnic tables allow you to sit and watch waves when the weather gets too raw for strolls along the beach. On good days, beautifully symmetrical breakers plunge ashore.

At the end of the point, the Point Reyes Lighthouse (built in 1870) is open from 10 A.M. to 4:30 P.M. Thursday through Monday. You climb three ramps and 307 steps to reach the lighthouse's base. Whale-watchers crowd here on winter weekends, so go early.

Limantour Beach and Estero (east of Drakes Beach) is the other spot on the seashore where wading and swimming are usually safe. Sun and stroll or watch the bird life; the estero is one of the few Pacific coast marshes not seriously altered by man. On summer weekends (July 4 to Labor Day) a shuttle bus runs between the Limantour parking area and the Bear Valley trailhead, making it possible to hike and ride through this region.

Point Reyes Bird Observatory is the only full-time ornithological field research station on the continent. You'll see land birds, shore birds, and waterfowl on the south end of the peninsula the year around. Take Mesa Road from Bolinas.

Point Reyes Beach, southwest of Inverness on the Sir Francis Drake Highway, is ruler straight, steep faced, current ridden, wind scoured; it has a haunting, austere beauty. Solitude and astonishingly high surf are rewards for your visit. Sometimes big waves roll up from distant storms during a spell of warm weather that comes nearly every February. Picnicking then is better than during almost any other month of the year. Water and rest rooms are available. Pounding surf at Point Reyes and McClures beaches makes them too dangerous for water activities.

McClures Beach, at the northern end of the peninsula, is usually deserted because the access trail is steep and narrow. There's no swimming here but plenty of rocks for shelter from the wind.

Bear Valley trails

Headquarters to the national seashore is a mile west of Olema at the old Bear Valley Ranch. The Information Center, open daily from 9 A.M. to 5 P.M., has maps, trail guides, nature books, and schedules of nature programs. Here you'll also find a seismograph registering any quiver of the San Andreas Fault. Near headquarters is a self-guided tour of Earthquake Trail and an authentic replica of a Coast Miwok Indian Village. At the nearby Point Reyes Morgan Horse Farm, self-guided tours and interpretive talks are offered at the stables.

Bear Valley trailhead is gateway for over 100 miles of trails for hikers, horsemen, and bicycle riders to enjoy. Some run through fir groves and meadows to the sea, others lead steeply up to panoramic vistas of the entire peninsula. You can spend an hour or days just roaming. Reservations are necessary at four hike-in camps. To obtain a permit, register at the headquarters.

No fees or permits are required for day hiking, but there are a few rules: don't bring animals on the trails, carry your own water, and stay back from the cliffs. Winds often pick up, so it's a good idea to carry a jacket.

To Tomales Bay for gapers

Its skinny profile and the sheltering bulk of Inverness Ridge make Tomales Bay a tranquil alternative to the oceanic edges of Point Reyes.

Tomales Bay State Park, just north of Inverness, is not a part of the national seashore but includes some fine stretches of pleasant sandy-bottom coves—Shell, Pebble, Heart's Desire, and Indian—offering the warmest and quietest salt-water swimming on the Marin coast. Rockier stretches below sandstone bluffs support fair-sized populations of rock cockles. In addition to its shoreside charms, the park is a preserve for the Bishop pine, which flourishes on the peninsula but is absent on the adjacent mainland.

Around on the east side of the bay is a county boat launch just south of the point where State 1 bends inland toward the town of Tomales. Beach areas all along the bay are accessible for cockling or the winter run of herring. You can buy oysters from one of the commercial growers in the town of Marshall.

Dillon Beach, a raffishly charming commercial establishment and summer village right at the mouth of Tomales Bay, is almost due west of Tomales on a spur road. Clamming for gapers on a low-tide island, fishing of various sorts, and swimming (for the hardy) are popular.

Sonoma's lovely coastline

Shorter and less developed than the Mendocino coast, its more famous neighbor to the north, the Sonoma coastline begins at Bodega Bay and runs north to the mouth of the Gualala River. Its principal attractions are a series of beach parks, awesome scenery, and Fort Ross, last surviving sign of the 19th-century Russian settlements in California. The Sonoma coast divides into three distinct parts—two lengths of coastal shelf divided by a spate of steep hills marching into the sea. The shelves extend from Bodega Bay to Jenner on the south, and from Fort Ross to Gualala on the north. Overnight accommodations are becoming more numerous, but it's wise to arrange lodging in advance.

Around Bodega Bay

The Bodega Bay-Jenner segment of the Sonoma coast is the most developed and easiest to view. A gently sloping shelf permits State 1 to run along a series of sandy beaches, only a little over an hour from San Francisco by way of Petaluma.

Bodega Bay, discovered by Spanish explorers in 1775, provides the only protected small boat anchorage of any size between San Francisco and Noyo in Mendocino County. Both charter and commercial boats operate out of Bodega, chasing salmon from May to October and bottom fishing when salmon are scarce. If you're in Bodega in the early afternoon, watch a party fishing boat unload the day's catch.

Perch feed in the lagoon shoals, especially along the west shore. A few gaper clams lurk along the shores, but most of them cluster offshore on a lowtide island. Outside the lagoon surfers can get up and ride toward the spit, starting at a point 400 yards east of the breakwater. Rock fishermen work the jetties and exposed side of Bodega Head. Parents and active children can romp endlessly in the rolling dunes that run all the way from the head north to Salmon Creek.

Doran Beach County Park occupies most of the curving sand spit that reaches across the bay toward Bodega Head, forming the inner lagoon where the moorages are. The outer beach is good for long strolls and rock fishing—sometimes for surfing. Inside, a boat launch adjoins the U.S. Coast Guard station. Camping is toward the tip.

Westside County Park adjoins a moorage in the lee of Bodega Head. In essence, it is a pair of parking lots, one for boaters and one for campers. Besides a launch ramp, it offers shore fishing for perch and quick access to Bodega Head's scenic beauties. You'll find picnic tables and trails down to open beaches.

Sonoma beaches—for variety

Small beaches, rocky headlands, and massive offshore rocks characterize Sonoma Coast State Beach. A collection of beaches and coves extends along State 1 from the village of Bodega Bay to the mouth of the Russian River, with over 14 miles of almost uninterrupted ocean shoreline in state park lands. Beachcombers and anglers find this stretch of coastline fascinating. For a park brochure, stop at the entrance station at Bodega Dunes or at park headquarters just to the north.

Bodega Head, the state beach's southernmost unit, is now public property. Here you can park your car and view the coast north as far as Fort Ross, south to Point Reyes. One mile north is Bodega Dunes, a state campground with over 100 units.

Salmon Creek is 1½ miles north of the town of Bodega Bay. Near the parking lot, Salmon Creek forms a summer wading pond. After fall rains break down the bar, it becomes a spawning stream for salmon and steelhead. Local surfers, night smelters, and surf fishers use the outer beach. Sand dunes roll away to the south, crisscrossed by foot and bridle paths.

Other beaches unfold in quick succession. Most are pockets of sand interrupted by outcrops of rock, good for surf or rock fishing.

Duncan's Landing is a dangerous section of coast. A large sign looms in front of a barbed wire fence, noting that a number of persons have been swept to their deaths in a pounding sea by unexpectedly high waves. Yet, there's plenty of safe rock fishing in these parks. On sandy beaches, surf fishing and dip-netting for smelts are good. Duncan's Cove, just in the lee of the point, is one of the most productive day smelt beaches in the region.

Wrights Beach, north of Duncan's Landing, is a camping unit of Sonoma Coast State Beach and a picnicker's favorite, as much for its broad, sandy strand as its facilities.

Goat Rock Beach is more than one thing—a protected cove, a long, sandy beach reaching out to form the mouth of the Russian River, and a sandy length of river bank. The road to it forks off State 1 near a long, upgrade crest and descends across nearly a mile of meadows to arrive at sea level. The northern end of the park is a popular daytime beach offering good smelt fishing in summer and steelheading in the winter.

From Jenner north, the coast is wilder, rockier; there are no easy returns to inland highways for many miles.

A Russian fort

Fort Ross is about 13 miles north of Jenner, where State 1 finally comes down from elevations that are either awe-inspiring or terrifying, depending on the density of the sea fog and the reliability of the driver. You see the stout, wooden buildings sitting high on the headlands before you reach them. The parking lot turnoff is just beyond the park.

A state historic park, Fort Ross was originally the North American outpost for Russian fur traders in the 19th century. During their reign the Russians and Aleut hunters wiped out the sea otter herds to the point of extinction, with help from American and British competitors. The Aleuts, skilled at hunting Alaskan otter herds, were deadly efficient. Fleets of two-man kayaks would form a circle and then start constricting the perimeter.

(Continued on page 68)

VISITORS INVADE *stout wooden walls of Fort Ross (above), perched high on sunny headlands overlooking Pacific Ocean. Once an American outpost for Russian fur traders, fort is now state historic park.*

WOOLLY SHEEP SCURRY *across Mendocino County road (above). Bucolic scene is common in area where quiet ranches dot rolling pastures and sheep raising is still lucrative.*

. . . Continued from page 66

When the animals surfaced to breathe, they were harpooned. Or hunters would take a live pup and use its distress cries to lure adult otters into range.

Painstakingly restored and reconstructed after the 1906 earthquake and several later fires, the fort now looks much as it originally did. A gated entrance leads visitors to a large new interpretive center containing exhibits, a gift shop, and a slide-viewing room. In the exhibit hall, artifacts and colorful displays illustrate the three major eras in the fort area's history—Indian, Russian, and contemporary logging and ranching.

The ⅔-mile paved loop walk between the center and the fort takes you through a grove of Monterey cypress and along the bluff. From here, you can view rockhounds foraging along the gravelly shore and divers working the rocks north and south in quest of abalone.

One of the more recent reconstructions in the compound is the Commandant's residence (Kuskov House), the first structure in the original stockade. The fort is open from 10 A.M. to 4:30 P.M. daily; there's a slight admission fee.

The northern beaches

From Fort Ross to Mendocino, the coastal shelf is generally narrow but gently sloping, sometimes wooded but mostly covered by meadow grass. Take along a picnic basket; eating places are few.

Immediately north of Fort Ross the land is privately held as part of the Timber Cove development. Walk around to the seaward side of the hotel to look at sculptor Beniamino Bufano's last finished work—a monument to Peace—that overlooks both land and sea.

Stillwater Cove County Park, 3½ miles north of Fort Ross, opened its cove and creek-front location for day use in 1975. A favorite of scuba divers, the park has tables, a canyon trail, and the old Fort Ross schoolhouse.

Salt Point State Park, midway between Jenner and Stewarts Point, is worth a stop, whether or not you plan to camp, picnic, or comb the beach. At the point you'll find open and secluded sites for camping, deeply cut coves rewarding to scuba divers (there's an underwater park here), small stands of pygmy pines and redwoods, and miles of hiking trails. This rich environment made Salt Point a pioneer unit in the state's marine park system.

Kruse Rhododendron State Reserve is at its best from April to June when plants are in bloom. You can wander along paths through more than 300 acres set aside to preserve shrubs as high as 20 feet. Sorry, no picnic facilities.

Stewarts Point and Sea Ranch show great architectural diversity. Stewarts Point's general store, hotel, and schoolhouse are late 19th or early 20th century vintage. At Sea Ranch, a private development just up the road, you'll see strikingly modern trendsetting vacation homes designed to blend with the landscape. The ranch's restaurant/lodge complex typifies the design approach that you'll see reiterated in many houses in the meadows and hills north to Gualala.

Gualala is an old lumber port between Anchor Bay and Sea Ranch. The county park occupies the headland and spit, forming the south side of the Gualala River and marking the northern boundary of Sonoma County. You can camp beside the river in which Jack London liked to cast for steelhead. Gualala has motels and the noble old Gualala Hotel, built in 1903, with a frontier-style bar, genteel dining room, and a few rooms to let. St. Orres, a small inn outside of town, is vaguely reminiscent of Fort Ross in its Russian-inspired architecture. The dining room offers fine coastal views.

Mendocino's magnificent coast

The spirit of independence still flourishes in Mendocino County. On December 31, 1974, some citizens of Mendocino "seceded" from the state and formed their own "state"—Northern California. The news elicited no official comment from Sacramento except one wry remark by a veteran observer that "the county's departure, if it ever goes, would scarcely be noticed, at least not until the fog lifted."

Foggy it may be during the summer, but Mendocino's 19th century charm and scenic beauty draw thousands of visitors yearly and a regular influx of new residents. Urbanization doesn't threaten yet; narrow, crooked roads help preserve its relative remoteness, and towns are still small and spaced well apart.

Blue sea and white surf contrast with deep green forests and weathered gray barns. In the 100 miles from Gualala to Rockport, the mood changes around every headland, making this a photographer's field day. Even the gap-toothed fences are appealing.

For most visitors the heart of this rugged coast is the short distance from Mendocino to Fort Bragg. At either end of this stretch, you'll find less deep sea fishing, less Victoriana, and less tourism but more expansive beaches for driftwood hunters and surf fishermen.

Highways and byways are more prevalent on this part of the coast than farther south. The southern boundary of the county lies only 125 miles north of San Francisco, the northern edge only 250 miles. And yet a weekend can often mean more hours on the road than on the beach. (For a delightful loop drive, head east from Mendocino to Comptche, south to State Highway 128, and west to Albion.) Most visitors find they need at least 3 days to linger leisurely in comfortable old inns, browse among art galleries, and picnic on pebbly beaches.

State 1 clings to the seaward edge of Mendocino County. Much of it is two lanes, within a mile of the sea and almost always in sight of it. Dipping and twisting across sharply ridged country and around deep coves, the highway takes you across the mouths of Mendocino's many rivers and creeks.

To reach the Mendocino coast you can join State 1 at its Leggett junction with U.S. 101 north of Fort Bragg or come up the Sonoma coast.

Two other routes provide easy access. State Highway

128 meanders north and west from Cloverdale on U.S. 101, passing through miles of rolling orchard and vineyard country before becoming a winding path through towering redwood forests. You pass through several hamlets along the 57 miles of well-paved, two-lane highway. State 20 is more direct and the area it passes through, less inhabited. The highway leaves U.S. 101 at Willits and joins State 1 just south of Fort Bragg-Noyo. Paralleling the route of the Skunk train, you'll travel 35 miles through fine stands of redwoods and Douglas fir. Watch for logging trucks on any road.

Accommodations center around the Mendocino-Fort Bragg area of the coast. You have your choice of old-time establishments or modern motels.

Inns in Little River, Elk, and Westport, as well as a hotel and several inns in Mendocino, recall the past (see page 77). If you wish to stay at one of these places, reservations are essential. Reservations are also advisable at motels in Fort Bragg and Mendocino. For a list of accommodations, write Fort Bragg-Mendocino Coast Chamber of Commerce, P.O. Box 1141, Fort Bragg, CA 95437.

Weather is variable. Your best chances for a good outing are in May and early June when blooming azaleas and rhododendrons are plentiful and summer traffic is not, or during September and October when the weather is balmy and the roads and campgrounds are less crowded. Tourist season runs from Memorial Day to Labor Day, even though the coastal fog bank often descends during summer months.

The rainy season begins around mid-October; most of the annual rainfall of 35 inches occurs between December and May. Winter days are usually in the 40°F/4°C to 50° F/10°C range; summer temperatures often get into the 70s.

Beach parks and campgrounds

Getting down to the shore or back into the forest is mainly a matter of getting to the public beaches scattered along the coast from Gualala to Fort Bragg. Ranging from flat, sandy coves to tunneled headlands, most of them have fine camping or picnicking facilities and abundant scenery.

(Continued on page 71)

SMILE, IF YOU CALL A MAN A *HAIREEM*

Like the Hawaiians with their pidgin and the cockneys with their rhyming slang, some of the people of Boonville speak a colorfully unique dialect. It's called Boontling, and when a real Boonter speaks it, there's an uneven lilt and a touch of humor that run all through the more than 1,000 words of the vocabulary.

Boonville, with a population of about 1,000, lies at the southern end of picturesque Anderson Valley in Mendocino County. It's no problem to find your way to the coast on State Highway 128 from Boonville, but if you ask directions of one of the oldtimers in town he might give them to you in Boontling and watch your surprise. It's a game they play, and one of the reasons the language developed.

Rumors are it had its beginnings in the Anytime Saloon, and evolved mainly from a desire to exclude outsiders. Some say it was a parent's form of pig Latin.

Boontling grew up in Boonville in the late 1880s when the men would meet in town and try to *shark* (stump) each other with a new Boont word. Origins of some words have been lost, for Boontling developed as a spoken language and has only recently been written. But the oldtimers have passed along most of the words to the new generations, and several logical patterns are apparent in word formation.

All through Boontling, names have become descriptive nouns, and a spirit of fun prevails. Those who speak it today do so strictly to entertain each other. These are some of the words they use:

A *Charlie Walker* is a photograph, after the one-legged photographer from Mendocino who took Boonville family portraits. A big mustache is a *Tom Bacon*—named for the man who could reputedly wrap his handlebar around his ears. Horace Greeley's name is used for any journalist, but especially to signify a newspaperman.

A *relf* is a rail fence, a *hairk* is a haircut, a *haireem* is a "hairy mouth" or dog, and *skipe* is a clergyman, from sky pilot. If you add the word "region" to these, a *hairk region* becomes barbershop and a *skipe region,* a church.

The remainder of Boontling is made up mostly of words or phrases whose connotation is immediately clear to a Boonter. *Featherlegged* means a know-it-all and comes from the strutting barnyard cocks. *Trashmovers* (big storms) tell something of winter problems in a rural community.

It's not easy to hear Boontling because Boonters speak it mostly to each other. But if you buy a cup of coffee or a sandwich in town, take a good look at the receipt. Across the bottom may be written: "Our Gorm is Boll, our Zeese is hot; some regions de-Hig you, but we will not." One hint: *Boll* means good.

BEHIND THE RED DOOR, Heritage House (below) epitomizes charm and warm hospitality of north coast inns.

FISHING BOATS SNUGGLE UP to peaceful dock (above) during golden moment at Noyo harbor, fishing center of Mendocino County.

HEADLANDS FRONT CLASSIC VIEW of quaint Mendocino (below), California's answer to a New England coastal village.

... *Continued from page 69*

Manchester State Beach has the first generous sand beach in Mendocino County and the last one south of Fort Bragg. Its 7 miles of wide shore run most of the distance between the Garcia River and Alder Creek. Middling good for sand castles, the beach is far roomier than its minimally developed campground, sheltered behind the dunes from the frequent winds. To the south lies Point Arena Lighthouse. There's a museum, lodging, and whale watching from the 115-foot tower.

Van Damme State Park, on scenic Little River, offers campsites, reasonably safe (but cold) swimming, and biking or hiking trails. One trail leads to an ancient pygmy forest of stunted conifers in the southeast quarter of the park. Its beach is a pleasant wayside stop but only a minor introduction to the main park on the inland side of the highway.

Mendocino Headlands State Park, whose splendor needs no superlatives, begins at the mouth of the Big River as a sandy beach, loops west beneath the bluffs as a wall of rock, and then broadens to cover the flat fields of the headlands, as well as their wave-swept edge. Heeser Drive, a loop road west of Mendocino town, circles along the edge of the bluff and down to the beach. This is a highly sculpted shore, with wave tunnels, arched rocks, narrow channels—even a few lagoons. Tidepoolers should have a "look but don't touch" attitude, and skin divers fare well. Watch an unusually picturesque surf pound its way ashore; the outermost point contends for honors as the finest wave-watching spot on the coast. Because offshore rocks or shoals temper the fury of onrushing swells, safe vantages are only a few feet away. At the north end of Heeser Drive, a public fishing access adjoins calmer seas.

North of Mendocino, another undeveloped unit in the state park system is Jughandle State Reserve. When the tide's out, you can picnic on a small beach.

Russian Gulch State Park looks back across a broad bay at Mendocino from the next headland to the north. It offers a compacted replay of the sheltered beach at Van Damme and the exposed headlands at Mendocino. A creek cutting out of the gulch pauses in a low, sandy spot so children may splash around in safety, and then slips into the sea in the lee of a craggy, lofty headland. A blowhole just north of the main overlook only works during storms.

From its dramatic edge, the main body of the park runs deeply inland; protected campsites nestle in the mouth of the canyon. It's an easy hike upstream to a lacy waterfall set amidst a forest underlaid with beds of ferns.

MacKerricher State Park begins north of Fort Bragg where Pudding Creek empties into the sea. Greatly enlarged in 1972, its headlands, beaches, surf, heavily forested uplands, and small lake for fishing and boating make it the most versatile of the parks. A road wanders down to the shore between a rocky beach to the south and sandy beach to the north, which runs all the way from the main parking area to Ten Mile River. Chief reasons for heading out along the dunes are smelt fishing or driftwood hunting. You can get to the Ten Mile River end of the beach from an old logging road off State 1.

Like Van Damme and Russian Gulch to the south, MacKerricher is popular and, despite three campgrounds, rarely has campsite vacancies in summer. For information on any of these parks, write to Department of Parks and Recreation, Mendocino Area State Parks, P.O. Box 440, Mendocino, CA 95460; call Ticketron for reservations.

Inland to Boonville

About 30 miles inland from the windy Mendocino coast lie the quiet ranches and hillside pastures of the Anderson Valley. Boonville, largest town on State 128 between Cloverdale and the ocean, was settled in the 1850s. Locals still make their living growing apples and raising livestock.

Special events are scattered throughout the year. In the spring when apple blossoms and native western azaleas color the valley pink and white against sheep-cropped, green hills, it's time for the local art show (March), the wildflower festival (April), and "Buck-a-roo Days," a rodeo in June. In July, sheep raisers gather to exchange gossip, compete for prizes, and feast on barbecued lamb. Held under tall shade trees at the Mendocino County Fairgrounds, this event attracts many visitors.

In the fall and winter, steelhead run in the Navarro River, and roadside stands sell the valley's fine apples. September is the month for the County Fair and Apple Festival; reminiscent of old-time fairs, it draws visitors from all over the West.

Camp and parks dot the roadside. Paul M. Dimmick Wayside Camp, a 12-acre redwood park between the highway and the river, makes a handy base for both trailer and tent campers. Forested Hendy Woods State Park has two camping areas, a stream for summer swimming and fishing, and stands of virgin redwoods.

From Mendocino to Fort Bragg

From Little River on the south to Fort Bragg on the north, Mendocino County reaches a sort of high point. These miles are the most populous, the most popular with tourists, and contain the two principal towns and the major fishing harbor. Progress is so complete that State 1 has been straightened and widened, bringing Mendocino and Fort Bragg within 15 minutes of one another. However, the best plan is not to hurry. There's variety to savor.

Mendocino: New England revisited

Almost startlingly in contrast to its time and place, this small cluster of wooden towers and carpenter's Gothic houses contains a contemporary society of artists and artisans. They share a view south across the mouth of the Big River and west across the grassy headlands to the sea. Amble through the numerous galleries and see how resident artists translate such scenes in oils, wood blocks, and water colors.

Settled as a mill town in 1852 by timber baron Henry Meiggs, Mendocino may look like a Cape Cod relic, but its weathered buildings are bursting with life. Park your car as soon as you get to town. Streets are short, narrow, and easily jammed by vehicle traffic. The terrain is good for biking.

A walking tour will take you to the Mendocino Art Center (heart of the coastal art renaissance), past homes of long-dead lumber barons, to art galleries, book stores, unusual shops, and coffee houses. Be sure to notice the Old Masonic Hall with its intriguing rooftop sculpture of Father Time braiding a maiden's hair.

Fort Bragg—for fish and flowers

Just up the road is the harbor town of Noyo, sportfishing center of Mendocino County. Charter boats operate out of a deep cove just inside the mouth of the Noyo River. Private boats go in free at a public launching ramp; charters go out for a half-day of salmon fishing. Fishing season runs from June until the first week in October (weekends only after school starts). Some of the best seafood restaurants are on the Noyo flat.

Fort Bragg, largest city on the coast between San Francisco and Eureka, was first settled as an army post in 1857, then resettled with the construction of its first sawmill in 1885. Paul Bunyan Days (Labor Day weekend) bring big crowds to watch modern loggers perform axe throwing, pole climbing, and log rolling. You can take a town walking tour, go picnicking or fishing, visit the Guest House Museum (a former lumber company guest house filled with displays illustrating logging and shipping history), hop aboard the strangely named "Skunk" train for an 80-mile round trip through redwood groves to Willits on U.S. 101, or visit the Mendocino Coast Botanical Gardens, a lavish, 47-acre display of plants and bulbs. On most summer weekends, you can enjoy an afternoon of music in the gardens. (Gardens are open daily; there's a moderate charge.)

Beyond Fort Bragg the coastal shelf narrows to next to nothing, then nothing. Weathered Westport's New England-style houses have changed little since the heyday of lumbering. Shore fishing is productive at Westport-Union Landing State Beach and South Kibesillah Gulch Coast Angling Access Area. A pair of unpaved parking lots alongside the highway give access to several hundred yards of vertical shore. Tiny Westport has a restaurant, grocery store (with gas pumps), café, and modest hotel.

The Redwood Highway

Before the Gold Rush brought a surge of new population to Northern California, a vast forest of the world's tallest trees—the coast redwood or *Sequoia sempervirens*—blanketed an area up to 30 miles wide, ranging 450 miles from the Santa Lucia Mountains south of Monterey northward into a corner of Oregon. The oldest known coast redwood was 2,200 years old when cut in the 1930s.

Civilization's demands have left only small parts of the forest primeval. The majority of the remaining redwoods are located along U.S. 101 from Leggett north to Crescent City. These giants grow naturally in no other part of the country.

The Avenue of the Giants, a 33-mile, alternate scenic route (254), roughly parallels U.S. 101. Winding leisurely through a cathedral-like aisle of 300-foot-high trees it offers a closer view of these "ambassadors from another age." The entrance is at Sylvandale, about 6 miles north of Garberville. The avenue ends about 5 miles north of Pepperwood (30 miles south of Eureka). Numerous turnouts and parking areas allow for "neck-craning"; trails lead you through tranquil glens and along bucolic river banks. If you take U.S. 101, you'll miss these sylvan glades, public campgrounds, picnicking and swimming facilities, and a few small towns on the way.

Although you can drive this route in an hour, you could easily spend a weekend sampling its attractions. At the southern end, children will enjoy several "curiosities," survivors from the days before the freeway was built—Living Chimney, Famous One-Log House, Shrine Drive-Thru Tree, Immortal Tree, and Eternal Tree House.

Logging still thrives, and visitors are not encouraged at harvesting areas. But you can visit demonstration forests, stop by reforestation displays, or visit the Pacific Lumber Company (one of the world's largest mills) at Scotia. At the main headquarters you get passes for self-guiding plant tours on weekends.

Weather is variable in redwood country. The finest season is autumn, when the crowds thin out, the air turns brisk, and the seasonal show of color brightens the countryside. Wildflower season along the coast often extends from March until August, but April to June is the best period. Expect rain and fog in summer; redwoods grow in moist climates.

Eureka, the major city in the redwoods, is one of the cooler places in the nation from June until October. From this city north to the Oregon border, the weather is much the same as the Mendocino coast. South of Eureka, after U.S. 101 cuts behind the coast hills, you experience an entirely different kind of climate. Because the mountains screen out the cooling ocean air, summers can be warm and dry.

Accommodations in redwood country are somewhat limited for the summer demand. More motels, hotels, and inns line this highway than appear along the Mendocino coast, but traffic is correspondingly heavier. Eureka and Arcata have a number of motels and inns; it's wise to have reservations. Without them, you'll have better luck finding a place to stay in Orick or Crescent City.

Pick a park

The best of the remaining coast redwoods are preserved in the Redwood National Park and in several state parks along the Redwood Highway section of U.S. 101. Parks are busy throughout the summer, offering informative naturalist programs, nature hikes, and evening campfires. If you're of the school that believes a family visiting the redwoods ought to have a square mile or so to itself, plan your trip in the off season.

South of Eureka, scenic attractions and the highway play tag with the South Fork of the Eel River. Sprawling Humboldt Redwoods State Park is the main attraction, but there are other good spots for campers. Several of the smaller parks contain awesome stands of old-growth redwoods and are frequently less crowded than the more publicized Humboldt groves. Standish-Hickey State Recreation Area, just north of Leggett, has plenty of camping but only one mature redwood among dense forest. Picnicking is popular at Smithe Redwoods State Reserve, a little farther north. You can hike to a waterfall or take a footpath down to the Eel River. The Benbow Lake State Recreation Area, south of Garberville, features picnic and limited camping facilities.

Richardson Grove State Park is relatively small (about 800 acres), but you can't fail to find it—the Redwood Highway goes right through it. Here are swimming holes along the Eel River's South Fork and highly developed campgrounds. Ten miles of trails make good hiking. Although it can be wet and chilly in the winter, Richardson Grove is open the year around. In winter, silver and king salmon and steelhead trout attract many fishermen.

Humboldt Redwoods State Park is scattered along most of the length of the Avenue of the Giants and the Eel River. Acquired piece by piece, the park complex now ties together more than 70 memorial groves. It begins unobtrusively at the Whittemore Grove across the river from the highway; take Briceland Road at Redway. Beyond Miranda, the groves are fairly continuous to the junction of the South Fork and the main Eel, with major breaks at Myers Flat, Weott, and the freeway overpass that has cut a tremendous swath between Founders Grove and California Federation of Women's Clubs Grove. At Burlington, in a dark copse of second growth, an all-year campground adjoins the park headquarters. Rangers give information on camping and picnic facilities in other parts of the park and, in autumn, tell where to see the best color display.

Highlights of the park include the Founders Tree, for many years considered the world's tallest (364 feet before a broken top brought the figure down to 347); the solemn depths of the Rockefeller Forest; the wide pebble beach of the Eel, where you can stand back and look at redwoods from top to bottom instead of being encircled and overwhelmed; and Bull Creek flats, where you can sit underneath the soaring trees and bask in the silence or stroll down to the site of the present "tallest" tree, Giant tree, and Flatiron tree.

Grizzly Creek Redwoods State Park, a small, secluded area along the Van Duzen River, is highly prized by picnickers and campers because of its climate, often warmer and less foggy than parks right along the coast. Its 234 acres include a virgin redwood grove, more than a mile of river front, hiking trails, and improved campsites—but no grizzlies. Summer trout fishing is fair to good; steelheading is good from mid-February to mid-April. The park is 18 miles east of U.S. 101 on State Highway 36.

For more information on these parks, write to California Department of Parks and Recreation, District 1 Headquarters, 3431 Fort Avenue, Eureka, CA 95501.

Eureka: A Victorian city

Lumbering and fishing built Eureka, largest city in Humboldt County, and are still its main industries. Sniff the air: the odors come from docks along Humboldt Bay or pulp mills south of town. Eureka is a midway point between San Francisco and Portland; you'll have to get off the main highway and drive through town to enjoy its charms. Here you'll discover many motels, a delightful Tudor-style hotel, charming inns, and several fine restaurants well known for their seafood.

For walking maps of downtown and driving maps of the waterfront and Victorians around town, stop by the Eureka Chamber of Commerce, 2112 Broadway, on your way into town. During the summer, the chamber offers a 5-hour bus tour of the area's attractions, including lunch and a bay cruise; the price is moderate and reservations are a must. A round-trip excursion train runs from Willits to Eureka during the summer. For more information, call (707) 442-3738.

Additional visitor information is available at Eureka-Humboldt County Convention and Visitors Bureau (1034 Second Street); phone (707) 443-5097.

Fort Humboldt State Historic Park, constructed in the 1850s and abandoned as a military post in 1865, is a half-mile off U.S. 101 on the southern edge of Eureka. Open daily from 9 A.M. to dusk, a small museum behind the park headquarters gives a brief history of the fort where Ulysses S. Grant spent several months just prior to his resignation from the army. On display is a selection of equipment used for turn-of-the-century logging near a reconstruction of a typical logger's cabin. On a clear day the view of Humboldt Bay is outstanding.

Sequoia Park (Glatt and W Streets) is a woodland oasis in the heart of Eureka. On these 52 acres, you'll find one of the best forests in this region. You can walk leafy trails past ferns and streams, stop at a zoo and children's playground, or feed ducks the remains of your picnic lunch. A shady haven on rare warm days, it's equally pleasant when the weather is cool and foggy.

Victorian-sighting is excellent in Eureka. Except for downtown thoroughfares, the town retains much of its original character. Brightly colored turrets, spires, and gables show up well against the often-stark sky. Most homes are well preserved or are being renovated. The largest concentration of Victorian homes is south of Seventh Street between C and K streets. Called the "queen" of Victorians, the flamboyant and much-photographed Carson Mansion is on M Street between Second and Third.

Now a private men's club, the mansion looks much as it did when completed by lumber baron William Carson in 1886. Decide for yourself whether it is the "finest example of Victorian Gothic architecture" or an "architectural monstrosity." The smaller house across the street was also built by Carson as a wedding gift for his son.

A self-guided tour highlights other examples of Victorian architecture throughout Eureka. Tour maps are available at the Eureka Chamber of Commerce.

Eureka's Old Town has come to life. Spurred by a concentrated redevelopment program, this once decaying waterfront district now boasts budding restaurants, specialty shops, new businesses, even a community art center.

Major renovation has focused on Second Street between C and M streets. At Second and F streets, Old Town Square features an open-air gazebo and meandering fountain. For some blocks in each direction you can glimpse restored vintage buildings.

Around the corner from Old Town Square the Humboldt Cultural Center (422 First Street) was a mercantile store in the 1870s. It now houses shows by local artists and craftspeople. Another popular stop is the Art Center, G and Second streets, which offers art supplies, gifts, and two galleries.

Also located in Old Town is the Clarke Memorial Museum at Third and E streets. The museum features extensive collections of Victorian, maritime, and pioneering relics, plus an outstanding native American exhibit.

Humboldt Bay

Just beyond the waterfront section of downtown Eureka and almost concealed from the highway is Humboldt Bay, largest deep-water port between Portland and San Francisco. You can explore the harbor on an old ferry, study the bay's birdlife, go boating and fishing, or beachcomb along the great stretches of sand guarding the harbor's narrow entrance.

Getting around the bay is easy when you take a narrated cruise; boats leave several times a day (1, 2:30, and 4 P.M.) from the foot of C Street. On the 75-minute trip, you'll see bay highlights and hear a brief history of the area. Watch the commercial fishing fleet coming into the harbor, nets still dripping from their catches, or view the large ocean freighters loading pulp on the peninsula.

Six boat ramps and two hoists make it easy to put your boat into the water. You'll find public ramps at several points: at the Eureka Mooring Basin, on the North Spit before the Coast Guard station, and at Fields Landing on South Bay. You can rent a skiff or charter a boat at King Salmon and use hoists and a ramp for a nominal fee.

Crossing the bridge to Samoa takes you over Woodley and Indian islands. Marshy Indian Island, part of the Humboldt Bay National Wildlife Refuge, is the site of the northernmost egret/heron rookery on the Pacific Coast. In a small grove of cypress, you may see hundreds of roosting birds, massed like a feathery white cloud. A sign at Samoa marks the turnoff to the Cookhouse, where you dine family style at one of the last lumber camp cookhouses operating in the West.

From Samoa you can continue along the North Spit across Mad River Slough to Arcata, where a self-guiding architectural tour takes you back to the time of Bret Harte and the heyday of gold mining. A few miles north of Arcata, the Azalea State Reserve bursts into bloom around Memorial Day. Trails lead you among masses of overhanging blossoms. Take the North Bank Road from either U.S. 101 or State Highway 299.

Picturesque Trinidad, settled in 1850, is one of the oldest towns on the north coast. Just minutes north of Eureka, this former whaling station is now a bustling fishing village. Colorful boats dot its sheltered harbor, and nearby Trinidad State Park offers day-use facilities. Fishing expeditions, gift shops, restaurants, and motels make Trinidad an inviting diversion at the north end of the bay.

A valley loop

A 73-mile trail loops through pastoral Mattole Valley to the sea and back into the redwoods. You can begin at Ferndale, about 15 miles south of Eureka.

Ferndale's freshly painted look is a study in carpenter's Gothic. Here you'll find some of the coast's best-preserved Victorians, from small white cottages to intricate gingerbread mansions. A stroll down Main Street reveals a menagerie of artisans working in stained glass, metal, even custom shirt design. Here, too, are antique and crafts shops, a western saddlery, several galleries, and a couple of restaurants worthy of a lunch stop. Zaniness prevails at the Kinetic Sculpture Race on Memorial Day weekend. The village also hosts the county fair in August.

For an overall town view (and a steep uphill climb), try 30-acre Russ Park. Take Ocean Avenue east from Main Street; your hike starts just west of the Catholic cemetery.

Driving over Bear River Ridge, you coast downhill through manicured pastures and finally reach the shore.

Heading back inland you'll pass through Petrolia, site of California's first drilled oil wells, and Honeydew, one of California's smallest towns. The village consists of a general store, gas station, and post office—all under one roof. Back in the redwoods, the road slants down to Bull Creek through Rockefeller Grove, meeting U.S. 101 about 2½ miles north of Weott.

Redwood National Park

A representative segment of old-growth redwood and the outstanding coastal scenery in Northern California are now being protected so that, generations from now, people will be able to view the magnificent trees and the plant and animal life which they nurture.

Stretching from above Crescent City at the north to below Orick to the south, Redwood National Park contains 106,000 acres (48,000 were added in 1978) of some of the West's finest scenic and recreation areas.

In 1985, the new Visitor Information Center opened on the beach beside U.S. 101 south of Orick. In addition to providing park information to help visitors effectively plan their stays, the center handles tickets for summer bus tours to the Tall Trees area. For further information, call (707) 488-3461.

A tour service offers bus trips highlighting Humboldt's north coast attractions. Starting from Trinidad, stops include selected state parks and sections of Redwood National Park. Reservations are suggested; price

SAND FLIES as young equestrians (left) trot onto sunny beach near Trinidad for a brisk bareback run.

LACED IN GREEN, majestic coast redwoods (Sequoia sempervirens) stand tall (right) in soft morning light of Richardson Grove State Park.

IMPOSING CARSON MANSION (above) is incongruous blend of turrets, gingerbread, gables, moldings. Built in 1886 for lumber baron William Carson, Eureka mansion now houses private men's club.

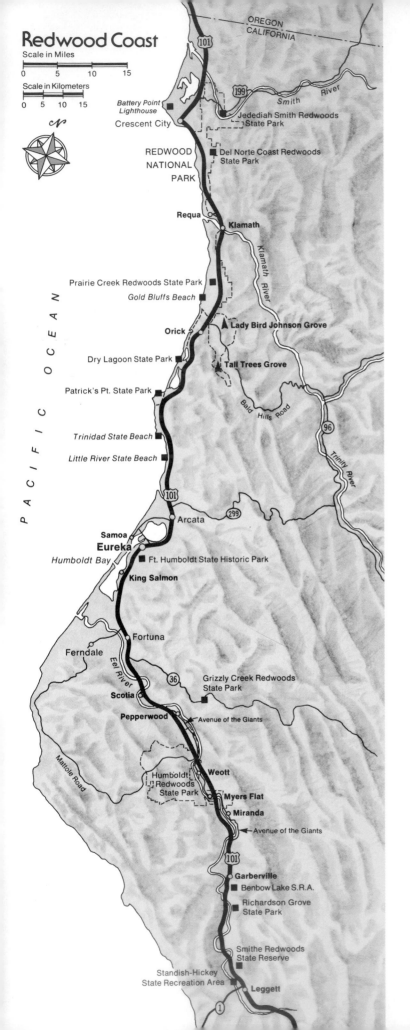

Redwood Coast

Scale in Miles
0   5   10   15

Scale in Kilometers
0   5   10   15

OREGON
CALIFORNIA

Smith River

Battery Point Lighthouse
Crescent City
Jedediah Smith Redwoods State Park

REDWOOD NATIONAL PARK
Del Norte Coast Redwoods State Park

Requa
Klamath

Klamath River

Prairie Creek Redwoods State Park
Gold Bluffs Beach
Lady Bird Johnson Grove
Orick
Dry Lagoon State Park
Tall Trees Grove
Patrick's Pt. State Park
Bald Hills Road
Trinity River

Trinidad State Beach
Little River State Beach

PACIFIC OCEAN

Arcata
Samoa
Eureka
Humboldt Bay
Ft. Humboldt State Historic Park
King Salmon

Fortuna
Ferndale
Eel River
Grizzly Creek Redwoods State Park
Scotia
Pepperwood
Avenue of the Giants
Mattole Road
Humboldt Redwoods State Park
Weott
Myers Flat
Miranda
Avenue of the Giants

Garberville
Benbow Lake S.R.A.
Richardson Grove State Park
Smithe Redwoods State Reserve
Standish-Hickey State Recreation Area
Leggett

---

is moderate. For more information call Northcoast Redwood Tours (707) 677-0334 or (707) 677-3470.

Klamath, at the mouth of the Klamath River, is well known for fine salmon and steelhead fishing. You can take a 64-mile jet boat trip up the river just to view the scenery. Tours leave one mile north of Klamath, on U.S. 101, from June 1 to the end of September.

Lady Bird Johnson Grove is located along the Bald Hills Road 2 miles east of U.S. 101 (just north of Orick). A half-mile trail will take you to the site where Mrs. Lyndon B. Johnson dedicated the national park on November 25, 1968.

Tall Trees Grove, home of the skyscraping sequoias, runs along Redwood Creek just west of Bald Hills Road. The tallest tree is 367.8 feet high and 14 feet in diameter. Primitive camping is available.

At one time the only way to see the world's tallest trees was a 17-mile round-trip hike along the creek. Now the park's new summer shuttle service takes you within a mile of these ancient giants. Every hour from 9 A.M. to 4 P.M. daily, passenger vans leave from the parking area 7 miles up Bald Hills Road to carry hikers to the grove's trailhead. The walk in is mostly downhill to the river. Once you reach the grove, a sign points out the world's tallest known tree.

Three parks within a park

Included within the Redwood National Park are three long-established state parks (Prairie Creek, Del Norte, and Jedediah Smith). In addition to being the nucleus of the national park, at present these parks have the only established camping. Federal recreation permits are not valid in the state parks, and summer reservations are a must for the 350-plus campsites.

Much of the redwood forest acreage of the state parks consists of memorial groves purchased by the Save-the-Redwoods League with donations from private individuals. Supplemented by state funds, this money is used to acquire more redwood groves and enlarge the parks.

Prairie Creek Redwoods State Park is a favorite of many campers. It does have more than its share of special wonders: a handsome creek, a herd of native Roosevelt elk, the wide expanse of sand at Gold Bluffs Beach (tent camping available), and scenic Fern Canyon. About 100 inches of rain falls on Prairie Creek most years, giving it rain-forest overtones; but high ground to the west protects it from most of the chilly ocean winds and fog. Hiking the more than 100 miles of trails (including one for the blind and a self-guided nature walk) is the best way to explore the park's interior. Two campgrounds offer a total of 100 sites.

Del Norte Coast Redwoods State Park lets you enjoy both a drive through rugged inland forest on U.S. 101 and vistas of Pacific shore from high turnouts south of the wooded section. Damnation Creek Trail will take you on foot through the dense forest to the ocean where the giant redwoods grow almost to the shore. From April to July, you'll see outstanding displays of rhododendrons and azaleas. Del Norte has excellent camping facilities at Mill Creek Campground.

Jedediah Smith Redwoods State Park is 9 miles northeast of Crescent City on U.S. 199. At the northernmost end of the Redwood National Park, Jedediah Smith presents views of skyline ridges still tightly furred with giant redwoods. The highway runs through hilly Tyson Grove and the National Tribute Grove (just two of 18 memorial groves in the park) and then out onto a magnificent flat, where some of the most imposing redwoods soar above vine maple, salal, Oregon grape, and ferns.

The Smith River provides good salmon, steelhead, and trout fishing in season and sandy beaches for sunbathing. There are numerous campsites and trails. Crescent City, at the northern gateway to the park, sits alongside a captivating harbor. Information on the area is available from the Crescent City Chamber of Commerce and the national park's headquarters and information center. For more information write to Redwood National Park, P.O. Drawer N, Crescent City, CA 95531.

Battery Point Lighthouse, built in 1856, stands on a small island approximately 20 yards from shore. Visitors may walk to it at low tide. Though your goal is the museum inside the lighthouse, most of the fun lies in getting there.

The small museum is open Wednesdays through Sundays.

INNS ARE IN—UP NORTH

Mellow old inns offer a warm welcome to North Coast visitors. Most hug the Mendocino area and serve as bases for exploring the countryside. Varying from the intimate home to the sprawling lodge with cottages, each hostelry has charm. Most operate on American (full meals) or modified (breakfast and dinner) plans.

A sampling of inns appears below. Plan to make reservations well in advance and note closed periods. Some of the well-known inns are booked completely for weekends a year in advance. For rates and additional information, write or call the inn directly.

Benbow Inn, Garberville, CA 95440; (707) 923-2124: Tudor inn in redwoods; Eel River forms lake and beach; 9-hole regulation golf course; large living room, restaurant, and lounge; open late March through November, Christmas.

Carter House Inn, Eureka, CA 95501; (707) 445-1390: Reconstructed three-story redwood mansion in Old Town; 7 rooms, 4 with private baths; art gallery, antique shop on lower floor; noted for breakfast; wine and hors d'oeuvres in afternoon; open all year; no children.

Elk Cove Inn, Elk, CA 95432; (707) 877-3321: Small Victorian home built in early 1880s sits in bluff hiding its private beaches; attractive annex up the street brings guest capacity to 14; breakfast and dinner served Thursday through Sunday; advance reservations only.

Gingerbread Mansion, Ferndale, CA 95536; (707) 786-4000: Much-photographed gabled house with English gardens; 4 rooms share 2 baths; afternoon tea, bathrobes provided.

Heritage House, Little River, CA 95456; (707) 937-5885: Original farmhouse built on the cove in 1877 by relatives of present owner; interesting names and architecture for all 46 units; beautiful living room, lounge, and dining room; notice plantings on sod roofs; closed December and January.

Hill House, Mendocino, CA 95460; (707) 937-0554: New inn with deliberate patina of age; ocean view from some units; 44 rooms with private baths; beautiful appointments; continental breakfast; open all year.

Joshua Grindle Inn, Mendocino, CA 95460; (707) 937-4143: Vintage 1879 home, now refurbished as most attractive inn; 7 rooms, each with private bath and distinctive decor, 2 with fireplace; full breakfast in cheerful dining room; children discouraged.

Little River Inn, Little River, CA 95456; (707) 937-5942: Maine-style mansion, vintage 1853, forms heart of complex offering "attic rooms," casual cottages, or contemporary hilltop rooms; 9-hole regulation golf course; open all year (lounge and dining room closed for a few weeks before Christmas).

MacCallum House, 740 Albion St., Mendocino, CA 95460; (707) 937-0289: Landmark house sold with treasure of contents is now enticing new inn; fruit bowls highlight breakfast in your room; dining room on premises.

Mendocino Hotel, Mendocino, CA 95460; (707) 937-0511: Lone survivor of hotels once lining Main Street; extensive renovation lends air of opulence; costumed staff; public restaurant.

Whale Watch Inn, Gualala, CA 95445; (707) 884-3667: 18 rooms with private baths, some with fireplaces, others with private spas; private decks overlook coast at Anchor Bay; guests dine in Whale Watch Room or on deck; no children or smoking.

The growing appreciation of wines in the United States has uncorked a new flow of visitors to California's vineyards and tasting rooms. Between 1½ and 3 million people visit the Napa and Sonoma wineries (backbone of the North Coast wine district) each year. Here you see vinous works of art created and sample the results of the creativity—a delicious way to increase your knowledge of wine.

Winery architecture is unexpectedly diverse. Handsome traditional buildings from the late 1800s show their European heritage; California ingenuity adds a variety of touches, ranging from mission to modern.

You could visit as many as 20 cellars in a day, if you planned your route with care. But you would miss the details—and details are what make wine. Don't try to visit more than three or four wineries in one day. Do plan to stop and visit other attractions in the area. The wine country lends itself to lazing; bring a picnic basket along or stop at bakeries, delis, or cheese shops along the way.

When to go? The best time to visit the wine country is the most active period—late September and early October—when the crush (the first step toward the new year's wines) takes place. The heady aroma of newly fermenting wine charges the warm afternoon air. Vines, stripped of their clusters of grapes, are tinged with gold and scarlet. Inside the wineries, in spite of hurried labor over the new wines, amiable guides welcome visitors as nonchalantly as they might in the still days of winter when the wines take care of themselves.

Divided into regions, this chapter points out typical wineries, lists main attractions, and offers a cool look at water sports, hiking and camping locations. Students of wine seeking a complete list of visitable wineries may write Wine Institute (165 Post Street, San Francisco, CA 94108) for a copy of *Wine Wonderland*. Enclose a stamped (39 cents), self-addressed #10 envelope. A complete tour book of all wineries in the state is *Sunset's Guide to California Wine Country*.

North of San Francisco lie the valleys and hills synonymous with California wine. Large and small wineries dot the countryside with architecture ranging from traditional European to refreshingly contemporary design. Leisurely savor the delights of winemaking by visiting three or four wineries a day. Autumn crush is the most picturesque and exciting season; hills blaze hues of red, orange, and gold, and fermentation sweetens the cool fall air. Sample other wine country highlights—walk around a small town, tour a museum or mission, raft down a river, or slither into a steaming bath of mud at a spa.

Napa Valley: For touring and tasting

Many people consider the Napa Valley synonymous with "The Wine Country"—and with good reason. The vine-covered floor of the valley, flanked with tall hills and dotted with evocative wineries, may have its peers, but it has few superiors.

Easy to get to, Napa Valley is most accessible from Sacramento, San Francisco, and Oakland on a combination of Interstate Highway 80 and State Highway 29 from Vallejo. Another slower, hillier, and prettier route from San Francisco goes across the Golden Gate and then north on U.S. Highway 101, State highways 37

REDS, YELLOWS, AND ORANGES light up Napa Valley vineyards when fall comes to the wine country. During harvest season, crushed grapes' piquant bouquet fills the air.

and 121. From the north, take U.S. 101 and State Highway 128 for a pleasant drive.

The greatest concentration of wineries open to visitors flanks State 29 north and south of the unhurried town of St. Helena. A parallel road, the Silverado Trail, has more wineries sprinkled on the slopes of the east hills. Elevated enough to afford panoramic vineyard views, most of the old stagecoach route has been widened and straightened to suit the modern automobile. Crossroads among the vines tie the two arteries together.

Though the city of Napa is by far the largest in the valley, its occupation with wine is minimal. The city has an impressive quarter of fine Victorian houses southwest of an agreeable shopping district, but most of the romantic traditions of the Napa Valley are to be found farther north.

The Napa Chamber of Commerce (P.O. Box 636, Napa, CA 94559) publishes brochures on lodging, restaurants, and attractions. For a look at valley history, stop by the historical society (1219 First Street) Tuesday or Thursday from noon to 4 P.M.

St. Helena—the wine center

The 1890s look of Main Street, St. Helena, is proudly maintained, and so is the century-old emphasis on wine. Oddly enough, the single sharpest focal point is the town's library building, 2 blocks east of Main Street via Adams. The building houses both a major collection of wine literature and an independent museum celebrating author Robert Louis Stevenson.

The Napa Valley Wine Library Association assembled —and continues to expand—the library's collection of wine literature. The association conducts several weekend courses in wine appreciation for members each summer; for details, write P.O. Box 328, St. Helena, CA 94574.

The Silverado Museum occupies a separate wing of the library building. Based on the collections of Norman Strouse, the museum houses a large display of Robert Louis Stevenson memorabilia including original manuscripts and letters, portraits and photographs of the writer, and a desk he used in Samoa. To find this museum here is historically fitting because the peripatetic author honeymooned in an abandoned bunkhouse of the defunct Silverado Mine on Mount St. Helena in 1880-81. In 1883 he recounted that experience in his book *Silverado Squatters*.

The Napa Valley Olive Oil Manufactory, on Charter Oak Avenue, is a grand place to pick up picnic fixings to go along with your wine tour. You'll find fragrant olive oil, cheeses, patés, dried mushrooms, and breadsticks.

The Hurd Candle Factory, in Freemark Abbey, is the center of a complex of shops offering foods, cookware, and wine accessories. Beeswax candles hang near good wine sleeping in cellars below.

To Calistoga for mud baths and geysers

St. Helena's life centers around grapes, Calistoga's around health. Situated at the foot of Mount St. Helena, Calistoga is famous throughout the country as a spa.

Mud baths bring thousands of tourists to this year-round resort. Visitors have been arriving ever since Samuel Brannan built his opulent spa in 1859. In addition to bath houses—where swimming pools may be mineral or hot spring water—motels, hotels, and resorts abound. Calistoga is a mecca for glider pilots. And you can take the scenic drive to the Petrified Forest, west of the city. Several charming hotels and inns plus some good restaurants offer choices for overnight stays.

Napa County Historical Society Museum is located in town. History buffs will find some fascinating facts on the life of the wealthy of the late 1800s.

California's "Old Faithful" geyser, impressive spectacle in a region of hot springs and fumaroles, spews a 60-foot shower of steam and vapor at 50-minute intervals. The eruption continues for about 3 minutes, after which the geyser retreats until its next performance. Visitors learn about the origins of geothermal steam. Located just north of town on Tubbs Road (turn east from State 128), the grounds are open from 8 A.M. to dusk; there's a slight admission charge.

Yountville—for food and lodging

Named for Napa County's first white settler, George Yount, this once-sleepy town has experienced a renaissance. After years of being geared to the pace of the nearby veterans' home, it is now enlivened by a rural counterpart to Ghirardelli Square and by several elegant inns and restaurants.

In 1870, G. Grozinger built a large brick winery here. His old cellar now stocks a collection of shops, galleries, and eating spots under the collective banner of Vintage 1870. Even a theater is tucked away in one cavernous corner of the place. Other shops and restaurants flank Vintage 1870.

Not far away, Yount's final resting place is in the local cemetery, hard by the land in which he planted the valley's first vines in the 1850s.

Hiking and camping spots

Beautiful weather, along with a variety of attractions, makes the Napa Valley an ideal place to spend more than a day. Fortunately you'll find a number of areas where you can pitch a tent, park a trailer, or unroll a sleeping bag. Hiking and biking are good ways to get around on the valley floor; heading up into the surrounding hills provides plenty of exercise. Swimmers, boaters, and fishermen will find natural and manmade lakes appealing.

Bothe-Napa Valley State Park, more than 1,000 acres of broad-leafed trees and conifers and second-growth redwoods, extends west into the hills. Facilities include camping and picnicking sites, hiking trails, and a swimming pool. The park is on the west side of State 29 about 4 miles north of St. Helena.

The Old Bale Mill, a short distance south of Bothe-Napa, was added to the park. Set in motion in 1846 for the convenience of nearby residents who needed their grain ground into meal, the grinding stones were active for more than 35 years.

Robert Louis Stevenson State Park, between Calistoga and Middletown, encompasses about 3,000 acres of wild area on the eastern slopes and around the summit of Mount St. Helena. A monument testifies that the author spent his honeymoon here. The site is undeveloped except for a fire trail leading to the remnants of his cabin and the old Silverado Mine. You can continue up to the lookout (about 4 miles) on top of this 4,344-foot peak that Stevenson called the "Mont Blanc of the Coast Range." Picnicking is permitted, but no fires.

Conn Dam Recreation Area, up off the valley floor in the east hills, is a stopping-off spot offering cool Lake Hennessey for bank fishing and picnicking. The turnoff from the Silverado Trail is marked State 128-Conn Dam.

Lake Berryessa, isolated in the dry, grassy hills that separate the Napa Valley from the Sacramento Valley, is principally a summer haunt of water-skiers and speed-minded boaters. But this popular, year-round fishing hole also has many quiet coves for hot-weather anglers.

All of the modest development is along 12 miles of the west shore, which falls into shadow while the east margin still bakes in the summer sun. A string of camper resorts can be reached by plainly marked stub roads leading away from State 128. Easiest access, especially for anyone trailering a boat or camper, is from Interstate 80. Accommodations range from campsites to motels. Fairly extensive stretches of shoreline are open to bank fishing and rough picnicking. The east shore is closed to all use because fire hazard is extreme.

Boating is the best way to explore the lake. Launches are spaced at close intervals from Markley Canyon near the dam up to Putah Creek. (All are operated by resorts and charge fees, with the exception of one unimproved ramp east of the bridge across a narrow arm just south of Putah.)

Fishing is principally for trophy trout and bass in this sun-warmed lake. Shore fishing is best on points jutting into the lake. Anglers working from boats try for blue gill, crappie, catfish, Kokanee salmon, and trout.

Clear Lake is the largest lake entirely within California. (Tahoe is bigger, but not wholly within the state.) A natural, fairly shallow lake, it's about 19 miles long and up to 7½ miles wide, with a shore amply developed for recreation. In summer the water temperature reaches as high as 76°F/24°C, ideal for water sports.

The direct route from the Bay Area to the southern tip of the lake (about 120 miles from San Francisco) is on State 29 through the Napa Valley. From the west, turn off from U.S. 101 at Hopland and follow State Highway 175 to the lake and south to the Cobb Mountain area.

Anglers flock to Clear Lake for some good bass fishing in spring and early summer. But October, with its balmy fall weather and scarcity of swimmers, speedboats, and water-skiers, offers the best fishing.

On the west side of the lake, resorts are concentrated from the junction of State 29 with State Highway 175 north to the boater's capital at Lakeport. At the north end, Lucerne, Nice, and Clearlake Oaks are centers of activity; Clearlake is on the east shore.

Clear Lake State Park covers two miles of shoreline at Soda Bay, on the west side.

In the Valley of the Moon

Historically, Sonoma is one of the most interesting towns in California. It's the site of Mission San Francisco Solano, last and northernmost of the 21 missions founded by the Franciscan fellows of Fra Junipero Serra. The Sonoma pueblo was headquarters for General Mariano Vallejo, the Mexican administrator at the time of the Bear Flag Revolt. It's where the Hungarian Agoston Haraszthy laid the groundwork for some premium California wines at his Buena Vista winery. And Sonoma was the last home of author Jack London, who so romantically named the valley.

Sonoma lies 45 miles north of San Francisco. U.S. 101 across the Golden Gate is the main northward artery; then take State 37 east to an intersection with State 121, which heads north toward the town of Sonoma. One more turn, clearly marked, onto State Highway 12 leads you right to the plaza.

The main approach from the north is State 12, cutting inland from U.S. 101 at Santa Rosa. Take the State 12 exit from the freeway. Coming from the east on Interstate 80, turn off onto State 12 and follow the signs to Sonoma.

Touring the wineries

Two separate clusters of wineries are open to visitors in the Valley of the Moon. One begins in Sonoma town and stretches a mile or two east. The other group is toward the head of the valley, north of Sonoma town along State Highway 12. In or near Sonoma: Sebastiani (sizable, with tours of a large cellar and tasting), Buena Vista (tours and tasting in the old cellar where Agoston Haraszthy did much to set north coast wine on its present road), Gundlach-Bundschu (tasting daily), and Haywood and Hacienda (tasting and picnic areas). To the north, from Glen Ellen to Kenwood: Glen Ellen, Smothers, St. Francis, and Grand Cru. All four offer tasting daily, but tours only by appointment. Chateau St. Jean has tasting and a self-guided tour. Between the two groups is the old-line family cellar called Valley of the Moon.

In and around Sonoma

The town of Sonoma embraces a spacious central plaza. Across from the northeast corner of the plaza stands the mission, founded July 4, 1823. Now a state historic monument and museum, it contains historic church vestments, early photographs and documents, and 62 oil paintings of the missions. The chapel is preserved, although it is no longer used for religious services. Museum hours are 9 A.M. to 5 P.M. Of several annual events staged on the plaza, the Vintage Festival in September and the Ox Roast in June are the most famous.

Pick up a walking tour map to points of interest; maps (slight charge) are available at the Sonoma Valley Visitors Bureau office on the plaza. Public parking is behind the Sonoma Barracks; turn into the driveway on First Street East just beyond Spain Street.

Sonoma State Historic Park includes a number of buildings in addition to the mission. The long, low adobe structure across Spain Street is the Blue Wing Inn, gambling room and saloon of the Gold Rush era. West on Spain from the mission, you pass Bear Flag National Historic Monument (in the northeast corner of the plaza park), Sonoma Barracks, Toscano Hotel, the servants' wing of Casa Grande (Vallejo's first home, most of which was destroyed by fire in 1867), Swiss Hotel (still in use as a restaurant), and the home of Salvador Vallejo.

For gastronomical rather than historical stops, try the French Bakery on the east side of the plaza or the Sonoma Cheese Factory on the north. The plaza is also surrounded by charming little shops, galleries, and restaurants.

General Mariano Vallejo's home is two blocks west and then north on Third Street West. Its name, Lachryma Montis ("mountain tear"), was suggested by the natural spring in the area. Adobe brick walls were covered by wood, so what looks like a conventional Victorian Gothic house is surprisingly cool inside on a hot day. Also on the site is a handsome old warehouse built in 1852 of timber and bricks shipped around Cape Horn. Eventually converted to residential use, it became known as the Swiss Chalet. Today it serves as a museum and interpretive center for the Vallejo Home Historic Monument (open from 10 A.M. to 5 P.M.).

Train Town is a private 10-acre park on State 12, about a mile south of the plaza. For a small fee, you can ride the reproductions of classic trains into a miniature mining village. The road is known as the Sonoma Gaslight & Western RR. The park is open daily in summer, on weekends from Labor Day until June.

Jack London State Historic Park is situated in the hills above the tiny community of Glen Ellen. The House of Happy Walls, built by London's wife, Charmian, after his death, is now a museum of the author's personal and professional life. The great rock walls and chimneys of Wolf House, which London planned but never occupied, are also in the park at the end of a ¾-mile trail beginning at the museum. London's grave, marked by a simple engraved lava boulder, is nearby.

To reach the park, turn off State 12 from Sonoma to Glen Ellen and continue uphill about a mile, following park signs. Hours are 10 A.M. to 5 P.M. except for major holidays.

Hiking and camping spots

Visitors to the upper end of the Valley of the Moon are near two large parks that invite both camping and picnicking. Equestrians find the parks particularly attractive—they can stay overnight in one park and ride extensively in the other.

Sugarloaf Ridge State Park is a 2,000-acre preserve of forest, field, and stream that reaches up oak-covered hills to edge over the Sonoma-Napa county line. Warm in summer, pleasant in spring and fall, it's likely to be wet in winter. A group campground invites equestrians to spend the night, ride over the meadowland, and view sites of old farm buildings. Stream fishing for trout is a good spring pastime.

You enter the park on Adobe Canyon Road, off State 12. The park gate is 2½ miles farther; the access road is not recommended for trailers.

Annadel State Park is for hikers, bikers, and riders—not auto explorers or campers. Keeping this in mind, you'll find plenty to enjoy in this almost 5,000-acre retreat of forest, lake, and meadow. Originally Pomo Indian land, it became part of a sprawling Spanish rancho and later a ranch called Annadel Farms. Rocky ledges around Lake Ilsanjo make welcoming picnic sites (bring your own water); no swimming, boating, or rafting allowed. Stocked in 1957, the lake still yields largemouth black bass and bluegill. Below Bennett Ridge, in the southeastern part of the park, is Ledsen Marsh—an ecological community of waterfowl and wildlife.

To reach the park from Oakmont, take State 12 toward downtown Santa Rosa; turn south on Los Alamos Road, which becomes Montgomery Drive. At Channel Drive turn left and follow signs to the parking lot. Here you can pick up a park folder and trail map.

Russian River's valleys

Early in the 1970s, the Russian River valleys began to emerge as a tourable wine district. The transformation from a region of bulk producers into one of bottled varietal wineries has been accompanied by an architectural flowering.

The most impressive wineries in the region are near Healdsburg, most of them along U.S. 101, but many lie to the west in Dry Creek Valley, and to the east in Alexander Valley. Still others are scattered across the plain west of Santa Rosa. Healdsburg is about 1½ hours driving time north of San Francisco on U.S. 101.

In and around Santa Rosa

Sonoma County's largest city and the county seat, Santa Rosa was founded in 1833 by General Vallejo. Its Spanish, Mexican, and early American periods are still reflected in its architecture. The Marshall House, 835 Second Street (near the center of town), is a charming and accessible example. Lunch is served daily (except Sunday) from 11:30 A.M. to 2:30 P.M. in elegant, spacious, high-ceilinged rooms with crystal chandeliers and other Victorian appointments. A second floor gift shop is open from 11 A.M. to 4 P.M.

Good picnic spots include Spring Lake County Park (swimming, camping) on the east edge of town and Mount Hood County Park (day use only) 5 miles northeast of Santa Rosa.

Howarth Memorial Park is Santa Rosa's biggest and most attractive. A 152-acre, tree-shaded retreat, it sits at the foot of the Coast Range. An imaginative, 20-acre children's area includes a pony ride, animal farm, merry-go-round, miniature train, and playground. Rides cost a minimal fee; other attractions are free.

A feature of the main park is a lovely 32-acre lake. Motorboats are prohibited, but you can rent sailboats,

SUN-DAPPLED tasting room at Sterling Vineyards (above) provides relaxing atmosphere to sample winery's wares—perfect finale for a tour-filled day.

MISSION'S RUGGED FACADE (right) brilliantly stands out against azure sky. San Francisco Solano, located in Sonoma on State Highway 12, is last and northernmost of 21 Franciscan missions.

canoes, and rowboats for a modest hourly charge. The park also has picnic areas, several miles of hiking trails, tennis courts, and a softball field.

You enter on Summerfield Road between Sonoma Avenue and Montgomery Drive, about 5 minutes from the freeway. Howarth Park is open daily the year-round; however, amusement rides and boat rentals are open daily in the summer but weekends only during spring and fall.

The Luther Burbank Memorial Gardens, now a city park, is a living testament to a great naturalist. Searching for the perfect climate and soil to start experimenting with plants, Burbank chose the Santa Rosa Valley. And it is here that he is buried, under a Cedar of Lebanon that he planted. Examples of his work are shown in the gardens.

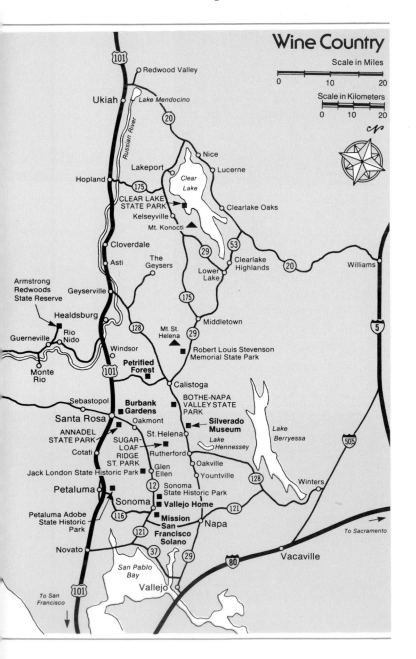

One block west is "The Church From One Tree," a chapel (complete with steeple) built from a single redwood; it's now the interesting Robert Ripley Museum.

Highways and byways lead north from Santa Rosa on U.S. 101, passing through Healdsburg, one of the few areas still holding a spring blossom tour. As a wine center, it also hosts a wine festival each May. At Geyserville, 7 miles north, is the turnoff for Devil's Canyon Geysers, 22 miles east. (This is the site of Pacific Gas & Electric Company's geothermal electric generating plant; there is no tour, and the sulfur fumes may keep you in your car, but the plant is spectacular for its roaring plumes of steam.) Cloverdale, once the northernmost of the country's commercial citrus growing areas, has the state's oldest fair, dating back to 1892.

South of Santa Rosa is Petaluma, a dairy center now, but in an earlier era a challenger to Detroit as one of the country's foremost carriage building centers. That and other prosperous times left an architecturally wealthy downtown, four blocks of it preserved as a historic site. Petaluma is also home to the world championships of wrist wrestling. Four miles east of town is Petaluma Adobe State Historic Park. Once General Vallejo's house and fort, it is now a museum furnished with period pieces and is one of the largest adobes still standing in California. Nine miles west of Petaluma on Red Hill Road is the over-century-old Rouge et Noir Cheese Factory. You can take a guided tour between 10 A.M. and 4 P.M., buy cheeses and other snacks, and have a picnic on the lawn overlooking the lake.

Sonoma County's back roads are good sources for fresh farm produce and handcrafts. For a free map and guide, write to Sonoma County Farm Trails, P.O. Box 6674, Santa Rosa, CA 95406.

Along the Russian River

To summer visitors who have swarmed there since the early days of San Francisco, "The River" is the 12-mile cluster of resorts from Mirabel Park to Monte Rio. The most direct approach from the south is U.S. 101 to Cotati (48 miles from San Francisco) and then left on State 116 to Sebastopol and the river.

For a more leisurely approach, take either Guerneville Road from Santa Rosa, Fulton-Trenton Road (3½ miles north of Santa Rosa), Eastside Road (3½ miles south of Healdsburg), or Westside Road from Healdsburg to Hacienda. Other minor roads crisscross the area.

West and north on the river's great semicircle, the mountains rise to a seemingly inaccessible steepness. You can explore them on a drive up narrow Mill Creek Road that starts 1½ miles from Healdsburg on Westside Road. Its 4 miles of pavement take you up into the tangy air and forest stillness of Mill Creek Canyon.

Guerneville is the center of the river resort area that extends as far east as Mirabel Park and west to Jenner, at the river's Pacific mouth. You will find restaurants and places to stay overnight in Guerneville. During the summer season, this is the scene of bustling activity, with thousands of vacationers seeking a variety of ways to relax. (Make reservations well ahead of time if you plan to stay overnight.) The area sponsors a big jazz festival the weekend after Labor Day. For information, call (800) 253-8800.

Farther upstream is good canoeing, where the Russian River flows through Alexander Valley. With a durable canoe or kayak, you can float between Asti and Healdsburg (where canoes can be rented) and Guerneville. River trips can last from 4 hours to 2 days. Be sure to include drinking water and a picnic, and wear protective clothing against the hot summer sun.

Touring the wineries

Wineries on or near U.S. 101 between Santa Rosa and Healdsburg include Piper Sonoma (picnic lunches served daily), Landmark, and Foppiano. From Healdsburg north to Cloverdale, the roster includes Simi, Souverain (with a major restaurant on the premises), Trentadue, Geyser Peak, and Cordtz Brothers. West of U.S. 101 near Healdsburg are Dry Creek Vineyard and Pedroncelli. East of Healdsburg on State 128 are Alexander Valley Vineyards, Field Stone, and Johnson's Alexander Valley. The venerable sparkling wine firm of Korbel is at Rio Nido, out in the plain west of Santa Rosa. Hop Kiln is also in the region. All the wineries mentioned above offer tasting; most offer tours, although some of the smaller cellars require appointments for the latter.

For years Mendocino County's vineyards were quite anonymous, an appendage to Sonoma County's. But in the early 1970s, vast new plantings brought new wineries and more tourists.

The Ukiah Valley is the smallest of this quartet, with the fewest of wineries to visit. At Ukiah: Parducci (tours and tasting at the patriarch of Mendocino cellars), Cresta Blanca (also tours and tasting), and Weibel (tasting only). A few miles south at Hopland are Fetzer (tasting and retail stores) and Milano (testing and tours of a dramatic cellar housed in a one-time hop kiln).

Camping in the redwoods, away from the river, is easy if you visit either of two nearby parks. Choose between cool, dark, dense redwood groves or rolling coastal mountain country.

Armstrong Redwoods State Reserve, 2 miles north of Guerneville, has a driving loop through dimly lit aisles of giant trees or hiking trails leading to park limits. Day-use picnic sites are among the trees or at the edge of a meadow.

Austin Creek State Recreation Area, really an extension of Armstrong Redwoods, has more than 4,000 acres (compared to Armstrong's 700) and a complete change of terrain. Much of it is meadowland with madrone, Douglas fir, and alder in the canyons. Three creeks and about 100 springs run all year. Unlike Armstong, it is warm in the winter. Equestrians use Horse Haven, a small primitive camping area.

To reach Austin Creek, stay to the right after entering Armstrong until you see the sign reading Redwood Lake Campground. From here, a narrow, steep, winding road (not recommended for trailers) runs 2½ miles to the top of a ridge, 2,000 feet above.

In and around Ukiah

Although wine touring is relatively new, Ukiah has ample history. A useful walker's guide to the town's old homes is available at the gift shop at Sun House, 431 So. Main Street (open Wednesday through Sunday from noon to 4 P.M.). This historic residence, once the home of painter Grace Carpenter Hudson, contains art and Indian artifacts; a small admission fee is charged.

Stop by the grand old turn-of-century bar at the Palace Hotel (closed for overnight stays) before heading out to manmade Lake Mendocino, 5 miles north of Ukiah on State Highway 20, for camping, picnicking, hiking, boating, and swimming.

HOW TO BECOME A WINE SNOB

Though wine tasting is fun, there's no short course in becoming a "pro." The complexities of enology take years to learn. Most wineries run tasting room with wines organized in a sequence so each sample shows off to advantage: dry whites first, followed by rosés, reds, appetizers, then desserts; sparkling wines come last.

Here are a few basic tests that may help make you more knowledgeable:

Sight—Look for color and clarity. The liquid should be clear. Table wines should not have brownish tints (whites range from pale gold to straw yellow, reds from crimson to ruby or slightly purplish, rosés from pink orange to pink). Most dessert wines will have a brownish or even deep amber tint, depending on type.

Smell—Is it fresh and fruity? Don't confuse *aroma,* the smell of the grapes, with *bouquet,* the smell of fermentation and aging. New wines seldom have bouquet; appetizer and dessert wines have little aroma and substantial bouquet.

Taste—It can range from sweet to sour, bitter, and salty. Most "taste" is an extension of smell. Some qualities can be perceived only after the wine is on the taster's palate; these qualities are acidity (liveliness versus flatness), astringency (young red wines will have a tannic puckeriness in all but the most mellow), and weight or body (light versus rich).

A last note. "Dry" simply describes the absence of sugar. Dry wines are sometimes considered sour because acidity and tannin are more evident.

Described as a "range of light" by the great naturalist John Muir, the Sierra Nevada is the largest single mountain range in the country. Rising gradually from the floor of the Central Valley, these mighty mountains ascend to jagged crests 7,000 to more than 14,000 feet high and then plunge almost vertically to desertlike Owens Valley to the east.

Glacial sculpturing is visible in many areas. Nearly every deep-cut valley owes its present configuration to glacial abrasion. The best-known evidence of glacial power is Yosemite Valley, formed by the cutting action of slow-moving ice during the Ice Age.

Higher elevations of the Sierra offer fishing in clear mountain lakes and streams, boating and water-skiing on large and lovely Lake Tahoe, and hiking trails into wilderness areas. In winter, skiers flock to its many snow-clad slopes. Awe-inspiring scenery attracts many visitors to Yosemite National Park, at its most dramatic in spring when waterfalls plunge over valley walls to splash rocks 1,400 feet below.

Along the Sierra foothills between Yosemite and Tahoe are reminders of bustling Gold Rush days. Small mining operations continue—every spring gold-seekers patiently pan for "color" alongside rushing streams. The old towns are well worth visiting. Many verge on ghost town status; some are covered by a façade of modernity. A few have been preserved in a state of arrested decay as state historic parks. One (Columbia State Historic Park) is being restored as a model of early days in California history when every would-be prospector's dream was "going to see the elephant" (anticipating experiences in the gold fields).

Largest single mountain range in the country, the Sierra Nevada boasts peaks of 14,000 feet. Stark and brooding from a distance, the Sierra unlocks a magical outdoor world. Stunningly blue Lake Tahoe provides a summer boating and hiking playground; in winter, skiers delight in its snow-covered slopes. Glacier-carved Yosemite National Park's massive cliffs, cascading waterfalls, and pristine high country make it the highlight of the central range. Snuggled into the Sierra foothills lie treasures of the Gold Rush country—historic towns, and clear rushing streams where visitors can pan for gold.

The Sierra

YOSEMITE

By any standard one of the most spectacular national parks, Yosemite has beauty of form in graceful domes and towering cliffs, beauty of motion in plunging waterfalls and rippling rivers, and beauty of color—from the red snow plant to the purple glow of sunset on canyon walls.

Only 7 of Yosemite's approximately 1,200 square miles are occupied by its famous valley. But here most visitors concentrate, missing other beauties and wonders—glaciers, giant sequoias, alpine meadows, and 13,000-foot Sierra Nevada peaks. Though the valley is a logical place to begin a visit, one should go to Yosemite with the knowledge that not all is found there.

A very popular vacation destination, Yosemite National Park offers an exceptionally wide variety of things to do and places to stay.

VERNAL FALLS' STUNNING BEAUTY veils sheer granite cliffs in Yosemite National Park. Hikers get close view along nearby Mist Trail.

If you drive to Yosemite, take State Highway 120 from Manteca or Modesto or State Highway 140 from Merced. From Southern California, take State Highway 41 from Fresno. During the summer when the road is clear of snow, you can enter from the east side of the park (via U.S. Highway 395) over Tioga Pass on State 120. U.S. 395, State 120, and State Highway 89 provide a scenic back road link between Yosemite and Lake Tahoe—particularly lovely in autumn.

Via Bus Company provides connecting bus service to Yosemite from Merced the year around. For information and reservations, write Yosemite Park and Curry Co. Reservations, 5410 E. Home Avenue, Fresno, CA 93727.

Timing your visit

June, July, August, and September are Yosemite's busiest months—especially in the valley. Though the Ticketron valley campsite reservation system (summers) helps relieve some park congestion, campsites are usually filled to capacity throughout the summer. Reservations for indoor valley accommodations are recommended weeks in advance and as much as 6 months in advance for the Wawona and Ahwahnee hotels. Make reservations through Yosemite Park and Curry Co. The phone number is (209) 252-4848.

If you're seeking a more isolated wilderness experience, escape the crowds and visit the high country. Yosemite offers miles of back country trails. Or visit the park during the off season (before Memorial Day and after October 1).

In the fall the valley quiets down and autumn reflections subtly color the Merced River. Winter gives Yosemite a fragile, fairyland look. Frosty weather makes difficult hiking but signals the beginning of snow fun. Major valley roads from the west are kept open (State 140 has first priority for snow removal); be sure to carry chains. A Yosemite spring is beautiful. Waterfalls splash through misty rainbows to the valley floor.

Lodging—luxury hotel to canvas tent

Yosemite offers a wide range of accommodations. Besides the valley, in summer months you may stay at Wawona (through October—you'll need reservations), Tuolumne Meadows, and White Wolf, which are often less crowded than valley lodgings.

In Yosemite Valley the Ahwahnee Hotel offers luxurious accommodations. Open the year around, except for a short time in December, the Ahwahnee has a gift shop, lounge, and spectacular dining room.

Popular Yosemite Lodge, with Yosemite Falls as a backdrop, is within walking distance of the village. Open all year, the lodge offers sleeping accommodations that range from attractive hotel rooms to redwood cabins with or without bath. Lodge buildings contain a lounge, shops, cafeteria, restaurants, and snack stand.

Curry Village, rustic and informal, has cabins, tent cabins, and some hotel-type rooms. Cabins come with or without bath and are available the year around.

At Wawona the hotel is informal but gracious. It has a dining room, swimming pool, tennis court, 9-hole golf course, and it is near stables. This area is popular partly because of its tree-fringed setting and relative isolation.

Above the valley floor, Tuolumne Meadows Lodge has simple tent cabins and a central dining hall where meals are served family style. White Wolf Lodge has both cabins and tents. Both Tuolumne Meadows and White Wolf are reached along the Tioga Road; Tuolumne, near the park's east entrance, is 55 miles from the valley, and White Wolf, near the Middle Fork of the Tuolumne River, is 31 miles away. Both lodges are open in summer only.

Campgrounds throughout the valley are open from Memorial Day through the end of September. At least two valley campgrounds and the one at Wawona are now open the year around. In the high country, campgrounds have a shorter season, and stay open as weather conditions allow.

During summer camping season, valley campgrounds are on a reservation basis. You may reserve campsites in person at Ticketron sales offices. You may also reserve campsites at the National Park Service Western Regional Office in San Francisco (see page 8 for address) or the field office at 300 N. Los Angeles Street, Room 1013, Los Angeles, CA 90012. A 7-day camping limit is enforced for all valley campgrounds; a 14-day limit for other park campsites. Trailers are accommodated in most campgrounds, but no utility hookups are provided except at a private camp at Wawona. Some campgrounds have sanitary stations. Pets are allowed only in specified campgrounds and must be kept on leashes and off trails.

Getting to know the park

Yosemite's wonders range wide over its 1,200 acres, from the majestic sequoias in Mariposa to the pristine Tuolumne high country. Yet, it's to the valley—less than 1 percent of the total park—that most of Yosemite's annual 2 million visitors flock. They come to relax in the valley's tranquillity, but they're sometimes met with the citylike hustle and bustle they sought to escape. In the past, horror stories were not of the bear that got away, but of accommodations impossible to secure, traffic jams, overnight vigils for a campsite, and lines at the village store that would rival any at a thriving supermarket.

If you haven't been to Yosemite recently, you'll be pleased to discover the park service has made changes. Foremost among them is a valley campsite reservation system designed to alleviate problems accompanying heavy park use, thus protecting the park's unique natural resources.

Protecting Yosemite against manmade intrusion is not a new idea. As early as the 1860s, President Lincoln set aside Mariposa and the Big Trees Grove from development. Scheduled for publication this year is a general plan describing the direction the park service hopes to take in Yosemite over the next 15 years. These are major points: Visitors will be encouraged to use public transit when touring the valley and to try to see Yosemite during the off season. An effort will be made to remove nonessential services from the valley, returning it as much as possible to a more natural state. Finally, new interpretive programs will expand visitor awareness of cultural, historic, and environmental aspects of the park.

Touring the park

Once you're in the park, make the visitor center at Yosemite Village your first stop. Here (as well as at the park entrances) you can pick up the free park newspaper, *The Yosemite Guide,* that lists monthly happenings. They include year-round programs by naturalists offering campfire talks, nature walks, and lectures.

Getting around the park is easy. Park your car and ride the free shuttle buses that run along the eastern half of the valley floor. Guided bus tours, full and half-day, jaunt to valley and other park highlights, such as Mariposa Grove and Glacier Point. Backpackers can take buses to major high-country trailheads.

An increasingly popular way to see the valley is by bicycle—roads are mostly level and easily pedaled. Bikes can be rented the year around at Yosemite Lodge (weather permitting) and in summer at Curry Village.

Saddle and pack animals are available at Yosemite Valley stables and outside the valley at Tuolumne Meadows, Wawona, and White Wolf.

For more information on bus and tour schedules, prices, and trail maps, contact the visitor information center or call (209) 372-4461.

Highlights of the valley

The 7-square-mile Yosemite Valley is neither the deepest nor the longest phenomenon of its kind in the Sierra, but of all the glacial gorges it exhibits the sheerest walls, the most distinctive monoliths, the flattest floor, the widest meadows, and the finest array of waterfalls.

The floor of the valley is a level meadow threaded by a dashing mountain river (the Merced) and diversified with groves of pines and oaks, thickets of shrubbery, and beautiful varieties of flowers, ferns, and grasses.

The valley walls rise, almost vertically, to a height of 2,000 to 4,000 feet above the meadow. Great domes and pinnacles stand out against the sky. Most conspicuous are El Capitan, Cathedral Rocks, Three Brothers, Sentinel Rock, and Half Dome.

Rushing waterfalls tumble from the cliffs, each with its own particular beauty. A ¼-mile walk to the rustic bridge over Yosemite Creek gives you an idea of Yosemite Falls' awesome power and volume. Bridalveil impresses, not because of its size but because of its sheer, lacy beauty.

The Indian Cultural Museum, located in the valley district building adjoining the center, displays exhibits of native American artifacts.

Happy Isles Nature Center is another valley museum. Ranger naturalists interpret park features and satisfy visitor curiosity. Happy Isles is also a trailhead for the John Muir Trail, Vernal and Nevada Falls (the Mist Trail), and the high country. Happy Isles itself is delightful, especially in early morning and evening— here, the Merced River breaks up into fingers and flows around several tiny islands. Nearby are the Indian Caves and natural Mirror Lake, worthy attractions in the upper valley.

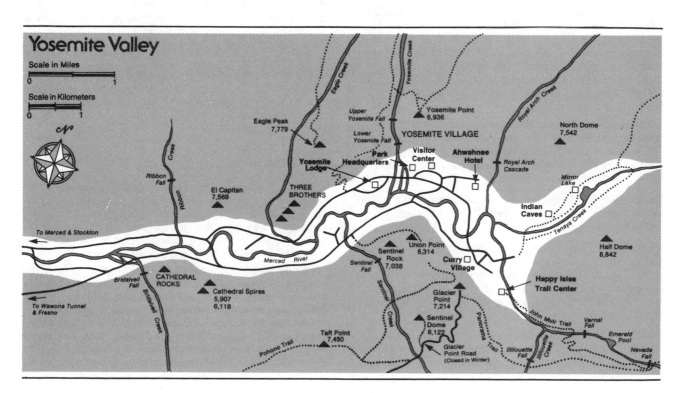

Wawona—home of big trees

Known for its grove of giant sequoias, the Wawona region, near the south entrance (State 41) at about the same altitude as the valley (4,000 feet), is a popular place to stay.

The Mariposa Grove, part of President Lincoln's original grant for preservation in 1864, is an outstanding feature. You may have heard about this grove because of its famous "tree you can drive through." A tunnel was cut in 1881 to permit passage of horse-drawn stagecoaches. Though the tree fell in the winter of 1969, you can still view the shattered trunk.

In the Mariposa Grove are over 200 trees that measure 10 feet or more in diameter, and thousands of smaller ones. The largest tree in Yosemite, and probably the oldest, is the Grizzly Giant, which approaches the size of the largest tree in the world (the General Sherman in Sequoia National Park).

Park private vehicles in the parking lot at the edge of the grove; free trams transport visitors through the trees, where the sequoia story is presented by park interpreters. Trams leave every 15 minutes in summer, hourly in spring and fall. Twice a day during summer rangers lead 2½-hour tram and walking tours through the big trees.

Pioneer Yosemite History Center, at Wawona, tells of man's role in the development of Yosemite as a national park. You'll see some of the first buildings, horse-drawn vehicles, and "living history" demonstrations during summer. To get to the history center, you cross a covered bridge, built in 1858.

Panorama from Glacier Point

The view is the thing at Glacier Point—a tremendous sweep of the length of the valley in both directions. Half Dome is at your front door; Vernal Fall is prominent; Nevada Fall's roar deafens; and beyond rise the snow-clad peaks of Yosemite's back country. You look down into a world of miniature people, cars, and buildings; the Merced River is like a tiny creek, and the roads are a network of dark ribbons.

The road to Glacier Point (closed in winter about a mile beyond Badger Pass Ski Area) winds through the forest and around lush meadow. After getting a ride to Glacier Point, you can hike down along one of several fine trails to the valley floor.

Four-mile Trail zigzags down the canyon wall to the valley floor about 2.2 miles west of Curry Village. Short and steep, it's about 4.6 miles.

Panorama Trail drops down into Illilouette Canyon and beyond, ending eventually at Happy Isles. Varied terrain makes all of this 8-mile route interesting—from infrequently seen Illilouette Fall across thundering Nevada Fall (a great picnic spot) and down the stone steps of the Mist Trail, wet from Vernal Fall.

Pohono Trail follows the rim for almost the full length of the valley, descending near the Wawona Tunnel (13 miles). It's particularly lovely when the wildflowers bloom in June and early July.

The high country—Yosemite's back door

If you leave Yosemite without a visit to the back country you're missing a large part of the park. Here miles of primitive wilderness offer a place for solitude and reflection, plus a hearty hiking challenge. With almost 800 miles of trails, almost any kind of hiking experience is possible—from short day hikes to trips of a week or longer. But 10 percent of the trails get 75 percent of the total use, with most hikers arriving on weekends. Crowded trails are the High Sierra Loop Trail, the John Muir Trail, the Cathedral Lakes area, Sunrise Meadows, Glen Aulin, and the top of Yosemite Falls.

To prevent overcrowding, wilderness permits are now required for all overnight back country trips. Permits are not required for day hikes. Free permits may be obtained by applying in person at any of the park's five issuing stations (Visitor Center, Tuolumne Meadows, Wawona, Big Oak Flat, and White Wolf). Dogs and other pets are not permitted in the back country, and groups of more than 15 should ask for the park's Backcountry Office. Call at least 2 weeks in advance.

Five High Sierra camps not accessible by road are maintained by the Yosemite Park and Curry Co. for hikers and saddle parties wishing to enjoy this country with maximum convenience. Camps at Merced Lake, Voglesang, Sunrise, Glen Aulin, and May Lake are about 10 miles apart. Dormitory tents cluster near a large central dining tent in which family-style meals are served. Reservations are always required.

Tuolumne Meadows Lodge is the gateway to the camps and to the high country. Fees at the camps include breakfast and dinner; box lunches may be purchased separately.

Several days a week during the summer, a 6-day guided saddle trip leaves Yosemite Valley and makes a circuit of the High Sierra camps, stopping one night in each camp. A 4-day saddle trip leaves Tuolumne Meadows with overnight stops at Glen Aulin, May Lake, and Sunrise camps.

For those who prefer to hike, there are guided 7-day trips leaving Tuolumne Meadows each Monday during the summer. Reservations must be made at least 6 months in advance for saddle or hiking trips. For rates, write to Yosemite Park and Curry Co. (see page 88).

Yosemite in winter

Yosemite Valley is especially splendid when snow fills the meadows and drapes the surrounding cliffs and sentinel peaks. In this picture-book setting, you can enjoy sledding, ski touring, and other winter activities against a backdrop of white-etched canyon walls and waterfall courses whitened by frozen mist.

Badger Pass, the ski area, is a 20-mile drive from the valley floor. Facilities include four double chair lifts, T-bar, rope tow, day lodge, snack bar, and child care center. More than 90 miles of cross-country trails are open—at Tuolumne Meadows, Glacier Point, Crane Flat, Mariposa Grove, and the valley floor. Cross-country skiing is taught by the Yosemite Mountaineering School at Badger Pass. Ski season usually lasts from Thanksgiving to mid-April. A bus goes from the valley to the ski area.

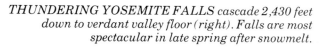

BRILLIANT ALPINE DAY greets backpackers in Tuolumne Meadows (above). Dense pine forests and spired peaks pierce horizon in Yosemite's high country.

THUNDERING YOSEMITE FALLS cascade 2,430 feet down to verdant valley floor (right). Falls are most spectacular in late spring after snowmelt.

AUTUMN LEAVES GRACEFULLY FRAME majestic Half Dome (above) in Yosemite Valley. Season's first snow dusts peak's famous face high above valley floor.

Wilderness north & south of Yosemite

Massive granite peaks along the Sierra's backbone tower above the pine forests, green meadows, and alpine lakes of the wild areas on both sides of the national park. Isolated in winter, except for skiing on the eastern side near June and Mammoth lakes, the peaks are penetrated during the summer by hikers, backpackers, and mountain climbers following well-marked trails.

Emigrant Wilderness

Emigrant Basin Primitive Area became Emigrant Wilderness in early 1975. Located just north of Yosemite National Park, it covers 105,000 acres—all within the Stanislaus National Forest. Elevations range from 5,200 feet near Cherry Lake at the south to 11,570 feet at Leavitt Peak at the northeast corner. Snow blankets the area from mid-October until June, covering some sections the year around. Summer temperatures fluctuate—from 90°F/32°C during the day to below freezing at night.

The basin was named for a party of emigrants seeking a short cut over the Sierra Nevada; a headstone marks the grave of one pioneer who died in 1853 near Summit Creek.

About 100 lakes in Emigrant Basin offer trout fishing; some of the larger lakes (Huckleberry, Emigrant, and Long) stretch over more than 100 acres. Nearest main highway is State 108, from which short stub roads lead to trailheads. Lakes, streams, and campsites are connected by 142 miles of trails. Though there are no improved campgrounds, some of the heavily used sites, such as Emigrant Lake, Cow Meadow, and Bucks Lake, have log tables and sanitation facilities. In most of the basin, you'll find plenty of wood and water.

Minarets Wilderness

From Yosemite the John Muir Trail enters the Minarets Wilderness at Donohue Pass (11,100 feet). The trail leaves the wilderness 4 miles northwest of the Devil's Post Pile National Monument. Elevations vary from 7,600 to 13,157 feet. Mount Dana, jewel of the north corner, stands over 13,000 feet, towering above its sister peaks—Mount Gibbs, Mount Lewis, and nearly a dozen more—all over 12,000 feet. Glaciers and barren peaks offer excellent mountaineering opportunities. Backpacking and camping traffic is heavy during summer.

Garnet Lake, Thousand Island Lake, and Shadow Lake are among the numerous lakes and large streams forming the headwaters of the Middle and North Forks of the San Joaquin River. Trout fishing is excellent in these 109,500 acres.

Access to the Minarets is from State 120 on the north, from State 203 through Mammoth Lakes on the east, and from Clover Meadow from the town of North Fork on the west. Commercial packers operate from Agnew Meadow and Reds Meadow on the east and from Clover Meadow on the west.

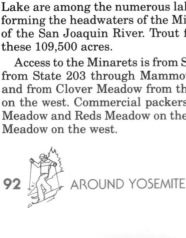

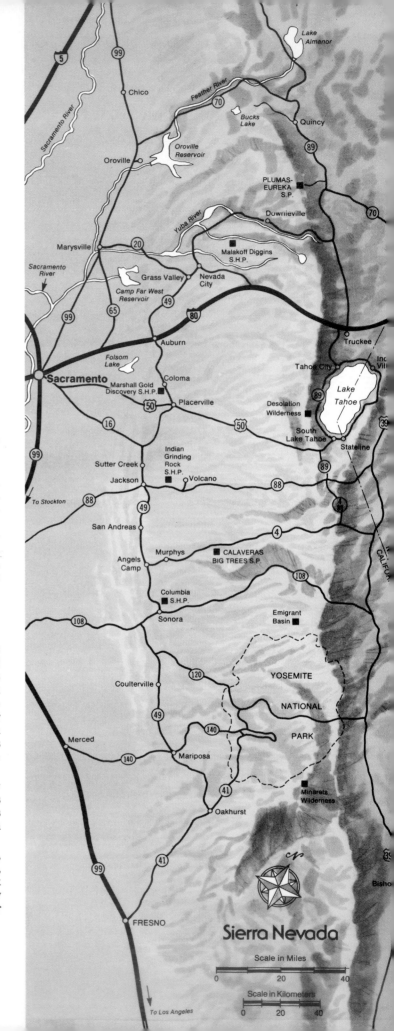

Sierra Nevada

Scale in Miles

Scale in Kilometers

GOLD COUNTRY

James Marshall changed the course of California history in January 1848 when he discovered gold in the millrace of Sutter's sawmill in Coloma. Within a year, California was known worldwide, and fortune seekers started the migration that would open the West.

Remnants of these tumultuous times still exist in the Gold Rush Country of the Sierra Nevada foothills. Appropriately numbered State Highway 49 runs through the heart of this rolling grassland and fir-clad hills, its elevation around 2,000 feet except where it dips into deep river canyons and climbs mountains above Downieville.

The Gold Country has comfortable, up-to-date hotels and motels and a few charming old inns. Camping is impractical in summer at lower elevations unless you're around a lake to cool off. But heading east from State 49 you can reach campgrounds at higher, cooler levels.

For a more detailed description of the Gold Country and for some of its rich history and lore, refer to the *Sunset* book *Gold Rush Country*.

Scouting the Southern Mines

The placer and quartz veins in the Southern Mines never rivaled those to the north. At the southern tip near Yosemite, the country was better known to Mexican ranchers and Indian traders than to gold seekers. Tourists arrived almost as soon as the prospectors did.

This section contains a large, active town, a few smaller communities, and isolated hamlets almost qualifying as ghost towns. Lively Oakhurst, Mariposa, and Sonora make good bases for exploring the surrounding countryside; elsewhere, facilities are limited.

Back roads from Oakhurst

The southern terminus of the Mother Lode Highway (State 49), Oakhurst—called Fresno Flats in its heyday—today shows little evidence of once-hectic mining activity. The original jail (now a shop at the Holiday Village center), the church down the street, and the developing Fresno Flats Historical Park at 427 High School Road are remnants of its more romantic past.

During the summer, Oakhurst presents melodramas Friday and Saturday evenings in a 19th century theater.

Coarsegold—8 miles south of Oakhurst on State Highway 41—survives. A single nugget worth $15,000 started the mining claim called Texas Flats—one of the oldest, deepest, and most extensively worked mines in this area. Rubble remains. One reminder of the past is a pump, dated 1852, that served a well dug in the middle of the main street.

A series of back roads northeast of Coarsegold leads through Knowles, with its landscape of granite, and Raymond, an early stage stop for Yosemite-bound travelers. Along Ben Hur Road, you'll pass crumbling remains of an early Chinese "stone wall"; workers received 25 cents for laying 25 feet of this wall daily.

Mariposa—a key to the past

Far from being a ghost town, Mariposa gets a sizable amount of traffic because of its convenient location halfway between Merced and Yosemite. Scattered along the sides of the valley enfolding Mariposa Creek, buildings are a blend of old and new. One of the Gold Country's choicest bits of architecture, the two-story courthouse at the north end of town has been in use continuously since it was erected in 1854; its tower clock has dutifully rung the hours since its installation in 1866. An excellent historical center and museum on 12th and Jessie depicts life over a century ago. Open daily May through October, it's closed in January, open weekends the rest of the year. The *Mariposa Gazette*, the town's newspaper, is California's oldest weekly publication, in continuous print since 1854.

North of Mariposa, watch for Mount Bullion, where more than $4 million in gold came from the now-vanished Princeton Mine. Mount Ophir, up the road, had California's first private mint, which supposedly produced $50 hexagonal gold slugs; none have been found.

A side trip to Hornitos can be made from Mount Bullion (13 miles) or from Bear Valley (11 miles). A small, lazy town, Hornitos has many charming old buildings framing its Mexican-style plaza. At High Street and Bear Valley Road is the outlet to an escape tunnel through which the Mother Lode's most famous badman, Joaquin Murieta, retreated from the fandango hall when things got too hot upstairs. Interesting remains include a grim little jail, now a museum; ruins of the Ghirardelli Store operated by San Francisco's chocolate king; St. Catherine's Church and the boot hill below; and the school, built in the early 1860s.

At Bear Valley, ruins strung along the highway include the Bon Ton Saloon (a café), a boarding house, Trabucco's store, and the Odd Fellows Hall which houses the Oso Museum. Nothing remains of John C. Fremont's "White House," from which he conducted his vast grant.

About 2 miles north of Bear Valley, a turnout off State 49 affords excellent views of the Merced River gorge below and the sinuous, 1,000-foot descent into Hell's Hollow. At the bottom are Lake McClure and the Bagby Recreation Area.

Coulterville is enriched by the presence of the old Jeffrey Hotel, built in 1851 of rock and adobe; the walls are 3 feet thick. Adjoining it is the Magnolia Saloon, displaying a fine collection of firearms, minerals, coins, and other memorabilia. Across the street are the remains of the Coulter Hotel and the Wells Fargo building, once operated by Buffalo Bill's brother. In front of these buildings in the small plaza are the local "hangin' tree" and a small steam engine once used to haul ore from the Mary Harrison Mine north of town. One Chinese adobe, the Sun Sun Wo store, is all that remains of a sizable Chinese population.

Chinese Camp lies 21 miles north of Coulterville along State 49. Driving north, watch for the Moccasin Creek

BUXOM BLONDE (below) belts out song and dance in Drytown melodrama. Claypipers, one of Mother Lode's oldest troupes, offer saucy Saturday night olios.

GINGERBREAD ICING, open balconies, and gothic windows make historic Red Castle hotel (above) a favorite with visitors to Nevada City.

ABANDONED STRUCTURES (below) peek through sun-bleached fields along rambling Gold Country back roads.

Power Plant where State 120 intersects State 49. A marker near the bridge tells of Jacksonville, a once-important gold town now inundated by the Don Pedro Reservoir.

Notice the "trees of heaven" in picturesque Chinese Camp. No one knows where the Chinese who settled here came from, but there were at least 5,000 mining the area in the early 1850s, and a full scale war once took place between two tongs. It's a popular place to explore; you'll find good ruins and a few homes along the tranquil streets.

History lives around Sonora

Sonora is as bustling today as it was a century ago. The county seat of Tuolumne and a trading center for the surrounding cattle and lumber country, Sonora has layered modern façades over the aged buildings lining Washington Street. Traffic moves slowly along the crowded thoroughfare, but a half-block drive off the main street takes you back to Gold Rush days.

The Big Bonanza Mine, one of California's richest, was out north on Washington Street, less than 100 yards from St. James Episcopal church. Built in 1860, the graceful church building is said to be the Gold Country's most beautiful frame structure. You can pick up a walking tour of all of Sonora's heritage homes at the century-old jail and museum on Bradford Street or at the Tuolumne County Visitors Bureau office in the Sonora Inn.

Jamestown, 3 miles south of Sonora, tries valiantly to retain its antiquity. Some of the best wood-frame structures have been destroyed by fires over the years, but a few proud buildings remain, among them three of the oldest operating inns in the Mother Lode. Here, you can pan for gold, browse through antique shops, or have a meal at one of several good restaurants.

At Railtown State Historic Park you'll find an historic 26-acre roundhouse and shop complex complete with steam locomotives and vintage rolling stock. Nearly 200 feature movies, television shows, and commercials have been filmed on the Sierra Railway, a narrow gauge line formerly connecting the Gold Country mines with San Joaquin Valley shipping centers. Rail excursions begin in spring and run through September.

Columbia State Historic Park is an ideal starting point for any Gold Country touring. Columbia will provide you with a sizable fund of knowledge about mining and miners' habits that will help you understand other, more confusing ruins and deserted mining camps.

Everything in Columbia is clearly labeled, and an abundance of maps and guidebooks explain attractions in detail. For best use of your time, stop by the park headquarters for a brochure that outlines an 1½-hour stroll. Children enjoy panning for "color," riding the jouncing stagecoach, sipping sarsaparilla at a saloon, or even getting a haircut at the State's oldest barbershop. Year-round theatrical performances have taken place at Fallon House for almost 40 years; the Fandango Hall houses melodrama; and the City Hotel is back in business as a hostelry and a fine restaurant.

Once called the "Gem of the Southern Mines" for its gold output, Columbia (4 miles north of Sonora) glitters today in its unparalleled collection of reconstructed buildings and mining artifacts.

Jackass Hill and Tuttletown, north of Columbia, acquired most of their fame from early residents. Mark Twain's cabin is reconstructed on its original site on Jackass Hill. Ruins remain of Swerer's store in Tuttletown, where Bret Harte was once a clerk and Twain a customer.

Central Mother Lode— heart of the Gold Country

Much of California's Gold Country was called the Mother Lode, but the section between Melones to the south and Auburn to the north contained the primary gold vein that gave the area its name. The most-visited part of the Gold Country, the Mother Lode contains most of the interesting, attractive historical towns that are relatively intact.

Here, too, is the largest concentration of little bed and breakfast inns (see page 100), restaurants, and shops. Colorful annual events include the crowd-drawing Jumping Frog Contest. Family recreational possibilities abound—fishing, boating, swimming, skiing, and more.

Angels Camp to San Andreas: From frogs to fandangos

Thanks to Mark Twain, Angels Camp is probably better noted for its frog-jumping contest in May than for its important Gold Rush background. In Angels Camp you'll find a few remembrances of the past—the Angels Hotel and jailhouse behind, foundations of the Angels mine (one of the best in the area), and a museum with a good collection of minerals and early-day artifacts scattered inside and outside a building at the north end of town.

At Carson Hill, south of town, a nugget weighing 195 pounds came from this richest of all Mother Lode camps. Fifteen miles of tunnels honeycomb the hill; they extend down as far as 5,000 feet.

Detour to Murphys (on State Highway 4), and you'll feel as if the clock stopped almost a half-century ago. Gingerbread Victorians peek shyly from behind white picket fences and the tall locust trees that line the main streets. It's a good town for strolling; tourists are treated like guests. Settled in 1848 by the Murphy brothers, Murphys claimed a population of 5,000 at its rollicking peak. The Murphys Hotel, opened in 1856 by James Sperry and John Perry, has an illustrious register of temporary residents—U. S. Grant, Thomas Lipton, Horatio Alger, "Charles Bolton" (better known as Black Bart, the notorious stagecoach robber), and many more. You, too, can spend the night, have a drink in the old bar, or eat in the casual restaurant.

Other buildings of interest include the Peter Traver building, housing the Old Timers Museum; the ever-present I.O.O.F. Hall; St. Patrick's Catholic Church; and the one-room jail.

Many caverns are found around Murphys. Mercer Caves (1 mile north) and Moaning Cave (on the Murphys-Vallecito Road) welcome amateur underground spelunkers for a modest fee.

Calaveras Big Trees State Park, about 15 miles northeast of Murphys on State 4, has the only groves of *Sequoiadendron giganteum* (the huge cousin of the coast redwoods) in a state park. By following the nature trail, you can climb a stairway to the top of a 24-foot-wide stump for a special look at these giants. Year-round camping allows for snow fun in winter and water play in summer on the North Fork of the Stanislaus River, which runs through the park. Both the river and Beaver Creek offer trout fishing. Two campgrounds provide 129 improved campsites; reservations are required during busy months.

Bear Valley, farther up the road, is not to be confused with the ghost town to the south. This is an all-year recreation area where you can ski Mount Reba's trails in winter or enjoy riding, swimming, and tennis when the snow melts. Lodging ranges from a hotel room to a mountain cabin. In August, Bear Valley presents a weekend concert series ranging from chamber music to light opera. For information, write Music from Bear Valley, P.O. Box 68, Bear Valley, CA 95223.

San Andreas, 12 miles from Angels Camp on State 49, can be reached by a series of interesting side roads east of the main highway. One leads through the little mountain towns of Sheepranch (where George Hearst, father of William Randolph, ran the profitable Sheepranch Mine, which helped enhance the great family fortune) and Mountain Ranch, where a former dance hall now respectably houses memorabilia.

Another interesting approach is the road paralleling State 49 between Altaville and San Andreas. You pass through sites of former mining camps of Dogtown, Scratch Gulch, and Brandy Flat. At Calaveritas you'll see the only tangible evidence of a once-flourishing gold area. Supposedly, Joaquin Murieta was a frequent visitor to the fandango halls; the old Costa store stands as mute testimony to these turbulent times.

Little of San Andreas shows its past. But the county museum, housed in the courthouse one block off Main Street, is worth a stop. Behind it is the old jail where Black Bart was held for trial. West of town is the Pioneer Cemetery, dating back at least to 1851. You'll find some intriguing inscriptions on the headstones still standing.

Cuisine & culture around Jackson

Jackson, the Amador County seat, has kept up with progress—but it's also trying to preserve some of its 19th century heritage. Although modern façades have transformed many of the old buildings along Main Street, a walk along side streets reveals a little of the flavor of the past.

One of the most interesting buildings in town is the Brown House, built in the 1860s on a hill about 2 blocks east of the main part of town. Today it serves as the county museum. On the narrow main street are the Odd Fellows Hall and the restored National Hotel. St. Sava's Serbian Orthodox Church may be tiny—but it's the mother church of the entire western hemisphere. Built in 1894, it's at the north end of town.

For many decades two great hard-rock mines—the Kennedy and the Argonaut—were very important to Jackson's economy, but neither has been worked in many years. The huge tailing wheels built to carry waste from the mines to a settling pond on the other side of the hills are still there (two in pieces); they can be seen from State 49.

For a closer view, drive out the Jackson Gate road northeast from town to Trailing Wheels Park. You can walk up to the large wheel on the hill or take the path across the street to a ridge overlooking the Kennedy Mine and two more wheels. Following Jackson Gate north, you pass several Italian restaurants, the county's oldest store, and an inn before the road curves around to rejoin State 49 at Martell.

At the Chamber of Commerce office (junction of State highways 88 and 49), you can pick up walking tours of Amador County towns, as well as a well-done area map. Cyclists will want a map of a 27-mile bike route. Brochures and maps are also available at the museum; check there if the chamber office is closed.

State 88 (open all year) heads east from Jackson over Carson Pass past several good summer trout lakes (Bear Reservoir, Silver Lake, and Caples Lake) and a couple of winter ski areas—the largest is Kirkwood at 7,800 feet.

Mokelumne Hill, 7 miles south of Jackson on State 49, has many buildings constructed of light brown stone (rhyolite tuff), a material common to much of the Mother Lode. The I.O.O.F. Hall was the first three-story building in the Gold Country. Once a tough, wild town, "Mok Hill" has had two racial strifes—the Chilean War, at nearby Chili Gulch, and the French War, on a hill overlooking town. A murder a week was not uncommon during the early days—hard to believe when you stroll through this most peaceful community.

Interesting buildings include the remains of the Mayer store, the beautiful wooden Congregational Church (oldest in California), and famous old Hotel Leger (still operating as an inn), which incorporates the building that was once the county courthouse.

Volcano, a side trip of about 12 miles east from Jackson off State 88 on Volcano Road, has many remains of the early town—the St. George Hotel, the old jail, a brewery built in 1856, the Odd Fellows-Masonic Hall, the Adams Express Office, and the assay office. Don't miss Old Abe, a Civil War cannon that might have won the Civil War for the Union Army.

Near Volcano are Indian Grinding Rock State Historic Park (camping, huge limestone outcropping, reconstructed Miwok village, and visitor center); Masonic Cave, where meetings were held in 1854; and Daffodil Hill, where you'll see a springtime explosion of color.

Sutter Creek, Amador City, and Drytown (north of Jackson) are meccas for antiquers. In addition to shops on tiny main streets, you'll usually find a flea market somewhere. Craft stores sell everything from hand-

loomed skirts to nugget jewelry. Sutter Creek and Amador City were important quartz mining centers; headframes attest to one-time mining activities. Both towns have interesting inns, and Drytown offers the famed Claypipers, performing summertime melodramas.

Poking around Placerville

Placerville, county seat of El Dorado County, was one of the great camps of the Gold Country. Founded in 1848, it was originally called Dry Diggin's because the miners had to cart the dry soil down to running water to wash out the gold. The next year some grisly lynchings gave the town a new name—Hangtown. In 1854 it became Placerville, a bow to self-conscious pride, but movement is afoot by some citizens to revive its previous foreboding name, even though today Hangman's Tree is marked only by a plaque.

The Old City Hall (built in 1857) and its next-door neighbor have been refurbished in 49er style and still serve as city offices. The Odd Fellows have been using their hall since 1859. The County Museum in the fairgrounds houses memorabilia of some of the men who began their careers here—Studebaker, Armour, and Stanford.

In Bedford Park, 1 mile north of town, you can don a hard hat and visit the old Gold Bug Mine, check out a gold pan and sift the sands of Little Big Creek, and drive up the hill to view the stamp press mill. The park is a good spot for hiking or picnicking.

Coloma, north of Placerville on State 49, is the birthplace of California's golden history. Now a state park, Coloma is one of the most important stops in the Mother Lode. Here James Marshall first discovered gold on John Sutter's land; here you will see Sutter's Mill reconstructed exactly to match the original. On the hill behind town is a bronze statue of Marshall, and down the road from the statue is the cabin he lived in after the gold discovery.

About 70 percent of the town of Coloma is within the park. Buildings are marked for easy identification, and rangers in the museum provide detailed maps showing the points of interest. The Coloma Crescent Players present melodrama during the summer.

Private campgrounds are scattered around the area of the American River, and you'll find two hotels: the Sierra Nevada House III (well-appointed replica of an old-timer) and the restored Victorian Vineyard House in Coloma.

Auburn, farther north at the junction of State 49 and Interstate Highway 80, is modern at the top of the hill and traditional below and west of the imposing county courthouse. To see the brick and stone structures built in the 1850s and 1860s, walk along Lincoln Way and Court and Commercial streets. You can pick up a complimentary "Guide to Auburn's Old Town" from the Chamber of Commerce at 1101 High Street. Look for the round-fronted brick Union Bar; the little frame Joss House, distinguished only by the plank with foot-high, incised Chinese characters above the door; the square, four-story firehouse; the Wells Fargo Office, now a gift shop; and the post office.

Deep-quartz mining was first developed in the Northern Mines. The area is also the birthplace of hydraulic mining, a highly destructive process in which entire mountain ridges are washed away. Summer is the time to visit this area because the best wanderings are on side roads, often impassable because of winter snows and spring runoff. Accommodations are primarily limited to the Grass Valley-Nevada City area. Make sure you have enough fuel and supplies for a day's outing; services are sparse. Plan a picnic beside a waterfall on a back road to Alleghany, or sift sands along a rushing river near Downieville.

Grass Valley & west

A disastrous fire in 1855 destroyed the early community of Grass Valley, leaving little to recall the town's mining camp days. But it still has narrow streets, scattered headframes, and the Empire Mine, now a state historic park. Today's visitors get a good look at what was once the state's oldest, largest, and richest gold mine.

Plan a stop at the best mining museum in the Gold Country—the Nevada County Historical Mining Museum in Boston Ravine (Lower Mill Street), open daily in summer. Even the most sophisticated tourist is impressed by the vast display of mining equipment.

West of Grass Valley off State Highway 20 are a few hamlets worth a slight detour. Rough and Ready seceded from the Union in 1850 and did not legally return until 1948. Three of the oldest landmarks are the schoolhouse, the I.O.O.F. Hall, and the blacksmith shop. The Old Toll House now extracts revenues from the sale of antiques. Smartville, Timbuctoo, and Browns Valley were once properous mining towns, but only a few structures and some ruins remain. Two miles southwest of French Corral, across the South Fork of the Yuba River, stretches the Bridgeport Bridge, longest (230 feet) remaining single-span covered bridge in the entire West.

Nevada City through Sierra City

Nevada City has a well-deserved reputation for beautiful homes, interesting shops, and carefully preserved antiquity. It's a good base from which to explore side roads east of State 49, and it's only a few miles to Malakoff Diggins State Historic Park, an impressive example of hydraulic mining.

Residential sections of town have many gabled frame houses; downtown are the Ott Assay Office, where ore from the Comstock Lode was first analyzed and found rich in silver; the National Hotel, whose balconies and balustrades reach out over the sidewalk; and the red brick Firehouse No. 2, now a museum with a collection of Gold Rush remnants.

For further exploration follow some of the side roads. You can reach the old high-country camps of Goodyears Bar, Forest, and Alleghany by turning south off State 49 on the Mountain House Road 3 miles west of Downieville.

Fire and flood have done their best to destroy the mountain settlement of Downieville, but it is still one of the most entrancing of the remaining gold towns. The old stone, brick, and frame buildings—many built in the 1860s or earlier—face on quiet, crooked streets and cling to the mountainsides above the Yuba River.

The towering, jagged Sierra Buttes, visible for many miles in all directions, overshadow the half-ghost town of Sierra City. Between 1850 and 1852, Sierra City miners tunneled through these dramatic granite peaks in their search for gold-bearing rock. In Sierra City are several structures of an early vintage—the largest is Busch Building, two stories of brick and a third of lumber, built in 1871.

FEATHER RIVER COUNTRY

Rich in scenery and history, the Feather River country presents a varied topography—rocky canyons, fern-filled ravines, high mountains, leaf-covered foothills, chaparral-swathed slopes, and second-growth forests of pine and fir. Through all this flows the Feather River.

Three major waterways form the Feather River: North Fork, Middle Fork, and South Fork. A lesser one flowing into the North Fork is the West Branch. State 70 follows the North Fork of the Feather and affords panoramic views of canyon country. The Middle Fork, the most rugged, offers some of the finest trout fishing in California. The site of early placer mining locations, the South Fork has many swimming holes and hiking trails. Along its stretches are seven reservoirs—the highest (5,000 feet) is 500-acre Grass Valley Lake.

Spanish explorer Don Luis Arguello named the river in 1820. He reached its lower end during the band-tailed pigeon migration and dubbed it "El Rio de las Plumas" for the feathers floating in it.

The Maidu Indians inhabited the area, hunting deer with bow and arrow, spearing salmon and steelhead, and searching the hillsides for acorns, roots, and herbs. These higher Sierra Nevada regions were the last to be prospected during the early days of the Gold Rush. One argonaut told the tale of discovering a lake whose shores were covered by gold. Though the lake was never discovered, the tale brought prospectors into the region. Because the Feather River was the site of major gold strikes, by 1860 the Indian way of life was destroyed by the hordes of gold seekers.

The Feather River Highway, State 70, connects the Central Valley and the Sierra. Following the deep canyon of the North Fork, it touches the edges of the upper Middle Fork, crosses nine bridges, and tunnels through three outcroppings of solid granite.

Along most of this route are a number of U.S. Forest Service campgrounds, major resorts, and cabin settlements. Most stretches along the way are heavily fished. Stub roads lead to old mining settlements, to pocket valleys that have been cultivated since 1850, and to trout-filled lakes beneath granite domes. Trails take off where roads end. You'll find a backpack handy for spur-of-the-moment hikes.

Oroville, 70 miles north of Sacramento on State Highway 70, is the gateway to the Feather River country. Today a lumber processing center and olive-growing area, Oroville first sprang up as Ophir City—a boisterous tent town of Gold Rush days. In the 1870s, when thousands of Chinese worked the diggings in the area, Oroville's Chinatown was the largest in California.

Temple, frame house & diamonds

The richest reminder of Oroville's past is the Chinese Temple, built in 1863. Now a museum of Oriental artifacts, it's at Broderick Street behind the levee of the Feather River. A more recent addition, Tapestry Hall, is connected to the temple by an open courtyard and garden with a graceful copper pagoda and small reflecting pool surrounded by Chinese plantings. At the entrance to the temple is a 2-ton brass incense burner said to have been the gift of Emperor Quong She of the Ching Dynasty. You can visit the temple from 11 A.M. to 4:30 P.M. Thursday through Monday, plus Tuesday and Wednesday afternoons.

Another Oroville landmark is the Judge C. F. Lott Memorial Home in Sank Park. Completed in 1856, the white frame dwelling is furnished with period pieces and sits among landscaped gardens. The house is open 10 A.M. to 4:30 P.M., Friday through Tuesday; 1 to 4:30 P.M. Wednesday and Thursday. A broad patio, added more recently, is the site of afternoon programs during spring and summer months.

North of Oroville, in the tiny town of Cherokee, you'll see a few more remnants of gold mining days—ruins of the Spring Valley Assay Office and an old hotel converted to a museum. The first diamonds discovered in the United States were picked out of a sluice box here in 1866, but no extensive diamond mining was ever done.

Superlatives apply to Lake Oroville

With a surface area of about 15,800 acres and about 167 miles of shoreline, Lake Oroville was created by the Oroville Dam, 5½ miles northeast of Oroville. Towering 770 feet above metropolitan Oroville, it is the highest dam in the United States and the highest earth fill dam in the world.

Much of the water stored in the lake is diverted into a system of aqueducts, tunnels, and basins extending the length of California. Adjoining the dam in the Feather River Canyon wall is a powerhouse that can generate enough electricity to supply a city of a million people. The dam offers a large measure of protection against river floods.

The lake, now designated a state recreation area, affords a variety of outdoor activities. Most popular are boating, water-skiing, swimming, fishing, and sailing. Picnicking and camping facilities are available, and there are reserved areas for boat-in camping and houseboat mooring.

(Continued on page 101)

TIME SOFTENS SCARS at Malakoff Diggins (above), former site of hydraulic mining. Once-barren cliffs and colorfully streaked slopes are reflected in rain-fed lake.

SIERRA STREAMS attract white water rafting enthusiasts in the summer. Some accessible rivers to run include the Stanislaus (shown at right), the American, the Mokelumne, and the Tuolumne.

GOLD COUNTRY HOSTELRIES

California's Gold Country has several mellow old inns scattered throughout a once-feverish mining area. These inns warmly welcome travelers and serve as bases for exploring the countryside.

All the inns listed (from north to south) are in towns on State Highway 49 or a few miles east or west. Reservations are always advisable; some hotels close for brief periods during the year.

Some of the hostelries have been in operation for more than a century; others are historic buildings more recently converted to accommodate guests. Accommodations range from rustic to opulent Victorian-style, but all the innkeepers work hard to preserve the feeling of old-fashioned hospitality.

Nevada City. National Hotel, Nevada City, California 95959; (916) 265-4551: Gold Rush exterior remains intact, and the interior furnishings are Victorian; private baths; dining room; pool.

Red Castle, 109 Prospect Street, Nevada City, California 95959; (916) 265-5135: Restored, 1860-era, private residence overlooks city; lovely antiques; suites have private baths; continental breakfast included; no children.

Coloma. Sierra Nevada House III, Box 268, Coloma, California 95613; (916) 622-5856. Well-appointed replica of an old-timer; private baths; old soda parlor serves meals; dining is also available (with reservations) in Gold Rush and Victorian rooms; price of room includes breakfast.

Georgetown. American River Inn, Box 43, Georgetown, California 95634; (916) 333-4499: Spacious, historic building; 11 rooms, 4 with private baths; swimming pool and heated Jacuzzi outside; full country breakfast.

Amador City. The Mine House, Box 226, Amador City, California 95601; (209) 267-5900: Formerly Keystone Mine offices; each of 8 rooms (with baths) named for original use—Vault, Retort, Assay, Stores, Grinding, Directors, Bookkeeping, and Keystone; morning coffee and juice brought to room; pool.

Sutter Creek. Nine Eureka Street, Sutter Creek, California 95685; (209) 267-0342: Private home turned inn provides 5 well-decorated rooms with baths; continental breakfast; sitting room for evening reading; no children.

Sutter Creek Inn, 75 Main Street, Sutter Creek, California 95685; (209) 267-5606: Eighteen rooms in this converted old home and outbuildings; intimate comfort is keynote; some rooms with fireplaces, some have private baths, others share bath; for fun, try the swinging beds; breakfast in kitchen included in price; no children.

Foxes, Box 159, Sutter Creek, California 95685; (209) 267-5882: Handsome two-story Victorian with over-garage extension takes 5 couples; large continental breakfast; next door to Sutter Creek Inn, close to downtown shops.

Volcano. St. George Hotel, Volcano, California 95685; (209) 296-4458: Venerable, three-story building; simple comfortable furnishings in rooms, with nearby bathrooms; dining room serves meals to those with advance reservations.

Jackson. National Hotel, 2 Water Street, Jackson, California; (209) 223-0500: Old-fashioned saloon entrance, 50 rooms upstairs, over half with private baths; Louisiana House, on lower level, serves dinner Wednesday through Sunday, breakfast on Sunday.

The Court Street Inn, 215 Court Street, Jackson, California 95642; (209) 223-0416: Five rooms furnished with antiques, three with private baths; breakfast included in price; no children; listed on National Register of Historic Places.

Mokelumne Hill. Hotel Leger, Mokelumne Hill, California 95245; (209) 286-1312: Handsome Victorian hotel; spacious rooms, 7 with private baths; pool; dining room open daily.

Murphys. Murphys Hotel, Box 329, Murphys, California 95247; (209) 728-3454: Two-story, 1860-era hotel; 12 rooms upstairs with 2 modern baths; 20 motel units with private baths; dining room open daily; historic guest ledger.

Columbia. The City Hotel was operating in the late 1800s. Nine rooms, furnished in that period, have wash basins and stools; showers are down the hall; dining room serves meals (closed Monday). For reservations, write City Hotel, P.O. Box 1870, Columbia, California 95310, or call (209) 532-1479.

Sonora. Gunn House, Sonora, California 95370; (209) 532-3421: Priceless antiques combine with modern conveniences in 1851 adobe hotel, once a private residence; 28 large, well-furnished rooms with private baths.

. . . *Continued from page 98*

The park's visitor center has interpretive displays and information on the dam and lake. An observation area affords a panoramic view of Lake Oroville on one side and Oroville and the remainder of the vast water project on the other side.

Across the Middle Fork arm of Lake Oroville is the Bidwell Bar Bridge. The suspension bridge, 627 feet above the river bed before the lake was full, is now only 47 feet above water.

If forest recreation attracts you...

Thousands of acres of forested land in the Plumas and Tahoe national forests offer trout fishing or swimming in mountain streams, camping in secluded spots, hiking or horseback riding, and skiing. Interstate highways 70 and 80 and State 49 and 89 are the main forest land routes. Much of the Plumas National Forest is in Feather River country; Tahoe National Forest extends south and east to the Nevada border. For a detailed map of roads, trails, campsites, and lakes, write to either Plumas National Forest, P.O. Box 1500, Quincy, CA 95971, or Tahoe National Forest, Highway 49, Nevada City, CA 95959.

Feather Falls—a picturesque leap

The Feather Falls Scenic Area is a 14,890-acre preserve of forested canyons, soaring granite domes, and plunging waterfalls in a remote section of Plumas National Forest just north and slightly east of Lake Oroville. Set aside by the U.S. Forest Service to preserve the special qualities of this segment of the Feather River drainage, the scenic area includes Feather Falls and Bald Rock Canyon.

Feather Falls, a 640-foot, plumelike cascade of the Fall River, lends its name to the scenic area. In the spring and early summer, you can see the falls by boating to the end of the Middle Fork arm of Lake Oroville and then climbing a hazardous ½-mile trail. For an eagle's-eye overlook, follow a 3½-mile trail from a road turning off at Feather Falls Village.

Along the Bald Rock Dome canyon rim, you'll catch some scenic views, but the canyon floor is primitive and inaccessible. Though the Milsap Bar Road crosses the Middle Fork at the upper end of the canyon, not even a foot trail descends to its inner depths.

To reach the Milsap Bar Bridge from Lake Oroville, follow the Oroville-Quincy Highway north for about 16 miles (along Berry Creek) to the Brush Creek Ranger Station. Then head east on the Milsap Bar Road about 7 miles to the river crossing.

Drop your line into Bucks Lake

Formed in 1929 when Bucks Creek was dammed, Bucks Lake is nestled in the Feather River country at a mile-high elevation. To reach the lake, follow the Feather River Highway (State 70) to Quincy and then turn west on the paved, 17-mile road to the lake. The lake can also be approached from Oroville on the Oroville-Quincy and Spanish Ranch roads.

Boating (rentals available), swimming, water-skiing, and fishing are prime attractions at the south shore resort area. Here, too, you'll find U.S. Forest Service and private campgrounds. For wilderness camping, cross the lake to the roadless north shore, where you'll find a number of excellent camping and fishing spots.

Hikers and equestrians can reach ten other lakes and numerous streams scattered through the back country. Good fishing destinations are Bear Creek, Grizzly Creek, and the Middle Fork of the Feather, reached on foot, by horseback, or by jeep.

At nearby Lower Bucks Lake, fishing is good for rainbows and browns. Undeveloped campsites are on the north side of this lake, too. Access is over a dirt road from Bucks Lake's south shore.

Plumas-Eureka State Park

On the slopes of Eureka Peak, surrounded by Plumas forest land, is the nearly 5,000-acre Plumas-Eureka

---

APPLES, WINE & TREES

Fresh-picked apples, apple pies, cakes, strudels, and cider tempt visitors to Apple Hill, that fabulously fertile stretch of land from Camino to Placerville off U.S. Highway 50. October is harvest month, but other attractions extend the season into December.

Though the emphasis is still on apples, many ranches have added other products for sale: pear juice, buckwheat honey, vinegar, pumpkins, gourds, and decorative Indian corn.

Several farms invite you to come to Apple Hill in December, cut your own Christmas tree, and enjoy apple goodies at the same time. Visitors find displays of handcrafted holiday season decorations.

Boeger Winery, reopened on Apple Hill, has a history of more than 100 years. The first wines were produced in the old winery building (now the tasting room) in 1872. If you look at the ceiling, you'll see the original chutes that dropped the grape juice into barrels. The old distillery up the hill still stands.

Four turnoffs from U.S. 50 at Camino provide access to Apple Hill; once you're off the freeway, roads are well marked. You can pick up brochures containing detailed maps at any stand or barn along the way. Pack a lunch to enjoy with your apples and wine at one of the many picnic grounds.

EMERALD BAY'S CLASSIC BEAUTY *enchants lone painter and young couple (above) at Lake Tahoe. Eagle Point boldly juts into water; beyond is Nevada shore.*

LONE SKIER GLIDES DOWN *one of Heavenly Valley's well-groomed slopes (right). Tahoe ski resorts offer exciting runs for all—hot dog to beginner.*

CARS ZOOM ALONG GLITTERING *strip of flashy hotels and casinos (below). Big name nightclub acts and the games people play keep Tahoe jumping all through the night.*

State Park. Park headquarters is at Johnsville (a partially state-owned town), 6 miles west from the intersection of State 70 and 89 near Blairsden. Hiking trails (many of them leftover roads from mining days) take you up Eureka Peak, Mount Elwell, and Mount Washington to the south. Picnic facilities are available, and there is a campground on Upper Jamison Creek. Trout fishing is excellent at Eureka and Madora lakes and in the numerous mountain streams.

The old mining town of Johnsville and the Plumas-Eureka stamp mill within the park recall gold mining days. The museum and hard-rock mining exhibit at park headquarters will interest California history buffs. Open from 8 A.M. to 4:30 P.M., the park charges a day-use fee for the campground.

After October 1 the campground closes, but the park is open all year. Heavy snowfall encourages skiing—even the miners of the 1850s raced down slopes. Eureka Bowl is open during the winter. Facilities include a rope tow, poma lifts, and an equipment rental concession.

LAKE TAHOE

Between the two main emigrant routes of California's early settlers (now U.S. Highway 50 and Interstate 80) lies Lake Tahoe. Surrounded by the heavily timbered Sierra Nevada, beautiful, unbelievably blue Lake Tahoe blossomed as a resort area in the 1870s when Lucky Baldwin built a large lodge and took guests out on the lake in his 168-foot steamer. Fifty years later skiing was introduced here, and roads to the lake were kept open in winter.

In the late 1950s and early 1960s the big boom began. Ski resorts and casinos dotted the basin, turning Tahoe into an all-year attraction.

Boating, swimming (the water is cold), water-skiing, hiking, and biking are the main summer activities; skiing is the prime winter attraction. Since Lake Tahoe never freezes, you can fish the year around.

Many people prefer to visit the lake in the spring or fall before the seasonal crowds arrive. Snow can fall from October to June. If you visit Tahoe during the winter, you should carry tire chains and check weather conditions that can make mountain driving hazardous. Snow conditions may force closing of the passes for short intervals.

Tahoe offers a variety of accommodations. You have a choice of resorts, motels, campgrounds (mostly summer only), or private cabins. For information on south shore accommodations and recreational facilities, write to South Lake Tahoe Visitors Bureau, P.O. Box 17727, South Lake Tahoe, CA 95706. For north shore information, write to Tahoe North Visitors and Convention Bureau, P.O. Box 5578, Tahoe City, CA 95730. Reservations are advisable the year around at the lake because of heavy use.

Part of Lake Tahoe is in Nevada, and on the Nevada side are gambling establishments that operate around the clock. Principal gaming areas are at Stateline at the south shore and Crystal Bay at the north shore.

Circling the lake

Lake Tahoe is 22 miles long and 8 to 12 miles wide. You can drive around the lake on a 71-mile shoreline road offering excellent views of the lake, its many coves, and the sheer mountain sides that plummet into the water. Occasionally winter snows may close a section of State 89 between Tahoe City and South Lake Tahoe around Emerald Bay on the west shore.

The lively south shore

Lake Tahoe's south shore is more heavily populated than the north shore. Resorts, motels, and private cabins are plentiful, there are a number of public beaches, and Nevada's Stateline offers gambling and nightclub entertainment in such high-rise hotels as Caesar's, Harrah's, Harvey's, Del Webb's High Sierra, and Lakeside Inn & Casino. South Lake Tahoe, sprawling against the California-Nevada border, is the major city.

Visitors to the area can get a quick introduction to its colorful historic past by browsing about the Lake Tahoe Historical Society next to the Chamber of Commerce.

To reach the south shore, take State 50 from Sacramento or State 88 and 89 from Stockton. Several intrastate airlines offer scheduled flights to Tahoe's south shore; many interstate air carriers fly into nearby Reno. Buses make daily runs into Tahoe from California and Nevada.

Emerald Bay, at the southwestern tip of the lake, is Tahoe's famed scenic attraction. The bay is entirely within Bliss and Emerald Bay state parks, and its waters surround Tahoe's only island—Fannette. The road around Emerald Bay is high above the water, and the view is unparalleled anywhere else on the lake.

Unseen from the road, at the southern tip of the bay, is a 38-room mansion called "Vikingsholm," once a summer residence. A striking example of Scandinavian architecture, Vikingsholm was patterned after an 800 A.D. Norse fortress. During summer the house is open to visitors daily. Park your car at Inspiration Point and then hike about a mile to the house. Daily excursion boats from South Lake Tahoe cross the lake, entering the bay.

At the head of the bay is a parking area for a short hike up to Eagle Falls. Picnic facilities are nearby, and camping units are located in both parks.

Sugar Pine Point State Park, up the road, is set in a dense grove of the trees for which it was named. Similar to other mountain parks in the vicinity, it is somewhat more protected from the heavy winter snows. Open all year, the park offers winter camping, cross-country skiing, and snowshoeing, in addition to its summer activities. The Ehrman mansion, acquired by the state with the property, is now an interpretive center and museum.

South of Emerald Bay you'll find several Forest Service beaches. The El Dorado National Forest Visitors Center, on State 89 north of Camp Richardson, offers slide presentations and group campfires at the Lake of the Sky Amphitheater; lecture programs at Angora Ridge fire lookout station; boat tours of Echo Lake; and short walks through surrounding meadows. Wilderness permits are available at the center.

A stream profile chamber allows you and the fish to exchange glances along an artifically created bypass of Taylor Creek, a natural trout and salmon spawning stream (October is peak season) flowing from Fallen Leaf Lake to Lake Tahoe. The visitors center is open from 9 A.M. to 6 P.M. daily mid-June to mid-September.

The South Lake Tahoe City Beach, on Lakeshore Boulevard, offers water-skiing and swimming. Picnic fires and overnight camping are prohibited on the beach, but approximately 150 campsites are within walking distance at the South Lake Tahoe El Dorado Recreational Area.

Nevada Beach Recreational Area, on the eastern side of the lake, is a popular picnic area for day-use visitors as well as a tent and trailer campground. Uphill from the beach, the U.S. Forest Service recently acquired 236 acres of meadows and pine forest that may be used to enlarge the campground.

Pocket resorts such as Zephyr Cove offer a campground, restaurant, swimming beach, and rental boats. Excursion boats dock here, including a paddle boat and sailboat.

What the north shore offers

The Crystal Bay area is a center of activity for the north shore. Here, motels, lodges, condominiums, cabins, and gambling casinos crowd State Highway 28 on either side. Once you cross into California, the casinos disappear, but the towns of Brockway, Kings Beach, and Tahoe Vista are fused to form a solid resort area.

A pine-forested area between Carnelian Bay and Tahoe City is relatively undeveloped. Tahoe City, closest town to Squaw Valley, Alpine Meadows, and other ski areas on the lake's west shore, offers shops, restaurants, and motels as well as winter and summer entertainment. You'll find a golf course, public beach, and state recreation area.

Tahoe State Recreation Area's beach and campground are nearly always crowded during peak summer season. The largest public beach at this end of the lake is sandy, 7-acre Kings Beach State Recreational Area.

Above the lake, the North Tahoe Regional Park in Tahoe Vista encompasses 108 sprawling acres of pines. There are hiking trails through the forest, a ½-mile nature trail, tennis courts, picnic area, and a demanding parcourse. In winter, there's a cross-country ski course.

Nevada's Incline Village complex, east of Crystal Bay on State 28, has a good family ski area. In summer you'll find golf (two 18-hole courses), tennis courts, riding trails, and bowling. Location scenes for TV's "Bonanza" series were filmed at the Ponderosa Ranch nearby.

Lake Tahoe Nevada State Park, south of Incline, makes up part of the northeastern shore, boasting rocky points (good for fishing), sandy beaches, launching facilities, and picnic grounds.

Summer fun on the lake

Lake Tahoe is a mecca for boaters and water-skiers. There's plenty of room for everyone, and the coves and harbors along the lake's shore are appealing. Many places around the lake rent boats. If you have your own boat, you'll find plenty of launching ramps, but during the busy summer season, you may have trouble finding a mooring. If a summer thunderstorm appears imminent, do not venture too far from shore; the lake can become very rough.

Lake Tahoe

Swimmers unaffected by icy cold water will find plenty of public beaches. At the south end of the lake are three Forest Service beaches (Pope, Baldwin, and Kiva). You can also swim at D. L. Bliss and Emerald Bay state parks, Sugar Pine Point State Park, and South Lake Tahoe Recreation Area. North shore offers public beaches at Tahoe City and Kings Beach. On the Nevada side, try Sand Harbor Beach State Recreation Area and Nevada Beach Campground. Many boat harbors also have beaches.

Fishing is good for rainbow, Mackinaw, silver, brown, eastern brook, and cutthroat trout. Local anglers report the waters from the mouth of Emerald Bay south toward Baldwin Beach are excellent for Kokanee salmon, introduced into the lake in 1940. California and Nevada fishing licenses are valid anywhere on the lake, but you must depart from and return to the state that issues the license. In the many lakes and streams close to Tahoe, you can trout fish from May to October.

Bikers may choose from more than 12 miles of safe, paved biking trails with great lake views. The longest paved trail runs 5.2 miles from Tahoe City to Homewood. Near Camp Richardson is a delightful 3.5-mile trail meandering through forest and streams close to three national forest beaches. For a free biking brochure on Lake Tahoe trails, write to Caltrans, Box 911, Marysville, CA 95901. You'll find a number of bike rental centers at both the north and south ends of the lake.

Hiking and riding trails around Tahoe are excellent. The Forest Service publishes hikers' maps. Inquire locally for other trips. You'll be able to rent horses at several spots around the lake.

Skiing Tahoe—something for everyone

The Lake Tahoe Basin is one of the most compactly developed ski regions in the world. Downhill skiers can enjoy a variety of terrain in a cluster of fine ski areas. For the Nordic enthusiast, Tahoe Basin boasts over 30 ski-touring centers, some of which are located at the major downhill areas. Most offer rentals, instructions, and group tours. For maps and ski information, write to the South Lake Tahoe Visitors Bureau and Tahoe North Convention and Visitors Bureau.

South shore's ski areas offer variety of terrain plus spectacular views. Heavenly Valley, Sierra Ski Ranch, Echo Summit, and Kirkwood have beginner to expert runs. Echo Summit and Kirkwood offer Nordic trails.

North shore has 14 ski areas—with wide, open bowls at Alpine Meadows and Sugar Bowl; wind-protected runs at Northstar, Homewood, and Tahoe Ski Bowl; gentle slopes at Mt. Rose and Ski Incline; and some of the country's most challenging runs at Squaw Valley. Seven cross-country ski areas provide groomed trails.

Squaw Valley, site of the 1960 Winter Olympics, is 8 miles south of Truckee. You turn off on a 2-mile side road from State 89. Squaw has facilities to challenge experts, nurture beginners, and satisfy everyone in between. You'll find restaurants and spectator centers from which you can watch the activity. For details, write Squaw Valley USA, Olympic Valley, CA 95730.

Branching out from the lake

Two popular destinations lie at either end of Lake Tahoe. Donner Lake, off Interstate 80, is surrounded by summer cabins. Desolation Wilderness, west of State 50, is popular with summer backpackers.

Donner Lake

Just 2 miles west of Truckee along Interstate 80, Donner Memorial State Park is a popular recreation area alongside Donner Lake. The park stands as a memorial to the members of the ill-fated Donner Party who camped here during the winter of 1846-47. Almost half of the 89 persons in the party perished in the severe Sierra's winter cold and heavy snows. A monument stands in the park on the site of the Breen family shack. Its stone base is 22 feet high—the depth of snow during that fateful winter.

The Emigrant Trail Museum in the park displays Indian and Donner Party relics. On display near the museum is a steam trailer that once hauled cut lumber on the eastern slope of the Sierra. Most of the park trails begin at the museum.

Desolation Wilderness

Just over the ridge along Lake Tahoe's southwest shore lies Desolation Wilderness, a favorite of Sierra high country devotees. "Desolation" describes the area's wild and lonely terrain, its huge boulders and glacier-polished slopes nearly devoid of trees. Elevations range from 6,500 to 10,000 feet, with Pyramid Peak dominating the four high summits on the southern end of the wilderness. The area also offers exceptional alpine beauty. Streams trace forests of fir, pine, juniper, and hemlock, and over 70 named lakes provide tranquil oases for fishing. In the spring, delicate wildflowers brighten Sierra meadows.

With so much to offer, Desolation Wilderness is—despite its name—ironically crowded, especially during the peak summer months. In recent years the area has become so popular that a campground reservation and wilderness permit system is in effect from mid-June to Labor Day. Campground reservations can be made through Ticketron up to 90 days and no less than 7 days in advance. Wilderness permits, necessary for both day and overnight use, are available at the area's district ranger offices and at the visitors center at Camp Richardson.

Within these 63,469 acres, you can hike about 50 miles of trails from five major trailheads. The much-used Tahoe-Yosemite trail connects many lakes. Backpack trips are extremely popular, or, you can try a stock trip, using animals to carry supplies.

For more information on the wilderness and backpacking trips, write to District Ranger, U.S. Forest Service, P.O. Box 8465, South Lake Tahoe, CA 95705, or call (916) 544-6420. For a wilderness permit, visit the Pacific Ranger Station at Fresh Pond, or call (916) 644-2348.

Northern Wonderland

Majestic mountains, pristine lakes, verdant valleys, and rushing streams embody California's Northern Wonderland. Fish the Klamath River, hike the Cascades and Trinity Alps high country, explore volcanic remnants in a national park, or houseboat on Shasta and Trinity lakes. And for the rugged mountaineer there remains the challenge of Mount Shasta's 14,162 feet. Whatever you choose to do, you'll find this "undiscovered" part of California a treasury of scenic wonders.

Splashing streams, towering snow-covered peaks, snug valleys encircled by forested slopes, miles of deep blue waters, and some of nature's most unusual attractions make up the Northern Wonderland, an area stretching from the Coast Range east to Nevada and from the upper Sacramento Valley to the Oregon border.

Outdoor recreation is unlimited. You can fish the Klamath, water-ski on Whiskeytown Lake, houseboat on Shasta and Trinity lakes, hike magnificent wilderness trails, sail at Eagle Lake, or camp along clear mountain streams. At Lava Beds National Monument and Lassen Volcanic National Park, you can see unusual land formations caused by volcanic action. Snow activities in winter center around Lassen Park. Try skiing, snowshoeing, or cross-country treks.

Interstate Highway 5 is the main north-south route through the northern mountains, and State Highway 299, the main east-west route. The highways join at Redding, hub of this outdoor playland, 234 miles north of San Francisco and 173 miles north of Sacramento. U.S. Highway 395 provides easy access to the northeastern part of the state.

For maps, brochures, and detailed information on this area, write to Shasta-Cascade Wonderland Association, 1250 Parkview Avenue, Redding, CA 96001, or stop by the offices at the corner of South Market and Parkview streets.

Bring a tent or trailer, backpack, and sleeping bag for delightful camping in the mountain country solitude. Accommodations are available throughout most of this region; it's advisable to plan ahead.

A water world

Boating is popular in the northland. Most of the activity centers at the lakes closest to Redding—Shasta, Whiskeytown, and Trinity. You can rent power boats, sailboats, or houseboats (Shasta and Trinity) and get water-skiing instruction at Shasta. Islands, inlets, and sandy beaches make picnicking popular. Campgrounds and marinas are plentiful and boat access is good.

Other good boating lakes lie north and east of Redding. Most are noted for fishing; several have good campgrounds and marinas; all are easily reached on good roads.

It's an angler's paradise. Mountain lakes and streams offer good catches all year. This is salmon and steelhead country; Chinook can weigh up to 55 pounds. Limits vary according to area. In some trophy waters, the limit is two trout. Anyone wishing to fish these waters should read the fishing regulations and restrictions on limits, size of hooks, type of lure, and stream closures.

Established in 1965 as part of the Federal Bureau of Reclamation's Central Valley Project, the Whiskeytown-Shasta-Trinity National Recreation Area consists of three units—Whiskeytown Lake, Shasta Lake,

YOUNG ANGLER TRIES HIS LUCK in crystal clear Hot Springs Creek near Drakesbad at Lassen Volcanic National Park.

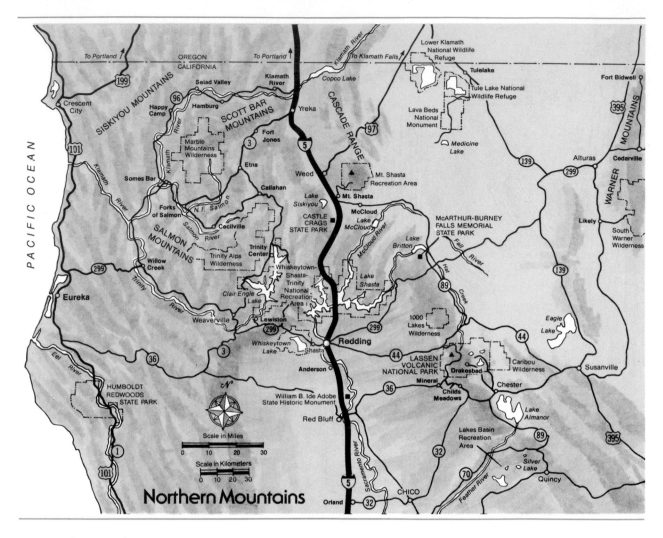

Northern Mountains

and Clair Engle (Trinity)-Lewiston lakes. All are popular summer destinations with boaters, campers, water-skiers, and picnickers. For detailed information on the recreation area, write to Shasta-Trinity National Forest, 2400 Washington Avenue, Redding, CA 96001, or to Shasta-Cascade Wonderland Association.

Whiskeytown Lake—try trout trolling

Eight miles west of Redding on State 299 is the Whiskeytown Reservoir, created when the Whiskeytown Dam was constructed to divert water from the Trinity River into the Central Valley. The lake is good for trout, Kokanee, bass, and bluegill fishing, especially in autumn and early spring. The 36-mile-shoreline, dotted with large and small coves, provides plenty of opportunities for water-skiing, scuba diving, swimming, and boating. Whiskeytown offers some of the top sailing waters in the northern mountains.

Two marinas—Oak Bottom and Brandy Creek—provide all services; boats launch from Whiskey Creek picnic area north of the highway. Other picnic and camping areas (some close to the beach) are designated; for reservations, call (916) 359-2085. No fires are allowed on the beach.

Some of Northern California's most beautiful scenery surrounds Whiskeytown Lake. A number of hiking and riding trails cross streams, climbing high enough to afford sweeping views of the lake's blue waters dotted with wooded islands.

The National Park Service maintains a visitor center just off State 299 on the east side of the lake. On the shore of the lake is the Kennedy Memorial, which commemorates President Kennedy's dedication of the dam and lake in 1963.

Below the dam, Clear Creek (once a major gold and silver-producing stream) winds through steep gorges and rocky hills. About 5 miles of the creek's waters are open to trout fishing. Check with the visitor center for gold-panning tours on this creek.

The choices at Shasta Lake

Nine miles north of Redding is Shasta, California's second highest dam, serving as the great barrier between the mountains and the valley. Behind it splays Shasta Lake, the largest unit of the three-lake national recreation area. Everything about Shasta Lake is on a grand scale. This great, four-fingered reservoir, the largest manmade lake in California, covers 30,000 surface acres and has 370 miles of shoreline. Shasta's many arms reach back into the canyons of the Sacramento, McCloud, and Pit rivers and Squaw Creek.

Shasta Lake is wide and unusually serene. Resorts on the lake (most clustered near Interstate 5) offer swimming, fishing, water sports, boating, and cruising aboard the *Bridge Bay Belle*. Rental craft range from canoes to cabin cruisers and modern houseboats that offer the convenience of a home with the advantage of providing movable scenery.

If you have your own boat, you'll find ramps at resorts and at several campsites along Shasta's shores. The Forest Service maintains a number of campgrounds around the lake. A few can be reached by boat only, and you may have to get your water from a spring or the lake itself. Several private campgrounds and trailer parks dot the lake area.

Shasta Lake is particularly inviting in spring when the redbuds bloom and in early autumn when the oaks change color. Summer is the heavy-use season: be sure to make houseboat, resort, or private campground reservations well in advance.

Lake fishing takes place the year around for 17 varieties of game fish, including German brown, rainbow, and Kamloops trout, black bass, Kokanee, and crappie. Since fish move frequently from one section to another, there's no "best place" for angling. Trout feed near the surface except during the summer, when they're found about 50 to 150 feet below. For crappie and bass, try angling around rocky points or where streams enter the lake. Limit is five fish.

Shasta Dam, the key structure in the Central Valley Project, is 602 feet high and two-thirds of a mile long at its crest. It's open daily; a model and film explain how the dam works. From here, you'll get a good view of Mount Shasta looming in the distance.

Shasta Caverns, a deep, complex series of limestone caves overlooking the McCloud River arm of Shasta Lake, are fun to explore; just getting there is an adventure. You travel first by boat and then by bus up a steep, 800-foot rise to the cavern entrance—a deceptively normal-looking "door" in the mountainside that leads to geological formations possibly a million years old.

Multicolored fluted columns, 60-foot-high stone draperies in symmetrical folds, and crystalline stalactite and stalagmite formations are featured on the 2-hour tour (including the cross-water trip). Knowledgeable guides take you through well-lighted tunnels and up stairs (over 10 at one point). Take a sweater, since temperature averages 58°F/14°C. The caverns are open daily the year around. From May 1 to September 30, tours start at 9 A.M.; service is reduced to three daily trips (10 A.M., noon, and 2 P.M.) from October 1 through April 30, weather permitting. Group tours are also available. Admission charges to the dramatic caverns are moderate.

To reach the caverns, take the O'Brien-Shasta Caverns offramp from Interstate 5 about 16 miles north of Redding. Follow the signs for about 2 miles to the visitor center. If you're boating, you can dock at the caverns landing on the east side of the McCloud arm.

WHAT IS A STEELHEAD?

Why do you find anglers wading waist deep in bone-chilling waters or huddled in drifting dories with numbed fingers, fumbling to refasten snagged rig or bait? They're out to catch the elusive steelhead coming in from the sea to begin their remarkable winter journey back to their birthplace. This is a fish with one purpose—to make its way up the river to spawn.

The steelhead, which many consider the most spirited fish in the West, is nothing more than a seagoing rainbow trout. Like any other wild rainbow, the steelhead begins life in the clear running water of a mountain stream. Completely indistinguishable from its stay-at-home neighbor, it shares the coloring and scientific name *(Salmo gairdnerii)*.

But after a couple of years, the young steelhead yields to some primeval urge to migrate. Drifting downstream on the first leg of a long trek to the Pacific Ocean, it pauses at the river mouth just long enough to undergo a remarkable transformation: the blue green of its back turns steely blue, the spots disappear from body and fins, and its lateral red line fades to silver. The rainbow has become a salt-water steelhead.

Little is known about how the steelhead spends its life at sea for the next couple of years, but a larger, stronger, and wiser fish returns from the ocean depths and, once again changing its markings back to those of a rainbow, is off on its difficult trek back to the ancestral spawning ground.

Arriving at last (unless interfered with by some wily angler), the steelhead spawns. Unlike the Pacific salmon that spawn only to die, though, the steelhead may spawn and return to sea. Steelhead rarely live longer than 8 years, but some manage as many as five complete spawning migrations during their life span. This is a remarkable fish.

Only along the coast of the Pacific Northwest do factors of topography and climate permit a public fishery for large migrations of these anadromous trout through the winter season.

HOUSEBOATERS AND WATER-SKIERS CRUISE Shasta Lake on clear summer day. Lake's serene turquoise waters are perfect playground for all aquatic sports.

Clair Engle (Trinity)-Lewiston lakes

Though Clair Engle Lake is the official name on most maps, residents of Trinity County still call this 16,500-acre impoundage Trinity Lake. By either name, it's the focal point of the Trinity National Recreation Area, a sparsely populated expanse of lake and forest. It offers excellent fishing for trout and smallmouth trophy bass, large and small campgrounds (some with sandy swimming beaches), marinas and launching ramps, swimming and sailing, water-skiing, and houseboat rentals (Cedar Stock Resort, Estrellita, Trinity Alps Marina, and Recreation Plus at Trinity Center). All facilities are on the west side of the lake in the shadow of the rugged Trinity Alps.

For information on the lake, write to the District Ranger, U.S. Forest Service, P.O. Box Drawer T, Weaverville, CA 96093, or to Shasta-Cascade Wonderland Association.

Lewiston Reservoir, downstream from Trinity Dam, is at an elevation of about 1,900 feet. Seven miles long, very narrow, and resembling a slow-moving river more than a lake, Lewiston offers good trout fishing. Trailer parks, campgrounds, boat rentals, and public boat-launching ramps sit on the west side of the lake. For additional details on the reservoir, contact the Weaverville Ranger District (address above).

To reach Trinity Lake, drive 49 miles west from Redding to Weaverville on State 299; then follow State Highway 3 about 15 miles to the lake. To get to Lewiston Reservoir, take State 299 26 miles east from Redding and turn right; it's about 9 miles farther.

A lake loop

Boaters, campers, and anglers all have their "favorite" lake. Here, singled out from the multitude of lakes in the north country, are some of the most popular, as well as a couple of the lesser known. Lodging is nearby.

Lake Siskiyou, a 430-acre impoundment of the Sacramento River in Box Canyon, was constructed solely for recreation purposes. Shoreline facilities include picnic and camp sites (RV hookups available), boat rentals, a ramp and wharf, and a spacious, sandy beach. Besides swimming and boating, the lake offers year-round trout fishing. No water-skiing is permitted.

To reach the lake, take the Central Mount Shasta off-ramp from Interstate 5 just west of the city of Mount Shasta.

Lake McCloud is a little off the beaten track, but this is part of its charm. Tarantula Gulch provides boating access for year-round trout fishing or just cruising in crystal clear, blue water. From Interstate 5, take State Highway 89 to the town of McCloud (9 miles) and follow Squaw Valley Creek Road heading south from town for about 12 miles. Watch for lumber trucks in summer; the road is sometimes closed in winter. On the way to the lake you'll pass a public, 9-hole golf course; it offers no sand traps but some challenging water hazards.

The quaint, gas-lighted town of McCloud nestled at the foot of majestic Mount Shasta was first built as a lumber town. Don't miss the local emporium containing everything from hardware to jewelry. Try the grand Guest House (five bedrooms with baths) for dinner or overnight stays. It was originally home to the president of the McCloud River Lumber Company.

Medicine Lake, about 500 years old, lies in what was once a volcanic crater. Burnt Lava Flow, to the south, has some of the most awesome lava formations in northern California. A high mountain lake, Medicine opens around July 1. Nights are chilly even in midsummer. Cold, clear, and deep, the lake is a popular fishing and boating area and even gets some hardy water-skiers. The Forest Service maintains a boat dock, ramp, and picnic area. The enclosed swimming area has a beautiful, sandy beach. From the south you can reach Medicine Lake by following State 89 east from McCloud to Bartle and turning north on a good (but not well-marked) road for 32 miles. From the north, take the marked road from Lava Beds National Monument or take State Highway 139 west from Perez.

Eagle Lake, in Lassen County, is one of California's largest natural lakes—and also one of its cleanest and least crowded. Here are plenty of spacious, tree-sheltered campgrounds and 27,000 acres of clear, blue water for excellent sailing. The lake also serves as a feeding ground for a rare breeding colony of osprey. Fishing is good for the large Eagle trophy trout, a natural hybrid that is the only game fish adapted to the unusually alkaline water. The limit is three, and catches up to 7 pounds are not uncommon.

Gallatin Beach, at the southern end of the lake, is a recreation center with store, marina, boat rentals, ramp, sandy beach, and shady picnic area.

From Interstate 5 take the Lassen Volcanic National Park turnoff from either Redding (State Highway 44) or Red Bluff (State Highway 36). The highways skirt the park on either side and join west of Susanville, closest town to the lake. The main beach and campground are reached on Eagle Lake Road. State 139 runs along the eastern shore.

Lake Almanor—52 square miles of azure water mirroring snow-capped Mount Lassen and rimmed with evergreen forest—is in Plumas County, 80 miles east of Red Bluff on State 36. Almanor, created by a dam on the Feather River, is also easily accessible from U.S. 395 and State Highway 70. Summer lake surface temperatures of 75°F/24°C make it ideal for swimming, water-skiing, and boating. Many resorts around the lake offer rentals, docking, and launching areas. A free public boat ramp is located west of the dam.

Fishing is excellent for trophy rainbow and brown trout, Kokanee, bass, catfish, and perch. Gould Swamp is a "hot spot" in spring, and summer night fishing near the shore is productive. During spring and fall, trolling for trout and Kokanee pays off. In addition to Almanor, there are about 50 lakes in the area and 500 miles of streams.

Additional recreational activities include a 9-hole golf course at Lake Almanor Country Club, holiday sailboat races, hunting, and rock collecting. Several nearby family ski areas (Stover Mountain, Lassen Park, Coppervale, and Eagle's Peak) operate during the winter. Slopes around the lake offer good tobogganing, sledding, and other snow fun.

Lakes Basin Recreational Area, almost on the border of Sierra and Plumas counties, is roughly halfway between Lassen Park and Lake Tahoe. A collection of small lakes conveniently located close to the road makes this a good family fishing and hiking area. A 23-site campground serves as a convenient base camp. Grassy Lake, the closest, is often overfished; nearby Big Bear and Little Bear lakes hold rainbow; in Cub and Silver lakes, look for brook trout; and at Long Lake, the largest, you can rent boats. Distances between lakes are short; you can hike, fish, and return to your car in the same day. There's trailside camping at Silver Lake; from there, it's an easy walk to less-fished lakes.

From State 89, turn off at Graeagle and follow Gold Lake Road south. From Lakes Basin you can continue south to Sierra City and State Highway 49.

Rivers for all anglers

Among the many rivers of the northern part of the state, a few stand out because of size, beauty, and accessibility, but primarily because of the fishing. Here you'll encounter the salmon and the steelhead (seagoing rainbow; see page 109), a challenge for any angler.

To see salmon spawned in a controlled environment, visit the Coleman National Fish Culture Station, the world's largest salmon hatchery, 6 miles off Interstate 5 at Anderson north of Red Bluff. (Or visit the new spawning channel at Red Bluff.) Spawning salmon provide a spectacular show during the fall and winter run. You can also get a good look at salmon in Redding's Caldwell Park, where manmade falls on the Sacramento River are lighted during spring and summer nights. Falls are dismantled in winter.

But it's in the rivers that you catch fish, and below we have listed the major streams. For angling information, check with the Shasta-Cascade Wonderland Association in Redding.

The Klamath, though not a long river, is an impressive stream within cliffed canyons. It offers some of the state's best steelhead fishing. The Klamath River winds through the mountains from Oregon and heads west to the California coast. Most of its course is paralleled by State Highway 96.

Along the highway, river communities offer lodges and resorts. Several Forest Service campgrounds spread out beside the river's banks. Try Happy Camp, Seiad Valley, Klamath River, Hornbrook, and Yreka for accommodations.

The most sought-after fish in the Klamath is the steelhead; next in popularity are the Chinook and silver salmon. Fishing is best from late summer to early spring for anadromous fish (fish going from the sea up rivers to spawn), mainly steelhead. Above Copco Lake the Klamath is a trophy fishing water.

The **Trinity River** also offers good steelhead fishing, particularly during fall and winter. Fishing for salmon is at its best in late spring and early fall. Much of the Trinity follows State 299; accommodations are available at small towns along the highway. Campgrounds are scattered along the river.

The **Salmon River,** in the mountains west of Scott Valley, has its main salmon run in late July, August, and September. Steelhead start moving in just behind the salmon. Check angling regulations; there are special closures on this river. Seemingly unknown Forest Service campgrounds are found in some of the most beautiful mountainous terrain. Resorts offer guide service, and small towns in the Scott Valley have limited accommodations.

The **Sacramento River** starts in the Trinity Divide country and ends up all the way down in the Sacramento Valley. This is California's major navigable recreational river. You'll see bountiful wildlife, including some endangered bird species.

Anadromous fishing (below the dams) is very good; several good salmon runs start around the latter part of August. This is when the big ones (up to 55 pounds) are caught. Spring runs begin the latter part of January and continue through March. Steelhead fishing is at its finest from mid-September into November.

Excellent trout streams abound in this great northern outdoorland. Anglers can usually wet their lines with good results. The season begins on the Saturday nearest May 1 and ends November 15. Here are a few favorite streams listed by county:
• *Lassen:* Willow Creek and the Susan River.
• *Modoc:* South Fork of the Pit River, East Creek, Mill Creek, Parsnip Creek, Pine Creek.
• *Plumas:* Middle Fork of Feather River, Nelson Creek, Yellow Creek upstream to Cottonwood.
• *Shasta:* Fall River (some trophy waters), Bear Creek, Hat Creek from Lake Britton upstream, upper Sacramento River including Castle Creek.
• *Siskiyou:* Scott River, McCloud River, Sacramento River, Butte Creek, Canyon Creek.
• *Tehama:* Deer Creek, Mill Creek, Battle Creek, Beegum Creek, South Fork of Cottonwood Creek.
• *Trinity:* Blue Tent Creek, Coffee Creek, Canyon Creek, Stuarts Fork Creek.

A wilderness experience

Few roads lead into the heart of the northern mountains. Three large mountain ranges—Klamath-Scott (including the Trinity, Salmon, and Marble mountains), Cascades, and Warner mountains—contain beckoning wilderness areas accessible only to packers and campers. You can sample the fringes by car. Resorts offer lodging, meals, and guides into the interior. Remember, you will need a permit to enter any wilderness area.

Only a handful of towns in the region offer tourist lodging. But take heart: these mountains can be more inviting than the towering Sierra range to the southeast. They are less crowded, generally less rugged, and more compact. Rivers and mountain streams offer excellent fishing, rafting, canoeing, and kayaking; the national forests invite camping and packing.

Snow melts around the lakes about mid-June, but sometimes not until the end of June. July through September is best for the trails.

Packers and hikers use these points: Happy Camp, Seiad Valley, and Hamburg on the Klamath; Somesbar at the confluence of the Klamath and Salmon; Forks of Salmon and Sawyers Bar on the Salmon River; and Etna, Greenview, Fort Jones, and Scott Bar along the Scott River.

Trinity Alps—hidden high country

The unexpectedly high and rugged Trinity Alps are camouflaged by lower mountains; you scarcely notice them from Interstate 5. An easy approach on cross-mountain State 299 has never brought them heavy traffic.

The Trinity Alps have some striking resemblances to the Sierra. Massive granite peaks soar from an alpine highland. Dozens of lakes pocketed in glacial basins feed the outlet creeks and rivers. Over 50 alpine lakes can be found east of Trinity Lake and west of Interstate 5, at about 6,000 feet. But the Trinity Alps are much more compact than the Sierra (trails to the high mountains are shorter) and, being closer to coastal moisture, Trinity has proportionately more and fuller streams, greener and thicker underbrush.

Trinity splits the difference between the dry heat of the upper Sacramento Valley and the damp coolness of the Humboldt coast. It has two zones—a low, warm canyon country and a high, cool mountain wilderness.

The Trinity Alps are a small Mother Lode. Three main roads form a circle around the Alps and link old gold towns. The principal road, State 299, parallels the Trinity Trail, famous as an Indian path, pioneer trail, and Gold Rush wagon road. The second, State Highway 3, was once part of the main route—the old California-Oregon Wagon Road—north from Shasta to Callahan and Yreka. The third road taps the Salmon River settlement and the north and west slopes.

Marble Mountains Wilderness

A loop road encircles the Marble Mountains, winding up the Scott River from Hamburg to Fort Jones and Etna, and down the North Fork of the Salmon River to Sawyers Bar, Forks of Salmon, and Somesbar.

With over 280,000 acres, the Marble Mountains are walking mountains, easier to get around in than the Trinity Alps to the south. You have to fight brush along the streams, and the trails are precipitous in places but, for the most part, scenic and easy to follow.

Almost in the exact center of the wilderness area are the Sky High Lakes, a hub from which main and spur trails go in all directions. Most of the trails wind through forests of fir, mountain hemlock, western white pine, black oak, and rare weeping spruce.

The Salmon-Scott Mountains, bordering the Marbles on the south, offer many fine lakes to fish and explore.

The wild Cascades

Extending all the way from British Columbia through Washington and Oregon, the Cascade Range ends at Lassen Volcanic National Park. Mount Shasta and Lassen Peak are the two outstanding mountains in Northern California.

Around Lassen are two wilderness areas popular with backpackers and fishers because of the large number of small lakes.

Thousand Lakes Wilderness, about 12 miles north of Lassen Park, has four major trails. Since all trails lead uphill, backpacks can get uncommonly heavy. But the pleasure of camping beneath lodgepole pines and the number of lakes in this valley compensate for the rigors of the hike.

Three-mile Cyprus Camp Trail, beginning at Cyprus Campground at the northwest end of the wilderness, is the easiest trail, climbing about 1,000 feet to Lake Eiler, the largest lake. At least six of the lakes provide consistently good rainbow trout action. Another campground (Bunchgrass) is south of the wilderness. You can drive to the wilderness on several unimproved roads from State 89; check with the ranger at Hat Creek.

Caribou Peak Wilderness, with easy access from Silver Lake in Lassen County, is a popular but still isolated wild area. Back to back with Lassen Park, Caribou contains a series of lakes along gradually sloping trails. Fishing for brook and rainbow trout is good.

Like Thousand Lakes, Caribou Peak is at its best from the latter part of June through the summer months. Several campgrounds are located close to Silver Lake.

Wandering in the Warners

If the Warner Mountains were near a large city, they would be famed for their scenery and aswarm with visitors. But because they are in Modoc County, in the northeastern part of the state, and reached by little-traveled highways, they still offer the adventure of discovery.

The topography may bring to mind parts of the Rockies—where unmodified rock strata slant steadily up to a summit ridge and break away abruptly on the other side. The long western slopes are carpeted in a random patchwork of pine, aspen, fir, juniper, sage, and grasses.

You won't find any resorts or lodges in the Warners. You can take one-day outings into the high country from Alturas, but if you want to remain in the mountains, you must camp out. Packers operate from Alturas.

The only paved road across the Warners is the Cedar Pass route, which descends into Surprise Valley, a ranching area. If you take this road to Cedarville (on State 299), you can return to U.S. 395 through Fandango Pass on a maintained gravel road. Cedarville's most historic building is the Bonner Trading Post, a log cabin built in 1865 as a trading post for early immigrants and settlers. At the valley's northern tip is Fort Bidwell, an army outpost from 1866 to 1892 and school for Paiute Indians from 1892 to 1930.

The highest part of the Warner Mountains is preserved as a 70,000-acre wilderness where no motor vehicles are permitted and the only signs of civilization are grazing sheep and cattle. Traversing the wilderness is the 24-mile Summit Trail, hugging the top of the range with views of Mount Shasta and Lassen Peak to the west and, to the east, Nevada in the distance and Surprise Valley 4,000 feet below. The trail skirts the three highest peaks—Squaw, Warner, and Eagle. All are climbable.

It takes 2 or 3 days to hike the entire trail; side trails lead to secondary roadheads that can shorten your trip. Side trails also lead to some fine trout fishing, especially in Pine, Mill, and East creeks and South Emerson Lake. Blue Lake (actually in Lassen County) is reached more easily on the road that goes from Likely toward Jess Valley, one of the prettiest spots you'll encounter.

From the south the Summit Trail starts at the Patterson ranger station, 42 miles by car from Alturas; it ends at Pepperdines Camp, 20 miles east of Alturas.

Nature's wonders

In California's far north you can discover some of nature's finest handiwork. Awe-inspiring Shasta's icy slopes still tempt the intrepid climber. Mount Lassen's snow-capped peak looms over a valley of bubbling sulphur pools, vestiges of volcanic activity of the not-too-distant past. Craters, chimneys, and cones of Lava Beds National Monument in the state's northeastern corner were the scene of California's only major Indian war. Not far away is the resting place for waterfowl traveling the Pacific Flyway.

It's a land of contrasts. You can climb the cluster of domes and spires that make up Castle Crags; hike down to Burney Falls, a scenic waterfall (familiar to many because it adorned a beer can); or take a lantern and clamber through Subway Cave, a lava formation set incongruously adjacent to Hat Creek just north of Lassen Volcanic National Park.

Mighty Mount Shasta

Lore and legend surround majestic Mount Shasta. This immense mountain, rising to 14,161 feet, dominates the landscape for more than 100 miles. Volcanic in origin, it is composed of two cones: Shasta itself, and Shastina, a small cone that rises from the western flank. Five glaciers mantle the eastern and northeastern flanks above the 10,000-foot level.

Mount Shasta City, on the west side of Strawberry Valley and right at the base of the mountain, was settled in the 1850s. When the Shasta route of the Southern Pacific Railroad reached the settlement in 1886, a townsite was laid out along the railroad. In 1924 the town took the name of the mountain that towers above it. Mount Shasta is considered sacred by many people; over a dozen sects flourish in the tiny town.

Mt. Shasta Ski Park, on the south side of the mountain (off State 89), offers over 200 acres of skiable terrain including a 1,150-foot vertical drop and one 1¼-mile-long run. Two triple chairs and one poma lift skiers from the lodge. Another ski area is scheduled to open in late 1986.

Perpetual glaciers, white water in deep canyons, jewel-like lakes, dense forests and open valleys, and wildflowers in spring call climbers to the mountain. Even though the angle of climb is rarely greater than 35 degrees, the ascent is taxing.

August is considered the best month to climb. Snow and ice are minimal then and weather conditions most stable. Special Forest Service brochures show recommended routes of ascent. Climbers are asked to check in and out at Mount Shasta City Police Department. Hiking equipment can be rented, and maps are available.

Lassen Volcanic National Park

Until May 30, 1914, Lassen's claim to fame was as a landmark for pioneer Peter Lassen, who guided emigrant parties over the mountains and into the Sacramento Valley. Then began the year-long eruptions of smoke, stones, steam, gases, and ashes that culminated in the spectacular events of May 19, 1915. On that day a red-glowing column of lava rose in the crater and spilled over the sides, melting the snow on the mountain's northeast flank and sending 20-ton boulders and devastating floods of warm mud 18 miles down into the valleys of Lost and Hat creeks.

Three days later, Lassen literally blew its top. A column of vapor and ashes rose 30,000 feet into the sky. A terrific blast of steam and hot gases ripped out the side of the mountain and rushed northeast, killing all vegetation in its path for miles. As far away as Reno, streets were buried under several inches of ash. Declining eruptions continued into 1917. On a visit to Lassen today, you will see striking examples of past volcanic activity, as well as evidence of present action.

One of the West's least discovered national parks, Lassen today has a sense of solitude and space. Over 150 miles of trails connect a rare combination of natural phenomena: glacial lakes, permanent snowpacks, boiling fumaroles, crashing waterfalls, and lush meadows.

Though much of the Lassen country is accessible only by trail, no point in the park's 163 square miles is more than a day's hike from the road. Permits are required to get into Lassen's wilderness area. A brochure available at the park entrance shows the self-guiding nature trails and key points of interest.

Lassen Peak road, linked at both ends to State 89, traverses the western part of the park between West Sulphur Creek and Manzanita Lake. It crosses a shoulder of the volcano at 8,512 feet. Winding around three sides of Lassen Peak, the road affords stunning views of the volcano, examples of its destructive action, and vistas of woods and meadows, streams and lakes. After the first snowstorm, the road is closed until late spring, except for the section leading to the park ski area.

A good trail takes you to the top of Lassen Peak. The hike is not difficult; it takes about 2 hours to climb from the highway—an ascent of 2,000 feet. From the highest point you will see not only the clear-cut evidences of the 1914–17 activity but also the distant Sierra Nevada in the vicinity of Tahoe, the Coast Range ascending northward to the Trinity Alps, and the icy cone of Mount Shasta.

Sulphur Works Thermal Area, near the park's south boundary, is the most accessible of the hydrothermal regions. North of here you pass Broke-off Mountain, Mount Diller, Mount Connard, and Pilot Pinnacle—peripheral remnants of the much higher Mount Tehama, a huge strato-volcano that collapsed perhaps 10,000 to 11,000 years ago.

Biggest and showiest of the thermal areas is Bumpass Hell. You'll first notice a vague smell of sulphur as you descend into a natural bowl eaten out of a hard lava rock by hot acids. The barren landscape includes violently roaring hot springs, boiling muddy pools, crystallized "solfataras," gurgling mud volcanoes, "morning glory" pools, deep turquoise waters over layers of fool's gold, and a mineralized "River Styx."

The eastern side of Lassen, from the town of Chester on State 36, is served by two main roads. On one road you drive 16 miles to Drakesbad, an old but comfortable summer spa. At Drakesbad is a 2-mile sign-guided trail around Boiling Spring Lake. A second road from Chester leads to Juniper and Horseshoe lakes. Horseshoe makes a good base camp for hikes to Snag and Jakey lakes.

Accommodations in the area include guest ranches, small lodges, and campgrounds. Drakesbad Guest Ranch, at the southern end of the park, accommodates over 50 in the main building and surrounding cabins. Guided saddle and pack trips can be arranged.

Manzanita Lake, in the northwest section of the park, has facilities and a campground. A few small to medium-size campgrounds are scattered around elsewhere— Summit Lakes, Sulphur Works, Lost Creek, and Crags along the Lassen Park road. Other camp grounds are in Warner Valley and at Juniper and Butte lakes.

For more lodging and camping information, write to the Superintendent, Lassen Volcanic National Park, Mineral, CA 96063.

Lassen in winter becomes a snow-covered, uncrowded, 106,000-acre playground. Winter activities are focused at the southwest park entrance (the main road through the park is closed). Entering the park at 6,700 feet, you'll find quiet, forested land where you can ski downhill or cross country, or take a ranger-led snowshoe walk. Ski tows and touring centers are open Wednesday through Sunday. Food, ski rentals, and lessons are offered. Overnight lodging is available at Mineral, Chester, and Mill Creek. For more detailed winter recreation information write to the national park headquarters in Mineral.

California's lonely corner

Centuries ago, flaming volcanoes in northeastern California spread rivers of liquid rock over the land below. Upon cooling, they formed one of California's most fascinating landscapes. It's a terrain made rugged by yawning chasms, cinder cones, and craters scattered

HISSING HOT SULPHUR SPRINGS, gurgling pools, and boiling mud volcanoes envelop visitors (below) to Bumpass Hell in Lassen Volcanic National Park.

MIGHTY MOUNT SHASTA'S snow-covered slopes provide awesome backdrop to simple country church in McCloud (right). Visible for miles, Shasta (14,131 feet) attracts intrepid climbers to its icy peaks.

RIDERS REST while horses graze at Patterson Lake (right) in South Warner Wildlife Area. Camping is the only way to explore this lonely northeastern California corner.

over the surface. The official name is Lava Beds National Monument.

Adjoining the monument on the north are Tule Lake and Lower Klamath national wildlife refuges. At these havens for millions of migratory birds, some 200 species have been sighted during flight season. Here, too, you can see the largest concentration of bald eagles in the continental U.S. Visits usually occur between December and March.

Lava Beds National Monument is an area of volcanic caves and plains in northeastern California. "Nobody will ever want these rocks. Give me a home here," declared Modoc Indian Chief Captain Jack. Not so: the area received monument status in 1872.

Just off State 139, almost to the Oregon border, these 72 square miles contain 1,500-year-old lava flows, high cinder buttes, pictographs and petroglyphs, and what may be the world's most outstanding exhibit of lava tubes. Lanterns are provided for self-guided explorations. The largest concentration of caverns is along Cave Loop Road near the monument's headquarters.

A campground is located in the southern section of the park near monument headquarters. Look for other lodging, food, and gasoline in nearby Tulelake.

Tule Lake and Lower Klamath wildlife refuges, north of Lava Beds, make the Klamath Basin in northern California a "stop off" for the largest concentration of waterfowl on the North American continent.

Lodging is available at Tulelake, Newell, and Dorris; a private campground and trailer parks are nearby. Get maps and regulations at the Tule Lake National Wildlife Refuge headquarters at the north end of the refuge.

Two great state parks

Castle Crags and Burney Falls are two gems that shouldn't be missed. Camp settings are particularly attractive.

Castle Crags State Park, a 3,447-acre reserve straddling Interstate 5 and the Sacramento River, rises in a cluster of gray-white granite domes and spires from an evergreen forest 48 miles north of Redding.

Long, warm summers and easy access make this park a popular place to camp or picnic from about the first of April to the end of October. Most popular activities are swimming and fishing in the river, hiking in the park or into the backcountry, and climbing in the Crags.

Though no hookups are provided, many campsites are large enough to accommodate trailers. Rest rooms, hot showers, and baths are nearby.

Burney Falls, one of the most beautiful natural phenomena in California, is the chief attraction in the McArthur Memorial Park, near the intersection of State 299 and 89. Burney Creek, welling up out of a subterranean source, divides into two fairly equal flows of water and goes streaming over a 129-foot cliff into an emerald pool. On sunlit mornings a little rainbow accompanies the mist blowing down the canyon.

The 565-acre park (open the year around) includes nearly 2 miles of frontage along Burney Creek, together with a bit of shoreline on Lake Britton, a 9-mile-long, manmade lake popular with swimmers, fishers, boaters, and water-skiers. Scattered throughout the forest are campsites (no trailer hookups); a grocery store and snack bar open from mid-April to mid-October.

BIGFOOT—MAN OR MYTH?

Leaving all the rest of California's scenic splendors behind, many people head for vacations spots among the relatively unspoiled wooded areas along the Trinity and Klamath river valleys near the state's northern border. Here, civilization encroaches slowly; much of the land is protected as a national forest and as a mecca for fishing, hunting, camping, or just getting away from it all. Yet there is one disconcerting, mysterious note in this idyllic scene—the occasional unexplainable footprints of Bigfoot.

Reported sightings of Bigfoot—supposedly a creature 7 to 14 feet high and weighing from 300 to 800 pounds—have spanned a century. The creature is said to be totally covered with hair except for his face, palms, and soles. Facial features are said to be more humanoid than those of apes or gorillas, with flat nose and broad nostrils, short ears, and dark, leathery skin. Photographs show that Bigfoot walks upright with an erect stance and a stride ranging from 4 to 10 feet long.

Nevertheless, the giant footprints are the most tangible evidence of this "monster" (perhaps a relative of the Abominable Snowman of the Himalayas). You can buy footprint castings in Willow Creek and Weaverville and on the Hoopa Valley Indian Reservation.

Over Labor Day, Willow Creek, gateway to Bigfoot country, has an annual festival—Bigfoot Daze—during which spectators are invited to compare their foot sizes with those of Bigfoot. Happy Camp and Weaverville also host Bigfoot celebrations on that weekend. Skeptics and believers are about evenly divided as to the creature's actual existence, but at least it's cause for a celebration.

HISTORIC SAMPLER

Turn back the clock in the north country by sampling remnants of yesteryear. A drive through now-quiet villages still shows evidence of the raucous 19th century when gold fever reigned. Visit the home of California's only president; photograph the roofless, grass-filled buildings of the one-time "Queen City" of the northern mines; tour a temple of Chinese worship; or wander around some of the gingerbread houses of early pioneers.

The Ide Adobe

Along the west bank of the Sacramento River, near Red Bluff, stands the William B. Ide Adobe State Historic Monument, a travelers' oasis. Picnic on verdant grounds overlooking the river, have a refreshing drink of cool water, or just stretch your legs by wandering through the shady 4-acre park, a landmark to the short-lived Bear Flag Party and California's president. The adobe ranch house is now a museum; a restored carriage house, smokehouse, and corral suggest ranch life in the 1850s. The park is open daily from 8 A.M. to 5 P.M.; admission is free. From Interstate Highway 5, take State Highway 36 through Red Bluff; turn right at Adobe Road. Mooring facilities for boaters are near the old ferry site.

Red Bluff Victorians

Of a later vintage are the grand Victorian homes of Red Bluff. The Kelly-Griggs House Museum (311 Washington Street) is a classic. Nearly 100 years old, it's open to the public Thursday through Sunday from 2 to 5 P.M. At the museum you can buy a Victorian "windshield tour" of central Red Bluff, including the cottage of Mrs. John Brown, widow of the celebrated abolitionist of Harper's Ferry.

Gold Country

Northern California's gold rush was never as well chronicled as mining in the Sierra Nevada. Yet many millions in gold were extracted by miners who thronged north in the 1850s. The La Grange Mine, started in 1851, was for years the largest operating hydraulic mine in the world. Two sample drives plunge you into Gold Country; one follows State Highway 299 within an hour's drive west of Redding; the other meanders through scenic Scott Valley at the foot of the Marble and Trinity mountains.

The Trinity Trail. Shasta, 6 miles west of Redding, is a mere ghost of its former lusty self. Today, shells and façades of "the longest row of brick buildings in California" speak for its prosperous past. Visit the Shasta County Courthouse (now a museum) to learn about Shasta's rise and fall.

Two tiny towns to poke around in are French Gulch and Lewiston. Both have historic hotels, picturesque churches, and one-room schoolhouses. Signs direct you to State 299 turnoffs.

Weaverville seems enchanted with its past. A hundred years have brought little change in its frontier-Victorian aspect except for the honey locusts grown tall shading the trim lawns, flowers, and picket fences. At the J. J. "Jake" Jackson Memorial Museum, open daily from May through November, you'll learn Trinity history amid nostalgic surroundings. Next door, across a pleasant park furnished with mining equipment, is the exotic Joss House, evoking memories of the important role of Chinese gold miners in California's history. Now it's a state historic park; rangers conduct guided temple tours daily.

Into Scott Valley. From Weaverville, State Highway 3 roams along the edge of Trinity Lake, through the mountains, and into peaceful Scott Valley. At Trinity Center the Scott Museum (open most of the year) gives you an idea of how it was to live during the days of the gold boom.

At the southern edge of agricultural Scott Valley, Callahan was a trading center for miners and ranchers. No traffic crowds the block-long main street. Several century-old buildings line the boardwalks. Plan to spend some time if you enter the Callahan Emporium, "Biggest Little Store in the World." Some of its wide variety of merchandise has been there for years.

Etna appears to be almost a metropolis if you see it after you visit Callahan. You'll enjoy many fine old buildings. A museum is usually open summer afternoons.

Fort Jones, up the road, was the site of an army outpost on the old stage road. You'll find an exceptionally fine Indian museum. Up the McAdam Creek Road are the remains of a couple of bullet-riddled cabins of Deadwood, where Lotta Crabtree danced and Joaquin Miller cooked.

Other towns offering turn-of-the-century nostalgia are Susanville and Alturas, now boasting museums filled with gold rush memorabilia. In the Yreka town courthouse, you'll find a fine display of nugget and placer gold.

The flat Central Valley provides strong contrast to its surroundings—the Sierra Nevada Mountains on the east, the Coast Range on the west. To the south rise the Tehachapis, and to the north the foothills of the southern Cascades and the northern Coast Range meet.

The Central Valley extends 465 miles from north to south and is 30 to 60 miles wide. The big valley actually includes two valleys—the Sacramento, through which the Sacramento River flows, and the San Joaquin, named for the river that runs part way through it.

Once called the Badlands, the Central Valley was changed by irrigation into the most fertile farm land in the world. Orchards, vineyards, and such staple crops as onions, sweet potatoes, and grain are the area's economic base. These lands are grazing grounds for dairy cattle and livestock. Two inland ports—at Sacramento and Stockton—provide the landlocked valley access to the sea.

Interstate Highway 5, on the valley's western side, is fast becoming the most traveled route between Southern and Northern California. A swift but lonely, monotonous road, it bypasses the towns that grew up along State Highway 99, which runs right through the valley. Feeder roads connect the two highways along their routes, leading through small agricultural communities.

Though the San Joaquin Valley extends south below Bakersfield, the section identified with Northern California ends at Fresno. For a description of the southern part of the valley, see the *Sunset* book *Travel Guide to Southern California.*

The Delta—a vast inland sea—offers miles of good boating and fishing. It's the Central Valley's greatest recreational asset.

The Sacramento valley – from gold to grain

The Sacramento Valley grew up during the Gold Rush days when river steamers and sailing schooners on the Sacramento and Feather rivers connected such communities as Marysville and Red Bluff to Sacramento. After gold panned out, agriculture developed. Grain ranches were built close to the Sacramento River, and grain soon became the valley's chief product

These large grain fields were later subdivided. Smaller, irrigated ranches became orchards, citrus groves, vineyards; alfalfa, vegetables, and some newcomers—cotton, rice, and sugar beets—were also planted. These crops remain the heart of the valley's agriculture.

The city of Sacramento, once a lusty boom town with its roots deep in the Gold Rush, soon emerged as an agricultural center and merchandising outlet for the rich valley. Some of its past still peeks out amidst the tremendous growth of its present.

SACRAMENTO'S GOLDEN-DOMED CAPITOL, completed in 1874, is outstanding landmark in downtown area.

Flatlands sprawl nearly 500 miles through the Sacramento and San Joaquin valleys; together they form the great Central Valley. Irrigation changed these once-barren "badlands" into acres of fruit orchards, golden grain fields, and rich pasturelands, turning the big valley into the nation's richest farming area. At the confluence of the Sacramento and American rivers lies Sacramento, the state capital. Here you'll find a modern metropolis studded with remnants of its rich gold rush past. And on the nearby Delta, an intricate network of lazy waterways, you'll discover exceptional fishing, water-skiing, and boating.

The Central Valley

California's capital city

Most of the major routes through central California pass through or around Sacramento, the state capital. To the east, Interstate Highway 80 and U.S. Highway 50 lead into the Sierra, to Lake Tahoe, and on to Nevada. For southern travel, State 99 and Interstate 5 are the main arteries. To the north, these highways, uniting at Red Bluff, lead into the northern mountains. The main route to the San Francisco Bay area is Interstate 80.

At the confluence of the American and Sacramento rivers, the city (whose summer temperatures soar into the 90s) offers skin diving, water-skiing, swimming, and all types of boating. You'll find public boat launches at Miller Park, Discovery Park, and Elkhorn Bridge, 10 miles north. For specific visitor information, write to the Sacramento Convention and Visitors Bureau, 1311 "I" Street, Sacramento, CA 95814.

The domed capitol building (9th Street between L and N streets), surrounded by its groomed park, has an impressive approach—across the Sacramento River on ornate Tower Bridge and east up well-landscaped Capitol Mall. A massive restoration involving 6 years and $68 million was completed in 1982. Today, the capitol again possesses the grace and beauty it originally had in 1874—magnificent dome, marble mosaic floors, crystal chandeliers, and polished wood appointments. In addition to museums depicting the heads of the state in early days, you can also see a film about the restoration.

The capitol is open daily at 9 A.M.; guided tours are offered several times a day. A series of 58 exhibits—one for each California county—displays the state's commercial, scenic, and recreational assets. You can also view the Senate and Assembly in action from their chamber quarters. When a measure comes up for a vote, the legislator pushes a button that flashes colors on a board—red for "no," green for "yes."

Capitol Park, an oasis on hot valley days, has 40 acres of more than 40,000 trees, shrubs, and plants. You'll see plants and trees from all over the world, including a collection of trees brought from Civil War battlefields. Among 2,200 plantings, more than 800 varieties of camellias bloom; peak season is February and March. The park includes a trout pond, several monuments, and lots of squirrels. At the State Police Office on the ground floor of the capitol, you can pick up a booklet suggesting three walking tours.

Sutter's Fort (2701 L Street) is the reconstructed site of the settlement founded by Captain John A. Sutter. Sacramento's story began with the splash of his anchor in the American River in 1839. Sutter had navigated a little fleet up the Sacramento River from San Francisco en route to the land grant he obtained from the Mexican government. On a small knoll not far from the anchorage, he built a fort to protect his 76-square-mile land grant, established an embarcadero, and started farming the area he called New Helvetia. Here in 1844 he entertained the United States exploring party led by John C. Fremont and his guide, Kit Carson. During the Bear Flag Revolt of 1846, General Vallejo was detained here.

The town of Sacramento sprang up around the fort after James Marshall discovered gold at nearby Coloma in 1848. After gold was discovered, Sutter lost his land to newcomers and later went east. Between 1891 and 1893 the state of California restored the fort, following sketches and plans from Sutter's day. Now the fort stands in the center of the city, housing a collection of historical mementos. Exhibits include carpenter, cooper, and blacksmith shops, a prison, and living quarters. Headsets allow visitors to tour at their own speed. The fort is open daily (except holidays) from 10 A.M. to 5 P.M.; admission, including headsets, is nominal.

The State Library (open Monday through Friday from 8 A.M. to 5 P.M.), housed in a handsome granite building adjoining the capitol, is worth a visit, especially for history buffs. The general reading room, adorned with a Maynard Dixon mural depicting California's growth, maintains an excellent file of present and past California newspapers.

The California State Archives (1020 O Street) also displays historic California documents and exhibits, including California's original constitutions of 1849 and 1879. Open Monday through Friday from 8 A.M. to 5 P.M., the archives are closed on major holidays.

The Governor's Mansion (16th and H streets) stands empty today. Built in 1877, it was acquired by the state in 1903 for Governor George Pardee. Home to 13 governors, the 15-room Victorian-Gothic structure, now a state historic landmark, is open for public tours daily from 10 A.M. to 5 P.M. (except Thanksgiving, Christmas, and New Year's Day). There's a slight admission charge for adults.

The State Indian Museum adjacent to Sutter's Fort, interprets the Indian way of life in California through the use of frequently changing exhibits ranging from archeology to mythology. The museum houses a variety of Native American artifacts, including a fine basket collection. Hours are the same as for Sutter's Fort. Admission is free.

The Crocker Art Museum (216 O Street), a large, stately Victorian mansion built by Judge Crocker in 1873 for his private art collection, is the oldest art museum in the West. The building's elegant interior—sweeping staircases, parquetry floors, repoussé ceilings, and grand ballroom—makes a perfect setting for the collection of paintings, drawings, decorative arts, and sculpture. Of particular interest are the Oriental and contemporary American art collections. A new wing increases exhibition space by nearly half. The gallery is open to the public Tuesday from 2 to 10 P.M. and Wednesday through Sunday from 10 A.M. to 5 P.M.

The Chinese Cultural Center (between 4th and 5th and I and J streets) features buildings of Oriental design, a mall with a Chinese garden, residences, stores, offices, and restaurants—a developing Chinatown set around the Confucius Temple at 4th and I streets.

The Sacramento Community/Convention Center (between J and L and 13th and 14th streets) frames the east end of the K-Street Mall. The handsome center consists of three main facilities: an exhibit building, an activity building, and the center theater—a stage for the performing arts. The center is located within walking distance from the capitol and capitol park.

For just 25 cents, you can ride the K-Street tram 14 blocks along the K-Street Mall from the center to Old Sacramento and a rendezvous with the 19th century.

Old Sacramento historic area

Old Sacramento (on the eastern bank of the Sacramento River between Capitol Mall and I Street, west of Interstate 5) is now a national historic landmark. Restored brick and frame buildings, gas lamps, plank sidewalks, and turn-of-the-century museums take you back to Sacramento's golden age between the 1850s and 1870s. Happily, Old Sacramento is not a fossil, but a living, self-sustaining district with unusual restaurants, "watering holes," gift stores, antique shops, and business offices that mirror the city of a century and a quarter ago.

The re-creation began in the late 1960s when Old Sacramento, then a scar of deterioration and neglect,

received a makeover from concerned and imaginative individuals. Now, nearly completed, the area boasts over 100 restored and renovated buildings, 41 of which are original structures.

Begin your tour at the John F. Morse Building on 2nd and K streets, originally built in 1865 for Dr. Morse, Sacramento's first physician and editor of the *Sacramento Union*. Here you can pick up an illustrated guide to the 28-acre area, with information on shops, restaurants, events, and historic landmarks.

Sacramento History Center (Front and I streets) exhibits much of the city's colorful history in an 18,000-square-foot museum. Five galleries have major displays, including Eleanor McClatchy's collection of Gold Rush newspapers and the Bank of America's gold and coin exhibit. The museum is open daily from 10 A.M. to 5 P.M. (small admission charge).

B. F. Hastings Building (2nd and J streets), completed in 1852, is the site of the first western terminus of the Pony Express and the first Sacramento office of Wells

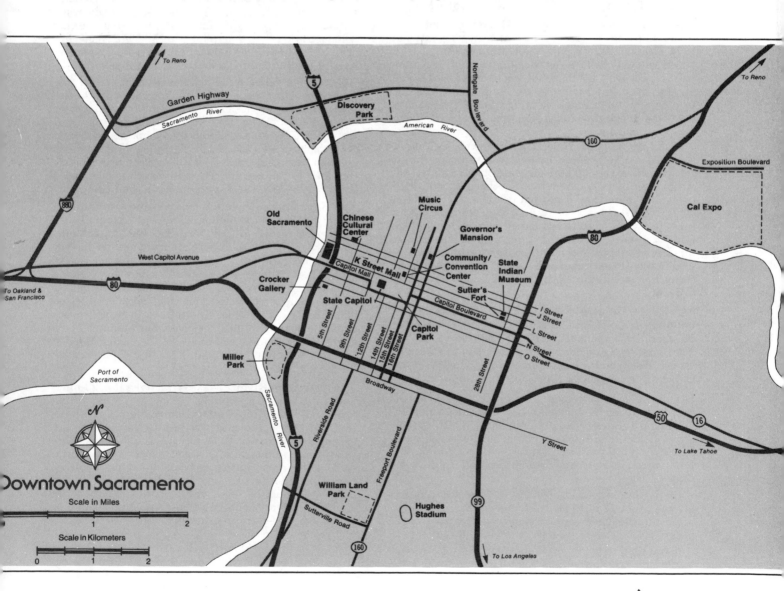

Downtown Sacramento

Scale in Miles

Scale in Kilometers

Fargo. The California Supreme Court convened here from 1855 to 1869. Inside you'll find museums commemorating these famous tenants as well as an early telegraph display. The museum is open daily from 10 A.M. to 5 P.M.; admission is free.

Across the street is the handsome statue of horse and rider memorializing the Pony Express, whose intrepid men rushed mail over 2,000 miles in just 10 days. Begun in 1860, the system lasted only 18 months, until the first telegraph message was received in 1861.

Old Sacramento Schoolhouse (Front and L Streets) evokes the atmosphere found in schools of the 1800s, with antiques and reproductions of the period. Bells call special classes to order between 10 A.M. and 4:30 P.M. Monday through Saturday, noon to 4:30 P.M. on Sunday; visitors are welcome.

Big Four Building, originally located in the path of Interstate 5, is now at I Street between Front and 2nd streets. One-time headquarters for the Central Pacific Railroad, the building now stands in tribute to the railroad's "big four"—Stanford, Huntington, Hopkins, and Crocker (Tuesday through Sunday 10 A.M. to 5 P.M.).

The California State Railroad Museum (Front Street between I and J streets) authentically re-creates an 1876 Central Pacific passenger station. Inside, train whistles blast, bells clang, dogs bark, and conductors yell "all aboard!" All these sounds serve as background for your recorded tour through the museum. You pick up a tour "wand" (actually a radio receiver) as you enter the depot. It explains the various exhibits and describes early railroad days.

In the railroad history section (adjacent to the passenger station), 21 restored locomotives and cars plus 46 exhibits fill up the 100,000-square-foot building. Rolling stock highlights include the Southern Pacific 4292 (weighing more than a million pounds), the luxurious *Gold Coast,* Lucius Beebe's lavishly decorated private car, the Governor Stanford steam locomotive, and the *C.P. Huntington.* In the wide screen movie theater, visitors learn the story of the 19th-century railroad era. One moderately-priced ticket admits you to the museum and the passenger station. Both are open daily from 10 A.M. to 5 P.M.

The Eagle Theatre (Front and J streets) was the first building in California to be constructed as a theater. Its doors first opened in 1849. Destroyed by flood in 1850, the wood and canvas structure has now been restored. Weekend evenings you can enjoy live plays and rollicking musicals of the Gold Rush era.

Dixieland jazz resounds through the streets of Old Sacramento each Memorial Day weekend when the Dixieland Jubilee begins. Sacramento's jubilee is rated tops by Dixieland buffs for its musical excellence and its growing international scope. Bands come from England, Japan, Canada, and Scotland, as well as the United States.

Festivities begin at noon on Friday and continue around the clock until early Monday afternoon. Crowds are not a problem since jazz rings out in as many as 25 different locations at once throughout Old Sacramento.

If you plan to go, buy tickets before May 15. Accommodations are tight so it's a good idea to make hotel and motel reservations well in advance. For more information on the festival and accommodations, write to the Sacramento Convention and Visitors Bureau, 1311 "I" Street, Sacramento, CA 95814.

Family fun

With a variety of outdoor activities to choose from, family outings are popular. Biking, hiking, boating, and picnicking are all within minutes from downtown.

William Land Park on Freeport Boulevard (State Highway 160 and Sutterville Road) in the southern part of the city is so vast it seldom seems crowded. It has pools, gardens, a 9-hole golf course, ball diamonds, picnic grounds, and a grove of Japanese flowering cherry trees among its 236 landscaped acres. Children's favorites include the large zoo, with fine reptile and feline collections, Fairytale Town (with child-size reproductions of fairy tale themes), kiddie rides in the amusement area, and pony rides nearby.

Gibson Ranch County Park, just north of Sacramento, is a child's delight. Youngsters can see domestic animals, peacocks, and pheasants or watch milking demonstrations. An 8-acre lake stocked with fish (children under 16 need no fishing license) makes a natural habitat for ducks, mudhens, geese, and muskrats.

One of the ranch buildings houses a historical museum displaying western objects. You can watch horses being shod in a blacksmith shop. Stables rent horses and ponies, offer hayrides, and provide riding lessons. On the 245 acres, you'll find many hiking trails and picnic spots. To reach the park, follow Watt Avenue north to Elverta Road. Turn left onto Elverta and follow this road to the entrance. Gibson Ranch is open daily from 7 A.M. to dusk. There's no admission charge.

The Sacramento Science Center and Junior Museum (3615 Auburn Boulevard at Watt Avenue), now in its new facility in northern Sacramento, contains many interesting displays of California natural history and has an excellent collection of live animals native to the area. Children will especially enjoy the weekend and holiday program, "Playtime with the Animals," when critters can be taken from their cages to be petted and touched. They'll also find it hard to resist the unusual library that lends not books but animals. For a slight admission fee, you can visit the center Monday through Saturday from 9:30 A.M. to 5 P.M., Sunday from noon to 5.

The American River Parkway, an irregular, 23-mile-long strip of green, stretches along the banks of the American River from Nimbus Dam to the stream's junction with the Sacramento River. Along the parkway are several county parks: C. M. Goethe County Park offers hiking and riding trails; Discovery Park, at the confluence of the rivers, provides boat launching facilities; and Ancil Hoffman County Park has an 18-hole golf course. Picnicking sites are plentiful. Fishing the American River yields catches of shad, steelhead, or salmon. Group float trips are popular with kayakers and rafters.

Winding its way along the river bank is the American River Bicycle Trail, which eventually will run the en-

"IT'S GOLD!" James Marshall exclaims to a pleased Captain Sutter in Gold Discovery Room, one of 38 exhibits at Sacramento's Sutter's Fort.

tire 30-plus miles from Discovery Park to Folsom Lake. For now, more than 20 paved miles are open, with picnic tables, restrooms, and other facilities along the way.

Nuts are the theme for two family fun destinations. At the California Almond Growers Exchange (18th and C streets), you can tour and taste in the world's largest almond "factory," open weekdays from 8 A.M. to 5:30 P.M., Saturday from 10 to 4. Plant tours start at 10 A.M., 1 and 2 P.M., weekdays only. Admission is free.

Thirty miles west of Sacramento is the Nut Tree, a restaurant *cum* amusement park, complete with train and airport—a popular fly-in destination for pilots. It all started with a single black walnut tree planted in 1860 to shade passers-by on the Emigrant Trail.

Folsom is fun. Shops on gas-lighted Sutter Street intrigue visitors. The structures are a mixture of old and new, set in western surroundings. Tourists flock to the Flea Fair in April and Peddler's Fair in October. In addition, famous Folsom Prison has a craft shop you may visit. Free area tourist guides are available in the old Southern Pacific Depot. Folsom is 15 miles northeast of Sacramento, off U.S. 50.

North of Sacramento

The major highways running north of Sacramento are Interstate 5 and State 99. Both leave from Sacramento, with Interstate 5 taking a more westerly course. In Red Bluff the highways converge, and Interstate 5 continues into Oregon. The Sacramento River runs between the two highways; the Feather parallels State 99.

The quiet towns and countryside along the banks of the Sacramento River seem to have changed little since the early 1900s. To discover the surrounding area, you'll have to stray slightly from Interstate 5.

Spring is a good time to drive State Highway 45—a two-lane, lightly traveled back road that follows the Sacramento's meanderings. Then the tall cottonwoods along the river have leafed out, fruit orchards are in bloom, crops have been planted, and summer's heat hasn't yet descended on the valley.

To reach State 45 if you're coming from San Francisco on Interstate 80, turn north at Davis on State Highway 113 and drive 22 miles to Knight's Landing. From Sacramento, take Interstate 5 to Woodland (home of some turn-of-the-century architectural gems) and then head north on State 113.

In Knight's Landing—a small river community somewhat reminiscent of towns along Mark Twain's Mississippi—turn left on Fourth Street, a narrow levee road running along the south bank of the river. Fourth Street soon joins State 45, which angles northwest across open farmland. Notice the rice "checks"—flooded areas of land surrounded by low levees.

Past Sycamore, turn east on State Highway 20, across a narrow swing bridge, to visit Meridian. Poke around the quiet, shaded streets. Near the river there's a small grocery store with ancient floors that creak, a lazy paddle fan above the door, and a selection of ice cream bars for a hot day. After you cross back over the river, Colusa is 5 miles north. State 45 continues as far as Hamilton City (between Chico and Orland). The only cable ferry left on the Sacramento River operates at Princeton, north of Colusa on State 45.

Colusa National Wildlife Refuge, 3 miles southwest of Colusa on State 20, is one of four Sacramento Valley refuges providing a winter home for millions of migratory wildfowl. You can pick up guide-yourself tour booklets at refuge headquarters. The area is open from dawn to dusk.

Gray Lodge Wildlife Area, just west of Gridley and 65 miles north of Sacramento near State 99, is one of the best places to watch the massive late autumn and winter migrations of ducks and geese from the Yukon, Saskatchewan, and British Columbia breeding grounds. Aquatic plants and cereal crops are grown on the 6,800-acre state reserve to entice wildfowl away from feasting in surrounding private fields. One portion of the reserve is a wildlife sanctuary; on a larger section, hunting is permitted during the season. You must obtain a pass before driving through on hunting days.

More than 200 species of birds frequent the reserve. The wildlife area is open daily during daylight hours. At the area headquarters is a small museum.

Up the Sacramento River

Upstream from Sacramento as far as Colusa, the Sacramento is a river of commerce, though the commercial traffic it bears today (mostly tugs and oil barges) is insignificant compared to that of the past. Remnants of yesteryear are visible along the river: occasionally you'll see half-rotting wharves through the cottonwoods and willows that mark the sites of forgotten towns. The tall piers where steamers tied up have been replaced by long floats for pleasure boating and fishing.

Swimming and water-skiing are possible anywhere along the Sacramento—the farther you are from Shasta Dam, the warmer the water. Colusa is a popular water-skiing center, with public floats and a jumping ramp.

The Colusa-Sacramento River State Recreation Area, a delightful, 67-acre oasis on the west shore, has a launching ramp, picnic sites, sandy beach, and unimproved campsites. In summer, a 140-foot floating dock makes boat tie-up easy.

Most of the towns and fishing resorts along the river have launching facilities for trailered boats. Motorless boats are suitable only for downstream trips. Rowing or paddling against the strong current is always difficult—at some points, impossible.

Woodson Bridge State Recreation Area, bisected by the Sacramento River, is just 3 miles west of State 99 at Vina or 6 miles east of Interstate 5 at Corning. The park is an almost unspoiled example of riverbottom lands. Part of it is covered with oaks; a flood plain section is densely wooded with willows, cottonwoods, and sycamores. In the park you can swim, boat, hike, and camp. Fishing is excellent.

In Chico, you'll find the most impressive and unexpected park in the whole valley. The green excitement starts downtown with the campus of the California State University at Chico and the grounds of the colonial mansion of town founder John Bidwell. Then Bidwell Park winds up Chico Creek, 10 miles into the foothills. Swimming, golf, and picnicking are popular.

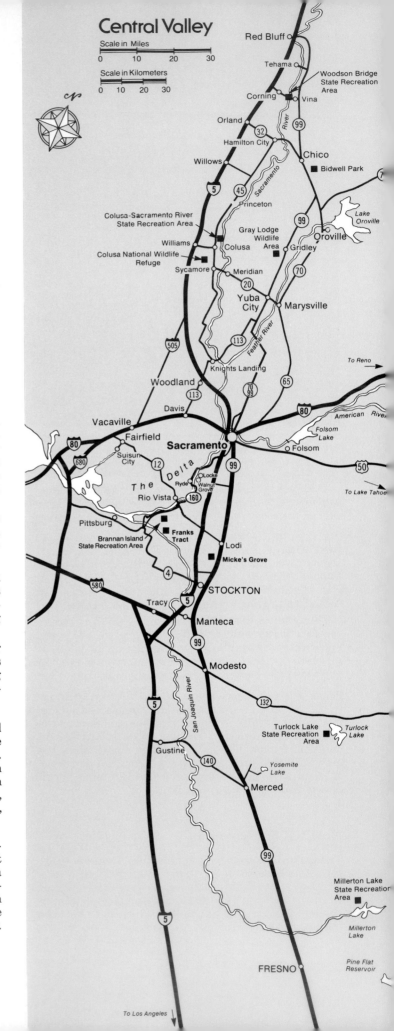

The delightful Delta

One of the most startling experiences for new visitors in the Delta region is to look across an island field of softly swaying grain and see the profile of a freighter moving silently along the levee top. Yet this is one of the Delta's most characteristic sights. Here, too, pleasure craft throw sudsy wakes across narrow sloughs and find hidden anchorages under bowing trees, where shipboard anglers throw out lines to hook lurking fish.

What is the Delta? The Sacramento-San Joaquin Delta is an irregularly bounded area of almost 740,000 acres that extends from Sacramento south a little beyond Tracy and from Pittsburg east to Stockton. About 50,000 of its acres are water, strung out in more than 700 miles of meandering channels bearing such astonishing names as Hog, Little Potato, Lost Whiskey, Little Conception, and Lookout Slough.

Once a great inland everglade densely forested with stands of valley oak and bull pine, the area was devoured by the furnaces of old river boats. Denuded expanses of mud that remained were later transformed into levee-rimmed islands (many still called tracts) that produced fortunes in asparagus and fruits for Delta farmers.

The first "resorts" in this area were farmhouses that just happened to have a boat or two for rent. After reports of excellent fishing began to spread, small, makeshift fishing camps sprang up along levee roads. Recreational fishing and boating became big business, and resort marinas replaced small fishing camps.

As you drive between Sacramento and Manteca on State 99, you're never more than 10 or 15 miles east of the Delta region, but you hardly know it's there. Until now, major highways have circumvented it entirely; however, Interstate 5 now crosses the heart of the Delta.

If you take the John A. Nejedly Bridge across the San Joaquin River to the scenic Delta Highway (State 160), you travel 45 miles along the meandering Sacramento River, skirting levees, drawbridges, and tiny Delta towns. It's a more scenic route to Sacramento from the Bay Area.

Cruises from Sacramento and Stockton let you tour the Delta and some of its old river ports. Trips are most popular during the spring months. Exploration Cruise Lines (1500 Metropolitan Park Building, Seattle, WA 98101) offers several 3-night, round-trip cruises from San Francisco to Sacramento and Stockton, with side-trips to Sausalito, Lodi, and Locke.

Cruise the Delta's rivers in anything from a simple fishing skiff to a deluxe houseboat. You don't have to be a boat owner to enjoy cruising on the Delta—more than a hundred marinas, resorts, harbors, and fishing camps rent boats. You'll find the rivers' waters also offer fine swimming, water-skiing, and fishing.

"Floating motels" range from small, nonpowered barges to luxurious, well-appointed floating homes (with electricity, running water, complete kitchens, and, in some cases, bathrooms) that sleep six or more people. Rental for one of these large, better-appointed houseboats runs

around $750 a week. However, rates vary according to the number of persons aboard and the season.

The remainder of the Delta rental fleet is an assortment of cruisers, ski boats, sailboats, and miscellaneous small craft.

There's not much chance of getting seriously lost in the Delta, but it is easy to become temporarily confused. A good map, marine chart, or guide book is essential for the newcomer. The basic guide to navigation in the Delta region is Chart 5527SC (San Joaquin River). For the chart, write to the Distribution Division (C44), National Ocean Survey, Riverdale, MD 20840. Chart 5528SC is a navigation guide to the Sacramento River from Andrus Island to Sacramento, including the northern reaches of the Delta. These charts indicate channel depths, bridge and overhead cable clearances, channel markers, and various hazards to navigation.

Though commercial traffic is found throughout the Delta, there are only two main deep-water channels. Pleasure craft are required to yield right of way to ships navigating these confined channels. For free pamphlets on California boating regulations and water safety, write to Commanding Officer (B), 12th Coast Guard District Office, 630 Sansome Street, San Francisco, CA 94126.

Swimming and water-skiing along the Delta's waterways are popular, despite the rather sluggish nature of the water. Considerate water-skiers avoid quiet anchorages where people are fishing.

Fishing is an all-year activity in the Delta, but spring is a peak season for one of the Delta's most sought-after game fish—the striped bass. Salmon and steelhead pass through the Delta on their fall migration up the Sacramento River, but the Delta itself seldom presents the ideal water conditions for trout fishing.

Most of the resort operators in the Delta have been there a long time and can guide you to the best fishing holes.

Sightseeing along the Delta can reap rewards. You can buy fresh produce at the roadside stands and pack a picnic to Brannan Island State Recreation Area (5 miles north of the Nejedly Bridge). Poke around small riverfront communities like Walnut Grove, Freeport, Locke, and Ryde. Here discover small cafés, asleep during the week, but roaring on a Saturday night.

Locke, a ramshackle Chinese community that may someday become a historic park (the state is making a study), is worth a visit. It's on River Road just north of Walnut Grove on the east side of the river. Its quaint two-story buildings rise only one story above the levee.

South of Walnut Grove, the small town of Ryde (population 60, elevation 1), is one of the few Delta towns offering overnight accommodations. Once a notorious hotel and speakeasy during Prohibition, the town's only hotel now re-creates the 1920s atmosphere while offering food, accommodations, and entertainment.

Accommodations in the Delta are not plentiful, but you'll find modern motels lying along the edge of the Delta, and some hotels in the towns along the Sacramento River. A few of the resort marinas offer housekeeping cabins or small campgrounds. Brannan Island

OPULENT RIVER MANSION (above) in fertile Central Valley is surrounded by pear orchards. German banker Louis Meyers built 58-room architectural extravaganza in 1917.

SLEEK SPEEDBOAT ZIPS symmetrical slalomers (right) around Delta waterway. Central Valley's popular aquatic arena is favorite spot for houseboating, water-skiing, fishing, swimming.

State Recreation Area (the only developed public campground in the Delta) has a 100-unit campground with room for trailers. Franks Tract Recreation Area, reached only by boat, is mostly underwater. There is a boat-in campground, but walk-around facilities are limited to a small dock, two picnic tables, and toilets.

Most of the larger resorts operate snack bars, and you'll find a few isolated cafés. The seasoned Delta sailor, though, brings provisions because stores are far apart and difficult to find.

The San Joaquin Valley

South of Sacramento the Central Valley follows the course of the San Joaquin River, which flows northward to meet the Sacramento. Agricultural development came later in this part of the valley. State 99 and Interstate 5 are the main routes south of Sacramento; Stockton and Fresno are among the largest valley cities.

The Lodi and Fresno areas are famed for their sweet appetizer and dessert wines. Long, warm summers give grapes their maximum sugar content. About a half-dozen wineries and tasting rooms are open to visitors in the Lodi area, home of the table wine pressed from the Tokay grape. Fresno, hub of the other wine district, also has wineries welcoming visitors. For a listing of wineries open for touring, write the Wine Institute, 165 Post Street, San Francisco, CA 94108, or consult the *Sunset* book *Guide to California's Wine Country.*

Stockton: A port city

Stockton was a booming mining town in the 1850s; today, it's an important port city delivering agricultural and manufactured goods to the San Francisco Bay Area by way of a 76-mile channel. Docks on the west edge of downtown Stockton serve around 700 cargo vessels a year. You can get out on the water on a cruise on the *Matthew McKinley* paddlewheeler (Waterfront Yacht Harbor, Dock A). The campus of the University of the Pacific, at Pacific Avenue and Stadium Drive, has ivy-covered Gothic buildings surrounded by expansive lawns and tall shade trees.

Victory Park, at North Pershing Avenue and Acacia Street, offers picnic tables under lofty trees, as well as playground equipment, a duck pond, open spaces, and a museum. In the Pioneer Museum and Haggin Galleries, you'll find an art collection strong in 19th century French and American paintings and usually a traveling or local art show. Several rooms depict Indian and pioneer life in the valley. Admission is free; hours are 1:30 to 5 P.M. Tuesday through Sunday.

Pixie Woods, in Louis Park 2 miles west of Stockton, is a children's fantasyland playground with dragons to climb on and a giraffe to slide down. Hours from mid-June to mid-September are 11 A.M. to 6 P.M. Wednesday through Friday, noon to 7 P.M. Saturday and Sunday; closed Monday and Tuesday. The park closes earlier the rest of the year.

Fresno's fresh face

Downtown Fresno radiates a parklike atmosphere. In the central business district—Fulton Street from Inyo to Tuolumne streets—you can stroll through a mall embellished with trees, flowers, fountains, and sculpture. Fresno's Museum of Art, History, and Science (1555 Van Ness Avenue), in the old *Fresno Bee* newspaper building, is worth a stop.

A pioneer nurseryman planted verdant Roeding Park with hundreds of trees, including lots of bark-shedding eucalyptus. A 157-acre oasis, it's great for a picnic; children can enjoy a zoo, amusement area, and boat rides.

Seven miles west of Fresno, at 7160 West Eucalyptus Avenue, is the Edwardian mansion and estate of wealthy land developer M. Theo Kearney; it's open to afternoon tours Thursday through Sunday.

Stops along the way

Often it's much easier, especially with children, to pack a picnic lunch on a long, hot trip. Even a stop to stretch your legs will be more pleasant if you know where to go. Here is a list of parks or stops to enrich your trip:

Lodi Lake, a big, tree-lined recreation spot on the north side of Lodi, offers boating, swimming, and picnicking.

Micke's Grove Park & Zoo, 5 miles south of Lodi and a mile west of State 99 by way of Armstrong Road, also contains an historical museum.

Caswell Memorial State Park, 16 miles south of Stockton and about 5 miles west of State 99, provides a cool place to picnic in a 258-acre park, 90 acres of which remain a primitive area.

Miller Ranch has an impressive collection of antique vehicles (farm machinery, horse-drawn vehicles, bicycles, tractors, and automobiles). The privately owned ranch, 10 miles east of Modesto at 9425 Yosemite Boulevard, also has antique household items, a general store, blacksmith shop, and old-time barbershop.

Turlock Lake State Recreation Area campsites are along the Tuolumne River; picnicking is on the lake. River fishing is good; you can also swim there during low-water season. On the lake side are swimming beaches, a water-ski beach, a boat harbor, and launching ramps. The park is 23 miles east of Modesto on State Highway 132.

Three state parks around Merced offer picnicking, swimming, and fishing alongside rivers. The first two have campsites: McConnel Park (a few miles east of State 99 on the south shore of the Merced River); George J. Hatfield Park (5 miles east of Newman on the San Joaquin River); and Fremont Ford Park (between Merced and Gustine on State Highway 140).

Seven miles northeast of Merced, just up into the hills, 400-acre Yosemite Lake is popular for boating, swimming, and shoreline picnicking

Millerton Lake, 22 miles north of Fresno, has campgrounds at the north shore (7 miles north of Friant) and boat and motor rentals on the south bay.

Index

Sunset
Southern California
TRAVEL GUIDE

By the Editors of Sunset Books
and Sunset Magazine

Lane Publishing Co. • Menlo Park, California

Hours, admission fees, prices, telephone numbers, and highway designations in this book are accurate as of the time this edition went to press.

Maps have been provided in each chapter for the special purpose of highlighting significant regions, routes, or attractions in the area. Check automobile clubs, insurance agencies, and chambers of commerce or visitors bureaus in major cities for detailed maps of Southern California.

Edited by Barbara J. Braasch

Design: Cynthia Hanson

Cartography: Ted Martine

Illustrations: Susan Jaekel

Cover: Excursion boat passes venerable Balboa Pavilion in Newport Beach. Photographed by Gerald R. Fredrick.

Thanks...

to the many people and organizations who assisted in the preparation of this travel guide. Special appreciation goes to the Greater Los Angeles Visitors and Convention Bureau, and to other city and county visitors bureaus and chambers of commerce throughout the area.

Photographers

William Aplin: 118 top. **Craig Aurness:** 50 bottom right. **Barbara Braasch:** 67 bottom. **Glenn Christiansen:** 19 top left and right, 55 bottom, 70, 78, 91 top, 99, 102 all. **Ed Cooper:** 91 bottom, 94, 115. **Disneyland:** 50 top right. **James H. Flanagan:** 83. **Gerald R. Fredrick:** 6 top right and bottom, 19 bottom, 22 bottom, 39 top, 47, 63. **Leland Y. Lee:** 42 bottom. **Martin Litton:** 118 bottom. **Long Beach Area Convention and Visitors Council:** 39 bottom. **Marie Mainz:** 14 top. **Steve W. Marley:** 107 bottom, 110. **MGM/Six Flags Movieland:** 50 left. **Josef Muench:** 86. **Norman A. Plate:** 126 all. **Bill Reid:** 3. **Sea World:** 75 top. **Jeffrey Stanton:** 11, 30, 55 top, 58, 75 bottom, 107 top. **Ted Streshinsky:** 34 all, 42 top. **Bill Tara:** 22 top. **Tom Tracy:** 6 top left, 14 bottom. **Mark Uhler:** 67 top. **Universal Studios:** 27 bottom right. **Robert Wenkam:** 27 top, 123.

Sunset Books
    Editor, David E. Clark
    Managing Editor, Elizabeth L. Hogan

Sixth printing April 1987
(Updated 1986)

Contents

Mission San Diego de Alcala

Special Features

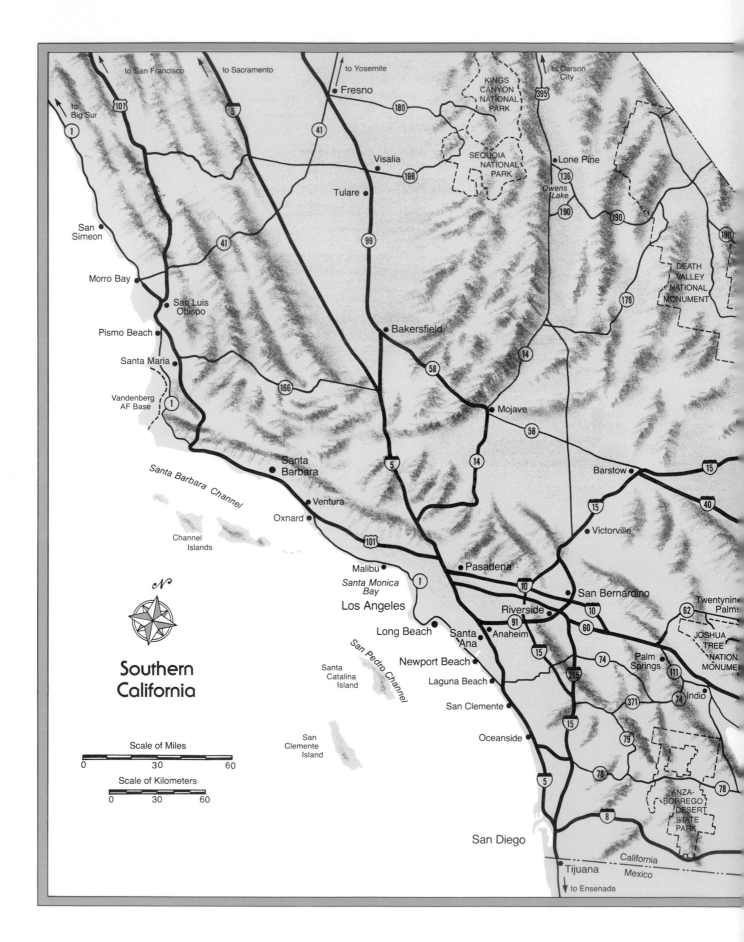

Southern
California

Scale of Miles

0   30   60

Scale of Kilometers

0   30   60

to San Francisco   to Sacramento   to Yosemite   to Carson City

Fresno

KINGS
CANYON
NATIONAL
PARK

to
Big Sur

Visalia

SEQUOIA
NATIONAL
PARK

Lone Pine

Owens
Lake

San
Simeon

Tulare

Morro Bay

DEATH
VALLEY
NATIONAL
MONUMENT

San Luis
Obispo

Bakersfield

Pismo Beach

Santa Maria

Mojave

Vandenberg
AF Base

Santa
Barbara

Barstow

Ventura

Oxnard

Victorville

Channel
Islands

Malibu

Pasadena

San Bernardino

Santa Monica
Bay

Los Angeles

Riverside

Twentynine
Palms

Long Beach

Santa
Ana

Anaheim

JOSHUA
TREE
NATIONAL
MONUMENT

Santa
Catalina
Island

Newport Beach

Palm
Springs

Laguna Beach

Indio

San
Clemente
Island

San Clemente

Oceanside

ANZA-
BORREGO
DESERT
STATE
PARK

San Diego

California

Tijuana

Mexico

to Ensenada

Areas of Interest

Hearst Castle—William Randolph Hearst's castlelike "ranch" above San Simeon, now a State Historic Monument; tours give a look at mansion's interior

San Joaquin Valley—southern half of California's Central Valley (state's major producer of cotton, grapes, rice, other hot-weather crops); Bakersfield, one of largest cities, is Basque center

Sequoia & Kings Canyon National Parks—end-to-end parks along Sierra Nevada ridge contain massive giant sequoias and Mt. Whitney, highest peak in the contiguous United States

Death Valley National Monument—legendary desert valley contains land of extremes, contrasts, and surprises: lowest point in Western Hemisphere, dramatic overlooks, rainbow-hued canyons, ghost towns, Scotty's Castle

Santa Barbara—red-tiled roofs and Spanish architecture add to beautiful city setting; drives from here take you up or down the coast on El Camino Real, or into back-country communities: Ojai Valley, Solvang

Los Angeles—West Coast's largest city; county encompasses some of the Southland's most fascinating inland cities (Hollywood, Beverly Hills, Westwood, Pasadena), the San Fernando Valley, plus back door mountains, front door beaches

Orange County—manmade amusement center for Southern California (Disneyland, Knott's Berry Farm, Movieland, and other attractions); great beach communities to intrigue surfers, snorkelers, sunbathers, shoppers, and fishermen

Catalina Island—Mediterranean-style isle just a helicopter, boat, or plane ride from the California coast; scenic drives and tours from town of Avalon; glass-bottom and flying-fish boat trips; snorkeler's and diver's paradise

Palm Springs—desert resort capital offers sunshine, sports, and easy access up mountain face by tram or into palm-filled canyons on foot or horseback; nearby are the Salton Sea, Joshua Tree National Monument, Anza-Borrego Desert State Park, date-studded Coachella Valley, and the Colorado River recreation area

Joshua Tree National Monument—high and low desert terrain protected in desert sanctuary; park headquarters at Twentynine Palms; dramatic wildflower show in springtime

San Diego—California's oldest city retains much of her Spanish heritage (Old Town, Cabrillo Monument, Presidio Hill, mission) in a lovely seaside setting; water sports and shows attract visitors, as do historic Balboa Park and the famous zoo; jumping-off spot for coastal and back-country trips plus jaunts across the Mexican border

Anza-Borrego Desert State Park—untamed desert marks one of California's last frontiers; Borrego Springs resort area provides base for exploring; unlimited camping

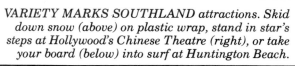
VARIETY MARKS SOUTHLAND attractions. Skid down snow (above) on plastic wrap, stand in star's steps at Hollywood's Chinese Theatre (right), or take your board (below) into surf at Huntington Beach.

Why visit Southern California? One reason might be that no other single area offers the environmental diversity, natural and manmade attractions, or social and cultural achievements that characterize this region. You could vacation here for a year without running out of exciting things to see and do.

Land of Variety

Nearly a century ago a massive advertising campaign by the Southern Pacific and Santa Fe railroads attracted thousands of settlers here with visions of swimming in the blue Pacific, picking oranges from acres of fruit-filled groves, and playing in the snow of nearby mountains—all in one day. It's still possible.

Variety in the Southland does not stop there. Large cities (each different in character) add overlays to the landscape between ocean and mountains, and desert meets the mountains at their north and east faces. In Death Valley, Badwater is 282 feet below sea level, the lowest point in the Western Hemisphere. Across the valley in the Sierra Nevada, Mount Whitney (14,495 feet) is the nation's highest point outside of Alaska.

Land of Sunshine

Southern California's biggest asset is its dry, subtropical climate—the only one in the United States. Very little rain, low humidity, little variation in temperature, and lots of sun make it possible to enjoy casual outdoor living the year around. Sunbathing around a back yard pool is in the best Southern California tradition.

Known around the country as the queen of desert resorts, Palm Springs offers most of the Southland's year-round outdoor recreational possibilities—golfing, tennis, swimming, horseback riding, biking, and hiking. At nearby Salton Sea you'll find boating and fishing.

On Southern California's beaches, bronzed beauties dot the sand, while surfers "hang ten," trying to avoid a wipeout. Each beach has its own character—Malibu has long been known as a playground for movie stars; Santa Monica is a show place for "muscle men"; Long Beach is home port for the ocean liner *Queen Mary* and the world's largest wooden airplane, the "Spruce Goose"; Newport hosts wildly colored sailboats and offers intriguing shoreside shopping; Laguna Beach inspires artists; San Diego's primary attraction is its beautiful harbor and manmade bay.

Land of Casual Culture

Mellowed by the fine weather, Southern Californians have adopted a new life style, becoming trend-setters in food, fashion, architecture, and gardening. In this capital of casual living, it's possible to enter a fine restaurant without a tie, and a dinner invitation usually means an outdoor barbecue on a garden patio.

(Continued on page 8)

In this chapter we present a sampling of Southern California's myriad attractions and define the boundaries of the Southland. (Also see map on pages 4 and 5.) Any time is the time to visit, and there is always something to see and do. Even residents may find a few "back yard" discoveries.

Introduction

. . . Continued from page 7

However, this region is a center of culture. You can discover some of the world's finest art museums, theaters, and music centers here. Outdoor pageants and "under-the-stars" performances are popular. In summertime, the Universal Amphitheatre provides a showcase for the biggest names in contemporary music. At Hollywood Bowl, the famed Los Angeles Philharmonic performs, while across the Hollywood Hills top-name entertainers draw crowds for evening concerts at the Greek Theatre. In San Diego you'll find performances in Balboa Park; at Hemet you can see the Ramona Pageant in a natural outdoor amphitheater; Santa Barbara offers song and dance spectacles at the Mission Bowl.

Land of Entertainment

Southern California sets the pace for other regions in family fun and entertainment. You'll find more man-made amusement parks and attractions here than anywhere else in the world—all within a few miles of downtown Los Angeles. With a magical wand, that great creative genius, Walt Disney, created the first and foremost of theme parks: Disneyland. Today, Disneyland stands amid a fantasyland of whimsical adventures and great amusement parks.

Whether your idea of adventure is a high-speed ride on Space Mountain, a stomach-jerking stop at the top of Montezooma's Revenge, a log-jamming water-flume run, jumping whales, a mock shark attack, or an eye-to-eye confrontation with a lion—you'll find it in Southern California.

Celebrity-hunting is a big game in Southern California. Many people come to the area hoping to rub elbows with movie and television stars. One of our special features—*Hunting for Celebrities*, page 28—gives some hints on the best places to "star-gaze."

Another special feature—*World of Entertainment*, page 29—tells you how to get tickets to television shows and which studios you can tour; in short, it's an introduction to the land of illusion.

Boundaries of a Land

Where is Southern California? Though actual boundaries do not exist, the area known as Southern California is nevertheless a real place—one defined as much by personality as by geography.

Our travel guide to Southern California covers a generous scope, stretching north to the San Joaquin Valley and Sequoia and Kings Canyon National Parks, and extending south across the Mexican border. In the east we draw the boundary a bit above Death Valley, taking in both Inyo and Mono counties, major recreation targets for Southland residents. Along the coast we inch north above San Luis Obispo (halfway between Los Angeles and San Francisco) to Morro Bay and San Simeon. The area north of this east-west line is described in the *Sunset* book *Travel Guide to Northern California*.

Beginning with the sprawling Los Angeles region, this book includes the ocean world and coastal resort towns, valleys fronting upon major mountain ranges, peaceful rolling hills with quiet villages and mission memories, desert resorts and wilderness, the winding Colorado River that divides Southern California and Arizona, and the grand southern section of the Sierra Nevada.

In addition to the general map of Southern California, other maps scattered throughout the chapters focus on local points of interest. Detailed street maps of downtown Los Angeles and Santa Barbara, with a general map of sprawling San Diego, aid in planning walking or driving tours. Freeways in the L.A. area are clearly marked to help motorists find their way around.

With each map in the book, a "Points of Interest" box keys some of the interesting attractions to their locations in that region. Many are famous, others not so well known. Intended only as suggestions, these attractions are explained more fully in the text.

When to visit

Any time of the year is good somewhere in the Southland. Summertime is more crowded, the desert is quite hot, and it's likely to be "smog season" around Los Angeles and environs. This is the time to enjoy the miles of white sandy beaches, dotted wih dramatic surfing areas, marinas, harbors, and noted coastal towns—Santa Barbara, Malibu, Santa Monica, Newport, Laguna Beach, La Jolla, and San Diego.

Desert parks and resorts are the goal of winter sun-seekers, while skiers head for the mountains.

Spring and fall provide the region's mildest weather and the choice seasons for most of the fairs and festivals. (For a calendar of monthly events, write the Greater Los Angeles Visitors and Convention Bureau, 505 S. Flower Street, Los Angeles, CA 90071.) Wildflowers carpet desert and higher elevations beginning in mid-February and lasting through June.

Since the sun season lasts all year, accommodations are not priced for a three-month "tourist season." Vacationers will find that dollars will stretch further in Southern California because many of its best-known features are free.

What to see

Entertainment centers are a part of the Southern California experience. Such magic words as "Hollywood" and "Rose Bowl" and "Sunset Boulevard" originated here. But don't overlook the natural attractions. Wilderness areas remain as they have for centuries—mountain peaks reach high above the roads and energies of man, lovely waterfall canyons elude all but the most probing eye, and the desert stretches for miles in sand and silence.

The Spaniards left their mark in California. Many towns grew up around the missions founded by Father Serra. A walk through San Diego's Old Town, Pueblo de Los Angeles, or the streets of Santa Barbara provides insight into the Spanish era's history and romance.

Southern California has something for everyone: from Marineland to missions; from the Hollywood Bowl concerts under the stars to the stars of Hollywood; from Sea World to sequoias.

How to get around

No matter how you arrive in Southern California (unless you drive your own car), you'll need some form of transportation to reach the many attractions in and around the major cities.

Never mind those hair-raising tales of L.A.'s freeway system. If you avoid the freeways at peak periods—7 to 9 A.M. and 4 to 6 P.M. weekdays—you will have no problem. Study a detailed map in advance, and stay in your own lane!

The Southern California Rapid Transit District operates a good bus system in Los Angeles, including a minibus service among points of interest in the downtown area. In Orange County, the Fun Bus whisks you to major attractions. From San Diego, you can take the Tijuana Trolley to the border city of Tijuana and back. Taxi service is good, but expensive; you'll find plenty of car rental agencies in each region.

Don't overlook tour facilities. In this land of multiple choices, sightseeing tours give background information and spotlight the high points of an area. They are usually good buys because they include admission prices (generally at reduced rates), where required.

Information for tourists and residents

Though this book is aimed primarily at the visitor and new resident, it includes information on possible discoveries for "back yard" vacations for those who have lived in Southern California for some time.

But if you are new to Southern California, no matter how you enter it—at its busy harbor, on its teeming freeways, or through its sprawling international airports—you'll sense immediately that this is a young and forward-looking region, a land with a well-grounded sense of the future. The past has been well protected, but not too many Southern Californians look back.

FESTIVALS & FESTIVITIES

The listings below provide a sampling of annual events and festivities of general interest to visitors. Dates change — it's advisable to check with the chambers of commerce of individual cities, or the Greater Los Angeles Visitors and Convention Bureau, 505 S. Flower Street, Los Angeles, CA 90071.

January
Palm Springs — Sled Dog Races, Aerial Tramway
Pasadena — Tournament of Roses Parade and Rose Bowl Football Game

February
Palm Springs — Bob Hope Chrysler Golf Classic and Desert Circus
Los Angeles — Chinese New Year, Chinatown; Mardi Gras, Olvera Street
Indio — National Date Festival
Kernville—Whiskey Flat Days

March
San Juan Capistrano — Fiesta de las Golondrinas (return of the swallows) at the mission
Los Angeles—International Film Festival

April
Blythe — Colorado River Country Fair
Del Mar — Jumping Frog Jamboree
Hemet — Ramona Pageant (through May)
Bakersfield—Heritage Days
Long Beach—Grand Prix

May
San Luis Obispo — La Fiesta
Bishop — Mule Days

June
Beaumont — Cherry Festival
Santa Barbara — Fishermen's Festival and Blessing of the Fleet
Ojai — Music Festival

July
Laguna Beach — Arts Festival and Pageant of the Masters (through August)
Lompoc — Flower Festival
San Diego — Mission Bay Sand Castle Contest
Del Mar—Thoroughbred Horse Racing

August
Newport Bay — Character Boat Parade
Los Angeles — Nisei Week, Little Tokyo
Long Beach—Sea Festival

September
Solvang — Danish Days
Pomona — Los Angeles County Fair
Julian — Wildflower Show

October
Borrego Springs — Desert Festival
Los Angeles — Double Ten Chinese Independence Day, Chinatown

November
Death Valley — '49er Annual Encampment
Hollywood — Santa Claus Lane Parade

December
Marina del Rey — Christmas Boat Parade
San Diego — Las Posadas, Old Town

Los Angeles

The West's largest city offers a great bill of fare for tourist and resident. Follow the steps of the Spaniards around Olvera Street in El Pueblo; enjoy star-studded performances at the Music Center; look up (or down) at L.A.'s new skyscrapers and subterranean shopping complexes; discover Griffith Park's secrets; and follow famous boulevards through Hollywood, along "The Strip," by the tar pits and Century City—all the way to the sea.

Big, bustling Los Angeles is a city in constant motion. The best overall view of the heterogeneous communities making up the metropolis of Los Angeles is from a plane, particularly at night. From nowhere else does the crisscrossing light pattern of the main street grid seem so extensive.

Sprawling inland from the Pacific Ocean over some 460 square miles, L.A. occupies as much land as the entire state of Rhode Island. The West's largest city is the focal point for one of the greatest population migrations in all recorded history. Over three million people call Los Angeles their home.

Why did they come? The Mediterranean climate was—and still is—the key. People found the year-round sun exhilarating; it stimulated the crops they planted. Citrus groves thrived; oil was discovered. Because they could operate all year, the cinema and aviation industries flourished, generating technological offspring—television and aerospace—that eventually outdistanced them.

L.A.'s genesis lives on in historic Pueblo de Los Angeles where cobblestoned streets and adobes mark its Spanish and Mexican roots. Just a few blocks away, Chinatown and Little Tokyo sweep visitors into different lands and cultures.

Architecture forms a large part of the city's heritage; it was the first major United States city to build *out* instead of *up*. Only recently have multistoried buildings changed the Los Angeles skyline.

Since the city has more cars than the entire state of New York, freeways play an important part in the Los Angeles lifestyle. Visitors find the freeway network a swift route among the multiplicity of attractions.

There's always pleasure to be found in Los Angeles. All you have to do is pin it down. You can sample the city in many ways: take in the basic natural gifts of sunshine and setting, or seek out the elaborate amusements of a city where entertainment is big business.

It takes a sense of humor to savor unpredictable, offbeat L.A. If you think museums and theaters are the measure of a city, you'll find some fine ones. But where else would you discover great art in a cemetery or look-alike replicas of once-trapped Ice Age creatures emerging from tar pits?

Getting there

Los Angeles has one of the largest and busiest airports in the country—Los Angeles International. Four other major airports in surrounding areas provide supplemental passenger service: Hollywood/Burbank, Long Beach, Ontario, and Orange County. You can make connections from one to the other by motor coach.

Within the airport, the Terminal Tram circulates every 10 minutes to all terminals. The charge is minimal for steps saved.

The city is also served by the nation's two big transcontinental bus companies (Continental Trailways and Greyhound) and by Amtrak rail service.

Settling in

First-timers and even those who haven't been to L.A. for a while may need some help in finding their way around

ON A CLEAR DAY, snow-capped San Gabriel range provides spectacular backdrop for city skyscrapers.

this large, ever-changing city. A few words of advice on touring and accommodations from those who know the area will make your visit much more enjoyable. The Greater Los Angeles Visitors and Convention Bureau offices at 505 S. Flower Street (Arco Plaza, Level B), Los Angeles, CA 90071, and 6801 Hollywood Boulevard (corner Hollywood and Highland), Los Angeles, CA 90028, offer free downtown and freeway maps, booklets, and current-event listings. (Some brochures are also available in the Tom Bradley International Terminal at L.A. International Airport.)

The Bureau's downtown office is open from 8 A.M. to 5 P.M., 7 days a week. Visit the Hollywood office weekdays between 9 A.M. and 4 P.M. (6 P.M. on Friday). The bureau's 24-hour Welcome Line phone number is (213) 628-5857.

Maps of greater L.A. are becoming more difficult to obtain; there may be a slight charge if you do find one. Motorists should come prepared with automobile club or Thomas Bros. maps.

Moving around

Once in Los Angeles, you can take guided bus tours of most major attractions. But if you plan any ambitious sightseeing, you will need a car.

Freeways are the lifelines of the city. Opinions vary as to whether they were designed by people of vision or madmen, but, at best, they get motorists long distances in astonishingly short periods of time. The often intertwining maze of routes may seem complicated at first, but a review of the freeway map on page 21 will help to simplify your driving. Try to avoid freeways during times of peak congestion—7 to 9 A.M. and 4 to 6 P.M.—when residents are traveling to and from work.

Touring Old Los Angeles

Los Angeles started as a Spanish village, then became Mexican, and finally Yankee. Today, the once somnolent Pueblo, aging but undergoing rebirth and restoration, is the nucleus of bustling districts. Close by, you can savor the sights and sounds, foods, and goods of Mexico and early California, the Orient, and the Mediterranean, all at the Civic Center edge of downtown L.A.

Pueblo de Los Angeles and vicinity

In 1781, 11 families recruited by the provincial governor, Felipe de Neve, concluded a 7-month colonizing expedition from Sonora, Mexico, to the banks of the Los Angeles River. They marked off the lots that gave birth to the Spanish village with the tongue-tangling name *El Pueblo de Nuestra Señora la Reina de Los Angeles* (the town of Our Lady the Queen of the Angels). Restoration of L.A.'s birthplace as a 44-acre State Historic Landmark is underway.

Walking is the best way to see El Pueblo. You can join a free guided tour departing from the visitors center (130 Paseo de la Plaza) hourly from 10 A.M. to 1 P.M. Tuesday through Saturday, or pick up a free map at the center and explore on your own.

The Plaza, once the center of activity for the whole town, is now closed to traffic and remains the heart of the Pueblo. On some summer Sunday afternoons, the circular, lacy *kiosko* may be the setting for an open-air concert of Mexican and Spanish music. Colorful fiestas are held throughout the year. Stroll around the square to view the varied topiary.

Southwest of the Plaza on Main Street stand three venerable structures: Masonic Lodge (dating from 1858); Merced Theater, the city's first; and Pico House—built over a century ago, it was the grandest hotel of its day. Under the theater and the Garnier Building an amazing labyrinth of basement shops and tunnels hid Chinese merchants during a period of oppression.

North of the Plaza, structures of interest include the Avila Adobe (see below) and Victorian-fronted Sepulveda House; a Siqueiros mural adorns nearby Italian Hall.

Old Plaza Fire House, on the Plaza at Los Angeles Street, is the restored station of Engine Company No. 1, the oldest Los Angeles fire station—serving from 1884 to 1897. Inside the two-story brick building is one of the first fire engines used in the city; the horse-drawn equipment was originally built in 1892 for the Chicago Columbia Exposition. Upstairs are the firemen's living quarters. The building is open Tuesday through Friday from 10 A.M. to 3 P.M., weekends from 11 A.M. to 5 P.M.

Plaza Church was first established as a chapel for the settlers in 1784. The diminutive church was originally only 18 by 24 feet. It was finally rebuilt in 1822 with proceeds from the sale of 7 barrels of brandy from Mission San Gabriel. In 1860 heavy rains nearly ruined the adobe walls, so the front was taken down and rebuilt with brick. In recent years other changes have been made, including the rebuilding of the bell tower to blend in with the church's original architecture. The door has the classic river-of-life design.

Olvera Street, a block-long, brick-paved pedestrian lane, is the greatest single magnet in the Pueblo and possibly the West's first pedestrian shopping mall. In its 50 years of existence, Olvera Street has developed its own distinct character, both Mexican and Californian, in shops, restaurants, color, and life. Visitors come, enjoy the experience, and return; the street is a continuous pageant. And its cheerful people are its greatest attraction.

Shop for candles, leather goods, silver jewelry, pottery, and Mexican candies. Or dine on good Mexican food with background music. The more Mexican way is to eat in one of the little food *puestos* along the street.

Watch the artisans at work. You may see a piñata being formed around a clay *olla* (you can have one made to order); wrought iron being fashioned; three players performing on one marimba; and candles, leather goods, blown glass, and pottery being made. Stalls and shops open at 10 A.M.

Avila Adobe, at 10 Olvera Street, is L.A.'s oldest dwelling (dating back to about 1818). During the American occupation of El Pueblo in 1847, it served as headquarters for Kearny, Stockton, and Fremont. Now restored, the house is a showcase of California living in the 1840s.

(Continued on page 15)

12 LOS ANGELES

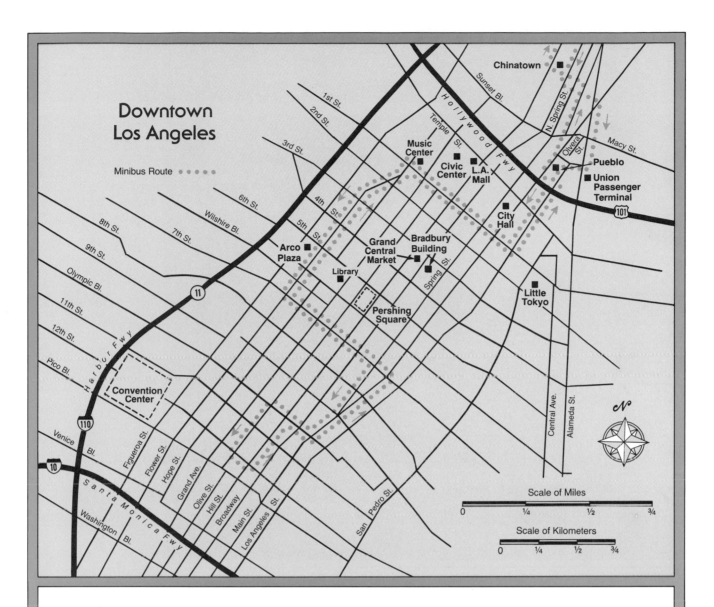

Downtown Los Angeles

Minibus Route •••••

Chinatown

1st St.
2nd St.
3rd St.
6th St.
Wilshire Bl.
8th St.
7th St.
9th St.
Olympic Bl.
11th St.
12th St.
Pico Bl.
Venice Bl.
Washington Bl.

4th St.
5th St.
Temple St.
Sunset Bl.
Macy St.

Music Center
Civic Center
L.A. Mall
City Hall
Pueblo
Union Passenger Terminal

Arco Plaza
Grand Central Market
Bradbury Building
Library
Pershing Square
Little Tokyo

Convention Center

Harbor Fwy
Santa Monica Fwy

Figueroa St.
Flower St.
Hope St.
Grand Ave.
Olive St.
Hill St.
Broadway
Main St.
Los Angeles St.
San Pedro St.
Spring St.
Central Ave.
Alameda St.
N. Spring St.
Olvera St.
Hollywood Fwy

11
110
10
101

N

Scale of Miles
0   ¼   ½   ¾

Scale of Kilometers
0   ¼   ½   ¾

Major Points of Interest

Civic Center (south of Hollywood Freeway)—panoramic city view from 27th-floor observation deck of City Hall; gardens, shops, restaurants, and Triforium in L.A. Mall around City Hall East

Pueblo de Los Angeles (north of Civic Center)—birthplace of L.A.; 19th century park restoration; Olvera Street, West's first mall with Mexican flavor

Chinatown—Little Tokyo (north and east of Civic Center)—smells, sights, and sounds of two cultures

Music Center (Grand Avenue at First Street)—L.A.'s cultural "in" place; Chandler Pavilion, Mark Taper Forum, Ahmanson Theatre

Arco Plaza (Atlantic Richfield and Bank of America twin towers)—home of Greater Los Angeles Visitors and Convention Bureau; interesting plaza sculpture and fountain; subterranean shops

Pershing Square (between Fifth and Sixth streets)—L.A.'s only downtown park; underground parking

Grand Central Market (Hill Street between Third and Fourth streets)—exotic food bazaar specializing in Mexican groceries

Bradbury Building (opposite Grand Central Market)—architectural landmark and background for movies and TV shows

DRAMATIC DESIGN marks
glittering Chandler Pavilion (above),
part of Music Center complex, and
Double Ascension sculpture fountain
(right) at Arco Plaza. Underneath
lies subterranean shopping complex.

. . . Continued from page 12

The interesting church on the east side of the entrance to Olvera Street is La Plaza Iglesia Metodista (Methodist Church). Built in 1929, its architecture is in the Mexican tradition. Services are conducted in Spanish.

San Antonio Winery, east of El Pueblo at 737 Lamar Street, is another historic site. The spot where it stands was once in the heart of Old Town's vast vineyards (now completely urbanized). A visit to the last producing winery in L.A. includes a tour of bottling, aging, and tasting rooms. It's open Monday through Saturday from 8 A.M. Self-guided winery tours take about 20 minutes; picnic grounds adjoin the main cellar.

Union Passenger Terminal, one of the last great rail depots built in the United States, is approaching the half-century mark. Soaring interior spaciousness, white-stuccoed towers, arches, and passageways, and a red-tile roof make the attractive terminal at 800 N. Alameda Street (east of the Plaza) one of the city's landmarks.

You can begin a walking tour of cosmopolitan Los Angeles from this stately terminal. It is a good place to park (for a modest fee); from here you can walk to Little Tokyo, City Hall, the Plaza, and New Chinatown. Taken in that order, the round-trip walking tour is about 3 miles long. The minibus route (see page 13) follows much the same route.

Chinatown

"New" Chinatown opened in 1939 to replace the Chinatown ripped out for the Union Station. Located off North Broadway near College Street, this 2-block-long pedestrian mall has small, shop-lined lanes with names like Gin Ling, Sun Mun, and Lei Ling.

Although devoted to much the same kinds of enterprise as Olvera Street, New Chinatown has not aged as well. The emphasis here seems to lean more toward tourism, but in a few shops you can find some excellent Oriental wares. Two food markets offer a wide variety of foods, teas, and utensils; there are good Chinese restaurants. One confectionary is a deservedly popular shop.

Liveliest at night, the main mall is bright with lights and often bustling with crowds of after-dinner shoppers and sightseers. The most colorful season here is during Chinese New Year week in late winter. But special occasions throughout the year are likely to bring forth firecracker explosions and parades.

The most authentic Chinese section of the city is on North Spring Street, southeast of New Chinatown. Here you'll see Chinese markets, restaurants, a Chinese cinema, and a fascinating juxtaposition of Chinese and Spanish-language signs.

Dodger Stadium

North of Civic Center and adjacent to Elysian Park (a good place for a picnic before a game) is Dodger Stadium, home of L.A.'s first major league baseball team. The cantilevered structure has a seating capacity of 56,000. You park your car on the same level as your stadium seat. Baseball season generally runs from April to early October; for schedules, call (213) 224-1400.

Around Civic Center

The scene of much redevelopment in recent years, Los Angeles' Civic Center is separated from the Old Pueblo area to the north by the Hollywood-Santa Ana Freeway. First Street is the southern extremity, while Figueroa and San Pedro streets are the western and eastern boundaries, respectively.

City Hall

For years L.A.'s 32-story City Hall was the tallest building in Southern California; a ruling against other high-rises kept the city low-roofed until the late 1950s. Set on one side of the City Mall (probable former site of the Indian village of Yang-na, which antedated El Pueblo), the City Hall tower provides a panorama of the city on a clear day. From the observation deck on the 27th floor, you'll see Union Station to the north and, 15 miles distant, Mount Wilson.

To the northwest is Hollywood along the Santa Monica Mountains and, closer in, historic Fort Moore Hill. The beach cities along the Pacific Ocean are 16 miles to the west. To the south you'll see Los Angeles Harbor and possibly Catalina Island. The imposing peak to the northeast is Mount San Antonio. To the east and southeast are the city's industrial sections. The observation deck is open from 8 A.M. to 4 P.M. on weekdays.

The Los Angeles Mall, or City Mall, a handsomely landscaped complex of shops and restaurants, covers 2 blocks—from the Hollywood Freeway to First Street between Main and Los Angeles streets. Containing sunken gardens and subterranean parking, the mall is served by the downtown minibus.

The Los Angeles Children's Museum, within the mall at 310 N. Main Street, is designed just for children. Here they can paint and paste, dress up in costumes, and enjoy displays that invite touching and exploring. Open daily, the museum charges admission.

The Civic Center complex, a multilevel maze of buildings, shops, restaurants, gardens, sculptures, and waterfalls, is dominated by the Triforium: a 60-foot tower at Temple and Main streets that delivers music and a simultaneous light show through colored glass prisms. Performances are generally held around lunchtime or early in the evening.

The Music Center—L.A.'s cultural heart

The cultural "in" place of Los Angeles, the Music Center at First Street and Grand Avenue, is a $34.5 million complex specially designed to accommodate theatrical and musical presentations.

The Dorothy Chandler Pavilion, an elegant marble and black glass music hall, is the home of the Los Angeles Civic Light Opera and Philharmonic Orchestra. Completed in 1964, it was the first of the three-theater complex, linked on the surface by a landscaped mall and underground by a parking cavern. Acoustics are close to perfection anywhere in the 3,250-seat hall.

The pavilion provides a glittering setting for opera,

symphony, musical comedy, and dance performances. Check newspapers for current attractions. Free guided tours are available on some weekdays and Saturdays throughout the year; phone (213) 972-7483 for times and reservations.

Mark Taper Forum, intimate and innovative, is usually committed to experimental drama by the resident Center Theatre Group, lured away from its longtime U.C.L.A. home. Occasionally the 750-seat building is used for lectures, chamber music, and opera.

The building is linked to its larger companion, the Ahmanson Theatre, by a lofty colonnade that echoes the design of the Chandler Pavilion across the court.

Ahmanson Theatre, a spacious 2,000-seat auditorium, completes the triple complex of the Music Center. Dedicated to attracting first-class plays and musicals, it is operated most of the year by the Center Theatre Group.

Little Tokyo

A Japanese neighborhood bounded by Central Avenue and Los Angeles, First, and Third streets, Little Tokyo offers a bit of local color. Its redevelopment has brought new restaurants, gardens, and office buildings. Adjoining the boldly modern New Otani Hotel stands Weller Court, a collection of shops, restaurants, and plazas.

Highlighting the area's Japanese American Cultural and Community Center complex (San Pedro and Second streets) is the handsome Japan America Theatre. In addition to traditional *kabuki*, the theater presents Asian music and films, as well as Western concerts. A highly sophisticated sound system provides simultaneous English and Japanese translations of performances. JACCC Plaza, an acre of rock sculpture and fountains, fronts the theater.

During Nisei Week in early August, colorful pageantry stresses cultural achievements and traditions of ancient Japan. On the final Sunday night, the *Ondo* parade sing-songs through the streets.

Downtown Los Angeles

Los Angeles is a fine example of downtown renaissance. Height restrictions previously placed on tall buildings because of earthquake scares were removed in 1957, and the city is growing upward. Today's skyline is dominated by towering office buildings with rooftop dining, futuristic hotels, and "in-city" apartments where elegant 19th century Bunker Hill residences once stood.

At the outskirts of the downtown center area, between 11th and Pico streets off Figueroa, sprawls the heavily used Convention Center—two spacious buildings with easy access and acres of parking.

Getting around

Finding your way around the downtown area is relatively easy. Traffic isn't bad, except during weekday rush hours. A planned subway transit system to link the Convention Center, shopping centers, and the financial district with the Civic Center and El Pueblo is still in the talking stages.

Tours on the DASH minibuses show you a fair sampling of the downtown sector: the retail district, from Fourth to Eighth streets; the World Trade Center and big new-generation high-rises on Figueroa, from Seventh to Fifth; the historic Bradbury Building and Grand Central Market, near Third and Broadway; and the Music Center and monumental Civic Center, on First from Flower to Los Angeles streets. You can also visit the L.A. Mall, the Plaza and Olvera Street, Chinatown, and Little Tokyo.

Buses run at frequent intervals on a continuous loop route from 7 A.M. to 5:30 P.M. daily (until 4 P.M. Saturday) except on Sunday and holidays. Bus-stop signs indicate the route and your location; you can get a pocket-size map on board. It's quite a tour for 25 cents a ride (you'll need exact change). There's a 12-minute delay at one end of a round trip.

Walking is still a good way to see some of L.A.'s landmarks. Leave your car in one of the city's many parking lots. Or take advantage of the downtown walking tours (Saturday only) offered by the L.A. Conservancy; make reservations a week in advance by calling (213) 623-CITY. (Costs are $5.00 for adults and $2.50 for children.) Near the heart of working Los Angeles, the buildings give you a sense of history; their architectural styles reflect both the economic boom of the 1880s and the building boom of more recent years.

Spring Street, on the eastern side of your downtown exploration, was once exclusively a financial district. At 202 W. First Street, off Spring, you can tour the *Los Angeles Times*, the nation's second largest newspaper. Free guided walking tours are offered weekdays at 11:15 A.M. and 3 P.M.; children under 10 are not permitted.

Broadway, once the main retail street from Fourth to Eighth, is still bustling, and crowded—and often nerve-jangling on Sundays, when people pack the sidewalks (Spanish is heard as often as English here). The Grand Central Market, between Broadway and Hill and Third and Fourth, is a food bazaar that could exist only in a metropolis. The giant market, open from 9 A.M. to 6 P.M. daily except Sunday and holidays, displays items you may not find anywhere else in town. One stall contains 13 kinds of beans, peas, and lentils; another offers 20 varieties of tea. You can look over rare spices and chilies, rice in all grain sizes, different blends of olive oil, and all the ingredients for Mexican cookery. Many stalls have bilingual signs.

The Bradbury Building, across the street from the market at 304 Broadway, looks ordinary from the outside. Once you're inside, though, you'll see why this almost century-old structure is a city cultural-historic monument. Ornate iron railings line a five-story skylit interior; metal tracery decorates the open elevator cages. One of the prototype hydraulic elevators is still in use. Once a fashionable address for law firms, the building houses offices today. You can look around (for a fee) Monday through Saturday.

Seventh Street, west from Broadway, is still a major downtown retail street, with several large stores and shopping complexes. It was intended as a great artery to the west. But the need to grade the hill on which the

Los Angeles Hilton was built slowed its development, and Wilshire overtook it as the main line.

Hill Street, between Sixth and Seventh streets, is the sparkling center for the Jewelry District. Though the stores cater primarily to the wholesale trade, individuals can also pick up some great discounts.

Pershing Square, called Central Park until 1918, is L.A.'s only downtown park (bounded by Hill and Olive and Fifth and Sixth streets). Facing Fifth Street is a statue of Beethoven, a reminder that the park was once downtown's cultural center. You can park underneath or in nearby lots for a few dollars a day (less on Sunday). Weekdays are liveliest here; Saturday is good for shopping. Sunday morning is a good time to experience the deep canyons of downtown without crowds.

The Los Angeles Central Library, at Fifth and Hope streets, is part of the largest public library system in the nation. Built in 1926, the fortresslike structure was designed by architect Bertram Goodhue, who achieved fame as the architect of the 1915 San Diego Exposition. Inside the library are detailed ceilings, pleasant gardens, an impressive second-floor rotunda, a mural-decorated History Room, and a wealth of books. You can visit every day except Sunday and holidays; guided tours are available. The library will move into temporary quarters in late 1986 during the expansion and renovation of the existing building; call (213) 612-3356 for information.

The Wells Fargo History Museum, in the company's headquarters at Fifth and Flower, includes a Concord stagecoach in the exhibition highlighting the bank's role in the "winning of the West." The free museum is open from 9 A.M. to 4 P.M. weekdays.

The World Trade Center, between Third and Fourth streets and Flower and Figueroa, is L.A.'s international business complex. Its two-level mall contains shops, restaurants, consulates, and a foreign currency exchange facility.

The Pacific Coast Stock Exchange, between Second and Third streets across the Harbor Freeway from downtown, recently moved into new quarters at 233 S. Beaudry. From the visitors' gallery on the 12th floor, you can get a first-hand picture of what's happening on the trading floor. The gallery's hours—6:30 A.M. to 1:30 P.M. Monday through Friday—coincide with those of the New York Stock Exchange.

Plazas and shopping centers

Indoor shopping malls are at their best in the downtown area. Multitudinous stores and restaurants crowd multilevel centers, either above or below sculpture and fountain-studded plazas. Elevated walkways or under-street tunnels connect many buildings.

The Arco Plaza (connected by a footbridge across Fifth Street to the Bonaventure Hotel) is marked by a striking sculpture and pool on the street level. Underneath the twin towers of the Atlantic Richfield and Bank of America buildings lies one of America's largest subterranean shopping centers, lined with stores and restaurants and featuring fashion shows, concerts, and art exhibits on a regular basis. Here, too, you'll find the Greater Los Angeles Visitors and Convention Bureau, a Catholic chapel, and a post office.

The Broadway Plaza's two-level mall on Seventh Street, between Hope and Flower, is topped by the large Broadway flagship store and the Hyatt Regency Hotel.

At Crocker Center, between Grand and Hope and Third and Fourth streets, a three-story, glass-enclosed atrium houses shops and restaurants.

Several more centers, including the California plaza atop Bunker Hill and the Pacific Plaza (between Seventh and Eighth streets, off Figueroa), also feature department stores, shops, and restaurants.

A major new museum on Bunker Hill, the handsome red sandstone Museum of Contemporary Art (250 S. Grand Avenue) is dedicated to art and culture of the past 40 years. Its previous location, a converted warehouse at 152 N. Central Avenue dubbed the "Temporary Contemporary" remains a part of the museum complex.

A look at lodging

There's a fine choice of lodgings in downtown L.A. for travelers, conventioneers, and those who appreciate a central location. These hotels offer restaurants and night spots that attract visitors from all over the area. Some of the most impressive are listed below.

The Biltmore Hotel, across Olive Street from Pershing Square, harks back to another era. Untouched by the splendid modernization applied to the hotel's rooms and halls, the lobby is ornate in the grand manner, as stunning today as it was in 1923.

The Bonaventure Hotel, a striking, contemporary downtown inn (between Fourth and Fifth streets and Flower and Figueroa), was designed by John Portman. Its five reflecting circular towers are your first step into a 21st century experience. Around the dramatic lobby atrium are five levels of shops. A ride in a glass elevator gives a good view of downtown, as do the rooftop restaurant and revolving cocktail lounge.

The Hyatt Regency, atop the Broadway Plaza, is a prime spot for one-stop shopping and landscape viewing. Its 26th-floor restaurant revolves, offering a good look at the downtown skyline.

The Los Angeles Hilton, on Wilshire and Figueroa, was one of the city's first high-rise hotels. Its convenient location and evening entertainment are perhaps more interesting than its architecture.

The New Otani Hotel (120 S. Los Angeles Street) combines attractive public and private facilities with shops and a lovely Japanese garden. Within the hotel and nearby are many good Asian restaurants.

The Sheraton Grande (Figueroa Street, connected by pedestrian walkway to the World Trade Center) is L.A.'s newest complex of rooms, theaters, restaurants, gardens, and office buildings. You can take tea in the striking sunken lobby lounge.

South of Downtown L.A.

South and west of downtown Los Angeles lie several of the area's Olympic sports centers, two big museums, one of the country's best known universities, the international airport, and other scattered attractions. All can be reached from several freeways—the Santa Monica (Interstate Highway 10), San Diego (Interstate Highway 405), Harbor (State Highway 11), and Long Beach (State Highway 7).

Exposition Park

A meeting place for nature, ideas and experiments, history, and activity, 114-acre Exposition Park is bordered by Exposition Boulevard, Figueroa Street, and Menlo and Santa Barbara avenues. A ramp from the Harbor Freeway takes you to Exposition Boulevard; the main entrance to the park is through the Memorial Gateway just west of the junction of Hoover and Figueroa streets.

In the center of Exposition Park, 16,000 fragrant rose bushes fill the Sunken Garden, a principal feature of the park's landscaping. The roses bloom from late spring through fall; all are identified.

The California Museum of Science and Industry, south of the Sunken Garden on State Drive, offers the opportunity for a do-it-yourself short course in basic science. It's a noisy museum: balls drop, a jet engine fires, a heart thumps. Some machines perform with soap bubbles and rubber balls. Others can be manipulated by a child to reveal the laws of orbiting bodies, to turn a car wheel or axle, or to play tic-tac-toe with an electronic brain that never loses. Major additions include the Mark Taper Hall of Economics and Finance; the California Museum of Afro-American Culture; and the Aerospace Complex, including the Mitsubishi IMAX Theater. The museum is open 10 A.M. to 5 P.M., 7 days a week; it's closed only on Thanksgiving and Christmas. Museum admission is free; there's a charge for entry to the theater.

The Museum of Natural History is on the west side of the Sunken Garden. It's filled with Egyptian mummies, reconstructed dinosaurs, glittering exhibits of gems, and dioramas of animals in natural settings. Other displays depict Southern California life in the Indian, Spanish, Mexican, and American periods. One-of-a-kind touches include such Hollywood memorabilia as W. C. Fields's billiard cue and Mary Pickford's curls. Museum hours are 10 A.M. to 5 P.M. daily except Thanksgiving and Christmas (small admission fee).

L.A. Memorial Coliseum, on the opposite side of the park from the museums, has an awesome seating capacity of nearly 95,000. The gateway to the park commemorates the Olympic Games. The stadium, built in 1928 and remodeled for the 10th Olympiad in 1932 and for the 1984 Games, covers 17 acres. The University of Southern California plays its home football games here; it's home for the Los Angeles Raiders pro football team, too.

Sports centers are numerous in this area. The modern indoor L.A. Memorial Sports Arena, in Exposition Park at the corner of Figueroa and Santa Barbara streets, has a seating capacity of 16,300. Collegiate and professional basketball, track meets, boxing matches (including the Olympic events), tennis tournaments, and special sports events and shows are held here.

Another outstanding sports center, the Forum, in Inglewood at the corner of Manchester Boulevard and Prairie Avenue, hosts Olympic and professional basketball and ice hockey, as well as ice shows, track meets, tennis, and boxing events. The Forum seats 18,600.

Southern California also boasts the first world-class velodrome in the western states. Built at the California State University Dominguez Hills in Carson, it was completed in 1983 for pre-Olympiad development of U.S. cyclists. The campus is east of the intersection of the Harbor and Santa Monica freeways.

University of Southern California covers several blocks along Exposition Boulevard opposite Exposition Park. Founded in 1876 by the Southern Conference of the Methodist Episcopal Church, it's the largest private university in California. Its architecture is a fine integration of old and new; notice especially Doheny Library and the campanile. U.S.C. is noted for its Department of Cinema, the oldest (1929), largest, and one of the most respected in the country.

Towers of Simon Rodia

In Watts, at 1765 E. 107th Street (Century Boulevard exit from Harbor Freeway, State 11), a group of unusual towers soar as high as 104 feet above the ground, a strangely beautiful symbol of a man's ambition "to do something big." The man was Sabatino (Simon) Rodia, an Italian tile setter who spent 33 years single-handedly building the towers. Rodia wired steel reinforcing rods together into a lacy structure, stuccoed them with cement, then studded the cement with broken bits of glass, tile, pottery shards, pebbles, and seashells.

After completing his work in 1954, Rodia quietly left town, and the future of the towers became uncertain. But the public became interested in preserving this forerunner of pop art. The towers' fate was settled when the steepest one was subjected to a "pull test" before television cameras and didn't budge.

You can visit the towers daily. An adjacent art center sponsors cultural events, exhibits, and classes.

Hollywood Park Race Track

Just east of the San Diego Freeway (I-405) at Century Boulevard in Inglewood, picturesque Hollywood Park features thoroughbred racing Wednesday through Sunday from mid-April to late July and from early November until late December. Harness racing goes on from mid-August to late October. Post time for the thoroughbred races is 2 P.M. weekdays and holidays, 1:30 P.M. weekends. The race track is famous for its beautiful infield.

Morning workouts (from 7 to 10 A.M. during the season) are open to the public. Activities are described over the public address system by a racing expert.

SUNSET BOULEVARD drive gives you a look at Griffith Observatory (left) on Mount Hollywood. To the north, sun lights up tennis courts (below) in Griffith Park. Farther west you drive by colorful Beverly Hills park (above).

North of Downtown L.A.

Just north and east of the downtown area, off the Pasadena Freeway (State Highways 11/110), you'll find a garden oasis and several spots of historical interest.

Lawry's California Center

Expanded from offices and a seasoning preparation plant, Lawry's handsome shopping complex offers a restaurant, wine shop and cellar, antiques, cookware, pottery, and plants.

The complex is open daily except major holidays. Shop hours vary according to the season. Lunch is served from 11 A.M. to 3 P.M. all year, dinner in the evening from May to November.

Lawry's plant can be toured weekdays only; free 45-minute guided tours start at 11:30 A.M., and at 1:30 and 2:30 P.M. For those who want to improve their culinary skills, Lawry's offers a schedule of cooking classes. Subjects range from the basics of food preparation to the esthetics of gracious serving. The fee covers both cooking demonstrations and the food you'll sample. For further information and reservations, call (213) 225-2491.

A hint of L.A.'s history

Though you'll find a scattering of historical monuments, museums, and parks in and around L.A., these three attractions are so conveniently located that they can become the focus of a single outing.

Heritage Square (east side of the Pasadena Freeway, Avenue 43 exit) is the beginning of the city's Victorian home preservation and restoration program. Several homes reflecting L.A.'s lifestyle from 1865 to 1914 now stand on this square. Guided tours are offered every Sunday; a small donation is requested.

Lummis Home (west side of the Pasadena Freeway, Avenue 43 exit), or El Alisal, is the two-story "castle" and surrounding 3 acres that belonged to Charles Fletcher Lummis, founder of the Southwest Museum (see below).

A native of Massachusetts, Lummis created the slogan "See America First"—and put his belief into practice by walking over 3,000 miles to reach Los Angeles. Here, he became the first City Editor of the Los Angeles Times. Two plaques on the walls of El Alisal list his achievements; one seals the crypt containing his ashes. Now a state park, the house and grounds are open Wednesday through Sunday from 1 to 4 P.M.

The Southwest Museum, at 234 Museum Drive, is north of the Lummis home. Established by Charles Lummis, it contains one of the country's outstanding displays of Western Indian artifacts.

Though there's a hillside parking lot above the building, it's more interesting to park below the museum and enter through a tunnel lined with dioramas showing American Indian life. An elevator whisks you up to the museum building and exhibits. The museum is open Tuesday through Sunday from 11 A.M. to 5 P.M.; admission is free.

L.A.'s Famous Streets

One of the best ways to see Los Angeles is to get off the freeways and drive its celebrity boulevards: Wilshire, Santa Monica, Sunset, and Hollywood. Each presents a different facet of city life. Almost every attraction in the western section of L.A. is on or near these thoroughfares.

Wilshire Boulevard

Stretching 16 miles from the city's center to the ocean, Wilshire Boulevard is one of the world's prestige streets, often compared to New York's Fifth Avenue. Launched in the 1920s with the opening of "Miracle Mile" (La Brea to La Cienega avenues), it soon began accumulating high-class shops, department stores, business firms, smart apartment houses, and plush restaurants. If you have time, you will want to stop at attractions along the way and explore interesting side streets. But even if you just keep driving, you will pass places closely identified with the growth of this city, along with some of the most interesting examples of new commercial architecture in the United States. Several well-known hotels have a Wilshire Boulevard address, starting with the downtown Los Angeles Hilton and including the farther-out Ambassador, Beverly Hilton, and Beverly Wilshire.

MacArthur Park, bisected by Wilshire Boulevard just west of Alvarado Street, was long known as Westlake, a country park at the westernmost edge of the city. Renamed for General Douglas MacArthur in 1942, the 32-acre park has a small lake and pleasantly landscaped grounds. Popular with the summer lunch group, it sports an open-air theater for Shakespearean and musical performances.

The Ambassador Hotel comes into view on the left soon after you cross Vermont Avenue. Set far back from ever-burgeoning Wilshire Boulevard amidst 27 protective acres of parklike grounds, the venerable old structure has long been a Los Angeles landmark.

Miracle Mile, locally renamed Mid-Wilshire, begins at La Brea Avenue and stretches for several miles to La Cienega. You'll recognize it by its median landscaped with palms. Though not as glamorous as in its heyday over 50 years ago, this section does have some outstanding attractions.

Hancock Park is one of the few remaining patches of greenery along Wilshire Boulevard. This is the site of the Rancho La Brea Tar Pits, where Pleistocene-era animals were trapped some 40 centuries ago. The collection of prehistoric animal skeletons that was found here is displayed in the George C. Page Museum on the park grounds, almost directly above the engulfing tar. Visitors can see films of the discovery of these remains and learn what life was like in the Los Angeles Valley over 14,000 years ago. The museum is open from 10 A.M. to 5 P.M. Tuesday through Sunday (except major holidays); there's an admission charge.

In Pueblo days, the Spaniards used *brea* (tar) from these pits to waterproof their roofs. Not until 1905 was it discovered that the bubbly, black pits had entombed such creatures as mastodons, dire wolves, and imperial

(Continued on page 23)

Van Nuys · to Bakersfield · Burbank · Griffith Park
to Santa Barbara · TBS · NBC · Ventura Fwy · 210
Universal Studios · Glendale · Pasadena · Colorado Bl. · Foothill Bl. · Azusa
Hollywood Bl. · San Gabriel · Arcadia · to San Bernardino
Chinese Theatre · Sunset Bl. · Hancock Park · Huntington Dr. · Alhambra · West Covina
Beverly Hills · Santa Monica Bl. · Century City · Wilshire Bl. · San Bernardino Fwy · to Pomona
Santa Monica · Farmers Market · Dodger Stadium · Pomona · to Riverside
Marina del Rey · Exposition Park · Inglewood · Whittier
L.A. Airport · Manchester Ave. · Watts · Norwalk
Manhattan Beach · Imperial Hwy. · Santa Ana Fwy
Hermosa Beach · Artesia Fwy · Buena Park · Anaheim
Santa Monica Bay · Redondo Beach · Torrance · Long Beach Airport · Lincoln Bl. · Santa Ana
Pacific Coast Highway · Garden Grove Fwy
Long Beach · to San Diego

San Pedro Bay

PACIFIC OCEAN

Scale of Miles 0 2 4 6 · Scale of Kilometers 0 2 4 6

Los Angeles Freeways

Major Points of Interest

Studio tours—behind-scenes peek at television and movie studios; largest tours at Universal, Burbank Studios (TBS), and NBC

Griffith Park (off Golden State Freeway)—L.A.'s superpark: zoo, Travel Town, Fern Dell, Griffith Observatory, Greek Theater

Chinese Theatre (Hollywood Boulevard)—celebrated movie house with forecourt of footprints and signatures of stars

Beverly Hills (Wilshire Boulevard)—hotels, restaurants, galleries, and shops of celebrities

Century City (Santa Monica Boulevard just west of Beverly Hills)—city of tomorrow on former movie lot; ABC Entertainment Center

Farmers Market (Third Street and Fairfax Avenue)—giant market-restaurant-gift shop complex started by farmers in Depression

Hancock Park (Wilshire Boulevard)—La Brea Tar Pits, site of prehistoric animals' entrapment; Page Museum; L.A. County Museum of Art, one of greatest U.S. art museums

Exposition Park (off Harbor Freeway)—California Museum of Science and Industry, Natural History Museum of L.A. County, U.S.C.

PAINTING receives earnest examination (left) from art patron at Los Angeles County Museum of Art. Shopping at Farmers Market often includes meeting a friend for lunch (below).

. . . Continued from page 20

mammoths that came to drink at the ponds 13,000 to 40,000 years ago, only to be caught and trapped in the seeping tar. Today, a strange, life-sized scene of the re-created ancient animals—including fiberglass imperial mammoths with tusks 12½ feet long—brings a touch of prehistory to busy Wilshire Boulevard. At the observation building in the northwest corner of the park, you can see the asphalt-laden water still bubbling and some animal bones still trapped in the tar. The tar pits are open weekends from 10 A.M. to 5 P.M.; Thursday through Sunday, guided tours of the grounds depart from the pits at 1 P.M.

Los Angeles County Museum of Art is the largest art museum built in this country in over 30 years. It is housed in several gleaming pavilions on a 3-foot-thick concrete slab atop the tar pits in Hancock Park. Glass bricks laid in ship's prow angles mark the entrance to the Robert O. Anderson wing. On the top two floors you'll view the museum's permanent collection of 20th century art, including fine modern works by Matisse, Mondrian, and de Kooning.

Though a latecomer in the art-collecting field, the museum has acquired some well-known artworks and features a range from prehistoric times to the present. Exhibits include Far Eastern art, American and European painting, sculpture, decorative glass, pre-Columbian art, photography, costumes and textiles, and Indian and Islamic pieces. The collection of Impressionism is particularly good and you shouldn't miss the renowned collection of Japanese Edo-period paintings and scrolls in the Japanese Pavilion.

A number of tours (free with admission charge) are offered daily. The art museum is open Tuesday through Friday from 10 A.M. to 5 P.M., and on weekends from 10 A.M. to 6 P.M. You can lunch at the cafeteria in the Leo S. Bing Center, which also has facilities for films, lectures, concerts, and changing exhibits.

Farmers Market is keynoted by its familiar white clock tower that rises above West Third Street and Fairfax Avenue and gives the busy neighborhood the air of a midwestern farming community. Words above the tower entrance read simply, "An Idea." The idea was to help Los Angeles-area farmers during the worst years of the Depression by letting them use a vacant field at the edge of the city to market their wasting crops.

The Farmers Market idea not only helped the 18 original farmers, but also grew into a giant market-restaurant-gift shop complex covering 20 acres and serving 20,000 visitors and shoppers daily all year. Although tour buses pack the parking lots around noon, most people here are from L.A.

Some of the original farmers and their families are still associated with the market, maintaining their widespread reputation by selling fresh food from all parts of the world. Here you can enjoy a tray of delicious food from any one of the market's 26 kitchens serving food from six countries. This is also the place to go shopping without a list, letting impulse be your guide through the tempting displays. You can buy a puppy, a fish, or an exotic bird here—but leave your pet at home. No animals are allowed to roam the premises.

The market is open Monday through Saturday from 9 A.M. to 6:30 P.M. during the winter; it stays open some-what later during the summer. Activity begins to slow down around 5 P.M. One restaurant offering varied entertainment is open until 2 A.M. For a map listing each merchant in the market, stop at the office just inside Gate No. 1. With the map, you can chart a course through the busy aisles that will take you past every stall and shop. With so many things to see and buy, a walk among the stalls takes about an hour. Allow plenty of extra time to visit the shops.

La Cienega Boulevard's loose Spanish translation, "the watering hole," is an apt one. Located about a mile past Fairfax Avenue, this is "Restaurant Row." The boulevard is more glamorous at night, when diners congregate in eateries on both sides of the street to enjoy some of L.A.'s best food.

Art galleries also abound on this fabled boulevard. You'll find a gallery row between Melrose Avenue and Santa Monica Boulevard. (Melrose has become the center of the design industry. The Pacific Design Center at 8687 Melrose, called the "Blue Whale" because of its glass skin and behemoth bulk, contains six floors of showrooms, most open only to the trade.)

Just east of La Cienega, at 6505 Wilshire Boulevard, you can visit the Martyrs Memorial & Museum of The Holocaust. Free guided tours are available weekdays and Sunday afternoons, except for major public and Jewish holidays.

Beverly Hills comes into view when you cross San Vincente Boulevard. The city's boundaries roughly extend from San Vincente west to Century City and Benedict Canyon Drive, and from Olympic Boulevard on the south to the hills above Sunset Boulevard on the north. But though Beverly Hills is surrounded by L.A., it has never surrendered its identity: there are no billboards, and buildings are lower. At the busy intersection of Olympic Boulevard and Beverly Drive is a "Monument to the Stars" honoring those who fought for the community's preservation when annexation to Los Angeles seemed likely.

Shop prowling is one of the city's main attractions for visitors. Beverly Hills is the place where New York stores open branches, fashion imports converge, and dining is cosmopolitan. Perhaps because this is the center of the affluent community, variety seems wider and specialities more specialized. Here more than elsewhere, shops project a heightened sensual appeal; even the most appealing goods play second fiddle to imaginative display. And where else would you need an appointment just to shop?

Wilshire Boulevard boasts many big stores, but *the* shopping street is 3-block-long Rodeo Drive—between Wilshire and Santa Monica boulevards. Though you might find valet parking service if you're a valued customer, it's best for visitors to park elsewhere. Check with the Beverly Hills Visitors Bureau, 239 S. Beverly Drive, for maps and locations of shops. Be sure to take a look at the architecturally unique Rodeo Collection, a recent shopping enclave.

Prefer to stay close to the action? Visit the Beverly Hills, Beverly Hilton, or Beverly Wilshire hotels, the city's largest.

Beyond Beverly Hills, Wilshire takes you past the exclusive Los Angeles Country Club; 18-hole golf courses line both sides of the boulevard.

Westwood Village, mecca for college students and a rather quaint community in its own right, nestles at the foot of the University of California, Los Angeles campus. Stop for a walk through the village and explore its inviting shops and eating spots.

Like a village within a village, Westwood's old Masonic Club, now called Contempo Westwood, is well entrenched as a shopping, dining, and arts center. Here you'll find the 500-seat Westwood Playhouse. Contempo Westwood is on La Conte Avenue across from the U.C.L.A. campus.

U.C.L.A. has grown in one generation from a cluster of four Romanesque hilltop buildings to a complete city of learning. The mammoth campus covers 422 acres of terraced hillside.

A major force in the city's cultural life, U.C.L.A. is a leader in drama, music, medicine, and the arts. The interesting architectural forms of the buildings are complemented by the fountain in front of Franz Hall, the Japanese Gardens, 8 acres of Botanical Gardens, and 4½ acres of 20th century art in the Franklin D. Murphy Sculpture Gardens. Of particular interest are the Dickson Art Center and the Museum of Cultural History.

For campus tour reservations, stop by the Visitor Center at 100 Dodd Hall or call (213) 206-8147. Free campus maps are available at parking kiosks; parking is free on Sunday. You can reach U.C.L.A. by turning north off Wilshire onto Westwood Boulevard.

Palisades Park in Santa Monica is the terminus for Wilshire Boulevard. Stretching for almost 2 miles along the cliff top, the park offers perhaps the most beautiful and familiar view of Santa Monica Bay. On a clear day you can see the Channel Islands, and on almost any day you can see the Santa Monica Mountains reaching out into the ocean to form the northern crescent of the bay. This corridor of green lawn, flowers, and tall palm trees is a pleasant area for a stroll or a picnic.

Before you explore the park, stop at the Tourist Information Center on Ocean Avenue just south of Santa Monica Boulevard and ask for a brochure. It will point out such features of interest as the sundial, the camera obscura, the totem pole, some of the trees and memorial plantings, and the park's seven monuments.

Santa Monica Boulevard

Originating in Silver Lake, the district east of Hollywood, Santa Monica Boulevard parallels Wilshire Boulevard heading north for a stretch, then turns south and cuts through Beverly Hills and across Wilshire on its way to the ocean. Though not particularly noted as a scenic thoroughfare, it does pass some interesting sights. If you have driven out Wilshire Boulevard, it's an alternate route back to Los Angeles or on to Hollywood.

Hollywood Cemetery, on Santa Monica Boulevard between Van Ness and Gower streets, is the final resting place for some legendary Hollywood film stars. Silent film star John Gilbert is buried here, as are Douglas Fairbanks and many others. This is where the mysterious lady in black paid her visits to Valentino's grave.

Paramount Studios, one of the few still left in Hollywood, is south of the cemetery. It is not open for tours.

The Mormon Temple, a monumental white edifice high atop a hill on Santa Monica Boulevard (a few blocks east of the Santa Monica Freeway), is the largest temple of the Mormon faith (Church of Jesus Christ of Latter-day Saints). The gold-leaf figure of Angel Moroni on top, once visible 25 miles out to sea, is now getting lost among the high-rises. You can tour the grounds but may not go inside the temple. Movies shown at the Visitor Information Center take you on a tour of the interior. The center is open from 9 A.M. to 9:30 P.M. daily.

Century City—a panorama of broad thoroughfares, sky-reaching buildings, green parks, and plazas—is a futuristic supercity being built on land once owned by a major movie studio. Turn onto the Avenue of the Stars from Santa Monica Boulevard (just south of Wilshire) to visit this trend-setting city within a city.

Based on the master plan of architects Welton Becket and Associates, Century City seems slightly larger than life. Traffic within the giant blocks is designed for the pedestrian; all parking on this 180-acre site is underground.

The land from which Century City rises was once the ranch of Tom Mix before it became the back lot of Twentieth Century-Fox Studio. In 1961 it was sold to the Alcoa Company for construction of a major new urban center in Los Angeles. Although the movieland sets were demolished, more than $1 million was invested in saving and replanting the unique studio tree collection.

Spread out like an oversized Japanese fan, Century City has as its crown jewel the Century Plaza Hotel and Tower, designed by architect Minoru Yamasaki. Surrounded by landscaped grounds and resembling New York City's Rockefeller Center, it was chosen as the location for the Presidential State Dinner honoring the first astronauts to reach the moon.

The ABC Entertainment Center, across the street from the Century Plaza Hotel, features the large Shubert Theatre, a setting for Broadway productions on the West Coast, as well as for other legitimate theater performances. There are also two first-run cinemascopic theaters. Twin 44-story triangular office towers rise in the background. Shops, restaurants, and clubs complement the theaters and face the plaza. The center is open daily, from morning well into the night. For information on a 1-hour multimedia tour, call (213) 553-0626.

Twentieth Century-Fox, one of the oldest and most prestigious movie studios in the industry, stands on one corner of the Century City property. Work still goes on here (television series and independent productions), and some movie sets are still standing. The studio fronts onto Pico Boulevard; from here, you can get a fairly good view of the prop lot (part of the lot can also be seen from the Century Plaza Hotel windows). At one time, Gray Line Tours conducted a walking tour through the studio back lot, but at present, tours are not offered to the public.

Sunset Boulevard

Gloria Swanson immortalized this street in the film *Sunset Boulevard*. She even lived on the famous thoroughfare (across from the Beverly Hills Hotel). Her home is gone, but other stars live nearby.

There's still a magic to the name "Sunset Strip," although its character has changed. Even if you're not a star-gazer, Sunset Boulevard is an interesting drive. Beginning at El Pueblo downtown, it proceeds through Hollywood and wanders along the foothills of the Santa Monica Mountains for 25 miles to its intersection with the Pacific Coast Highway.

The boulevard intersects with the canyon roads that cut across the mountains to the San Fernando Valley. "Hideaway" homes are built along these winding roads. Perhaps the best known residential area is exclusive Bel Air.

Angelus Temple and Echo Park are just south of Sunset Boulevard on Glendale Boulevard. Although Angelus Temple is visually unprepossessing, in the 1930s it presented one of the greatest shows in Los Angeles—a nightly, slightly edited version of the life of Aimee Semple McPherson, complete with full cast and scenery. Aimee, a self-appointed faith healer, is gone, but the temple lives on.

South of the temple is Echo Park, a pleasant haven of greenery complete with a small lake for boating in a sylvan setting. It is notable for its lotuses which flower in July. Sometimes stocked with fish, it's the meeting place for small children.

Hollywood flavor is not seen along Sunset. You'll catch it on the next main street north: Hollywood Boulevard (see at right). You will see bulky buildings housing film, television, radio, and recording studios, plus a concentration of camera shops.

Sunset Strip in its heyday was one of the plushest stretches of the boulevard. Within this 20-block area were a trio of famous nightclubs: Trocadero, Mocambo, and Ciro's. Fans gathered here to watch the comings and goings of the movie colony. With the gradual demise of Hollywood as a film center, the Strip has exchanged its Rolls Royce culture for a Volkswagen one.

There's still action at night, but it centers on the young and hip strolling in and out of the numerous loud, gaudy lounges and glorified hamburger stands. The view over L.A. is still good, but people don't seem to notice; they're too distracted by the colorful costumes and the theatrical billboards.

Sunset Plaza is an oasis of delightful small stores just past La Cienega. You can buy and browse among boutiques and art galleries, eat at some very good restaurants, or sit at a sidewalk cafe and "people-watch."

A mile past Sunset Plaza, you reach the end of Sunset Strip. Suddenly the towering buildings are replaced by the gracious green spaces surrounding the lovely homes of residential Beverly Hills in one of the most dramatic urban transitions to be seen.

"Where do the stars live?" is a frequently asked question here. Street-side vendors will provide you with addresses (not particularly accurate) for a price. You can also pick up a brochure on the stars' homes from the Sunset Plaza merchants or from the Greater Los Angeles Visitors and Convention Bureau in downtown L.A.

Lionel Barrymore's former home and garden is now Butterfield's Restaurant (8426 Sunset Boulevard) below the Strip. On the hill above Sunset Boulevard and Doheny Road stands Greystone Mansion—a "castle" which cost Edward Doheny of Teapot Dome notoriety $4 million to build. Because of its tremendous size, the mansion later became a white elephant on the market. Eventually purchased by the city of Beverly Hills, the gardens around the house are open daily except holidays from 10 A.M. to 5 P.M. A series of concerts takes place here during the summer; information on times and tickets is available from the Beverly Hills Visitors Bureau at (213) 271-8174.

The Beverly Hills Hotel (at Beverly Drive and Sunset Boulevard) enjoys a lush, green 16-acre setting across from a park. This pink palace, set back from a busy intersection (also the entrance to Coldwater Canyon), looks like a stage setting. Not camera shy, it has been used in films many times. It has also been home to a multitude of famous personalities at one time or another.

Will Rogers State Historic Park will expose you to the wit and personality of humorist Will Rogers. At the main house (filled with mementos of the "cowboy philosopher's" busy life) of this Pacific Palisades estate, a curator is on hand to tell you about the paintings, Navajo rugs, lariats, saddles, and other objects.

In the stable area, you'll still find polo ponies in the corrals and exercising and roping rings. Riding and hiking trails circling the low hills above the ranch houses invite exploration. The park is open every day except major holidays. Admission is free; there is a small fee to see the main house (open from 10 A.M. to 5 P.M.). No picnicking or camping is permitted on the grounds. The entrance road to the park is located at 14235 Sunset Boulevard.

Self-Realization Fellowship Lake Shrine is one of the hidden treasures along this route. A small natural lake, fed by springs, it is set in a garden that almost succeeds in shutting out the traffic noise of busy Sunset Boulevard. Look for the 10-acre meditation gardens at 17190 Sunset Boulevard in Pacific Palisades, just up from the coast highway.

The fellowship is devoted to yoga. Its miniature park, dedicated to all religions, is open free of charge to everyone daily except Monday from 10 A.M. to 5 P.M. You walk a lakeside path past shrines, along garden slopes, and past a small houseboat, being rewarded with vistas of gazebos, a chapel in a windmill, and a waterfall.

Hollywood Boulevard

A comparatively short street, Hollywood Boulevard is perhaps the best known of all L.A.'s thoroughfares because it leads directly to the place most people visit first—Hollywood. Pedestrian-looking architecture? Perhaps. But Hollywood Boulevard still manages to retain a little of the sparkle of yesteryear.

Look at the hills to the north. Those large letters spell out the name of the town. Look underfoot. The bronze stars studding the sidewalk mark the names of the film, radio, and television actors who gave the name "Hollywood" its special romance.

Barnsdall Park, once the haughty stronghold of Olive Hill at Hollywood Boulevard near Vermont Avenue, ceased to be forbidden ground when the city of Los

Angeles inherited it from the late Aline Barnsdall in 1927.

Hollyhock House, one of Frank Lloyd Wright's early achievements, sits atop the summit. Extensively restored in 1975, it's now open to the public for touring from 10 A.M. to 1 P.M. Tuesday and Thursday, and noon to 3 P.M. Saturday and the first three Sundays of each month. Visitors pay a small fee.

Here also is L.A.'s handsome Municipal Art Gallery, first major art gallery to be built in the city since 1965. Opened in 1971, it replaces a smaller pavilion also designed by Wright.

This two-story gallery, designed by architect Arthur Stephens, harmonizes well with the other buildings on the hill: Hollyhock House and the Junior Arts Center. The gallery does not have a permanent collection but presents a series of changing exhibitions. Films and dramatic and musical performances take place in the 300-seat auditorium. The gallery is open from 12:30 to 5 P.M. Tuesday through Sunday; guided tours start at 2 P.M. There's a small admission charge.

For one week in the summer, an All-City Outdoor Art Festival exhibits sculptures, paintings, and other works of art.

Hollywood and Vine may disappoint you. At first glance the boulevard looks like any Main Street of any town. But look north on Vine Street at the Capitol Tower, a circular-shaped structure appropriately resembling a neatly piled stack of records. The light atop the building blinks out "Hollywood" in Morse code.

The first Academy Awards (1928) were presented at the grand, recently renovated Hollywood Roosevelt Hotel at 7000 Hollywood Boulevard. The James Doolittle Theatre, among the best in Los Angeles, is at 1615 N. Vine Street; the grand art deco showcase, Pantages Theatre, stands at 6233 Hollywood Boulevard.

The Hollywood Wax Museum, 6767 Hollywood Boulevard near Highland Avenue, has life-sized figures of movie personalities, presidents, and historical personages. The Chamber of Horrors features the coffin used in the movie *The Raven* and a scene from *The House of Wax* with Vincent Price. In the Oscar Movie Theatre, you can see a film that spans more than 40 years of Academy Award winners and presentations.

Mann's Chinese Theatre (formerly Grauman's Chinese), at 6925 Hollywood Boulevard, is a testament to a real showman—Sid Grauman. Grauman first built the Egyptian Theatre, a replica of a palace in ancient Thebes, on the south side of the boulevard; he then outdid himself by creating the Chinese Theatre, a model of a Chinese temple with imported Oriental pillars, across the street. The hand, foot, hoof, and face prints (even Jimmy Durante's noseprint!) and the signatures of well-known stars are imprinted in the concrete courtyard, tracing the history of Hollywood cinema since this celebrated movie house first opened its doors in 1927.

Hollywood Fantasy Tours leave from 1721 N. Highland Avenue for a 2-hour, 17-mile ride overlooking the streets and landmarks where Hollywood's realities spawned its myths. City tours depart five times daily; call (213) 469-8184 for information and reservations.

The Hollywood Bowl, built in a natural amphitheater in the Cahuenga Hills, grew from a simple bandstand in a weedy dell into an open-air concert theater with seating capacity of 20,000. The bowl's natural acoustics are responsible for its success; modern technology is trying for even better amplification. The "Symphonies Under the Stars," its noted summer series, features the Los Angeles Philharmonic Orchestra. The most notable annual event is the pre-dawn pilgrimage to the bowl for the memorable Easter sunrise service.

The bowl is on the west side of Highland Avenue, north of the Hollywood Boulevard intersection. A 20-minute film in the museum at the entrance gives its history; it's open concert days and Wednesday through Sunday from 10 A.M. to 5 P.M.

Mulholland Drive, within the city, then Mulholland Highway beyond, winds along the summit backbone of the Santa Monica Mountains, L.A.'s own mountain range. Driving its whole 55-mile length starting from the Hollywood Freeway in Cahuenga Pass is one of the easiest ways to get a view of the wilderness so threatened by urban pressure. The only longitudinal route along the Santa Monicas, this highway is one of the traditional scenic drives in Los Angeles.

At Topanga Canyon, you can follow winding Topanga Canyon Boulevard down to the ocean, emerging just east of Malibu, or continue on through the mountains, ending up at Leo Carrillo State Beach. You can also reach the sea on Malibu Canyon Road. The road past Topanga Canyon Boulevard is slow and the countryside almost wild.

You can get onto Mulholland Drive from the Hollywood Freeway in Cahuenga Pass, or you can avoid some of the tortuous course through residential areas by joining it farther west, at Laurel Canyon, Coldwater Canyon, Benedict Canyon, or Beverly Glen. Or enter Mulholland Drive from the San Diego Freeway.

Griffith Park

Griffith Park is a superpark, once the largest municipal park inside any city in America. Comparable in area with the cities of Beverly Hills and Santa Monica, on a fine weekend it may attain a population midway between the two (58,000).

Straddling the eastern end of the Santa Monica Mountains, the park was begun over 80 years ago with a gift to the city of some 3,000 acres by Colonel Griffith J. Griffith. The gift included a trust fund used since for the acquisition of more land and for building the grand old Griffith Observatory and Greek Theatre.

Although rising to just 1,625 feet at the summit of Mount Hollywood, the mountains in the park are steep and rugged. Such topography has helped to preserve nearly three-fifths of the land in a nearly natural state. Until the era of the bulldozer, it was simply too vertical for conventional city-park development. Most of the mountain heartland remains a sort of domesticated wilderness.

The perimeter of Griffith Park is very accessible. To the north is the Ventura Freeway, to the east the Golden

TOP VISITOR ATTRACTIONS *include film festivals at ABC Entertainment Center (above) on the Avenue of the Stars in Century City. The waters "part" (right) for tram trips through Universal Studios' back lot.*

State Freeway, and to the west the Hollywood Freeway. Both Western and Vermont avenues enter the southern park edge. Western leads to Fern Dell and the Nature Museum, Vermont to the Bird Sanctuary and Greek Theatre; both reach the observatory. Well-marked freeway exits lead to other points of interest.

Griffith Observatory, high on a promontory, commands a vast panorama, spectacular at night. The observatory's large dome contains a 500-seat planetarium theater; two smaller domes are for telescopes and the Hall of Science. Visiting hours vary by season; generally, the observatory is open from around noon until 10 P.M. daily. Admission to the museum is free, but you will pay for theater shows (children under 5 are admitted only at the 1:30 P.M. show).

Greek Theatre, at 2700 N. Vermont Avenue, seats 4,500 people for drama, music, and dance performances in a natural canyon amphitheater. Check local newspapers and city guides to find out what's playing.

Fern Dell is reached through the next canyon to the west, another access to the upland. Called Western Canyon, its road begins off Los Feliz Boulevard just east of the end of Western Avenue. You'll find Fern Dell to be a natural, spring-fed fern bower with a collection of exotic ferns. Here you can walk a half-mile past waterfalls and terraced pools.

A good place to start exploring the park is the Fern Dell Nature Museum. Its exhibits describe plant and animal life in the park and some of the area's geological features. On weekends you can attend free showings of travel and nature movies in the museum. Its hours are from 1 to 5 P.M., Wednesday through Sunday; admission is free.

Griffith Playground means business. Intense recreational activity concentrates in the flatland along the eastern and northern edges of the park. The southeast-ern tip is one of the liveliest parts of the park, at least when a soccer game is in progress. Here, along Riverside Drive south of Los Feliz Boulevard is Griffith Playground, which contains a swimming pool, tennis courts, playing field, and other activities. Across Riverside Drive are the Cultural Arts Center and the Mulholland Fountain, a memorial to the father of the Los Angeles Aqueduct.

North of Los Feliz Boulevard, Riverside Drive becomes Crystal Springs Drive. After passing a miniature train ride, a children's pony ring, and one of three nine-hole golf courses, you'll come to the venerable 1926 Spillman merry-go-round, still one of the best of its era. This is also the site of a nature center and park headquarters. Beyond are two 18-hole golf courses.

Los Angeles Zoo (exit on Zoo Drive at the junction of the Golden State and Ventura freeways) draws more people than any other park attraction. First all-new zoo of its size to be built in modern times, it features over 2,000 birds, mammals, and reptiles in 113 acres of attractive grounds. Moats and natural settings replace bars and cages. Among the most popular zoo spots are the Children's Zoo and the Koala House. You can walk (mostly uphill) or take a tram to see the five continental areas.

You'll pay an admission fee plus an extra charge for the tram; parking is free. The zoo is open daily (except Christmas) from 10 A.M.; picnic areas are nearby.

Travel Town, at the northwest corner of the park, is home for antique trains and airplanes. Youngsters enjoy the ride; rail buffs enthuse over the rolling stock. The free exhibit is open daily except Christmas.

The Equestrian Center, at Riverside Drive and Main Street, lies across the river from Train Town. Here you'll find a training area, jumping course, and indoor arena; you can also rent horses and ride along 53 miles of park bridle trails. Weekend activity is intense.

HUNTING FOR CELEBRITIES

People-watching is Los Angeles' most popularly practiced spectator sport. Residents and tourists are equally avid participants in a game—most appropriately titled "star-gazing"—that can be played at any hour of the day or night.

Since Los Angeles and environs abound with entertainment and sports world luminaries, sightings of famous faces have been recorded throughout the area.

However, if your observation time is limited and your curiosity piqued, you might visit a few of the haunts favored by these celestial beings, or drop by places where they shop and work.

Most of the well-known faces hide out in the hills above Hollywood, in the canyons of Bel Air, around the crest of the Santa Monica Mountains, in Beverly Hills, or farther west near Pacific Palisades and Malibu. Tours past some celebrities' homes are offered (see facing page).

Even celebrities go out to shop and eat lunch. Try the eateries around the various studios. Farmers Market is close enough to CBS for a lunch break.

Some expensive restaurants are frequent haunts of stars. You'll have to buy a meal for the dubious chance of glimpsing your favorite, and reservations are a must. A sure way to be asked to leave is to bother a star inside the restaurant.

The following eating and sipping spots are among current favorites. In Los Angeles: Jimmy's (201 Moreno Drive), L'Ermitage (730 N. La Cienega Boulevard), Matteo's (2321 Westwood Boulevard), Morton's (8800 Melrose Avenue), Scandia (9040 Sunset Boulevard), Spago (8795 Sunset Boulevard), and Trumps (8764 Melrose Avenue). In Beverly Hills: La Scala (9455 Santa Monica Boulevard), Le Bistro (246 N. Canon Drive), Max au Triangle (233 N. Beverly Drive), and Trader Vic's (Beverly Hilton Hotel).

WORLD OF ENTERTAINMENT

Movie making in Los Angeles is the great fascination of visitors, but many residents consider it old hat. These same residents, however, often know little more than the average tourist about how to see "the industry."

Below is a rundown of studio tours, television facilities, and ways to see something of the stars—their homes, their footprints, and how they look (in person and in wax).

Movie studios

The motion picture industry's sound stages are scattered over an area that includes not only Hollywood but also most of its neighboring cities.

Universal Studios (Lankershim Boulevard just north of the Hollywood Freeway) offers elaborate tours. Over a million people a year enjoy a ride through the studio's 420-acre lot on guided, candy-striped trams that pass by TV and sound stages, false front sets, stars' dressing rooms, warehouses, and labs. You'll experience a flash flood, a shark attack, and The Battle of Galactica, and watch live shows.

During the summer, tours run daily from 8 A.M. to 5 P.M.; the rest of the year they operate from 10 A.M. to 3:30 P.M. VIP tours (for 6 or more) are expensive, but may give you a chance to dine with a celebrity in the commissary. For specific information, call (818) 508-9600.

Burbank Studios (Warner Bros., Columbia Pictures, and several independents) offers an intimate view of movies and TV. You are taken through the lot in vans and on foot, observing whatever is going on in the day's production schedule. You may or may not see actual filming; nothing is scheduled for the tour. Often you'll walk quietly on either a sound set or recording stage. You'll tour prop and special effects shops and an historical back lot.

The cost is fairly high (especially if you reserve lunch in the Blue Room), and children under 10 aren't allowed—but you'll see things you won't see anywhere else. Two-hour tours are offered on weekdays, by reservation, at 10 A.M. and 2 P.M. (There are two additional tours during the summer.) Enter at the Hollywood Way gate just off the Ventura Freeway. Call (818) 954-1744 for reservations and information.

Television studios

Many popular TV shows originate here, and you can be part of the audience if you first get advance tickets, offered free by most studios. The Greater Los Angeles Visitors and Convention Bureau,

505 W. Flower Street, Los Angeles, CA 90071, has a limited number available.

For tickets to a specific broadcast, it is necessary to write several months in advance to the broadcasting network from which the program originates. Enclose a stamped envelope, giving your address in the L.A. area. Tickets will not be mailed to out-of-state addresses.

Ticket requests should be mailed to: ABC, Guest Relations and Ticket Office, 4151 Prospect Avenue, Los Angeles, CA 90027 or ABC Vine Street Theatre, 1313 N. Vine Street, Hollywood, CA 90028; CBS, Ticket Division, 7800 Beverly Boulevard, Los Angeles, CA 90036; and NBC, 3000 W. Alameda Avenue, Burbank, CA 91523.

NBC Television Studio tours depart daily (except major holidays) for a 1¼-hour behind-the-scenes look at set construction, special effects, make-up, and wardrobe; you'll also see how you'd appear on camera. Don't expect to watch a show being taped—for this you'll need studio audience tickets (available early in the day at the studio). For information on tour cost, call (818) 840-3537. The studio is located at 3000 W. Alameda Avenue (it's visible from the Ventura Freeway at the Buena Vista exit in Burbank).

Wax, footprints, and star trips

If you've been to a wax museum, you may have loved it or hated it; the figures recall certain characters and movies accurately, but obviously they're not real. Six Flags Movieland, 7711 Beach Boulevard, Buena Park, is about the best (see Orange County chapter for details). Hollywood Wax Museum, 6767 Hollywood Boulevard, competes for the tourist who wonders where the stars are if they're not on the boulevard.

At Mann's Chinese Theatre, 6925 Hollywood Boulevard, foot, hoof, and palm prints of the stars have been collecting tourist stares for over 50 years. The forecourt is always open.

A rib-tickling tour by Starline Sightseeing Tours leaves from the front of the theater for drives past stars' homes.

Gray Line Tours offers a look at Hollywood and Beverly Hills; call (213) 481-2121 for information. Hollywood Fantasy Tours (1721 N. Highland Avenue) provides a 2-hour view of Hollywood's past, present, and future from a double-decker, open-top bus.

Hollywood on Location provides information about filming around L.A.; for a fee, they'll provide movie and show names, shoot times and locations, names of stars, and maps to sites. Call (213) 659-9165 between 3 and 5 P.M. for an idea of the next day's activities. Pick up the package around 9 A.M. the next morning from the offices at 8644 Wilshire Boulevard.

CROWDS THRONG to L.A.
area's wide sandy beaches.
Lifeguards staff stations, ready
to rescue swimmers, surfers
from tugging tide.

An impressive dimension is added to Los Angeles by an array of beaches and mountains ringing the L.A. Basin.

Southern California beaches are hardly a discovery. If you've ever been caught in a coast highway traffic jam on a summer Sunday afternoon, you know that the shoreline of the Los Angeles city region is perhaps the greatest summer recreational resource in California. What is surprising is the variety of ways you can enjoy the coastal area. Ranging in topography from wide, sandy stretches with gentle waves to narrow, rocky strips with explosive surf, these beaches invite every aquatic pleasure: swimming, boating, fishing, surfing, scuba diving, snorkeling. Though the shoreline is mainly urban, on a few stretches you can be amazingly alone.

Three high mountain ranges separate Los Angeles from desert lands to the north and east, forming an imposing backdrop for the teeming city. The San Gabriel, San Bernardino, and San Jacinto (page 89) ranges rise abruptly to peaks over 10,000 feet. At low elevations, the frontal slopes of these mountains are closed because of fire danger from July 1 to the first rainfall (usually in November). But in winter, residents head for the hills for snow fun: belly-thumping down the slopes on improvised sleds at such resorts as Lake Gregory, Lake Arrowhead, and Big Bear—easily reached from the valley floors.

The Santa Monicas, a fourth mountain range, march right into the Pacific Ocean west of the city, their rocky tops forming the offshore Channel Islands. Where mountains and beaches meet at Point Mugu, this chapter begins, tracing the metropolitan coastline first east, then south. Then the chapter shifts its focus to the attractions in or near the three mountain ranges surrounding Los Angeles.

Beaches and mountains at L.A.'s front and back doors lure escapees from city living. Long stretches of sand and water — dotted with fishing piers, marinas, museums, and shopping complexes — invite exploration. Mountain ranges provide summer and winter fun. Valley cities like San Fernando, Van Nuys, Burbank, Glendale, Pasadena, and Riverside include family amusement centers, gardens and parks, and museums in or near their boundaries.

Along L.A.'s Beaches

Southern California's beaches see action every month of the year. The huge Los Angeles population makes full use of the sea as a coolant when summer heat builds. Water temperature is around 67°F. from July until fall. Air temperature at Santa Monica will reach an average maximum of about 75°, even as the temperature in inland Pasadena rises ten degrees higher.

Winter weather is cyclic, with clear, warm air and a glassy sea often following a blustery rainstorm. Although few swimmers brave the 55° water for a dip, wet-suited surfers, surf kayakers, wind-surfers, and lightweight-catamaran sailors turn out in force.

Here are some highlights of a coastal tour of Los Angeles County from Santa Monica Bay in the west to Long Beach Harbor in the south.

West of Santa Monica

The south slope of the Santa Monica Mountains drops abruptly to the sea on the first section of this east-west Los Angeles area beach tour. Its western half is rocky headlands and coves; it runs to good swimming beaches at the eastern end. Point Mugu to Malibu has the cleanest ocean along the metropolitan coast, offering clear water, healthy kelp beds, the best shore and offshore fishing and diving, and some very good surfing.

Variety of activity and topography marks the beaches west of Santa Monica Bay. You can camp at Point Mugu State Park and at Leo Carrillo State Beach, venture up into the hills, sand-ski, and try your luck at gliding from bluff to beach. Facilities vary, but lifeguards are on duty during the summer.

Zuma Beach, just west of Point Dume off State Highway 1, is L.A.'s largest county-owned beach. An excellent swimming beach (except for occasional summer riptides), it offers ample parking for about 2,500 cars (at a small charge) and modern facilities.

Dume, next door, is a long, steep-sided finger of sandstone pointing prominently to the south. Flocks of pelicans and cormorants perch on rocks a few hundred yards offshore; meanwhile, flocks of surfers are hurtling toward broad, sandy beaches or paddling away from them. Swimming is good; so are the tidepools.

Santa Monica Bay: Home of surf and stars

Along this crescent-shaped bay, almost all the coast is sandy with wide beaches. About half of it is set aside for public use, and used it assuredly is: its total annual visitor count numbers about 50 million. Day-use parks usually offer excellent swimming, good surfing, sunbathing, and beach play. Hang gliding is good at two spots: Dockweiler and Torrance beaches. (The latter discourages the sport during the crowded summer season.) Although the beaches are fairly similar with sandy stretches below high bluffs, facilities differ. Some charge admission; others do not. Lifeguards are generally on duty during the peak season.

In 1983, winter storms destroyed or damaged some of the area's fishing piers (and a few private residences); but repair and restoration work got underway almost immediately.

Malibu has long been known as a "getaway" spot for movie and TV stars; their houses line the road for several miles and perch precariously on the cliffs above it. Zonker Davis Accessway, one of many new public-access footpaths along the coast, links Santa Monica Bay and the Pacific Coast Highway, threading between Malibu residences and passing a restaurant.

Malibu Lagoon, a 35-acre state beach with a ⅔-mile ocean frontage, offers good swimming (one area is for surfers only). Restrooms, concessions, and parking are along the highway.

At Malibu's private pier, you'll find sportfishing boats, an excursion boat, and a restaurant; you can fish from the pier if you have a license.

J. Paul Getty Museum, at 17985 W. Pacific Coast Highway in Malibu, received worldwide attention upon Getty's death in 1976. An American industrialist (often called the richest man in the world), Getty left the bulk of his estate to the museum, ensuring its future expansion. At present, several hundred million dollars are represented in his collection of rare tapestries, Greek and Roman statuary, Louis XV and XVI furniture, and valuable paintings by Italian and Dutch masters.

The museum itself is a replica of the Villa Papyri (a large villa at Herculaneum destroyed by the eruption of Vesuvius in A.D. 79); about $17 million was spent in its construction.

From June through September, the museum is open from 10 A.M. to 5 P.M. Monday through Friday; from October through May, hours are 10 A.M. to 5 P.M. Tuesday through Saturday. There's no admission charge, but you'll need a parking reservation. Call (213) 459-8402 at least a week in advance of your visit.

Will Rogers State Beach, at the intersection of the coast highway and Sunset Boulevard, is beneath the Pacific Palisades (so close that slides have forced several relocations of the highway a few feet south, into some badly needed parking lots). Lifeguards and restrooms are provided on the beach, and restaurants line the highway nearby.

Santa Monica

At Santa Monica the shore turns southerly for a splendid sweep of 20 miles of almost wholly accessible, broad, sandy beach encompassing eight public beaches, five fishing piers, and two small craft harbors. Then it rounds the Palos Verdes Peninsula for 15 rocky miles as the road rides high above the cliffs before losing itself among the channels of two big harbors—Los Angeles and Long Beach. A bike path stretches 19 miles from California Avenue to the bluffs at Palos Verdes.

Shops, restaurants, and boutiques line Santa Monica's Main Street, Montana Avenue, and Third Street. The free Heritage Square Museum (2612 Main Street) gives a look at the area's past; it's open Thursday through Saturday from 11 A.M. to 4 P.M., Sunday from noon to 5 P.M.

Santa Monica State Beach, adjacent to Ocean Avenue, has been the most frequented of the bay beaches since the 1860s. It has picnic tables, fire rings, and playground equipment, and is handy to restaurants.

Santa Monica Pier, hard hit during the 1983 storms, is now on the way back to its former glory. It's a gathering place for tourists as well as locals, for bathing-suited beachgoers and more fully clad sightseers. The pier, the esplanade below, and the cliffside park above are colorful, and bustling. Some activities are free—you don't have to pay to fish from the pier, or to watch surfers, volleyball players, and amateur acrobats at what used to be Muscle Beach. For a fee, you can go out on a fishing party boat.

Venice—California's answer to Italy

Perhaps one of the most unusual beachfront communities in the West, Venice-by-the-Sea was the dream of Abbot Kinney, a wealthy Easterner, who, in 1892, induced the Santa Fe Railroad to extend its tracks to these 160 acres of sand dunes and salt marsh. Here he built his dream city of homes, hotels, interconnecting canals plied by a fleet of gondolas, amusement halls, and a large Chautauqua auditorium. Unfortunately, engineering mistakes caused the canals to deteriorate. Venice began to decline, and oil developments ended the dream.

The pier, at the foot of Washington Street, is organized for round-the-clock fishing. Bays at short intervals expand its perimeter to a length of about 400 yards.

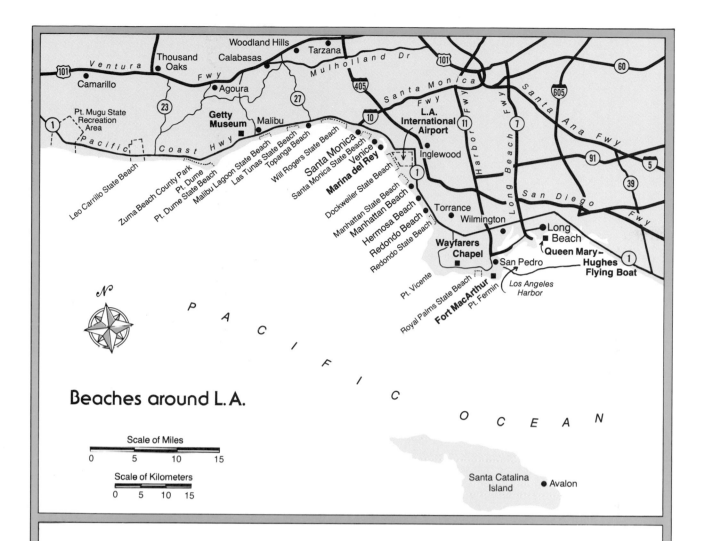

Beaches around L.A.

Scale of Miles

0 5 10 15

Scale of Kilometers

0 5 10 15

Map labels:

Ventura Fwy, Thousand Oaks, Woodland Hills, Calabasas, Tarzana, 101, *Mulholland Dr*, 101, Camarillo, 101, Agoura, 23, 27, 405, *Santa Monica Fwy*, 10, L.A. International Airport, 11, 60, 605, Getty Museum, Malibu, Inglewood, 7, *Santa Ana Fwy*, Pt. Mugu State Recreation Area, 1, *Pacific Coast Hwy*, Las Tunas State Beach, Topanga Beach, Will Rogers State Beach, Santa Monica, Santa Monica State Beach, Venice, Marina del Rey, 1, 91, 5, 39, Leo Carrillo State Beach, Zuma Beach County Park, Pt. Dume, Pt. Dume State Beach, Malibu Lagoon State Beach, Dockweiler State Beach, Manhattan State Beach, Manhattan Beach, Hermosa Beach, Redondo Beach, Redondo State Beach, Torrance, Wilmington, *Harbor Fwy*, *Long Beach Fwy*, *San Diego Fwy*, Long Beach, Wayfarers Chapel, San Pedro, Queen Mary–Hughes Flying Boat, 1, N, Pt. Vicente, Royal Palms State Beach, Fort MacArthur, Pt. Fermin, *Los Angeles Harbor*, PACIFIC OCEAN, Santa Catalina Island, Avalon

Major Points of Interest

J. Paul Getty Museum (Malibu)—replica of ancient Roman villa houses priceless statuary, furniture, paintings

Santa Monica—splendid public beaches, fishing piers, boat harbors, waterfront carnival

Marina del Rey—home port for over 10,000 boats; Fisherman's Village houses shops, restaurants, galleries; take harbor cruise

Palos Verdes Scenic Drive—15 miles of varied spectacular marine and mountain views; see Wayfarers Chapel

L.A. International Airport—area's largest air terminal; shuttle service to downtown, connections to outlying airports

Los Angeles Harbor—maze of channels, inlets, and islands covers 50 miles of waterfront; takeoff site for Catalina Island; deep-sea fishing; shopping at Ports O' Call nautical village

Long Beach—naval center and major port; good swimming, boating, fishing. Shoreline Village shops; two former Spanish ranchos now open for tours

Queen Mary (Long Beach)—fabled British ocean liner; tour decks, shops, museum; dine and sleep aboard

Spruce Goose (Long Beach)—Howard Hughes' Flying Boat, world's largest wooden plane, on exhibit next to Queen Mary and LondonTowne

Catalina Island—getaway island 21 miles offshore; tour Avalon, island interior; take boat trips to seal colony and undersea gardens; overnight accommodations, good boating and swimming

ARCHITECTURAL CONTRASTS,
*Wayfarers Chapel (right) in Palos
Verdes, and J. Paul Getty Museum
(below) in Malibu, are open to
visitors. Call ahead for museum
parking space.*

Seaside shopping

Between Marina del Rey and Long Beach, you'll find a number of ocean-oriented shopping complexes. Marina del Rey's Fisherman's Village (137263 Fiji Way) combines waterside shopping with a boating enclave. From promenades you overlook some 7,000 yachts.

On the waterfront at Redondo Beach's King Harbor, 167 acres contain all forms of watery sport and recreation. Here, too, are restaurants, hotels, and sportfishing boats.

In addition to San Pedro's Ports O' Call Village (see page 36) the south bay offers a turn-of-the-century waterfront center in Long Beach featuring shops, restaurants, and a beautifully restored carousel.

Marina del Rey

It's easy to believe that Marina del Rey, home port for more than 10,000 boats, is the largest manmade pleasure boat harbor on the Pacific Coast.

One of the most dramatic waterfront scenes in the world is the huge armada of boats of all types heading out to sea or parading placidly up and down the main channel.

Shopping centers abound in Marina del Rey; hotels and motels face beach and waterfront.

Harbor cruises leave Fisherman's Village—a Cape Cod collection of shops, restaurants, and art galleries—every hour. The harbor cruise gives you a close-up look at many celebrities' boats, as well as Chinese junks, catamarans, antique and classic craft, and old, square-rigged Scandinavian schooners.

Large public launching ramps allow boat owners to truck or trailer in their boats. Power and sailboat rentals are available for marina cruising and for offshore deep-sea fishing.

The famed Marina del Rey waterfront restaurant row is one of the largest concentrations of casually elegant eating places in the Greater Los Angeles area.

Manhattan, Hermosa, and Redondo

At this trio of beaches you'll find more youthful beach aficionados per square yard than almost anywhere else along the coast. Both Manhattan and Hermosa beaches have public fishing piers. Much like other piers in the region, each has a bait and tackle shop, rest rooms, and a snack bar for the comfort of anglers.

Redondo State Beach adjoins a marina complex (King Harbor) of restaurants, motels, yacht clubs, and boat facilities. Next to it are the shops and restaurants that line two piers extending out over the water, giving a good view of the 1½-mile beach.

Palos Verdes to Long Beach

Following the scenic drive around the Palos Verdes Peninsula is a pleasant alternative to continuing on the coast highway. You pass several interesting tourist attractions, as well as many ocean overlooks. You're on your way to the busy ports of Los Angeles and Long Beach. Attractive seaside shopping, good fishing spots, a marine museum, and the imposing ocean liner *Queen Mary* are only some of the ocean-front attractions. You'll also find some historical surprises.

The plush Palos Verdes Peninsula, below Point Conception, is the most prominent projection on the coastal map—about 15 miles of rocky shore with a few sandy beaches. Informal access at several points has been made by tidepool probers, rock fishermen, skin divers, and surf scanners. A spectacular scenic drive through this area—along Palos Verdes Drive—is one traditional attraction of the Los Angeles region. The road begins in parklike Palos Verdes Estates and ends in Point Fermin Park in San Pedro. In between, it follows the rugged cliff top for a 15-mile stretch, offering you varied and spectacular views of the sea and mountains.

Other parts of the drive take you through beautiful residential areas and flower fields; there are ocean view turnouts at several spots. You'll pass such points of interest as the Point Vicente Lighthouse and the Wayfarers Chapel (overlooking Abalone Cove) en route to San Pedro and Long Beach.

Less frequented is the relatively isolated seacoast 100 feet below the cliffs. Since accessibility to this shore is limited by tides, all of the beach areas are hard to explore in one day. Newspapers publish exact times of tides for each day. Fires and overnight camping are prohibited.

South Coast Botanic Garden (26300 Crenshaw Boulevard, Palos Verdes) exhibits over 150,000 plants. One of the first experiments in land reclamation, it was built on what was a mine, then a sanitary landfill. The garden is open from 9 A.M. to 5 P.M. daily except Christmas. There is a small entrance fee. Call (213) 772-5813 for information and directions.

Point Vicente Interpretive Center (31501 Palos Verdes Drive W.) features exhibits and displays focusing on the peninsula and environs: formation and erosion, Portuguese Bend slide activity, tidepool ecology, kelp beds, the California gray whale, and famous peninsula shipwrecks. The center is open weekdays from 1 to 7 P.M., weekends 10 A.M. to 7 P.M. There's a token admission fee.

Point Fermin Park offers a place to picnic and watch the hang gliders. The Old Point Fermin Lighthouse (built in 1874 of lumber brought around Cape Horn) is restored, but it's not open to the public.

Royal Palms State Beach, 2 miles northwest of Point Fermin off Paseo del Mar (extension of Western Avenue), offers one of the few places to swim on the south coast of the peninsula. Space and facilities are limited.

Wayfarers Chapel is set on a hill at Portuguese Bend (a mile east of Marineland), looking out over the ocean and Palos Verdes Drive. Glass walls, redwood beams, and a white-rock campanile bearing a gold cross make this a striking structure. The grounds are set with plants mentioned in the Bible. The chapel is open daily from 11 A.M. to 4 P.M. for self-guided tours. Swedenborg Reference Library and Museum is located just east of the chapel.

Architect Lloyd Wright (son of Frank Lloyd Wright) designed the unique chapel for the Church of the New

Jerusalem as a memorial to Emmanuel Swedenborg, but it is intended as a place of worship and meditation for people of all faiths.

Los Angeles Harbor: An aquatic freeway

The Port of Los Angeles and the Port of Long Beach share the world's largest manmade harbor. Its maze of channels, inlets, and islands covers 50 miles of developed waterfront, shielded by a 9-mile breakwater. Newest of the major western ports (started in 1889), Los Angeles is a leader in total tonnage processed and in modern handling techniques. It is the center of the country's seafood canning industry. The Port of Los Angeles includes the Terminal Island, San Pedro, and Wilmington districts.

Terminals at the San Pedro port are currently being expanded to service up to 12 cruise lines. The new World Cruise Center, encompassing hotel and entertainment facilities for both cruise customers and day visitors, will be completed in 1989. Walkways and a shopping promenade encourage strolling and sightseeing.

Soaring 185 feet above the harbor's main channel is the Vincent Thomas Bridge, a replacement for an auto ferry. This handsome suspension bridge connects San Pedro with Terminal Island, location of most of the harbor's large shipping berths and warehouses. Under the bridge's western end is the Catalina Terminal, where ferries and seaplanes depart for Catalina Island. You'll pay a small toll to cross the bridge.

The area off Harbor Boulevard in San Pedro flanks the main channel of Los Angeles Harbor and makes dock-watching a breeze. There's a little park where Sixth Street runs into Harbor; at its south end is the Los Angeles Maritime Museum, where you'll see detailed models of the supertankers *Aurora* and *Torrey Canyon*. The museum is open from 9 A.M. to 4 P.M. weekdays and from 12:30 to 4 P.M. on weekends; admission is free. There's a small observation deck.

Fort MacArthur, near the harbor entrance, once helped protect the harbor. Headquarters of the 47th Artillery Brigade, it's also an air defense center.

Cabrillo Beach, just south of the fort, is usually crowded with people, cars, and boat trailers. You'll find picnic tables and barbecue pits. In addition to a still-water beach inside the breakwater, there's a surf beach on the ocean that's popular with fishermen. On the harbor side are a public boat launching ramp and a fishing pier paralleling the breakwater. The free Cabrillo Marine Museum, across from the beach at 3720 Stephen White Drive, offers L.A. Harbor and maritime lore in general. There you can look at seashells, ship models, marine specimens, and navigation equipment. Summer museum hours are 10 A.M. to 5 P.M. Tuesday through Sunday; winter hours are shorter.

Ports O' Call Village, an extensive shopping complex, faces the harbor's main channel at Berth 77 on Harbor Boulevard. There's a lot here: restaurants, import shops, and craftspeople combine with harbor tour boats and nautical memorabilia. You can hover over the harbor in a helicopter or shoot to the top of a sky tower—and when a crisp day brings on the urge to head out to

sea, an hour-long cruise aboard one of the ships sailing from piers 76 and 77 may be the answer.

Banning Park is located on the Pacific Coast Highway 2 blocks east of Avalon Boulevard. General Phineas Banning, a fabled host who founded the town of Wilmington, built a 30-room colonial showcase in 1864 and landscaped it with acres of beautiful gardens. Now restored, the mansion is a museum exhibiting furnishings from the last century. The home and grounds are open to the public daily. On Wednesday, Saturday, and Sunday, free tours are offered at 1, 2, 3, and 4 P.M.

Long Beach: A city on the rise

Long important as a naval base, major port, and manufacturing center, Long Beach is again surfacing as a major resort and recreational area. California's fifth largest city is linked to Los Angeles (21 miles to the north) by the Long Beach Freeway. The Pacific Coast Highway and San Diego Freeway cut east and west through the city. Direct flights to the Long Beach Airport avoid the Los Angeles traffic.

Thanks to thoughtful planning, Long Beach is no longer known as the "Coney Island of the West"; today, it's one of Southern California's most attractive, progressive communities. An extensive 421-acre redevelopment project has changed the whole face of the city, from the downtown center to the harbor. An attractive pedestrian mall and boardwalk runs from downtown Long Beach Plaza (and the amphitheater adjoining it) to the shoreline.

The city's transit system is California's most sophisticated. A several-block-long stretch of First Street—between Pine Avenue and Long Beach Boulevard—is for buses only. Lining the "bus mall" are brightly lit passenger shelters, where video information systems display up-to-the-minute routes and schedules for transportation throughout the city, as well as to L.A. and Orange counties.

The redevelopment program includes the restoration of some of the city's more historic buildings; but it's the new business and residential high rises that have really changed the Long Beach skyline. Even the oil drilling rigs that dot the harbor have been cleverly concealed behind facades on palm-studded, manmade islands.

Along Ocean Boulevard, across from the city's municipal offices, stands the handsome Convention and Entertainment Center—the site chosen for two of the 1984 Olympic events (volleyball and fencing). Here you'll find the Terrace Theater (home of the symphony, civic light opera, ballet, and grand opera), the more intimate Center Theater, and the Arena.

Farther east, at 2300 Ocean Boulevard, the Museum of Arts is quartered in a charming turn-of-the-century house. The museum and adjoining bookstore and gift shop are open Wednesday through Sunday from 1 to 5 P.M. Visit nearby Bluff Park Historic District for a look at several blocks of carefully preserved early 1900s residences.

At the waterfront, imaginative harborside development has resulted in new parks, marinas, tourist-oriented shopping complexes, and hotels. On the water side of the Convention and Entertainment Center is Shoreline Park, a 100-acre aquatic playground with fishing platforms, picnic sites, and a recreational vehicle park. Next door, lushly landscaped Rainbow Lagoon Park boasts paddle boats and biking paths.

Shoreline Village, at the foot of Pine Avenue, resembles an early 1900s seaside hamlet. Specialty shops and restaurants cover 7 acres along the water. A ride on one of the hand-carved Looff carousel animals (vintage 1906) is sufficient reason to make the trip.

Every year in April, the Toyota Grand Prix is held along Shoreline Drive. The nerve-jangling, ear-popping race attracts visitors from all over the world. For information, contact the Long Beach Area Convention and Visitors Council, 180 E. Ocean Boulevard, Suite 150, Long Beach, CA 90802; or call (213) 436-3645.

Across the channel looms the regal *Queen Mary*. Near the retired Cunard liner, and perhaps almost as famous, is Howard Hughes' "Spruce Goose"—the world's largest wooden airplane, now housed under the world's largest clear-span aluminum dome. Little LondonTowne, a replica of an English village, sits beside the two attractions.

The *Queen Mary* is open daily for tours and dining; you can even sleep aboard, in staterooms run as a hotel. A self-guided tour (ticket office open 10 A.M. to 8 P.M. in summer, until 5 P.M. the rest of the year) covers the bridge, engine room, officers' quarters, and upper decks. If you prefer, just stroll around the venerable ship, peeking into some of the shops and enjoying a meal in one of the on-board restaurants.

A one-hour water tour departs from the bow of the *Queen Mary*—daily during summer, Saturday and Sunday the rest of the year.

On a visit to the *Spruce Goose,* the wooden flying boat owned by Howard Hughes, you can enter the enormous plane and peer into the cockpit, see a cutaway engine display, and view films from Hughes's aviation career. Hours are 10 A.M. to 9 P.M. in summer, until 6 P.M. the rest of the year. You'll be charged admission to both the *Queen Mary* and the *Spruce Goose;* a combination ticket reduces the prices.

To reach both attractions, exit the Long Beach Freeway at Harbor Scenic Drive and follow the signs, or cross the Queen's Way Bridge from Shoreline Drive.

Along the beaches inside the harbor breakwater, there's almost no surf, making the 5½-mile arc of white sand attractive to swimmers and sunbathers. Between Redondo and Park avenues, the Belmont Fishing Pier extends out into the harbor. At Alamitos Bay, you'll find marinas, restaurants, yacht clubs, and a couple of on-the-water shopping complexes—Seaport Village and Marina Pacifica Mall. On Naples Island, you can dine in a restaurant, picnic in a park, or take a gondola ride along the waterways.

Two Spanish ranchos evoke the past. Rancho Los Cerritos, at 4600 Virginia Road, is one of the finest of the L.A. area's restored adobes. Built in 1844, the delightful Spanish-style house was once surrounded by acres of rolling hills and lush grazing land. You can still view the original garden today; some of its trees are over a century old. Los Cerritos is open Wednesday through Sunday from 1 to 5 P.M.; there's no admission charge.

Rancho Los Alamitos, located atop a knoll, has become a city museum-park. A visit to the ranch will transport you back over a century: the adobe's history goes back to 1806. Once owned by Jose Figueroa, an early California governor, it was a working cattle ranch until 1953. The Bixby family (donors of the property) left the house equipped with family possessions that span many generations.

Free, 1-hour guided tours are given between 1 and 4 P.M. Wednesday through Sunday. To reach the adobe, take Palos Verdes Avenue south from the San Diego Freeway. At the intersection of Anaheim Road you'll see a "private road" sign; just keep going 1 more block to Bixby Hill Road, then turn left to the entrance.

Catalina Island: A nearby getaway

Once a hideout for buccaneers and smugglers (though only 21 miles from shore) and the site of an unusual aquatic gold rush, Santa Catalina Island has been a popular visitor destination ever since 1887, when the resort town of Avalon was opened and steam service started from the mainland. Except for Avalon, the 21-mile-long island consists of mountainous wilderness and calm coves.

Crossing the sea. Just getting to Catalina is an enjoyable experience. You'll have your choice of conveyances—from sleek turbo jets to whirling helicopters, from stubby amphibian boats to modern excursion vessels. Boats depart year-round from terminals at San Pedro and Long Beach; from April through October, there's a boat from the Balboa Pavilion at Newport Beach. The sea crossing takes about 2 hours.

For fares and schedules, call Catalina Cruises at (213) 514-3838 or (714) 527-7111; Catalina Channel Express at (213) 519-1212, or (in season) Catalina Passenger Service at (714) 673-5245.

If you fly to Catalina, you'll get there in only 20 minutes. Seaplanes leave from the Long Beach Airport; helicopter service is available from Long Beach and San Pedro.

For all travel information, call the Visitors Information and Services Center at (800) 428-2566.

Avalon is still chiefly geared to the pedestrian, but motor traffic is increasing; tour vehicles line up to greet debarking steamer passengers. Shops and restaurants along Crescent Avenue offer good souvenir shopping. The visitor information and services center on the Green Pleasure Pier makes a good first stop.

Still the landmark to visitors arriving in Avalon Harbor is the fortress-like Casino—really a movie theater topped by a vast, open ballroom. On the first floor is the free Catalina Museum.

Exploring the island can be a short or long-term experience. On a half-day stop you can combine a trip on a glass-bottom boat with a scenic tour of the Wrigley residence and your choice of a Casino tour or a coastal cruise (summer only).

If you're staying for a full day or overnight (be sure to make reservations), you'll have time for further explorations of the island's coastline or interior.

Around L. A.'s Mountains

Our tour of the mountains encircling the Los Angeles region extends from the San Fernando Valley in the west to the Upper Santa Ana River Valley in the east. We begin with the westernmost Santa Monica Mountains, move on to survey the San Gabriel Mountains and their environs, and end by exploring the recreationally rich San Bernardino Mountains.

Along the way you'll find many diverse parks, gardens, resort areas, and landmarks, as well as some of Southern California's most famous smaller cities. In or near these mountain chains are such familiar names as Griffith Park, Burbank, Pasadena, San Marino, Mount Wilson, Pomona, and Lake Arrowhead.

In these mountains, sportsmen can hike and ride over hundreds of miles of trails, try their luck in the stocked streams of national forests, and hunt for various wildlife. Motorists and sightseers can take scenic walks, picnic, explore a wilderness area, or drive through picturesque thoroughfares. Angeles National Forest, a giant preserve in the San Gabriel Mountains, includes nearly a fourth of the area of Los Angeles County.

Santa Monica Mountains

Los Angeles has a mountain range in its midst. Even those who have never heard of the Santa Monicas by name probably know Griffith Park, Mulholland Drive, and Sunset Boulevard, all within or bordering this island of emptiness that reaches into the heart of L.A.

The Santa Monicas are unusual among American mountains in that they run east and west: 47 miles from the Los Angeles River to the Oxnard plain. Some of the best beaches in the northern section of the Los Angeles coast abut the Santa Monicas.

In a drive through the Santa Monicas, you can see Griffith Park; three great canyons (Sullivan, Rustic, and Topanga); the Claretian Seminary (former palatial estate of King Gillette of razor blade fame); and Tapia County Park. You'll also see familiar gorges and rock formations at Malibu Creek State Park, formerly the 20th Century-Fox movie ranch; the Paramount Ranch (now a park, once a location for movies and TV); Lake Sherwood (one of six impoundments of Malibu Creek and tributaries open to the public for a fee); and Malibu Canyon and Point Mugu on the coast.

Griffith Park now has an extensive system of hiking and bridle trails. Inquire at the park ranger office on Griffith Park Drive. Will Rogers State Historic Park also has trails for horses and hikers that ascend to good view points.

San Fernando Valley

The San Fernando Valley section of Los Angeles (220 square miles bounded by the Santa Monica, Santa Susana, Verdugo, and San Gabriel mountains) only 60 years ago comprised open wheat fields, farms, and a few small towns. Since the area was annexed by the city of Los Angeles, it has grown to a population of over a million. Despite the valley's tremendous growth, there are still charming remnants of its past and some appealing oases of the present. You can reach the valley from downtown Los Angeles on the Hollywood or San Diego freeways. From the north, you enter on the Golden State Freeway (Interstate Highway 5); from the west, on the Ventura Freeway (U.S. Highway 101).

Famous landmarks of Southern California history have been preserved in and near the valley. You'll find the original San Fernando Valley mission, some famous stagecoach stops and movie sites, and, to the north, the site of Southern California's gold discovery. Parks and gardens in the valley are varied. Two of the most familiar are Forest Lawn, an unusual cemetery in Glendale, and Valencia's Six Flags Magic Mountain, a family amusement park.

To simplify the location of these historic landmarks, we have organized the section from west to east. It starts where you would arrive in the valley on the Ventura Freeway, from the west, and on the Golden State Freeway, from the north; continues through the middle of the valley; and ends in the Arroyo Seco foothills.

At the western end of San Fernando Valley, three historic sites and one movie location bring back the past.

• *Newbury Park's Stagecoach Inn*, built in 1876, has seen action as a country hotel, stage stopover, military school, Scottish gift shop, and finally, the stately museum it is today. Part of a 4-acre park, the grounds also contain a collection of carriages, stagecoaches, and wagons. Nearby, a small Chumash thatched hut, an adobe, and a homesteader's cabin represent early California's three cultures. The inn is open Wednesday, Thursday, Friday, and Sunday. Admission is free. From the Ventura Freeway, exit left on Lynn Road to Ventu Park Road; turn right and look for the sign on your left.

• *Simi Valley's Strathearn Historical Park* centers around a residence that's actually two structures: a pre-1800 adobe with a grand two-story Victorian attached to its south side. The residence is full of turn-of-the-century furnishings, most of which belonged to the Strathearn family. In the yard, a lineup of antique ranching equipment awaits inspection. Here, too, you'll find the original Simi Valley Library and an 1880s Colony House, one of 12 prefabricated houses moved (in pieces) to this area from Chicago.

Strathearn Park is open Sundays from 1 to 4 P.M. Admission is free. From the Ventura Freeway, take Topanga Canyon Boulevard north 7 miles to State Highway 118. Drive west to Madera Drive near the freeway's end, then south on Madera to Strathearn Place.

• *Wildwood Park in Thousand Oaks* was the location for more than 300 movie and TV westerns. As you enter the park, look to the cliffs at your right—smoke signals were often filmed rising from these crags. A mile into the park are Stagecoach Bluffs; from here, film crews rolled countless wagons into the canyon below. From the Ventura Freeway, take Lynn Road north 2.2 miles and turn west on Avenida de los Arboles.

• *Calabasas* was a stage stop a century ago, days out from Los Angeles on the road to Monterey. Fifty years ago it was the last stop in the San Fernando Valley for motorists heading west on U.S. 101. Today it is by-passed by the Ventura Freeway, and its visitors are those who deliberately seek it out.

(Continued on page 40)

WATER-ORIENTED DESTINATIONS include Avalon Bay at Catalina (above) and Long Beach's mighty Queen Mary (right). Dome covers Howard Hughes' "Spruce Goose"; LondonTowne lies in foreground.

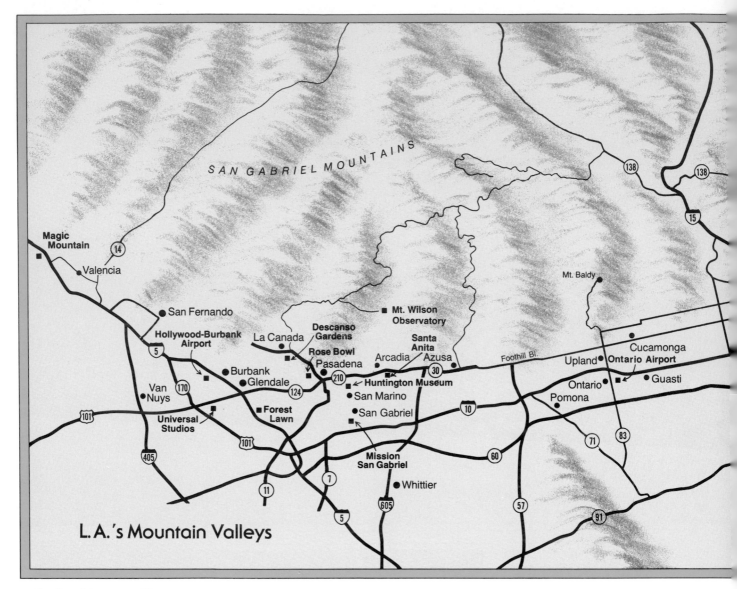

L.A.'s Mountain Valleys

...*Continued from page 38*

The gem of Calabasas is the Leonis Adobe. Tucked away among tall trees, this ranch house is a monument to Miguel Leonis, a contentious Basque land baron who played a colorful part in the region's history. Restored and furnished, it is open from 1 to 4 P.M. on Wednesday and weekends. A small donation provides maintenance. Take the Mulholland Drive-Valley Circle Boulevard exit from the Ventura Freeway.

Los Encinos State Historic Park (16756 Moorpark Street, Encino) is the place where the valley's recorded history began over 200 years ago. The Portola party stopped here, beside an Indian settlement built around a spring that's still flowing. Here, the bustle on the boulevard seems far away. Encircled by old olive trees and tall grevillias are turn-of-the-century sheep ranch buildings and the 1849 Osa adobe. Some of the rooms in the Osa adobe are furnished; recorded voices describe their contents. Los Encinos is open Wednesday through Sunday from 10 A.M. to 5 P.M. Expect a small admission charge.

Six Flags Magic Mountain, located near the Golden State Freeway in Valencia, features "white-knuckler" rides as well as more gentle family adventure rides, live shows, and a 6-acre children's area.

You can experience white-water rafting, take a splashing dash through a water flume that climaxes with a 90-foot plunge, race through a mine in a runaway car, ride aboard a water-jet boat, or try the skydiving thrill called "Freefall." Among the park's five roller coasters are the new stand-up "Shock Wave" and "Colossus," one of the world's largest wooden coasters. Small fry will love Bugs Bunny World and the petting zoo in the Animal Farm.

All this is part of a 260-acre family amusement park, the Southland's newest. The entrance fee includes unlimited use of rides, attractions, and entertainment (food, games, and shopping aren't included). The park is open daily mid-May through Labor Day from 10 A.M., weekends and holidays only during the remainder of the year.

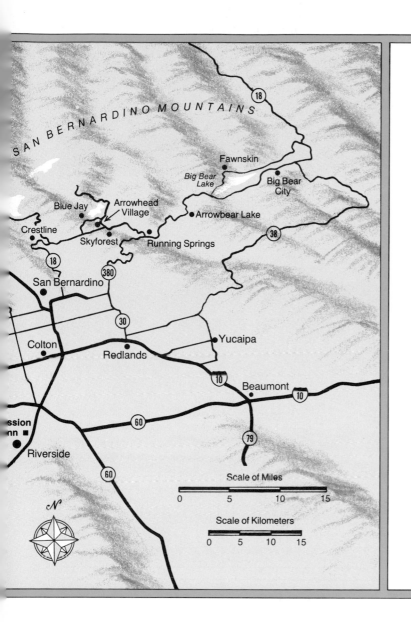

Major Points of Interest

Magic Mountain (Valencia)—260-acre family amusement center; top summer-night entertainment

Descanso Gardens (La Canada)—acres of camellias and rose gardens offer year-round blooms; Japanese tea pavilion

Rose Bowl (Pasadena)—stadium for New Year's football game; tour Football Hall of Fame inside

Norton Simon Museum (Pasadena)—controversial architecture; superb collection of art, sculpture, paintings, medieval tapestries

Forest Lawn (Glendale)—memorial park noted for statuary, church replicas, art works

L.A. State and County Arboretum (Arcadia)—see plants from every continent of the world; take guided tram trip through outstanding plantings; historic buildings

Santa Anita Race Track (Arcadia)—thoroughbred horse racing December to mid-April on well-landscaped grounds; no charge for watching morning workouts and touring stables

Huntington Library (San Marino)—also art gallery ("Blue Boy," "Pinkie") and botanical gardens on 200-acre estate

Mission San Gabriel (San Gabriel)—restored mission was once known for ancient vineyards; unique architecture and paintings attract visitors

Mission Inn (Riverside)—tour landmark hotel housing treasures from 1875

Rim of the World Drive (San Bernardino Mountains)—scenic route to Lake Arrowhead and Big Bear resort areas

William S. Hart Park, northwest of the valley at the junction of Newhall Avenue and San Fernando Road in Newhall, was originally Horseshoe Ranch—property of William S. Hart, Western star of the silent screen. He left the 253-acre estate to Los Angeles County, with instructions that it be preserved as a park.

The original ranch house at the bottom of the hill contains mementos of the star's motion picture career and is flanked by a corral filled with gentle livestock for the delight of children. Shaded picnic areas are nearby. Hart's home atop the hill, a Spanish-Mexican style mansion called "La Loma de Los Vientos" (Hill of the Winds), houses historical weapons, American Indian artifacts, Western art (including paintings by Charles Russell and Frederic Remington), and other Western Americana. A herd of bison roams the hills.

The ranch is open from 10 A.M. to dusk daily; free mansion tours run every hour between 10 A.M. and 5 P.M. weekends, and between 10 A.M. and 3 P.M. Wednesday through Friday. There's no admission charge. A free shuttle service brings visitors from the park entrance.

Placerita Canyon State and County Park memorializes the golden dream of Don Francisco Lopez. In 1842—6 years before the Sutter's Mill gold strike—this weary shepherd stopped for a nap under an oak tree near what is now Newhall. As the story goes, Lopez dreamed of gold as he slept. When he awoke, he was hungry and pulled up a clump of wild onions growing nearby. Gold nuggets clung to the roots—the first glimpse of an $80,000 deposit. The gold is gone now, but the tree—called the Oak of the Golden Dream—still stands in this small park about 5 miles east of Newhall, off U.S. Highway 14.

The park is a pleasant place for a picnic or a hike (you can pick up a trail map at the nature center). Scenes for the Cisco Kid movie series were filmed here.

Mission San Fernando is the focal point of the valley's oldest settlement. Founded in 1797 by Father La-

ART AND GARDENS attract tourists to the San Gabriel Valley. Sculpture garden (above) is part of Pasadena's Norton Simon Museum of Art. Teahouse (right) sits among Descanso Gardens in La Canada.

suen, California's 17th mission was known for its hospitality (it was a Butterfield Stage stop) and its fine cattle. The mission subsequently served as headquarters for Governor Pico, and later for Colonel Fremont during the Mexican-American War. Allow at least an hour for the well-marked walk through the extensive buildings and grounds. Located on San Fernando Mission Boulevard between the San Diego and Golden State freeways, the mission is open daily from 9:30 A.M. to 5 P.M. A small donation is requested.

Across the street in Brand Park is the Memory Garden, with a statue of Father Serra. From there, go south on Columbus Avenue 2 blocks to the YMCA field for a look at the Andres Pico Adobe. Its exterior shows how a typical adobe house grew. The oldest portion was built about 1834 by former mission Indians; later in its long career, lean-to rooms and a second story were added.

Forest Lawn in Glendale, east of Griffith Park, is the first of the extraordinary Forest Lawn Memorial Parks (open to visitors from 9 A.M. to 5 P.M. daily). These superbly landscaped 206 acres form what is probably the best known, most visited, and most controversial cemetery in the world. There are no tombstones here; instead, you'll see an unusual collection of statuary, memorials, shrines, and replicas of famous churches. The collection includes reproductions of Michelangelo's sculpture and of the famous "Last Supper" stained-glass windows. Forest Lawn is also the home for the world's largest religious painting, "The Crucifixion," which is 195 feet long and 45 feet high. The park's entrance is on Glendale Avenue, northeast of the terminus of Glendale Boulevard at San Fernando Road.

Forest Lawn-Hollywood Hills, noted for its patriotic theme, features a Court of Liberty with a 175-foot Birth of Liberty Mosaic, a Monument to Washington, and a Lincoln Terrace. The Hall of Liberty Museum and various churches house historical memorabilia. A free patriotic movie is shown daily. Forest Lawn-Hollywood Hills is located at 6300 Forest Lawn Drive.

Additional art treasures may be viewed at Forest Lawn-Covina Hills and Forest Lawn-Cypress.

Burbank — where entertainment begins

Satirized for years as "beautiful downtown Burbank" on a television show, this city is really the center of the movie and television industry. Film studios are based here and stars live nearby in the Toluca Lake area. The Hollywood-Burbank Airport is one of the busiest in Southern California, and even the formerly drab downtown section has become a delightful shopping mall.

Burbank is one place where you can tour the studios (see page 29). Universal City (the world's largest studio), Burbank Studios, and NBC Television Studios offer guided tours.

San Gabriel Valley

The San Gabriel Valley is certainly the most lush, in terms of greenery, and the most plush, in terms of wealth and architecture, of the three Los Angeles area valleys. It contains the oldest valley settlements in the L.A. region, some of the area's finest museums and estates, and some of the oldest architecture and gardens.

Pasadena, the *grande dame* of the area, is perhaps best known for the colorful Tournament of Roses Parade and Rose Bowl game held on New Year's Day. But primarily it is an attractive residential community with stately trees and old buildings at the base of the San Gabriel Mountains. Driving through the quiet streets, you'll find many places of architectural interest, including the Gamble House at 4 Westmoreland Place, one of the best-known works of architects Charles and Henry Greene. The house is open for 1-hour guided tours (for a fee) from 10 A.M. to 3 P.M. on Tuesday and Thursday, and from noon to 3 P.M. every Sunday except major holidays; call (818) 793-3334 for further information.

• *The Pasadena Historical Society Museum*, at 470 W. Walnut Street (across Orange Grove from Gamble House), is another example of the gracious mansions that once lined the streets. Guided tours are from 1 to 4 P.M. Tuesdays and Thursdays; donations are requested.

• *The Tournament House*, at 390 S. Orange Grove Boulevard, contains Rose Bowl memorabilia. From February through September, free ½-hour tours are offered on Wednesdays between 2 and 4 P.M.

• *The Pasadena Library*, a grand-manner City Hall, and the Civic Auditorium are all set in a row along a short stretch of Garfield Avenue. All were built between 1925 and 1932 to become the heart of a formal civic center, a plan which never materialized. Around the remodeled Civic Auditorium, the Pasadena Center, with its shops, meeting rooms, and landscaped gardens, provides a focal point for access to the civic center.

• *The Norton Simon Museum* (at Orange Grove and Colorado boulevards), one of the most important new museums of art in California, symbolizes the new architectural look coming to Pasadena. The cornerless, tile-clad museum baffles design critics, but most admit that its positioning and classic setting are superb. The collection ranges from Indian and Southeast Asian sculpture to European old masters, impressionist and modern paintings, and medieval tapestries. Galleries and gardens display sculpture. The museum is open Thursday through Sunday from noon to 6 P.M.; there's a modest admission charge for anyone over 12.

• *Brookside Park and the Rose Bowl* in its center cover more than 500 acres in Arroyo Seco Canyon. Here you'll find picnic areas, playgrounds, hiking trails, a swimming pool, and a municipal golf course, in addition to the famous Rose Bowl. Seating 100,000 spectators, the stadium is the home of a climactic intersectional football game played every New Year's Day. During the rest of the year, it is the site for other football games, political rallies, civic events, and, on the second Sunday of every month, a gigantic swap meet. The stadium entrance is on Rosemont Avenue.

• *Descanso Gardens*, at 1418 Descanso Boulevard in La Canada, was formerly a private estate and is now 165 acres of magnificent beauty any time of the year. From late December through March, the vast collection of camellias is in bloom. A Japanese tea pavilion is nestled here in a camellia forest.

The beautifully landscaped historical rose garden features species planted in chronological order to demonstrate the development of modern hybrid tea roses. The peak of the blooming season is May and early June. Through the archway opposite the historical roses are group plantings of each of the All-American Rose Selection winners chosen since the program began in 1940. Unlike many of the old roses, these specimens bloom from May until December. Descanso Gardens is open from 9 A.M. to 5 P.M. daily except Christmas. Take a guided tram tour (extra charge) between 1 and 3 P.M. Tuesday through Friday or between 11 A.M. and 4 P.M. on weekends and holidays. A small admission is charged.

Huntington Library, Art Gallery, and Botanical Gardens inspire many superlatives. Located at 1151 Oxford Road north of Huntington Drive in San Marino, the home and 200-acre estate of Pacific Electric tycoon H. E. Huntington were willed to the public, so you may visit them without charge. The Art Gallery in the mansion is composed of seven large and fifteen small galleries. Acknowledged as best in the country, the 18th century British art collection exhibited here includes "Sarah Siddons as the Tragic Muse," "Blue Boy," and "Pinkie."

In the library (a large, white classical building), you'll see selections from the outstanding collection of half a million volumes of rare books and 5 million manuscripts, some as old as eight centuries. Among the fascinating works are a Gutenberg Bible, a "First Folio" of William Shakespeare's plays, Benjamin Franklin's hand-written autobiography, and George Washington's genealogy in his own hand.

The acres of rural and formal gardens on the estate have a number of highlights: the desert garden, the palm garden, two types of Japanese gardens, the circular Shakespearean garden with a bust of the poet and flowers and shrubs mentioned in his works. Also included are the herb garden, the first commercial avocado grove in Southern California, and an orange grove — but not a producing one.

Huntington is open to visitors Tuesday through Sunday from 1 to 4:30 P.M.; tours are offered at 1 P.M. weekdays. L.A. County visitors need Sunday reservations. Donations are requested.

Mission San Gabriel, fourth mission to be dedicated in California (1771), was moved to its present site 9 miles east of Los Angeles in 1775. Its location at the crossroads of three well-traveled trails (now 534 Mission Drive in San Gabriel) made it a busy place. It was once known for its extensive vineyards and winery, the oldest and (at one time) the largest in the state. The mission's winery helped to finance the Plaza Church in the Pueblo of Los Angeles.

Architecture of the church is unlike that of other missions: the facade is on a side wall, and there are Moorish-capped buttresses and long, narrow windows, reminiscent of a cathedral in Cordova, Spain, where the mission's main builder received his training. Notable attractions include its bells and early California religious and historical treasures. The tradition-minded Claretian Fathers restored the mission and maintain it today, conducting masses every Sunday. Mission San Gabriel Arcangel is open to the public daily except for major religious holidays, from 9:30 A.M. to 4:30 P.M. There's a small admission charge.

Los Angeles State and County Arboretum, at 301 N. Baldwin Avenue, between Huntington Drive and Colorado Boulevard, includes 127 acres of plants grown in every continent of the world. The Demonstration Home

Gardens, jointly sponsored by the Arboretum Foundation and *Sunset* Magazine, display take-home ideas in garden design. Peacocks roam the grounds, and historic buildings date from the time the property was Rancho Santa Anita. Guided tram tours leave from the entrance during mid-day. The gardens are open from 9 A.M. to 5 P.M. daily.

Santa Anita Race Track is just across Baldwin Avenue from the arboretum. During the thoroughbred horse racing season from December 26 to mid-April (with a special meet in October), throngs of racing fans jam the 500-acre track. Well-landscaped grounds include nearly one million special Santa Anita pansies in peak bloom for the season. The track entrance is on Holly Avenue. Gates open at 11 A.M. During the season you can watch morning workouts (7:30 A.M. to 9:30 P.M.) free of charge; on weekends, you can take a free "back stretch" tour.

San Gabriel Mountains

Stretching from seaward slopes to the Mojave Desert, the San Gabriel Mountains form the northern border of the Los Angeles area. The most accessible of high mountain ranges near Los Angeles, these mountains have been called the city's mountain playground, offering back-country hiking and riding, camping, picnicking, wilderness areas, and short walks to scenic waterfalls.

You can see some of the high country by car, but the best is seen on forest trails leading to the heights. The middle high country (or mid-range) is reached by the Angeles Crest Highway, the eastern high country by San Antonio Canyon Road. Both are within an hour's drive from the edge of Los Angeles. For information and maps, write to Angeles National Forest Supervisor, 701 N. Santa Anita Avenue, Arcadia, CA 91006.

Angeles Crest Highway, State 2, originates in La Canada and connects the most popular sites and activities in the San Gabriel Mountains. At Vista, one of the picnic areas on the range crest, you may catch sight of bighorn sheep.

Of the crest peaks, Mount Williamson and Mount Islip are the closest to the highway and the easiest to climb. Vincent Gap, 5 miles from Big Pines, is the starting point of a popular hike to the old Big Horn — a fairly easy walk that takes less than an hour. Mount Baden-Powell, a steep, 4-mile trip each way, is second perhaps only to Old Baldy as a worthy climb.

Mount Wilson Observatory, reached by the Mount Wilson Road which leaves State 2 at Red Box, is world renowned for the 100-inch, 100-ton Hooker telescope camera and its magnificent views. The observatory is open free of charge from 10 A.M. to 5 P.M. daily. It lies beyond Mount Wilson Skyline Park, which has a pleasant picnic area. No fee is charged.

San Gabriel Wilderness, an area set aside to preserve the wild, rough mountain country, requires accomplished hiking skill and good maps to explore. Automobile sightseers can sample the flavor of this area on a drive of about 25 miles from La Canada on State 2, or 20 miles from Azusa on State 39. You'll enjoy panoramic rim views (especially at Jarvi Memorial Vista) across to rugged Twin Peaks and down into awesomely steep Devil and Bear canyons.

Pomona-Walnut Valley

Along the base of the San Gabriel and San Bernardino ranges is a valley usually designated as Pomona-Walnut by weather forecasters. Vineyards are losing out to urban pressures in what was once one of the great wine-producing areas. You'll still find a few wineries to visit in the Cucamonga-Guasti area.

Pomona, a center for horses and higher education, is also the site of the huge Los Angeles County Fair every September. Largest county fair in the nation, it underscores an often overlooked fact: the urbanized Los Angeles area is still a significant agricultural producer.

At 2 P.M. on the first Sunday of the month (except in July, August, and September) you can watch an Arabian horse show at Cal Poly near Pomona. The shows (small charge) have been held since 1925, when the campus was still part of the Kellogg ranch.

Rancho Santa Ana Botanic Gardens, on Foothill Boulevard just west of the turnoff to Padua Hills, is devoted exclusively to native California plants. A short, well-marked nature trail, beginning near the giant sequoias west of the administration building, takes you past a cone collection, home demonstration garden, and through woodland, rock, dune, and desert areas. Try to see it in the spring when the California poppy is in bloom. It is open daily from 8 A.M. to 5 P.M.

The San Bernardino County Museum shouldn't be missed. You'll see a mixture of animal, vegetable, and mineral exhibits, as well as the largest egg collection in the U.S. Located at 2024 Orange Tree Lane in Redlands, the museum is open Tuesday through Saturday from 9 A.M. to 5 P.M. and Sunday from 1 to 5 P.M. Next door is the Edwards mansion, a classic example of Victorian architecture. (The mansion is now a restaurant.)

Historical countryside

If you drive from L.A. to the mountains or desert through Riverside, Perris, and Hemet, expect to see some historical countryside. Allow time along the way for such attractions as California's first navel orange tree, the famous Mission Inn, and Mount Rubidoux—site of an annual Easter sunrise pilgrimage.

Riverside is the birthplace of California's multimillion dollar navel orange industry. One of two original trees brought from Brazil in 1873 is still bearing fruit (at the corner of Magnolia and Arlington streets); the other, transplanted to the courtyard of the Mission Inn by President Theodore Roosevelt in 1903, died in the late 1920s, but the trunk is still preserved.

The Mission Inn, modeled after the California missions, is a stunning sight. Begun as an adobe cottage in 1875, it grew to become one of the showplaces of the countryside. Covering a square block bounded by Sixth, Seventh, Main, and Orange streets, this former resort houses many treasures, including the Patio of the Fountains, the Garden of the Bells, and the St. Francis Chapel. One-hour tours leave the lobby twice daily on weekdays and three times a day on weekends.

Ramona Bowl focuses on Indian history in the Hemet and San Jacinto area, where the local residents have been staging California's greatest outdoor play, *Ramona*, since 1923. It is generally held on three successive weekends starting in late April. Early reservations can be made after January 31 by requesting an application from the Ramona Pageant Association, Box 755, Hemet, CA 92343; enclose a stamped envelope.

San Bernardino Mountains

Highest of the mountain ranges surrounding Los Angeles, the San Bernardinos are another part of the mountain barrier between coast and desert. Past them are two major automobile routes: Cajon Canyon north to the Mojave Desert and San Gorgonio Pass east to the Coachella Valley. Peaks are high: Mount San Gorgonio (called Old Grayback because of its high expanse of naked granite) is 11,502 feet; many peaks on the south face reach over 10,000 feet. The San Bernardinos are rich in history, scenery, and recreation.

From Interstate Highway 15 you can get into the mountains on scenic Rim of the World Drive; the interstate also provides an easy "back door" to both the San Bernardino and San Gabriel mountains.

Rim of the World Drive (State Highway 18) is the famous route leading to the best-known locations in the San Bernardino Mountains. The scenic road winds up to elevations of 5,000 to 7,200 feet. As you start your ascent from San Bernardino, note the "arrowhead," a natural landmark on the mountain face.

For spectacular views along your way, take short side roads up to fire lookout stations on top of Strawberry Peak (most accessible), Keller Peak, and Butler Peak. Rim of the World Drive takes you near Crestline, Lake Gregory (site of an old Mormon settlement and today a favorite swimming destination), Blue Jay, Lake Arrowhead, Running Springs, Arrowbear, Big Bear Lake, and other small mountain resorts.

Lake Arrowhead is a manmade recreation lake and all-year resort, offering water sports and beautiful scenery. A marina has water-ski instruction, boat rentals, and swimming and fishing areas. You'll find a golf course, theaters, abundant restaurants, motels, stores, and private cabins here. At the south end of the lake, the resort center village is a picturesque, Alpine-style town but also contains a bit of bustling civilization, especially on weekends. The resort is open in the winter for skiers.

Big Bear Lake, farther east, is another resort development and scenic spot for water activities. In the village on the west end of the lake are motels, shops, and restaurants, many with lake views. Staying in the village, you can walk to theaters, a bowling alley, and an ice rink. South of Big Bear, manmade Cedar Lake, complete with an old waterwheel and mill, was the locale for the first technicolor movie.

Nearby Snow Summit ski resort runs its lifts in the summer for views of the lake and mountains at an 8,300-foot elevation. Good ski areas abound in the area; most are along the south shore. Depending on the weather, the season runs from November to March. From the mountain ridge south of the lake, you can look across Barton Flats to the vast white dome of San Gorgonio, summit of a snowy wilderness that is a goal for rugged hikers and backpackers.

Orange County

Mickey Mouse, a gathering of wax stars, and a berry farm with theme park — this is part of Orange County, center for family fun and fantasy. Orange groves may be scarce, but the swallows still return to Capistrano; surfboards jockey for the high "comber"; brightly colored sails weave in and out of Newport and Dana Point marinas; and Laguna hosts a time-honored art festival.

Once little more than a sleepy agricultural county scented by orange blossoms, Orange County was transformed by the magic wand of Walt Disney in the 1950s into one of the largest tourist meccas in Southern California.

Today, Orange County possesses one of the greatest collections of manmade amusements to be found anywhere. The county has become a sort of spread-out, continuous world's fair: in addition to renowned Disneyland, its boasts ever-expanding Knott's Berry Farm and several major specialty attractions.

But there's more. There's the great Golden Coast — extending from north of Huntington Beach (surfing capital of the world) through the seaside communities of Newport and Balboa and the art colony of Laguna south to San Clemente. This generous stretch of beach world produces many of Southern California's famous golden tans.

Among the rolling hills on the former Irvine Ranch is a University of California campus, part of a dynamic master-planned community. You'll also find remains of mission days at San Juan Capistrano, where the famed swallows return annually to visit.

Visitors return again and again to Orange County. There are always new additions to the amusement parks or new restaurants and shops to browse. You can't see it all in a day or even several days. You'll find many attractive, moderately priced hotels and motels clustered around the inland amusement parks and also along the beach highway.

During the summer — peak tourist season — most places you visit will be crowded. Summer temperatures rise to the high 80s and up inland; at the ocean it's much cooler, but beach space is often at a premium. In winter, you'll have plenty of elbow room, but amusement park hours are shortened and it's likely to be cold along the shore. Still, a visit to Orange County at any time of the year guarantees a fun-packed vacation.

A Mecca for Diversion

The possibilities for entertainment in Orange County are unlimited. Take a stomach-jerking parachute ride, hear the cheers for jousting knights, eat a slice of boysenberry pie while strolling the streets of a ghost town or listening to Wagon Camp music, view a lagoonside water and light show, or watch Dorothy and her friends tread the "yellow brick road" — and this is only a sampling of the many attractions centered in the region. Surprisingly, none of the above-mentioned adventures occurs in Walt Disney's "Magic Kingdom," a major amusement area that would bring fame to any county.

Threaded by freeways, the area is accessible from anywhere in Southern California. You can drive, take a bus, or fly directly to Orange County.

By car from Los Angeles, take the Santa Ana Freeway (Interstate Highway 5) or the San Diego Freeway (Interstate Highway 405), which joins I-5 in southern Orange County. North and southbound freeways (Long Beach, San Gabriel River, Orange, and Newport) connect with the coast highway and freeways north of Orange County.

NEWPORT'S BUSY BAY is *best seen from boat deck. Catch a cruise at venerable Balboa Pavilion, harbor's focal point.*

The easiest route from the east is along Interstate Highway 10 (San Bernardino Freeway) to the Riverside Freeway (State Highway 91).

Bus transportation is both national and local. Orange County is served by Trailways Bus Service and Greyhound, both of which operate with national schedules. Trailways has terminals in Santa Ana and Laguna Beach. Greyhound has stations in Santa Ana, Anaheim, Laguna Beach, and Fullerton for through, not local, traffic. (You can't take Greyhound from Los Angeles to any Orange County town closer than San Clemente.)

The Southern California Rapid Transit District has direct service from its main Los Angeles terminal (located at 6th and Los Angeles) to Disneyland, Knott's Berry Farm, and the Movieland Wax Museum.

Airlines serve Orange County from major California cities. From Los Angeles International Airport, you can take commuter flights or helicopter rides to Fullerton Airport and to John Wayne/Orange County Airport in Santa Ana. The flight takes about 25 minutes.

You can also fly directly to Orange County on Air Cal, American, Frontier, Imperial, PSA, Republic, and Western. For further information on these flights, see your travel agent or airline representative. Several airport coach services make daily scheduled runs between Los Angeles International Airport and John Wayne/Orange County Airport and the Anaheim area. Limousines and taxis are also available for hire.

Once you're there, check with your hotel or the visitors and convention bureau (see below) about rental cars and the numerous sightseeing services.

Orange County has one of the best transit systems in Southern California. Buses cover every area of the county, and booklets with maps are distributed widely. Any city hall, large hotel, or civic center will have them. You can pick them up at the Convention Center in Anaheim. For a moderate fee, you can ride The Fun Bus from all major hotels and motels to and from major attractions in Orange County and Los Angeles. Phone (714) 635-1390 for details.

Three other commuter buses offer service between local hotels and regional shopping centers: the City Shopper (also goes to Crystal Cathedral), the Anaheim Plaza Express, and the South Coast Plaza Shuttle. Check with your hotel for schedules.

Tourist World

Consider time and money when you plan a foray into Orange County's amusement centers. You'll need both.

Many major attractions are clustered around Buena Park, 20 miles southeast of Los Angeles and just a tempting 5 miles from Disneyland in Anaheim. Amusement centers, special-interest museums and theaters, a glass cathedral—even if you have unlimited stamina, you'll never see them all in one day. In this entertainment mecca, a full weekend only allows you to scratch the surface.

Tour companies offer limited-time visits to major attractions. If you prefer a more leisurely pace, go on your own—but bring a good map to help you get around.

Anaheim Convention Center

Located at 800 W. Katella Avenue (directly across from Disneyland), the convention center makes a good first stop for your Orange County tour. Here, the Anaheim Area Visitor & Convention Bureau offers free information on lodging, restaurants, and attractions. Call the Visitor Information Line at (714) 635-8900 for a 2½-minute recording giving attraction hours and information relating to sports and special events.

The sporting life

Sports events draw many visitors to the area. In addition to water-oriented activities along Orange County's beaches (described later in the chapter), you'll find plenty of tennis courts (including Tennisland Racquet Club, 1 block from Disneyland) and more than 20 public golf courses.

Anaheim's two professional sports teams play at the Anaheim Stadium, 2000 S. State College Boulevard, just north of the Santa Ana Freeway. The California Angels' baseball season begins in April and runs through September. The Los Angeles Rams, Anaheim's football team, play from August through December.

At Los Alamitos Race Course (4961 Katella Avenue, Los Alamitos), quarter horse races are held nightly except Sunday, from May to August and from November to January. Harness races take place from February to May. Thoroughbreds race from mid-October to November during the Orange County Fair.

The Orange County International Raceway in Irvine is a drag strip for autos, motorcycles, and go-carts. Call (714) 552-5514 for current race information. To get there, head north off the Santa Ana Freeway at Moulton Parkway. In Costa Mesa, motorcycles race every Friday evening from April to October at the Orange County Fairgrounds, 88 Fair Drive. Midgets compete at the El Toro Speedway, 23001 S.E. Valencia.

Let's go shopping

Orange County's shopping facilities range from waterfront browsing to the latest in air-conditioned malls to quaint villages. For great gifts, try The City in Orange, Anaheim Plaza, and Westminster malls—and be sure to include a stop at South Coast Plaza, one of the county's busiest (and largest) shopping showplaces. Across the street, South Coast Plaza Village adds more stores.

Along the waterfront are Old World Village in Huntington Beach, super-chic Fashion Island and Lido Marina Village in Newport Beach, and Laguna Beach's one-of-a-kind shops. Check with the Anaheim Area Visitor & Convention Bureau for brochures.

Performing Arts Center

The curtain will rise on the Orange County Performing Arts Center in the autumn of 1986, ushering in the area's first major theater complex. Situated on 5 acres adjacent to South Coast Plaza in Costa Mesa (Bristol exit from I-405), the center includes a 3,000-seat multipurpose theater for symphony, opera, ballet, and Broadway show performances.

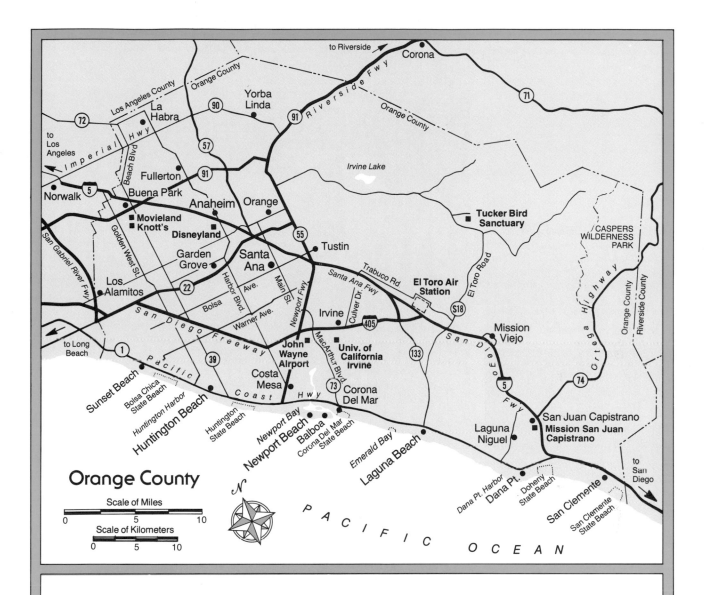

Major Points of Interest

Movieland (State 39, Buena Park)—best collection of Hollywood stars in wax; horror in the Black Box; star hand and footprints

Knott's Berry Farm (State 39, Buena Park)—one-time berry farm turned theme park; old-time nostalgia, new rides, shows, music

Disneyland (Santa Ana Freeway to Anaheim)—seven "lands" of make-believe; new rides; fireworks display summer evenings

Huntington Beach—surfers' "capital"; good Pismo clamming

Newport Beach—boating playground; Newport Center shops, restaurants, art museum

Balboa Peninsula—colorful community of shops and homes; Balboa Pavilion, famous landmark; Balboa ferry ride between Balboa Island and peninsula; dory fleet goes to sea daily for fishing

Laguna Beach (on Pacific Coast Highway south of Newport Beach)—Southland's prominent art colony, summer resort, lovely beach

Dana Point Harbor—the only Southern California marina landscaped as park; picnic facilities, bike trails, restaurants, still-water beach, fishing pier

San Juan Capistrano (off San Diego Freeway)—home of "Father Serra's Chapel" in California's 7th mission; stop by renovated railroad station

MICKEY MOUSE (right) leads parade down Disneyland's Main Street while Dorothy and friends (below) invite you along Movieland's yellow brick road. Plummeting rides (below right) are only part of Knott's Berry Farm's family entertainment complex.

Disneyland–
Best-known Park of All

The father of "theme parks" springing up around the country, Disneyland has been world-renowned for over 20 years for its combined use of technology and imagination to control the environment and to achieve illusion. Disneyland is at its best in creating a three-dimensional illusory experience you move through, most masterful of which is the Haunted Mansion. A disembodied head speaking from inside a glass sphere, a ballroom full of transparent dancers, and spirits perching on the back of your moving chair are all part of the hair-raising experience.

In Disneyland, an enjoyable ride becomes a trip into history, space, fantasy, or a foreign land. An entire area becomes a reproduction of a well-known fairy tale.

Disneyland even undergoes marked seasonal changes outdoors when only subtle changes have occurred in the weather, producing Easter blooms in spring, flashing autumn colors after Labor Day, and displaying brilliant poinsettias at Christmas time. The park has truly become what Walt Disney intended: a place enjoyed by adults as well as children, actually drawing more of the former than the latter.

On your first park visit, consider the 2½-hour small-group guided tour, which will introduce you to all seven "lands" in the Magic Kingdom. The tour costs about $4 more than the Passport alone (unlimited admission ticket to all events), but it offers a good overview of the park, making it easier to return to attractions you'd like to experience again.

Main Street 1890 in Home Town, U.S.A. is your first stop in the park. The colorful Disneyland Band, known for its showmanship as well as its musical skill, often marches here—in front of the nostalgic old ice cream parlor and silent movie house, or in the Town Square and depot (departure point for the Disneyland Railroad's park tour). At the opera house, see the Walt Disney Story, climaxed by the animated show "Great Moments with Mr. Lincoln."

Adventureland offers a jungle boat ride and safari in alligator, gorilla, and elephant territory; the opportunity to climb the treehouse of the shipwrecked and industrious Swiss Family Robinson; and a visit to the "enchanted" Tiki Room.

New Orleans Square, with the Mississippi steamwheeler, Blue Bayou Restaurant, exciting Pirates of the Caribbean ride, and eerie Haunted Mansion, evokes the glamour of the French Quarter of this Louisiana city.

Frontierland, the haunt of Tom Sawyer and Davy Crockett, is your target for a ride on the sailing ship "Columbia" or on the riverboat "Mark Twain" (both pass Tom's island). Take a raft across the river and explore Fort Wilderness, or steam across the land on the Big Thunder Mountain Railroad's runaway train.

Bear Country features a Country Bear Jamboree with such characters as Swingin' Teddi Barra, and offers canoes you can paddle along the rivers of America.

Fantasyland—that make-believe world of Peter Pan, Alice in Wonderland, and other storybook characters—is reached by crossing a moat and entering Sleeping Beauty's Castle. Recently renovated, this "land" now resembles a Bavarian village; existing rides have been lengthened and changed, and new ones have been added. You can still enjoy your old favorites—but don't miss trying Pinocchio's Daring Journey, Snow White's Scary Adventures, and the other recent additions.

Tomorrowland requires continuous renovation to keep up with advances in the exciting world of science. It now offers a monorail, a submarine voyage, a Mission to Mars, an Adventure through Inner Space, and a Peoplemover. Towering over Tomorrowland is Space Mountain, a rocketing race through the galaxy.

Each land has restaurants and refreshment stands, musical entertainment, shops, services, and free exhibits. You won't see all of Disneyland in a day, so either return again or plan ahead, being very selective for your only visit. Disneyland changes continually—whenever inspiration and imagination ignite.

Daytime or evening can be equally engrossing in Disneyland. In the summer, music of the Dixieland band is prominent in the night air, and name bands entertain. Multicolored fireworks light the sky at 9 P.M. every night. You'll spend a lot of time waiting along the parade route to see such popular evening attractions as the Electric Parade meandering through the park.

Disneyland is less crowded in winter (as well as in the fall and early spring). Lines are shorter, and streets offer you more strolling room. It's also cooler then, but there's less entertainment.

The park is open daily most of the year (occasionally closed on Monday and Tuesday in the winter), but schedules vary according to the season. From October through February, hours are 10 A.M. to 6 P.M. weekdays, 10 A.M. to 7 P.M. weekends. From March to mid-June, the park is generally open longer on weekends. During the summer, hours are extended from 9 A.M. to midnight or later. To get to Disneyland, take I-5 to the Harbor Boulevard exit in Anaheim. There's a parking charge.

The Disneyland Hotel

Across the street is Disneyland Hotel—the largest hotel in the county. It's connected to the park by a fast monorail from Tomorrowland. Your monorail ticket allows you to stop off at the hotel for a visit.

More than a hotel, this 60-acre resort complex features 16 theme restaurants and lounges, a marina, and a multitude of shops. On the full-size marina, live outdoor amusement includes a free summer Polynesian show. "Seaports of the Pacific," a waterfront bazaar, is set among lush tropical gardens, waterfalls, and a palm-studded beach, Koi swim in their own pond, and twice nightly the pulsating Dancing Waters and Lights Fantastic Show (no charge) fascinates visitors.

Need some exercise? You can swim in one of three pools, rent a pedalboat, or take advantage of nearby Tennisland's courts.

You don't have to be a guest to enjoy the marina activities and evening shows. The hotel is also a good spot for watching Disneyland's nightly fireworks during the summer.

Knott's Berry Farm

Knott's, at 8039 Beach Boulevard in Buena Park, is the oldest of the county's amusement parks. It began in 1920 as a berry farm with a little roadside shed where the Knott family sold their produce. A restaurant was added in the early '40s; it attracted such crowds that founder Walter Knott decided to provide guests with amusements while they waited for Mrs. Knott's chicken dinners.

From these humble beginnings, the farm has grown into a 150-acre combination "ghost town," theme park, and restaurant and shopping center—still operated as a family enterprise.

Five theme areas offer everything from Wild West shows to Snoopy. Most of the 165 rides, shows, and attractions are concentrated on one side of Beach Boulevard, but some spill across the street to an area with lagoons and a full-scale reproduction of Independence Hall, built with handmade bricks and featuring a Liberty Bell (authentic down to the crack).

Everything is designed for family enjoyment, from the vaudeville show in the Calico Saloon (where the strongest drinks served are sarsaparilla and boysenberry punch) to the Good Time Theatre, a 2,150-seat, air-conditioned showcase for top stars.

Ghost Town, an authentic reproduction of a mining town, started it all. Here you can ride "shotgun" on a stagecoach, pan for gold, or ride an ore car through a mine or a "log" down a water flume. Passengers on the Denver & Rio Grande—a real, smoke-belching narrow-gauge train—will be suitably affrighted when gun-firing bandits enter the car.

At Fiesta Village, you can shop, watch Mexican artisans, take a stomach-gripping swoop on Montezooma's Revenge, and enjoy a Mexican meal.

The Roaring '20s, featuring bumper cars, old Model A Fords, and a large game arcade, provides a tongue-in-cheek look at an uninhibited period of American history.

Knott's Airfield salutes the days of early aviation with a collection of awesome thrills including the Corkscrew and the 20-story Parachute Sky Jump; you'll find soapbox racers here, too. The latest attraction is a performing dolphin and sea lion show in a marine stadium.

Camp Snoopy, one of the newer areas, is set among tall trees, waterfalls, streams, and a lake. Bobbing pontoon bridges, swaying suspension bridges, and a sky-high playground add to its appeal. The Old Wooden Mill fun house is one of 30 attractions in this area.

Ride a steamboat, stern-wheeler, train, balloon, mule-powered carousel, roller coaster, or pony. Slides and tunnel shoots invite squeals. Snoopy strolls through his kingdom, greeting guests and posing for photos.

The entrance fee to Knott's Berry Farm includes unlimited use of all rides and adventures except panning for gold and the shooting gallery. During the summer, the park is open daily until midnight (later on weekends). Winter hours are 10 A.M. to 6 P.M. Monday through Friday; 10 A.M. to 10 P.M. Saturday; and 10 A.M. to 9 P.M. Sunday.

Additional Attractions

Several inland visitor destinations are clustered around Knott's in Buena Park. Others are scattered around the towns of Garden Grove, Santa Ana, Costa Mesa, and Anaheim. It's a diverse collection, ranging from knights on horseback to airplanes, cars, wax images, and a cloud-reflecting church.

Six Flags Movieland

Just a few minutes' drive north from Knott's, at 7711 Beach Boulevard, is the Six Flags Movieland—the biggest gathering of celebrities in the world. Featured are over 230 wax likenesses of Hollywood stars in scenes from memorable movies and television shows. Here you'll find more glitter and glamour than in Hollywood, and you'll encounter more stars than on the busiest day at any studio lot: Judy Garland and friends in *The Wizard of Oz*; Sophia Loren in *Two Women*; Clark Gable and Vivien Leigh in *Gone with the Wind*; Paul Newman and Robert Redford in *Butch Cassidy and the Sundance Kid*. Visit with some of your favorite TV stars—Ed Asner, Carol Burnett, Redd Foxx, Mr. T., and others. One warning: The settings seem so realistic that you may be tempted to touch the figures. Try not to touch, though—if you do, you'll trigger an alarm.

In the terrifying Chamber of Horrors (an optional part of the tour), you'll experience the thrill of such movies as *Psycho* and *The Exorcist* and meet Elvira and Vincent Price.

Movieland is open daily from 9 A.M. in the summer, from 10 A.M. in the winter. On the premises are a snack bar and several shops.

Medieval Times

Medieval Times lies across the street from Movieland, at 7662 Beach Boulevard. The latest attraction in this 70,000-square-foot facility is a dinner theater. A one-price ticket includes a 2-hour banquet with entertainment featuring knights on horseback competing in sword fighting, jousting, and medieval games. For information on prices and reservations, call (714) 521-4740; in California, call (800) 438-9911 toll-free.

Crystal Cathedral

A tall glass edifice stands at Chapman and Lewis streets in Garden Grove. It's the Crystal Cathedral, home of the Reformed Church in America. Free, hour-long tours of the glass-paned church and grounds include a look at one of the world's largest pipe organs. Tours are offered between 9 A.M. and 4:30 P.M. Monday through Saturday, between 12:30 and 4:30 P.M. Sunday.

Annual Easter and Christmas pageants include live animals, flying angels, and incredible sound effects. For reservations, call (714) 54-GLORY.

A look at planes and cars

Movieland-of-the-Air, at the John Wayne/Orange County Airport, contains one of the country's largest

collections of antique aircraft. More than 50 airplanes (many originals) are on display in this museum. Open daily from 10 A.M. to 5 P.M. during the summer, it's closed Monday and Tuesday during the rest of the year.

The Briggs Cunningham Automotive Museum, at 250 E. Baker Street in Costa Mesa, is one of the finest in the world, focusing on some 100 cars that were industry leaders in performance, looks, and technical features. Featured are a 1927 Bugatti, a Hispano-Suiza, and other sports, racing, and classic cars. The museum is open from 9 A.M. to 5 P.M. Wednesday through Sunday.

Museums for dolls and soldiers

Hobby City Doll and Toy Museum (1238 S. Beach Boulevard, Anaheim) displays more than 3,000 dolls and toys in a half-scale model of the White House. The collection includes antique dolls, teddy bears, and toy soldiers. The museum is open daily from 10 A.M. to 6 P.M.; there's a small charge for admission.

The Museum of World Wars and Military History (off Beach Boulevard at 8700 Stanton Avenue, Buena Park) contains more than 200 military figures in over 100 realistic settings. It opens at 9 A.M. during the summer months and 10 A.M. the rest of the year. Admission is moderate.

Wild Rivers

One of America's largest water parks and Southern California's newest family attraction, Wild Rivers is located on the former Lion Country grounds at 8800 Irvine Center Drive, Laguna Hills (adjacent to the San Diego Freeway at the Moulton Parkway offramp).

Here you'll discover a watery world, with 40 rides and attractions for visitors of all ages. Experience the excitement of white-water rafting on the Wild Rivers Run, be fired from the Shot Gun, or float along the Lazy River and work on your tan. The children's area features water slides, innertube runs, pools, and waterfalls.

Gift shops provide suntan lotion, towels, and even swimsuits. Changing rooms, showers, and lockers are also available. If you don't want to get wet, you can simply stroll through the park, have a snack, or try your luck in the video arcade.

The park is open daily from June through mid-September, weekends only to mid-October; for information on operating hours and price of admission, call (714) 768-WILD.

The Present...

The northwestern section of Orange County is crowded; you'll find little evidence of the bean fields that once flourished for miles. As urban sprawl spread southeastward, "instant cities" sprang up, land sites decreased, and people began to fear this once-beautiful countryside would suffer the fate of surrounding areas.

Irvine Company—owners of an 83,000-acre ranch comprising one-fifth of the area of Orange County—in 1960 retained William L. Pereira to prepare a broad, general plan for the land, designed to stop or at least to integrate the urban sprawl. Within this framework, the Irvine Company planners, working with other consultants, prepared a more detailed plan. A comprehensive look at the total environment, the plan established building and population density limits and provided greenbelt areas, effective traffic flow, and esthetic balance. Billboards, overhead power lines, and TV antennas were forbidden. Both shopping centers and wildlife preserves were included in the mountains-to-ocean scheme. Still being modified to conform with state and regional planning commissions, the plan is a model for the rest of the country.

The University of California at Irvine enjoys the unique advantage of being developed within the master plan. Its 1,500 acres (over twice the area of U.C.L.A.) are the focal point of the city of Irvine, which one day will incorporate some 53,000 acres of the ranch. By the turn of the century, the community is expected to have 100,000 people, the university 27,500 students.

...and the Past

Where are all the orange trees? Many are gone, though a few groves survive on the Irvine Ranch and some still hold out around the Santa Ana area. And faint traces of a distant past still linger among the mission ruins at San Juan Capistrano. Other historical attractions also exist, and looking for them is part of the fun. The Diego Sepulveda Adobe (1900 Adams Avenue in Anaheim) stands on old Indian grounds.

The Orange County Experience, a very special historical tour that includes stops for freshly squeezed orange juice at the old Irvine headquarters and for wine atop a Dana Point bluff, is operated by a history professor. Designed for small groups, the tour provides a 4½-hour dip into the past and a glimpse of what's ahead for Orange County. For details, call (714) 680-3556.

For a tour on your own, visit Heritage Hill Park in El Toro—the county's first historic park, comprising an original adobe and three restored turn-of-the-century buildings. From I-5, take the Lake Forest Drive exit east for 2 miles, then turn left on Serrano Road. Tours are given at 11 A.M. and at 2 and 3 P.M. daily; the park is open from 8 A.M. to 5 P.M. Just down the road is Serrano Creek Park. A 1½-mile jogging trail runs through its towering eucalyptus grove; shaded tables invite picnicking.

The Charles W. Bowers Memorial Museum, in Santa Ana, offers a look into Southern California's past. The mission-style structure has galleries devoted to natural history, archeology, early and contemporary California art, and artifacts of the Southwest. Here you will find an extensive collection of early Spanish and Mexican documents, among them deeds to area ranchos.

The Bowers Museum, at 2002 N. Main Street, is just south of the Main Street offramp from the Santa Ana Freeway. Hours are 10 A.M. to 5 P.M. Tuesday through Saturday, noon to 5 P.M. Sunday. Admission is free; donations are accepted.

Venerable San Juan Capistrano

The village of San Juan Capistrano has been a favorite stop for travelers ever since its mission was founded in 1776, the year of American independence. About midway between Los Angeles and San Diego, it's by-passed by I-5. Even so, its streets fill up on weekends and holidays with people who come to see the picturesque mission, shop, eat, or break up a longer journey.

The town is small enough to cover on foot. Horseback riders from nearby rural communities and cyclists in from the lightly traveled old highway are part of the traffic. On the street you still hear the Spanish language, and you can see the influence of Mexico in the restaurants, the craft and fashion shops, and in the building design.

Architecture. The sweep of California history is displayed in the architecture of San Juan, from the mission and adobes of the Spanish and Mexican eras to the Egan house and the railway station dating from the late 19th century. Nondescript buildings remain from the time San Juan was a farm with a main highway running through it. Now, with architectural controls in effect, some handsome new structures are appearing in the mission district.

The most impressive structure is the new parish church at the northwest corner of the mission grounds. Though built in the likeness of the original "Great Stone Church," it's considerably larger. A dramatic bell tower rises 104 feet above the ground. Across the street is the architecturally striking public library, oriented around a central courtyard with a reflecting pool, stream, and fountain.

On the main street, south of the mission, are almost all the adobes—some still family occupied, some converted into businesses, some in ruins. All are labeled. Just around the corner from the train depot is Los Rios Street, a charming pocket of the past. The city's historical society is housed in the O'Neill Museum, a restored 1880s house. The well-furnished museum is open Tuesday to Friday from 9 A.M. to 1 P.M., and Saturday and Sunday from noon to 3 P.M. Admission is free.

You may want to sample the shops along Camino Capistrano, where you can buy goods both old and new: Navajo rugs, pottery, saddles, Indian jewelry, and Western wear.

Mission San Juan Capistrano is the great attraction of San Juan Capistrano. The mission was founded in 1776 by Father Junipero Serra. The seventh in the California mission chain, it was completed in 1806 after a decade of work, but much was destroyed in an earthquake only 6 years later.

A small admission charge takes you through the gates. For another small fee you can rent cassettes to guide you through the legendary ruins and restored gardens. Fluttering white pigeons splash in the mossy fountain; they're so used to visitors that they may eat out of your hand. Past the fountain, broken, ivy-covered walls are all that remains of a stone church that was once the most magnificent in the mission chain. Today, the ruined walls hold the mud nests of the legendary swallows of Capistrano.

Four bells, saved when the original bell tower collapsed, today ring out in a campanile. Behind the campanile are a small tranquil garden, a fountain, and the mission museum.

Having survived the rigors of neglect and time, the modest mission chapel is believed to be the oldest church in California. The adobe chapel, called "Father Serra's church," is the only extant place where he is known to have said Mass. Inside, the 300-year-old giltwork *reredos* (altarpiece) from Spain was added during the mission's restoration in the 1920s.

Outside you may stroll through a shady arcade (a remnant of the original mission) and along flower-bordered paths past ivy and rose-covered walls. Other buildings and excavations of tallow vats and working parts of the mission are open to visitors. The mission grounds are open from 7 A.M. to 5 P.M. daily.

The legend of the swallows of San Juan Capistrano is known through stories, songs, and poems. Supposedly, the swallows return to their nests every year around St. Joseph's Day; actually, the majority of cliff swallows do return on March 19, but some of the group also arrive a little earlier or later. The swallows leave their mission nests for an unknown southern destination around October 23 (date of the death of the patron saint of the Mission, St. John of Capistrano).

The town's 1894 rail station is on the Amtrak line between Los Angeles and San Diego; both northbound and southbound trains stop here five times daily. Part of the depot is now a restaurant.

It is also a museum of railroad memorabilia. On the roofed loading platform you sit on old-time depot benches or on an old shoeshine stand while waiting for a table. A freight-weighting platform holds a combo at night. A caboose, boxcars, and a dining car now house shops and eating space.

Caspers Wilderness Park

Another bit of old California, this park is reached 7 miles in from San Juan through the lovely pastoral land beside the Ortega Highway (State Highway 74). Here the county has set aside a 5,500-acre former ranch as a wilderness preserve. You can picnic free beside the highway; there's a fee for picnicking in meadows farther into the park and for camping.

Caspers Park is a hiker's and horseback rider's park, with almost no development, including water—so bring your own. You walk beside the creek of Bell Canyon—which flows in winter—through grassy meadows, into oak and sycamore woodlands, up through chaparral to low ridges for a view of the mountains and the sea.

Tucker Wildbird Sanctuary

Just past the charming old town of Modjeska (named for the great actress who lived nearby) is a beautiful oasis of trees, flowers, plants, and wildlife, operated by California State University at Fullerton. You can walk along a lovely stream and listen to the birds sing. The sanctuary is open from 9 A.M. to 4 P.M. daily except Mondays; a small donation is requested for upkeep.

Getting into the back country is done by following narrow roads along gentle hillsides. The ride is best in spring.

PIGEONS PERCH on fountain (left) in Mission San Juan Capistrano's courtyard. You can rent a gondola (below) to cruise the waterways of Naples, near Long Beach.

BED & BREAKFAST—SOUTHERN CALIFORNIA STYLE

Bed and breakfast inns may not have originated in the Southland, but the area soon discovered their appeal and added unique touches to attract travelers. Some inns are just a stone's throw from beaches, some are located in historic homes or buildings, and others resemble intimate hotels. All offer breakfast; most provide wine or "high tea" upon guests' arrival. Flower-filled courtyards and fruit or plant-filled rooms remind vacationers that Southern California is a horticultural center.

Part of the small hostelries' charm is the opportunity to learn about the area from the host or other guests. It's a good way to exchange ideas on restaurants, modes of transportation, or "must sees." Inns seem to attract a compatible crowd.

A sampling of inns appears below. Plan to make reservations well in advance of your trip; some of the long-established hostelries are soon completely booked for summer weekends. For rates and additional information, write or call the inn directly.

Britt House, 406 Maple St., San Diego, CA 92103; (619) 234-2926: Beautifully restored Victorian; 8 rooms and cottage, each with distinctive decor; most share baths. Delicious afternoon tea; breakfast served in rooms or parlor. Parking is on the street; you'll need change for meters during the day.

Heritage Park, 2470 Heritage Park Row, San Diego, CA 92110; (619) 295-7088: 1889 charmer moved to Old Town; 9 rooms (6 baths) with antique furnishings (all antiques and furnishings for sale). Breakfast in bed or garden, on sundeck or veranda; dinner in rooms by arrangement; 30s movies at night.

Carriage House, 1322 Catalina St., Laguna Beach, CA 92651; (714) 494-8945: Imaginatively furnished New Orleans-style colonial; 6 spacious suites with kitchens and baths; more suites on Spanish-style property a block away. Breakfast in Grandma Bean's Dining Room off lush courtyard; children and pets accepted.

Eiler's Inn, 741 S. Coast Highway, Laguna Beach, CA 92651; (714) 494-3004: Turning its back to busy highway, inn offers 11 small rooms and 1 suite (all with private baths) around central courtyard. Buffet breakfast, afternoon tea; sun deck; library.

The Old Seal Beach Inn, 212 Fifth St., Seal Beach, CA 90740; (213) 493-2416: Garden entrance sets tone for French Mediterranean ambience; 23 rooms with private bath (some with kitchens). Breakfast room; swimming pool; 1 block from ocean; no smoking.

Salisbury House, 2273 W. 20th St., Los Angeles, CA 90018; (213) 737-7817: 1909 house featured in movies, good city location; 5 rooms, private and shared baths; complimentary beverage; full breakfast.

The Parsonage, 1600 Olive St., Santa Barbara, CA 93101; (805) 962-9336: Queen Anne Victorian originally built as parsonage for Trinity Episcopal Church in 1892; 5 rooms, 3 with shared baths; restored with period furnishings, original redwood interior; location between downtown and foothills offers panoramic views, convenient shopping, touring.

Bayberry Inn, 111 West Valerio St., Santa Barbara, CA 93101; (805) 682-3199: 1904 Colonial-Federal house, once a boarding school, then a sorority; 7 rooms, some with private bath; parlor with fireplace. Croquet; pick-up service from train station, airport; bikes for rent.

Villa Rosa, 15 Chapala St., Santa Barbara, CA 93101; (805) 966-0851: Historic hotel, now elegant inn; 18 rooms with private bath; fireplaces; pool and spa; wine; continental breakfast; just a few steps from beach.

The Glenborough Inn, 1327 Bath St., Santa Barbara, CA 93101; (805) 966-0589: Turn-of-the-century house (4 rooms, shared baths, fireplace, hot tub) and 1880s cottage (4 rooms, private baths, New Orleans-style garden). Evening wine in parlor; no smoking; full breakfast in room or gardens.

The Old Yacht Club Inn, 431 Corona Del Mar, Santa Barbara, CA 93103; (805) 962-1277: Built in 1912 as private residence, temporary yacht club in 1920s; 1½ blocks to beach; 9 rooms, some shared baths. Big breakfast, dinner by arrangement; bike rentals.

Ballard Inn, 2436 Baseline, Ballard, CA 93463; (213) 659-6495: Newly built, hidden retreat convenient for wine touring, back-country exploring, Solvang shopping; 15 well-decorated rooms with baths; fireplace, complimentary wine; full breakfasts.

Union Hotel, 362 Bell St., Los Alamos, CA 93440; (805) 344-2744: 1880s way station for stage route was destroyed by fire, rebuilt in 1915, then abandoned. Third incarnation open 3 days a week: 12 rooms, 2 with private baths; swimming pool; Victorian gazebo; hideaway spa; full breakfast.

The Rose Victorian Inn, 789 Valley Road, Arroyo Grande, CA 93420; (805) 481-5566: Lawn with arbor and gazebo surrounds former pioneer rancher's home; 8 rooms on 3 stories, 5 with private bath; restaurant; antiques; no smoking.

Along the South Coast

Orange County's coast has two faces. The shore of the Los Angeles plain, as far south as the Balboa Peninsula, has the heaviest-use beaches. The more picturesque bluff coast begins at Corona del Mar, with a rocky shoreline dotted with small-coved beaches. This coast is the summer resort capital of Orange County, with most activity centering around the county's north end (on beaches that are not the most attractive part of the coastline).

Watch your driving along these beaches, for cars park wherever there's an available inch of space, and it's not uncommon to see a horizontal surfboard with legs attached dashing across the highway between bursts of traffic.

Terrible storms battered the coastline in early 1983, sweeping away beaches, destroying the Seal Beach pier, and rupturing Huntington Beach's pier. The sand has returned, though, and the piers will soon be repaired or replaced.

Seal Beach abuts the Los Angeles County line and is just south of Long Beach. Along the inland side of the highway, the coastal route from this point south almost to Huntington Beach bears the constant reminder of the oil industry—with operating pumps, refineries, and storage tanks. But modern technology has enabled the beach towns and parks to continue serving the populace with no greater inconvenience than a lingering odor of petroleum.

Seal Beach and Sunset Beach (just south of Seal Beach) are beach towns in the full sense of the word. The coast highway follows along just behind the rim of sand, lined on either side with refreshment stands and places offering any kind of beach gear for sale or rent. At Seal Beach, summertime surfing takes place early or late in the day between the pier and jetty areas.

Sunset Beach has a marina (reached from the coast highway) and an aquatic park (west on Edinger Avenue from Bolsa Chica Road), as well as a launching ramp and space for parking car trailers.

Bolsa Chica State Beach is 6 miles long, but only the northern end—a 3-mile-long strip between ocean and highway—is lined with sun-lovers in the summer and on warm weekends the year around. This part of the beach is an extension of the general shoreline, a 300 to 360-foot-wide strand of sand adjacent to the highway; it has fire rings (common to several beaches in this region), rest rooms, and lifeguards. Exclusively a day-use park, it closes at midnight.

At the southern end, steep cliffs between the road and the beach make access difficult. Some trails and one stairway near 16th Street penetrate the bluffs. A biking path and walkway extends the entire length of the beach. Clamming, diving, and fishing are popular here; grunion runs occur between March and August.

On the landward side of the highway across from the beach is Bolsa Chica Ecological Reserve, a series of spreading salt marshes that provide a landing site on the Pacific Flyway.

Huntington Beach

In 1901 Philip Stanton organized and helped settle a town site on the coast of Shell Beach. The new town,

---

ART FESTIVALS IN LAGUNA BEACH

Laguna Beach is a city created by artists. Attracted by her curving bay setting, one of the most picturesque sections of the Pacific Coast, they came to capture the magnificent, unspoiled beauty of the sea and land on canvas, and remained to form the nucleus of a town. From their first humble art shows has grown one of the oldest and most exciting spectacles in the state—the Festival of Arts and Pageant of the Masters. Launched out of Depression desperation, the show now attracts some 300,000 spectators annually.

From mid-July to late August, the entire city is alive with art. In addition to the more famous exhibition, you can browse through two other art shows, all running simultaneously: Art-A-Fair, a traditional exhibit of arts and crafts, and the zany Sawdust Festival, an unstructured, unjuried, and uncensored art show.

The Festival of Arts and Pageant of the Masters is an ambitious cultural festival.

From 10 A.M. until 11:30 P.M. daily, visitors stroll through a tree-shaded park among booths displaying works by local artists in all media.

Children can take a fling at creativity in an art workshop—smocks, paints, and canvases are provided. A marionette show plays in a little theater. At 8:30 P.M. the Pageant of the Masters begins. Masterpieces of painting, sculpture, and tapestry are re-created by living models in a 2-hour tableau. Staging, lighting, costumes, music, and commentary add to the effect.

So popular is this evening performance that tickets are sold out months in advance. You can get an application form for next year's show while you're there or write (several months in advance to be sure of tickets) to Festival of Arts, 650 Laguna Canyon Road, Laguna Beach, CA 92651. Prices include the admission fee to the grounds.

Parking is limited, so plan to arrive early. Park along Laguna Canyon Road or (for a fee) in a lot across the street from the grounds.

SECLUDED COVE below bluff near Laguna Beach expands when tide goes out, accommodating both watcher and walker.

named Pacific City, was intended to rival Atlantic City on the East Coast. In 1902, Henry E. Huntington of Pacific Electric Railway bought a controlling interest in the project and renamed the community.

The beach is famous today, but not for the same reasons as its East Coast counterpart. To intrepid surfers world-wide, it's "the capital"—home of the summer international surfing competition—where they can tackle some of the greatest combers along the coast. Most of the surfing activity centers around the Huntington Pier site (at the foot of Main Street). If you want to get a good look at man and board, come early in the morning or later in the evening (after the swimmers and sunbathers have gone).

You won't be alone, even on a foggy morning, for here flock the fishermen, outfitted with folding stools, tackle boxes, and lunch sacks, to settle in for a long peaceful day. When the weather is less calm, a good place to fish is at the flood control levee of the Santa Ana River. A trail along the riverbank ultimately ends at Yorba Linda, many miles inland.

The state beach, stretching for 2 miles south of the pier, is spectacular on summer nights, when its 500 fire rings are ablaze with bonfires.

Newport Beach and Balboa

The opulent homes, handsome yacht clubs, and mast-studded harbor you see here would appear to have little connection with Newport's salty past, when the town was literally a "new port" between San Diego and San Pedro. Yet some of its original character still remains, or is being recultivated, if you look carefully.

In 1863, Captain S. S. Dunnels pushed the sidewheeler *Vaquero* past the mud flats into the harbor at the mouth of the Santa Ana River, unloaded lumber from San Diego, and picked up a cargo of produce from the inland fields, marking the beginning of a prosperous trading era. James and Robert McFadden bought that boat and landing in 1888, contracted for another steamer, built a long wharf on Newport Bay, and laid out a town. This was the beginning of Newport Beach.

Balboa Peninsula no longer boasts of sidewheelers, but thousands of boats still use the harbor. Pleasure craft of every description are anchored in channels dredged from former flats on land created by the dredging and planted with homes. It's the biggest yachting harbor on this section of the coast, berthing some 8,000 boats. Whatever land is left sells by the square foot—perhaps one of the reasons this area is called the Gold Coast.

Most of the tangible glimpses of yesteryear are on Balboa Peninsula (on the ocean side of Newport), a long skinny sandspit stretching out to sea, the tip of which is called Balboa.

If you turn south on Via Lido at the north end of the peninsula, you cross a humpbacked bridge leading to Lido Isle, a posh residential area dredged up from the harbor's bottom. Almost every waterfront home has a boat at its back door.

For a new look in shopping centers, start at Lido Village, a cluster of former apartments transformed into a labyrinth of shops and patios against the seawall. This is one of the more unusual cityscapes in California:

street and sidewalks are paved in brick and are outfitted with street lamps, trees, bedded and hanging flowers, benches, and bike racks. Fountains grace the walkways. It takes some looking, upstairs and down, to find the more than 75 shops, ranging in scope from a yacht dealer to boutiques specializing in intimate apparel.

On the peninsula is the site of McFadden's Pier (west of the intersection of Balboa and Newport boulevards). The original pier was destroyed by fire and rebuilt as a fishing spot with tackle shops at its foot. But many buildings around the area date back to the original waterfront days and are now being restored as Cannery Village, a charming conglomeration of boutiques, restaurants, boatyards, and antique shops. One cleverly converted warehouse, The Factory, has over 30 tiny shops under one roof.

The dory fleet which works from the beach adjoining the pier is the last of its kind on the West Coast. Each day at dawn, fishermen shove off in their small wooden boats, working alone 5 to 10 miles out to sea to set trawl lines with thousands of baited hooks for rockfish, halibut, mackerel, flounder, sea trout, and sand dabs. With luck, the fishermen head for shore by midmorning, helping one another through the surf onto the beach, where the area quickly turns into one large, open-air fish market. To the delight of camera-clicking customers, this picturesque fleet has now been designated an historic landmark.

The Newport beach, extending 5¼ miles, is narrow at the northwestern edge and broadens farther south and east. There are fire rings near Balboa Pier, farther out on the peninsula. The largest parking areas are at Palm and Balboa boulevards and at 26th Street. Surfing is popular in the morning in the Newport Pier area, in late afternoon from 30th Street west, and all day at the mouth of the Santa Ana River.

The peninsula's jetties supposedly tamed what was once considered some of California's best surf. But a rock extension of the jetty created a phenomenon called The Wedge, where large breakers are further amplified into a maelstrom. Expert body surfers challenge the waves even during the winter.

Balboa Pavilion, focal point for the Newport Beach playground area for over three-quarters of a century, once was the terminus of the big red streetcar line, Pacific Electric, from Los Angeles. It also served as a bath and boathouse for stylish bathers in ankle-length bathing togs. Since then, the venerable pavilion, with its much-photographed cupola, has been the scene of many "firsts," including the first Surfboard Riding Championship Races in the U.S. in 1932. The Tournament of Lights yachting celebration, held in December, began here in 1908.

When the Big Band sounds echoed across the nation in the 1940s, the pavilion resounded to thousands of dancing feet as the Balboa Peninsula became known as the place that gave birth to a dance that swept the nation—the Balboa Hop.

Recently redecorated, the pavilion still preserves its original 1905 look. It has a restaurant, gift shop, and banquet room; it also serves as headquarters for fishing charters, whale-watching cruises, and harbor excursions, and as the Newport terminal for Catalina tours. At a nearby dock, you can rent all types of water craft.

Harbor cruises are perhaps the best way to see Newport Bay. You won't get a look at all of Newport's 13 square miles (2 of which are underwater), but you will see its small islands and blufftop subdivisions. Harbor cruises leave from the "Fun Zone Dock" near the ferry landing—about 20 daily in the summer, fewer on weekends the rest of the year. On a 45-minute narrated cruise (moderate charge for adults and children), you'll see waterfront homes of motion picture and television stars and many of the boats berthed in the area. For a 4-hour evening cocktail cruise, complete with dancing and live entertainment, you'll pay a bit more.

Balboa Ferry has little three-car ferries (the last on the southern coast) which have been transporting residents and vacationers between the peninsula and Balboa Island since 1919 (small fee for cars, even smaller charge for walk-on passengers). Instituted by a petition signed by the entire island population (then 26 strong), the ferries are still the most interesting way to get to the island, now connected to the mainland by a two-lane bridge and a road from the highway.

Balboa Island has an artsy-craftsy shopping center with a European flavor crunched into about 3 short blocks. Parking is almost impossible on summer weekends. For exploring, your best bet is to park on one of the side streets lined with small wooden houses, and walk. A bayfront boardwalk circles the island, offering fine views of the harbor.

Just across the bridge separating the upper and lower harbor is the *Reuben E. Lee*, replica of an old-time riverboat, now a three-deck, floating restaurant.

Newport Center

Overlooking the ocean and bay to the south is Newport Center (on Irvine land)—a vast shopping, business, professional, and financial complex. Fashion Island, one of the largest and most tastefully designed shopping centers in the West, features interrelated malls and plazas, one equipped especially for children.

But the big thing is the stores. Designers are deserting Beverly Hills and Pasadena in favor of high fashion for the Newport-Irvine-Laguna crowd. First Bullock's Wilshire swept onto Fashion Island with higher price tags than those normally seen in these beach towns. It was quickly followed by other large stores like Robinson's and Neiman-Marcus. The latest—and grandest—addition is the beautiful Atrium Court, housing chic shops and the Irvine Ranch Market.

In addition to stores, there are fine restaurants and the Newport Harbor Art Museum (open Tuesday through Sunday; patio lunch served weekdays only).

Upper Newport Bay

Just south of the bridge crossing, the upper bay arm on the east side of the coast highway has a park within a bay. A commercial enterprise called Newport Dunes Aquatic Park, it offers numerous ways of getting out on the quiet, warm waters of the 15-acre lagoon. For a small entry fee, you can use the beach, dressing rooms, playground, wading pool, fire rings, and launching ramp.

You can also rent paddleboards, kayaks, sea cycles, and sailboats. The park is an attractive overnight camping spot for trailers and campers.

For a real surprise in the midst of all the resort hubbub, take Backbay Drive, off Jamboree Boulevard. It leads you along the east shore of Upper Newport Bay—a vast estuary scarcely touched by man and nearly invisible except from here because it is surrounded by bluffs. It is islands and channel at low tide, a minisea at high tide. There are always birds in action, but in fall it swarms with ducks, geese, and other users of the Pacific Flyway. The area is a wildlife preserve. Guided tours take place on Saturday during the winter.

Water sports enthusiasts have to do their waterskiing on the ocean; speedboats are not allowed on Upper Newport Bay.

Corona del Mar

Corona's state beach, just south of the breakwater, is operated by the city of Newport Beach. Wide and sandy with palm trees, its ½-mile total frontage is divided into two parts. Big Corona is at the east jetty; Little Corona is around the point to the east. The beach is very popular all year; there's a charge for parking. To get there, turn west off the coast highway on any of the streets named for flowers in Corona del Mar between Orchid and Iris.

Look for attractive shops and restaurants along the coast highway in Corona del Mar. Sherman Garden and Library, at 2647 E. Coast Highway, makes an interesting stop for horticultural enthusiasts and for photo buffs. The gardens are open daily; there's an admission charge. Plant lovers will also enjoy nearby Roger's Gardens, which contain 7½ acres of plants.

Development is taking place on the hills to the east of the highway, and your view to the sea is often blocked by exclusive residential development. The topography changes from low, lagoon-backed seashores to a continuing rank of steep bluffs. Irvine Ranch properties account for a considerable stretch of empty shore between Corona del Mar and Laguna Beach, the next town south.

Laguna Beach offers more than sand

Long known as an art colony, Laguna Beach is now a city aware of its French Riviera setting, as well as its problems. Not the least of these is traffic. To follow the coast highway through town on a summer weekend is to experience an interminable series of starts and stops. There are a number of stores where you'll want to pause and take a look.

Painters' galleries are numerous throughout the town. An art lover's first stop might be at the Laguna Beach Museum of Art, 307 Cliff Drive. Open Tuesday through Sunday from 11:30 A.M. to 4:30 P.M., it features an ever-changing variety of media.

The ceramics industry was pioneered here, and many other types of crafts now compete for space with galleries. Often you can watch artisans creating handcrafted pottery, jewelry, clothing, leather goods, rugs, or other articles.

Remote and inaccessible, Laguna Beach was discovered in the 1890s. First-comers built summer homes on the hills, which were followed by more pretentious residences. The colony's boutiques, galleries, little theaters, and coffee houses that sprang up were popular long before Greenwich Village began attracting attention.

Unlike many beach resorts which hibernate during the winter, Laguna holds a Winter Festival in February and March, a May Faire, as well as its famous Festival of Arts and Pageant of the Masters in the summer (see page 57). Since 1932, thousands have gathered annually to see the local residents don costumes and become living pictures. So professional is the performance that it's hard for visitors to believe these "paintings" are really alive.

Laguna has increased its stretch of public beach. Use was formerly limited by the scarcity of street parking. The main beach is along the coast highway in the center of town; it has become a beguiling "window to the sea" park, now that a number of buildings that blocked it have been torn down. To the north are Crescent Bay, Divers Cove, and Heisler Park (with bluff-top fire rings and picnic tables); to the south are pocket beaches such as Woods Cove and Victoria Beach. Surfers and scuba divers are active early in the morning.

In South Laguna is Aliso Beach Park, a ¾-mile frontage with lifeguards, a few fire rings, and a handsome fishing pier. Adjacent Camel Point and West Street pocket beaches have similar small frontages.

Dana Point

Once a cliff over which cowhides were thrown to waiting traders (see references to Point San Juan in Richard Henry Dana's *Two Years Before the Mast*), Dana Point subsequently became a lonely cove frequented by abalone hunters, a park, and now the site of a luxurious marina with accommodations for over 2,000 boats. You can rent one for the day to explore the harbor area.

A manmade harbor created a vast marina, divided into east and west basins, with some 2,500 slips. Encircling the marina are three yacht clubs, a great variety of boating services, docks for sportfishing excursions, several dozen specialty shops at Mariners Village and Dana Wharf, numerous restaurants, and a motel.

At the end of Del Obispo Street, the Orange County Marine Institute offers excursions, sailing lessons, and overnight adventures for children aboard a replica of Dana's ship. You'll find aquariums, marine exhibits, art work with a nautical theme, and a pond where you can touch tidepool creatures. The free museum is open daily except Sunday.

Several miles of paved pathways are popular among roller skaters (rentals are available), and grassy picnic spots dot the areas off Del Obispo Street and Dana Drive. But one of the most popular amusements is simply boat watching. Many Newport-based boats sail down the coast for lunch; you'll see some fancy deck picnics as you walk along the piers.

A trio of beaches

These last three Orange County beaches are good for swimming, and camping is also allowed.

Doheny State Beach is next door to Dana Point. Popular and crowded, Doheny offers camping combined with a safe beach and good surfing. The lagoon on San Juan Creek at the north end of the park is a wild bird habitat. Surf fishing (once better than it is now) and a fair grunion run are attractions.

The park is near the junction of State Highway 1 and I-5 at Capistrano Beach in Dana Point.

San Clemente State Beach is really a dual-purpose park, similar to Doheny. Campsites perch on the edge of a bluff, shaded and separated with mature trees and shrubs. Because the beach is extremely popular, camping reservations are important. For information, write to Pendleton Coast Area Office, 3030 Avenida del Presidente, San Clemente, CA 92672.

Well-established footpaths lead from the cliffs to the beaches below; don't stray off the trails, for the bluffs are crumbly. Swimming is good (lifeguards are on duty), but watch for occasional riptides.

San Onofre State Beach (formerly part of the Camp Pendleton Marine Corps base) was opened for public use in 1971. The beach is not visible from I-5. Take the Basilone Road exit off the highway and follow signs past the nuclear power plant. Campers and trailers occupy the by-passed old coast highway, and three trails lead about ¼ mile down to a usually broad beach.

From Orange County to San Diego

Three routes lead through Orange County to San Diego. All have their advantages. Your choice is determined by your time.

The coast highway. Driving the Pacific Coast Highway takes you by all the beaches and shoreside cities mentioned in the South Coast section. It's a pleasant drive, but if you are in a hurry to get through Orange County to San Diego, or if you wish to avoid the summertime beach crowds, it would be easier to take Interstate 5 (Santa Ana Freeway) or Interstate 405 (San Diego Freeway) to its junction with I-5.

The freeways. These routes take you through Orange County's largest cities, but you won't see many attractions unless you get off. To reach most of the county's main diversions, the freeways are the easiest approach. Most directions to attractions are given in terms of freeway offramps.

The Santa Ana Freeway divides the county in two, with most of the inland points of interest located on nearby main streets. The San Diego Freeway more closely parallels the coast highway, joining I-5 before it heads south to San Juan Capistrano.

The back roads. Still another way to head south through Orange County toward San Diego is on the back country roads. Much of the southeastern part of Orange County is still undeveloped, and meandering roads lead through canyons, over hills, and beside lakes. At times the only companions you'll meet along the route are some uninterested cows.

Eventually to head south you will have to join one of the canyon roads leading toward the freeway. Many of the back country routes end abruptly. Unless you are out for a jaunt, not caring too much about where or when you'll end up, be sure you have a good map of the county with you. Automobile clubs, the Anaheim Area Visitors and Convention Bureau, and Thomas Bros. have the best maps.

San Diego

An illustrious past, a scene-stealing setting, and historic and aquatic parks lure visitors to San Diego. Up the coast lie beach cities, an oceanside racetrack, a rare pine preserve; inland roads lead to Palomar Observatory, an unusual wild animal park, Indian camping grounds, and century-old mining villages. To the south, sample Old Mexico, right across the border.

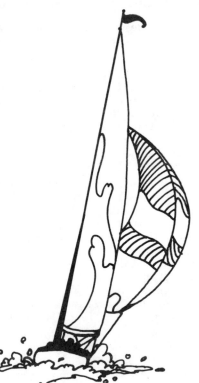

San Diego is constantly changing and consistently charming. At first glance, the city's modern facade belies its old age. But California's oldest town is ever mindful of her rich Spanish-Mexican heritage. Monuments report it and buildings preserve it. A legacy of Spanish place names, graceful architecture, and a relaxed life style reflect San Diego's pride in her past.

California's history began here when Juan Rodriguez Cabrillo landed at Point Loma in 1542. Sixty years later, Sebastian Vizcaino also reached the bay he named San Diego. But the West Coast's first settlement was not established until 1769, when Father Junipero Serra, a member of Portola's expedition, founded Mission San Diego de Alcala on Presidio Hill. The village that grew up around the mission became the anchor point for Spanish domain in California and a terminal point of the famous El Camino Real (the King's Highway), now U.S. Highway 101.

Thanks to a splendid natural setting, an equable climate, and early city planning, this once sleepy little seaside community is now the third largest city on the Pacific Coast. Constant sea breezes keep the air clear and fresh. An average temperature of 70°F. and a low humidity level make San Diego an all-year vacation city.

Water-oriented San Diego also owes her growth to a great harbor. Vast, natural, and almost landlocked, San Diego Harbor is one of the world's best deepwater anchorages. Host to ships from all ports, it is also home of the 11th Fleet, the U.S. Navy's largest.

Up the coast are gems of seaside villages, colorful flower fields, and wide, sandy beaches. The interior, or back country, holds a wealth of surprises, ranging from San Diego's impressive Wild Animal Park to the old-fashioned mountain mining village of Julian.

Across the border lies the fascination of another country—Mexico. This chapter takes a look at several Mexican towns, only a convenient drive from San Diego.

Entertainment. San Diego offers plenty to see and do. Many inexpensive recreational activities are easily accessible; some of the finest attractions are free. San Diego County claims more good public bathing beaches (70 miles) than the rest of California. Boating centers around the harbor and Mission Bay to the north. In the heart of the city are Old Town (the original village) and Balboa Park, location of the San Diego Zoo—one of the largest collections of wild animals in the world.

A sports center, San Diego has major league football, baseball, and soccer, as well as a stadium and a sports arena. You can play tennis, soar, skin dive, deep-sea fish, or sail any time of the year. Golfers will find that one of the 66 courses will suit them to a tee.

Biking enthusiasts and joggers have a choice of several scenic routes marked by signs along the ocean and through the Presidio and Balboa Park. One bike trail stretches south along San Diego Bay from the Naval Training Center estuary.

Moving around is easy in San Diego. The International Airport (Lindbergh Field) is near downtown; a network of freeways, ringing the city, can take you anywhere within minutes. In about 20 minutes, you've crossed the Southern California border into Mexico or driven up the coast to Del Mar. For the most part, hotels and motels are clustered around the San Diego harbor, Mission Bay,

SAN DIEGO SKYLINE and bay boating provide exceptional views for landlubbers on manmade Harbor Island.

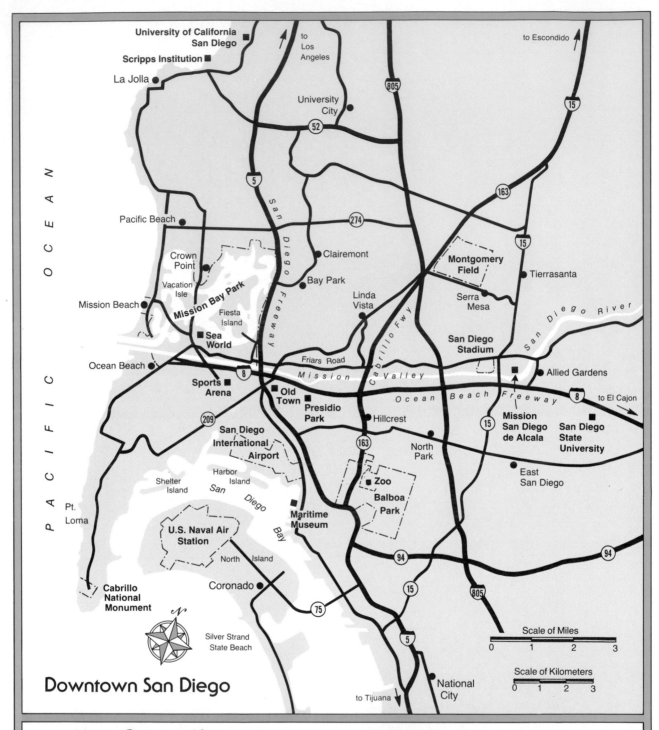

Downtown San Diego

University of California
San Diego ■

Scripps Institution ■

La Jolla ●

to
Los
Angeles

to Escondido

805

15

University
City ●

52

5

274

163

Pacific Beach ●

Clairemont ●

15

Montgomery
Field

Tierrasanta ●

Crown
Point ●

Bay Park ●

Serra
Mesa

San Diego River

Vacation
Isle

Mission Bay Park

Linda
Vista

Mission Beach ●

Fiesta
Island

San Diego Freeway

■ **Sea
World**

Friars Road

**San Diego
Stadium** ■

Allied Gardens ●

Ocean Beach ●

8

Mission *Ocean Beach Freeway* 8

Cabrillo Fwy

Valley

to El Cajon

**Sports ■
Arena**

■ **Old
Town**

Hillcrest ●

15

**Mission
San Diego
de Alcala**

**San Diego
State
University** ■

209

**Presidio
Park**

163

North
Park ●

**San Diego
International
Airport**

Zoo ■

East
San Diego ●

Shelter
Island

Harbor
Island

**Maritime ■
Museum**

**Balboa
Park**

Pt.
Loma

San

Diego

**U.S. Naval Air
Station**

94

94

North Island

Bay

Coronado ●

75

15

805

**Cabrillo
National
Monument**

N

5

Silver Strand
State Beach

Scale of Miles

0 1 2 3

Scale of Kilometers

0 1 2 3

to Tijuana

National
City ●

Major Points of Interest

Mission Bay Park — aquatic playground with vacation hotels, campgrounds, water sports

Sea World — aquatic shows, exhibits, rides, pearl divers, performing killer whales, shark exhibit

Old Town — State Historic Park offers views of yesteryear San Diego; restored adobes, shops

Harbor Island — manmade isle with hotels and restaurants; excellent harbor view

Shelter Island — glamorous restaurants in a pleasure boat harbor setting

Cabrillo National Monument — commemorates California's discovery; lighthouses, museum, major whale-watching point

Coronado — island setting for West's Victorian-style architectural wonder, Hotel del Coronado

Balboa Park — home for museums, galleries, theaters, San Diego Zoo

Mission San Diego de Alcala — oldest California mission

Mission Valley, and downtown. Close to major freeways, they are easy to locate. Campers will find a wide selection of sites; one campground will rent whatever you forget to bring—including the camper.

Visitors can receive specific information by writing to the San Diego Convention and Visitors Bureau, 1200 Third Avenue, Suite 824, San Diego, CA 92101. A visitor information center is located at 11 Horton Plaza. For recorded information on what's happening around town, call (619) 239-9696.

Motorists can follow a 52-mile scenic drive all around town and the surrounding area. Just start anywhere and follow the road signs bearing a white sea gull.

The Tijuana Trolley connects downtown San Diego with the border town of Tijuana, Mexico. Trolleys depart several times an hour all day long from the Santa Fe Depot (Broadway and Kettner streets). The run to the border takes 35 minutes, including frequent stops (seven in downtown San Diego) for loading passengers. Trolley cars run every 15 minutes from 5 A.M. to 1 A.M. You'll need exact change for the trip. For additional information, call (619) 231-1466.

The Water World

San Diego should be viewed from the water. The beautiful harbor is a notable exception to the rule that waterfronts are necessarily ugly and conceal the fascination of great ships. San Diego's provides both visual and recreational amenities for people against a colorful backdrop of commercial and naval vessels. It offers parks where you may stroll and play, a pier and embankments for fishing, boat launching, a small beach, and places to watch the big ships go by or to take a closer look at yachts, tuna clippers, oceanographic crafts, and an antique sailing ship. And it offers thriving complexes of marinas, hotels, shops, and restaurants oriented to a water view.

Shops and restaurants built in Victorian and Spanish styles re-create the past in Seaport Village, a shopping complex at Pacific Highway and Harbor Drive. A turn-of-the-century carousel from Coney Island is a highlight amid the 14 acres of bayside browsing.

Harbor tours

The best way to get your bearings is on a harbor excursion. Both 1 and 2-hour cruises loop close along the shoreline, exposing a full range of air, surface, and undersea craft and harbor activity otherwise hidden from sight.

Boats leave from the well-marked dock on Harbor Drive at the foot of Broadway. In summer, short cruises leave at 45-minute intervals; 2-hour cruises leave twice daily weekdays, more often on weekends and holidays. Cocktail and dinner cruises and whale-watching trips (in season) are particularly popular.

Embarcadero

North of the excursion boat dock is the former square-rigger *Star of India*, probably the oldest (1863) iron-hulled merchantman still afloat. Go aboard for a hint of sea life over a century ago. Now painstakingly restored, the ship is moored as part of a Maritime Museum Fleet. You can also visit two other ships in the fleet, the 1800s San Francisco ferryboat *Berkeley* and the vintage steam yacht *Medea*. The museum is open daily; admission is nominal.

Walk north to see some picturesque action on weekdays at the net yard on the seawall dock for long-range tuna clippers. You must stay outside the fence to watch the fishermen mending huge nets.

Don't miss Broadway Pier—San·Diego's unique park-on-a-pier—where a lot of net handling takes place and sleek cruise ships are often berthed.

Sport fishers can board a deep-sea fishing charter from several points around the harbor and from Mission Bay. Many excursions fish the Mexican-owned Coronado Islands, 18 miles off the coast. You'll need a license and permit.

Waterfront dining is good along the Embarcadero. A Mediterranean-style seafood complex offers visitors a choice of buying fresh fish to take home or dining near the water on seafood delicacies.

Shelter Island and Harbor Island

Two manmade vacation "islands" in San Diego Bay accommodate boaters, sailors, sportsmen, and atmosphere-seekers. Though they once were mud and sandpiles built up by dredging operations in the bay, Shelter and Harbor islands are now attractive resort areas studded with forests of boat masts.

Shelter Island offers a fishing pier, attractive marinas, boat launching ramps, restaurants, and hotels. Tropical blooms, torches, and "Polynesian" architecture give the island a South Seas flavor. Winding paths provide good strolling, biking, and bay-watching sports. Friendship Bell is here, the gift of Yokohama, San Diego's sister city in Japan. Really a peninsula, Shelter Island is connected to Point Loma by a salty causeway.

Harbor Island, located opposite the San Diego International Airport, can be viewed from a peaceful vantage point in Spanish Landing Park on Harbor Drive. The island features high-rise hotels, restaurants, parks, and marinas. On the western tip of the island, a Spanish-style building houses a combination lighthouse and restaurant.

The Navy

San Diego is home to the large 11th Naval District, as well as to many other military installations. Though no longer known primarily as a Navy town, San Diego is still influenced by the activities that the Navy brings.

Naval vessels moored at the Broadway Pier on Harbor Drive hold open house from 1 to 4 P.M. on weekends.

Both the Naval and Marine centers in San Diego present colorful, full-fledged military reviews every Friday. Parades begin at about 2:15 P.M. at the Naval Training Center and at 10 A.M. at the Marine Corps Recruiting Depot. Both centers are located off Pacific Highway; to reach them, drive southwest on Barnett Avenue and enter Gate 4.

Coronado

Coronado's relative isolation gives it the flavor of an island. Actually it's connected to the mainland by a long, scenic sand spit and a graceful bay bridge. Low guard rails on the sweeping span open up a panoramic view reaching from the San Diego skyline south into Mexico.

Hotel del Coronado. Coronado was a sterile, wind-blown peninsula, populated with jackrabbits, coyotes, and occasional wildcats, when Elisha Babcock and H. L. Story bought the 4,100 acres (including North Island) in 1885. Babcock's dream—to build a hotel that "would be the talk of the Western world"—came true in the form of the striking, red-roofed Hotel del Coronado, still operating as the focal point of this area and now a State and National Historic Landmark. Distinguished guests over the years have included United States presidents, Thomas A. Edison, Henry Ford, and Robert Todd Lincoln.

You can rent cassettes from the lobby shop and take a self-guiding tour of this Victorian-style wooden wonder, exploring the intricate corridors and cavernous rooms at the completely self-contained hotel.

Around the peninsula. Across from the hotel, a picturesque boathouse (now a restaurant, designed to match the Victorian architectural style of the hotel) sits at the edge of Glorietta Bay, a small boat harbor that contains a public launching ramp. Adjoining it are a municipal golf course and a public bathing beach (caution: watch for sting rays early in the season). Facing the bay, the Glorietta Bay Inn (formerly John D. Spreckels's home) hosts visitors. At the north end of the peninsula is the Naval Air Station, one of the oldest in existence. For a map of the island, stop by the Coronado Chamber of Commerce, 720 Orange Avenue.

Silver Strand State Beach. Millions of glittering seashells gave their name to this 5-mile-long ocean beach, one of America's finest day-use beaches. It stretches almost the full length of the sand spit connecting the tip of the peninsula to the mainland.

The sand is dotted with nearly 400 fire rings and picnic units; the parking lot has space for almost 2,000 cars, and the climate is almost always very good.

Pedestrian underpasses cross beneath State Highway 75 to the bay side, where there is quieter water, good for swimmers and water-skiers.

Point Loma

The high promontory that shelters San Diego Bay from the Pacific Ocean offers a great view of the harbor. On a clear day you can see from the mountains of Mexico to beyond the La Jolla mesa and from the sprawling city of San Diego to the Coronado Islands and out to sea.

Cabrillo National Monument. At the tip of Point Loma is Cabrillo National Monument, one of the smallest, most historic, and most visited monuments in this country (outdoing even the Statue of Liberty).

Cabrillo's statue, a gift from Portugal (homeland of the great navigator), faces his actual landing spot at Ballast Point. The nearby visitor center explains Cabrillo's discovery of San Diego Bay and the events following

it. A glassed-in observatory at the monument gives fine views of the whale migration that occurs each year from mid-December through mid-February. On the high bluff stands a well-preserved lighthouse; it was used from 1855 until 1891, when the waterside lighthouse (still in use) was built.

The monument has a nature trail, a surprisingly unique plant community, and some of the best tidepools left in Southern California (marine biologists invite you to look but not touch). The monument is open daily from 9 A.M. to 5:15 P.M. To reach it from San Diego, go southwest on Rosecrans Street and follow the signs; from Mission Bay, take Sunset Cliffs Boulevard to Catalina Boulevard.

To the tip. A drive through residential Point Loma takes you past the U.S. Navy reservation and through Fort Rosecrans.

A Look at the Past

In 1769, Father Serra chose a hill site overlooking the bay for a mission that would begin the settlement of California. A presidio was also built to protect the mission; this site is now called Presidio Hill. Soon a town began to sprout at the foot of the hill, with a plaza, a church, and the attractive tile-roofed, adobe homes of California's first families.

Spanish, Mexican, and American settlements thrived here; buildings and relics of these periods survive. Some have been restored or reconstructed with adobe bricks shaped at the same site which furnished the original bricks. Much of the restoration is within Old Town San Diego State Historic Park, an area of 6½ blocks bounded by Wallace, Congress, Twiggs, and Juan streets. Old Town is bordered by old residential areas and two modern freeways, Interstate Highways 5 and 8. Its streets are for strolling only.

Old Town

Old Town is no sterile museum display; many shops and restaurants are housed in the district's original buildings and patios. The shopping area, once confined mainly to Squibob Square on San Diego Avenue, has been extended by the addition of Old San Diego Square, at Juan and Harney streets, and Bazaar del Mundo (located in the famous Casa de Pico hacienda). At Bazaar del Mundo you can dine (the Mexican restaurant overlooks the garden), browse in high-quality shops, and mingle with shopping San Diegans. The multilevel Old San Diego Galleria complex provides much-needed underground parking. Squibob Square's wares are displayed in false-front stores.

Highlights. Walking is the best way to savor the historical flavor. Do it on your own—or take the free walking tour that departs at 2 P.M. every day from the Machado y Silvas Adobe across from the plaza.

Visitors will find the flavor of Old Town one of its fascinations: you can observe bread baking in the outdoor oven behind the Machado house on Saturday, as well as brick making, candle dipping, and wool spinning. You can also take a horse-and-buggy ride (for a

DAYS OF FATHER SERRA are recalled in museum (above) on Presidio Hill, site of first mission. You can take a buggy ride (left) among Old Town Historic Park's restored and reconstructed adobes.

slight fee). These are some of the Old Town sights you'll see.

• *El Campo Santo*, at San Diego and Linwood, is the easternmost landmark in Old Town. This adobe-walled, Mexican Catholic cemetery (1850-1880) was the final resting place for many founding fathers, as well as for a few bandits. It's hard to tell how many people are buried here because so many headstones are missing.

• *The Whaley House*, at the corner of San Diego and Harney, is the oldest brick structure in Southern California. The American-style mansion, the only one of its kind in San Diego, has served as a dairy, funeral parlor, theater, saloon, courthouse, and as the city's first Sunday school. It is reputed to be haunted. The restored house and premises, including such historical relics as a yellow streetcar, are open Wednesday through Sunday from 10 A.M. to 4:30 P.M.

• *The Derby-Pendleton House* (entered through the Whaley House) is perhaps the first prefabricated building in California. The New England-style home was shipped around Cape Horn and put together with wooden pegs. It is now a museum. Your admission fee to Whaley House includes this visit.

• *Chapel of Immaculate Conception*, at San Diego and Conde, was Old Town's first church, converted from an old adobe house and dedicated in 1858. Father Ubach was reputedly the inspiration for "Father Gaspara" of Helen Hunt Jackson's novel *Ramona*—he claimed to have known the characters in the story and their families.

• *Casa de Altamirano*, at San Diego and Twiggs, site of the first printing of the San Diego Union in 1868, is restored as an early day printing office. Originally a home, the building was used as a store before the newspaper was located there.

• *Casa de Pedrorena*, at San Diego between Twiggs and Mason, is a large, restored adobe that is now a popular Mexican restaurant with courtyard dining.

• *Casa de Estudillo*, east of San Diego on Mason, built of logs and rawhide on a lot granted by the governor, was the home of Captain Jose Estudillo, commandante of Monterey and San Diego. The first Spanish *casa* to be constructed on the plaza, it was robbed of roof tiles and reduced to ruin after the family abandoned it in 1881. Extensively restored, the house and garden afford a glimpse of how a comparatively wealthy rancher once lived. Admission includes entrance to Seeley Stable.

• *Casa de Bandini*, at Mason and Calhoun, originally a one-story adobe, gained a second story when it became a stagecoach station in the 1860s. Built by wealthy Don Juan Bandini (known for his lavish fandangos and dinners), the house was Commodore Stockton's headquarters during the American occupation of California in 1846. Kit Carson also visited here. The adobe now houses a popular Mexican restaurant.

• *Plaza Vieja*, or San Diego Plaza, was the center of town. A comfortable and verdant stop for walkers today, it was once the noisy scene of bullfights and other entertainments. Among the lacy pepper, eucalyptus, and graceful palm trees stands the flagpole that has flown Spanish and Mexican flags for two centuries; the American flag was added in 1846.

• *Casa de Machado*, at San Diego between Wallace and Mason, was built in 1832 for a Spanish Army soldier and his wife. Scarcity of wood required use of adobe in most of the early homes, and here you can see some of the original adobe bricks, formed and placed by the good soldier Machado.

• *The Mason Street School*, west of San Diego on Mason, was the city's first public school building. When replaced, the quaint one-room schoolhouse became a tamale factory. Now restored, it displays mementos of the early San Diego school system.

• *The Machado-Stewart House*, on Congress between Wallace and Mason, was built by Jose Manuel Machado for his daughter, who married John C. Stewart, a shipmate of Richard Henry Dana. Dana described his 1859 visit to the house in *Two Years Before the Mast*. In contrast to the most elaborate Estudillo residence, this small clapboard adobe displays how a man of moderate means may have lived.

• *The Seeley Stable* and barns, at the corner of Juan and Twiggs, is another Old Town attraction. It's a replica of the stables of Albert Seeley, who operated a stagecoach line around 1869. The stable houses the Roscoe Hazard Museum; here, you can see a collection of horse-drawn vehicles and Western artifacts.

• *Casa de Lopez*, a longtime local favorite sometimes called Flynn's House of 10,000 Candles, is a State Historic Landmark at the deadend of Twiggs Street. Walk-through tours are conducted daily.

Heritage Park

In this historic park on the outskirts of Old Town (at Juan and Harney streets), a haven is being established for some of San Diego's oldest Victorians. Currently seven restored structures house shops, offices, and a bed and breakfast inn.

Presidio Hill

Just five years after Father Junipero Serra and the Spanish soldiers set the Royal Standard, raised the cross, and dedicated the first mission in California, the site was already too small for the mission's growing members. Out of a need for fresh water and in order to be closer to Indian settlements, Mission San Diego was moved in 1774 from Presidio Hill 6 miles east up Mission Valley. The presidio and the old American garrison (Fort Stockton) have long been covered over. Their foundations are outlined in the grassy mounds on the hill. Diggings in the area are archeological excavations.

The birthplace of California is now the home of handsome Serra Museum, a Spanish Colonial structure; of lush Presidio Park; and of the Serra Cross. Made of bricks from Spanish ruins, the cross marks the site of the original mission chapel.

Standing prominently at the heart of the hill and gleaming white in the sun, the Serra Museum exhibits the area's history from mission days through pioneer times. The museum is open from 9 A.M. to 4 P.M. Tuesday through Saturday, noon to 4 P.M. Sunday.

Mission San Diego de Alcala

The San Diego Mission was the first in the long line of 21 missions built in Alta (upper) California.

The restoration of the "Mother of the Missions" retains the simple facade of the original mission and is characterized by a strikingly graceful campanile. Here you'll discover a museum containing original mission records in Father Serra's handwriting, relics and art from the early days, a reconstructed Indian village, and olive trees from the mission's original grove. Recent restoration includes a visitor center with a mural depicting San Diego's early history.

Sunday services are still held in the original chapel. The mission is open daily to the public. Tote-a-tapes for self-guided tours are available.

San Diego Mission is best reached by taking I-8 to Murphy Canyon Road; watch for mission exit signs.

Downtown San Diego

In the past few years, downtown San Diego has received a thorough facelift. A revitalized central core, restored historical buildings like the refurbished U. S. Grant Hotel, and the dramatic Horton Plaza shopping center have combined to make the downtown area attractive to both residents and visitors.

As the city's skyline continues to grow upwards, restaurants are being opened atop skyscrapers to take advantage of fine views. Theater, dance, and symphony performances bring added life, as do sidewalk cafés, jazz bistros, and street performers.

Horton Plaza (bounded by Third, Fourth, Broadway, and E streets) is a good place to start your investigation. The 11½-acre complex includes major department stores and 180 smaller shops; restaurants and several theaters occupy a top floor. At the entrance to Horton Plaza, a stairway and plaza lead to the Lyceum Theater.

The Gaslamp Quarter, a 16-block restoration (bounded by Fourth and Sixth and Broadway and the harbor), is worth a look. In an area frequented by Wyatt Earp late in the last century, splendid representations of Victorian architecture house art galleries, antique shops, restaurants, and the Gaslamp Quarter Theatre. "Beat cops" costumed in 1890s dress patrol the area as goodwill ambassadors.

The Charles C. Dail Concourse (formerly Community Concourse) is the center of downtown. Covering more than a full city block (bounded by A and C and First and Third streets), it includes a Convention and Performing Arts Center, as well as the City Administration Building. The 3,000-seat Civic Theatre is home for the San Diego Symphony, San Diego Opera Company, and city and state ballet companies. A huge parking facility tops the concourse.

Two fine hotels highlight downtown's redevelopment. The Westgate Hotel (Second and C streets) is one of the world's leading hostelries. A true luxury hotel, it's full of "wasted" space and such appurtenances as Aubusson tapestries, Baccarat crystal chandeliers, and famous paintings. The U. S. Grant Hotel (across Broadway from Horton Plaza), a San Diego landmark since 1910, has been restored to its original glory and is attracting lots of attention—and plenty of guests.

San Diego Public Library (corner of Eighth and E streets) is one of the most modern and well-stocked

---

THE SPA SITUATION

You don't have to worry about gaining weight on at least one kind of San Diego vacation. Because of its mild climate, this area has more than its share of health spas, often referred to as "fat farms."

Spas come in all sizes and shapes—from glamorous resorts to more modest settings. Those listed below are only a sampling of what's available in the area. But don't expect to just drop in for a week or a weekend—you need advance reservations.

According to the dictionary, a spa means "any locality frequented for its mineral springs," and at the modest Hotel Jacumba, in San Diego's back country, people still come to "take the waters." Carlsbad, up the coast, built its early reputation around the similarity of its mineral spring to the waters in Karlsbad, Germany.

Couples frequent Fallbrook's Pala Mesa Spa, an attractive secluded oasis about a mile from a lodge and 18-hole championship golf course. Women check in for a full spa program (exercise, water workouts, and salon service) from 8 A.M. to 5 P.M. daily while men enjoy golf and tennis at the clubhouse. They overnight at the lodge, with separate menus for spa guests and spouses.

The Golden Door in Escondido is frankly for the wealthy and not *too* lumpy. This women-only retreat is decorated in Japanese chic. According to patrons, the mini-meals are worth the very high price of the visit.

Rancho La Puerta, across the border in Tecate, is an earlier, earthier version of the Golden Door. Largest health resort in North America, it exudes a homey atmosphere among 600 acres of unspoiled Mexican countryside. This is one place for the entire family. Hiking, pool activities, yoga, and a vegetarian cuisine highlight the stay.

At elegant Rancho La Costa, up the coast, you'll find a complete spa plus plush extras. Men make up much of the clientele. People not on the spa program also come here to enjoy the 25 tennis courts, dancing, and nightly entertainment. Not too private, it has an atmosphere that at times resembles a large convention. It's a frequent stop for sightseeing buses.

LAGOON REFLECTS
arcade and towers of 1915
exposition building in
Balboa Park.

libraries in the country. It's open daily except Sunday. Its collection goes back 4,000 years to Sumerian cuneiform tablets (though you can't withdraw them on your library card).

The Firehouse Museum, at 1572 Columbia Street, reveals a glittering array of major pieces of firefighting equipment. You'll even find such oddities as a notorious New York false-alarm box. You can visit the museum on weekends from 10 A.M. to 4 P.M. Admission is free.

Villa Montezuma, considered one of the city's finest Victorian mansions, has been partially renovated and refurbished; it's open for public tours from 1 to 4:30 P.M. daily except Monday and Saturday. Located at 1925 K Street, the restored Victorian features a fine stained glass collection.

Two Great Parks

Two of the city's most outstanding attractions are examples of careful planning and foresight. Balboa Park, conceived in the 1880s, and Mission Bay Aquatic Park, developed a century later, are destinations for millions of tourists yearly.

Balboa Park

The park came first. Then the city was built around it. Transformed from rattlesnake-infested, hilly chaparral to a public garden with sky-high eucalyptus trees, lush tropical plants, and Mexican Churrigueresque buildings—this is century-old Balboa Park, one of the nation's greatest. Avenues curving through verdant foliage and grassy fields take you to almost any recreational or cultural activity you might seek: art galleries, science and natural history museums, an innovative space theater, the world's largest zoo, a merry-go-round, a picnic grove, and a golf course.

How it began. Optimism and foresight helped shape Balboa Park. In 1868, the city fathers set aside 1,400 acres (nine large lots at a time when the city had only 915 houses) "to be forever a public park." For 20 years the unimproved land supported a dog pound, a trash dump, and a gravel pit until horticulturist Kate Sessions set up a nursery on a few acres in exchange for doing a considerable planting in other areas of the park. By 1910, community planning and action had formed a park.

Two world's fairs added the massive and ornate structures for which the park is known. The 1915 Panama-California International Exposition, commemorating the completion of the Panama Canal, attracted 3 million visitors and is survived by the attractive Cabrillo Bridge (through which most out-of-town visitors enter the park) and much of the cultural center along the Prado area, still the park's center of activity. The Spreckels Pavilion contains the world's largest outdoor organ. Donated in 1915, it has provided Sunday recitals ever since. Built as the only permanent structure of this fair, the unique California Building (home of the Museum of Man), with its familiar Spanish-Renaissance tower rising above the treetops and its ornamental facade depicting California history, has become the symbol of the city of San Diego. Its openwork tiers contain a carillon that proclaims the hour and enlivens the area with a daily noontime concert.

In 1935, the California-Pacific International Exposition contributed a series of structures representative of Southwest history. Added then were the building complex south of the Prado known as the Palisades area, the Old Globe Theatre, and the Spanish Village.

Getting in and around. Four million visitors a year sample the attractions at Balboa Park, and countless more stroll the beautiful paths and picnic in special groves or on the lawns. You can spend an active or a leisurely day here. Walking is the best way to enjoy the lovely park, since the latest phase of development has now closed half of the Prado to cars during the day, creating a pedestrian promenade. The Prado is located east of the central plaza in front of the Fine Arts Gallery.

Scattered through the broad mesa tops and canyons are plenty of recreation spots for golf and tennis, field and target archery, baseball, roque, lawn bowling, shuffleboard, horseshoes, and badminton.

You enter Balboa Park from either 6th Avenue and Laurel Street or Park Boulevard and El Prado. There are big parking lots in the Palisades area, at the zoo, and along Park Boulevard.

Highlights. On the plaza along El Prado, the House of Hospitality has free maps and information on the park. These are some of the major attractions:
- *The Museum of Man,* a must for anthropology buffs, is known for its research on the Indian cultures of the Americas. It includes an exhibit of mummies and offers demonstrations of historical crafts. The museum is open daily from 10 A.M. to 4:30 P.M.; there's a small admission charge.
- *The Old Globe Theatre,* in a grove behind the California Building, was built for Shakespearean productions. Destroyed by fire in 1978, it was rebuilt in 1982 and is now part of a complex of three interconnected stages known as the Simon Edison Centre for Performing Arts. The complex also includes the outdoor Festival Stage, home for the annual summer Shakespeare Festival (mid-June to September), and the intimate Cassius Carter Centre Stage.
- *The San Diego Museum of Art* collection spans the ages—from early Asian art to 20th century pieces (on display in the west wing). There's also a small sculpture court and garden. You'll discover a fine collection of old masters and a special gallery for American artists. Located on the north side of the plaza, the museum is open Tuesday through Sunday from 10 A.M. to 5 P.M. You'll pay an admission charge.

The adjacent Timken Art Gallery houses a collection of American and European art, including a large number of Russian icons. It's open from 10 A.M. to 4:30 P.M. Tuesday through Saturday, and on Sunday from 1:30 P.M. to 4:30 P.M. Admission is free.
- *The Aerospace Museum* greets visitors with a replica of "The Spirit of St. Louis," Lindbergh's famous plane. Its exhibits cover the whole history of flight, from gliders to space capsules. The Hall of Fame salutes aviation pioneers. Open daily from 10 A.M. to 4 P.M., the museum charges admission.

- *Casa del Prado* (next to the Botanical Building), a complex of buildings, arcades, and courtyards, in 1971 replaced the decrepit Food and Beverage Building from the 1915 exposition. Casts of existing plaster ornamentation on the building were made for reproduction in permanent materials.
- *The Natural History Museum* has something for all kinds of explorers. Extensive exhibits and a large research library fascinate visitors, and bimonthly nature walks attract adventurers. Ask at the museum for a self-guided horticultural walk around the Prado. This museum on the Southern California environment is open from 10 A.M. to 4 P.M. daily (admission fee).
- *The Reuben H. Fleet Space Theater and Science Center* is a later addition. In the theater, the screen is a tilted hemisphere; image and sound surround you. Not confined to showing the sky as seen from earth, the theater's microprocessor-controlled system of more than 80 projectors takes you into space, past planets, in view of stars changing configuration as you move. In the adjoining science center, you operate ingenious gadgets demonstrating principles of sensory perception. Listen to your heartbeat; look at the inside of your eye; create pop art with a harmonograph; or match wits with a computerized teaching machine. The center is open from 9:45 A.M. daily. Sunday through Thursday it closes at 9:30 P.M.; on weekends it's open until 10:30 P.M. Showtimes vary; call (619) 238-1168 for a schedule.
- *San Diego Zoo* is extraordinary. Here one of the world's largest collections of wild animals lives in surroundings as natural as man can provide. Lions roam freely behind good-sized moats, and exotic birds fly free in a tropical rain forest. You may even see a guinea fowl strutting independently on the walk, helping to hold down the insect population. This manmade jungle holds some of the rarest animals in the world.

High above the zoo canyons, an aerial tramway called Skyfari whisks you on an exciting ride over the grottos and mesas that are home for the animals in this cageless zoo. The Skyfari leaves near the zoo entrance over a lagoon colored by Chilean flamingos and black swans, rises over the nearby seal show (free performances are held in the afternoon), and travels above the active and popular residents of the Great Ape Grottos in Monkey Mesa. When you're not looking closely at animal activity beneath you, you can enjoy a spectacular overview of Balboa Park.

The orange gondolas reach their highest point of 170 feet over Stock and Crane Canyon and terminate at Horn and Hoof Mesa, where inhabitants include antelope, bison, kangaroos, and wallabies. If you do not choose to make the return trip immediately, you can disembark here and tour the western end of the zoo before returning by tramway or walking back.

On the ground, you can see the 128-acre zoo on a guided tour bus that takes in 3½ miles in 40 minutes, including areas not easily reached by walking. You can save steps and time this way, planning where you'd like to revisit and also catching a performance by stagestruck bears or other animals that are cued by your guide.

The zoo is open all year, from 9 A.M. to dusk. Deluxe admission packages include entrance to the zoo, guided bus tour, round-trip Skyfari ride, and admission to the Children's Zoo.

- *The Children's Zoo,* a wonderful zoo within a zoo, puts the four-year-old nose to nose with the animal kingdom's younger members. Benches and drinking fountains are also appropriately scaled down. Garden paths wind through an aviary in which tiny, colorful finches fly overhead and perch in nearby branches and birdhouses, past swimming turtles, to the baby elephants begging peanuts. A cuddly but lazy koala sleeps in the V of a tree, a tolerant Galapagos tortoise offers a ride on his great hulking shell, and friendly little deer and barnyard animals come to be petted and fed by their equally friendly little visitors. One of the most delightful attractions is the small hatchery where you can watch baby chicks peck out of their shells. If you wish, you may hold some of the fluffy yellow newborns in your hands. Another treat is the nursery for baby animals unable to be cared for by their mothers. Here you're likely to see diapered infant chimps and orangutans romping in playpens with their toys, anticipating the bottle of milk administered by nurse attendants. Signs identify the "babies" by name and give their birth dates, weights, and feeding schedules.

Mission Bay Aquatic Park

Mission Bay, now a beautiful aquatic playground right on the edge of downtown San Diego, was once a vast and productive estuary, home for resident waterfowl, resting place for migratory birds, and nursery for fish and other sea creatures. Originally named "False Bay" when Cabrillo mistook it for San Diego Bay, it degenerated into a silt and trash collector, popular as a fishing hole for those who could brave the mosquitoes, until community action finally transformed it into one of the most beautiful resort areas on the coast.

Twenty years of dredging and development have created a maze of islands and lagoons, 27 miles of beaches, free public boat-launching ramps, picnic areas, campgrounds and trailer park, children's playgrounds, golf courses, a marine park, and miles of beautifully landscaped, grass-covered coves.

Hotels and campgrounds. The hotels of Mission Bay are worth seeing for their unusual architectural qualities, as well as for their location. Many have now gone high-rise to take advantage of the view. Vacation Village makes extensive use of streams and lagoons for landscaping. Mission Bay Visitor Information Center, just off I-5 at East Mission Bay Drive, provides information on hotels and maps of the park. Reservations are a "must" during peak summer months and three-day holiday weekends.

Vacationers who like to "rough it" can easily settle in at Campland, on the north shore of the bay by way of Olney Street. Here resort-equipped campsites rent for $20 and up a night (prices are highest in summer). Nearby are a parking area for boats, a swimming beach, and complete rental facilities—for everything from campers and bedding to boats and skis. To reserve a site, write Campland on the Bay, 2211 Pacific Beach Drive, San Diego, CA 92109; or call (619) 274-6260.

Water sports are Mission Bay's reason for being. At the many marinas, visitors can rent paddle boats or ocean-going sloops—any type of boat they desire. Traffic on the bay is organized so that one water activity is separated from another. Water-skiers use a 1½-mile course with several beaches reserved as pick-up and landing areas; power boats roar over the same 3-mile course used by hydroplanes and competition speedboats during organized races; sailboats reign in the western cove of the bay. Small racing sloops, tiny dinghies, exotic outriggers, and swift catamarans dart across the cove all year long.

Fishing is enjoyed from a comfortable lawn chair on the beach, from a small skiff, or from the deck of a sportfishing boat. Within the bay, fishermen land halibut, flounder, bass, croaker, and perch.

Sea World makes a big splash. San Diego's 135-acre aquatic park within a park is one of the world's largest oceanariums, featuring some popular added attractions as well. Besides outstanding aquarium exhibits and a variety of water shows, you'll find a Japanese Village, an innovative children's playground, a sky tower, an aerial tram, and hydrofoil boats.

Water show stars include Shamu, a remarkably agile black and white killer whale; Google, a trained elephant seal weighing 1½ tons; a water-skiing chimpanzee; a penguin on skates; and a live shark exhibit. At the Water Fantasy Show, colorful lights and explosive dancing fountains perform like fireworks set to music. All shows are free. Presented on the hour and half-hour, they average 20 minutes in length; to see them all, consult your time schedule and the map distributed at the gate.

One of the park's finest exhibits is the Penguin Encounter. Inside the building, an Antarctic ecosystem has been created for some 400 birds. Thankful that you're on the room-temperature side of the glass, you glide on a conveyor belt past penguins flapping in an "ocean," waddling on snowy banks, and screeching in rookeries. The catchy exhibit includes six 6-minute films on the birds and their habitat.

The Sky Tower ride, highest of its kind in the United States, makes slow turns up and down its 320 feet, giving you an unobstructed 360° view of Mission Bay and surrounding territory. The Skyride tram takes you up 70 feet over the waters of Mission Bay to the Atlantis Restaurant for lunch or sightseeing. Hydrofoil boats zoom over the bay's famous speed course.

An exotic feature of Sea World is the Japanese Village, which flies the giant Koinobori fish kite. Here Japanese pearl divers will retrieve a pearl-bearing oyster for you from the bottom of the pool. You can have the pearl extracted on the spot and mounted into jewelry.

Walking through mature gardens between the arenas and exhibits, visiting the manmade tidepool, and shooting pictures at pre-picked spots will be a pleasant part of your visit. Sea World's horticultural exhibitions are outstanding. If you need to, rent a whale stroller for the small ones and check out the diaper changing facilities on your map before you begin your stroll.

It takes about 5 hours to see all the park, open daily from 9 A.M. until dusk. To get a behind-the-scenes peek at marine mammals, waterfowl, and other sea life, take a 1½-hour tour (additional charge).

The one-price park admission currently runs around $15 for adults, $12 for children over 3. Sea World is on Perez Cove at the southern edge of Mission Bay Park; to get there, follow Sea World Drive.

North of San Diego

Many of the area's attractions are located north of San Diego—off Interstate Highway 5 and along the coast on State Highway 21; inland on Interstate Highway 15 and State Highway 78. You could make a fast loop trip in one day, but you may want to take more time to visit quaint seaside communities, flower fields, a famous biological institution, an oceanographic museum, rare Torrey Pines, and the large San Diego Wild Animal Park.

Captivating La Jolla

Fronting the sparkling Pacific and its broad beaches and built over beautiful coves, caves, and cliffs, La Jolla is aptly named. It means "hole" or "caves," according to Indian legend, but the more common interpretation today is from the Spanish word meaning "jewel" or "gem." La Jolla is not a touristy place. It is the quiet edge of the big city of San Diego, a 5-mile section of Mediterranean California at its most beguiling.

If you come north from the main part of San Diego—as most visitors are likely to do—the quick route is by I-5, taking the Ardath Road exit. You can also drive the older, longer route up La Jolla Boulevard from Pacific Beach. Neither route reveals much of the La Jolla experience, which begins when you get out of your car.

The sea beauty of La Jolla is the reason for everything else here. You'll find all the beach pleasures: swimming, diving, surfing, rock fishing, tidepool exploring, beach walking.

The beaches are a magnet here, and every beach has a character of its own. Some vary considerably with the tides, as well as with the seasons. Below Prospect Street, which curves through the heart of the old village, the beaches nuzzle under sandstone bluffs in a series of small crescents and coves. If you stand on the sidewalk on Coast Boulevard and look over the railing above La Jolla Cove (the northernmost of the beaches below the city proper), you'll see why it has been a favorite for years of sunbathers, swimmers, and skin and scuba divers. Intimate and protected, it has a gentle surf. The clear water and undersea gardens hold such prizes as spiny lobster and abalone. On the bluff above the cove is Ellen Browning Scripps Park, where you can stroll green lawns or sit and enjoy the sea air, watching the beach below.

South of Boomer Beach (ideal for the expert body surfer) and connected to the park and the cove by a promenade is the Children's Pool. This small beach has a curving breakwater that keeps the surf gentle enough for small children.

At the foot of Bonair Street is Windansea Beach, celebrated as one of the best places on the coast for surfing. Swimming here can be dangerous.

To visit one of the La Jolla caves, go to the end of Coast Boulevard and enter through a curio shop, descending 133 wooden stairs (not recommended for the infirm). You pay a small admission charge. Just seaward of the cave entrance, a bluff-top trail (part of an ecological reserve) runs easterly through about a half-mile of semiwild city park past a rocky gorge called Devil's Slide. The view of

La Jolla Bay is spectacular from this sometimes dizzying overlook. Close by, on the sheer face of the cliffs, you'll see birds—cormorants, pelicans, sea gulls—watching the waters for fish.

There's no beach at the foot of these cliffs. You have to get well north of the village before you see the second kind of La Jolla beach—wide, hard-packed sand with shallow water some distance out. Kellogg Park and the La Jolla Shores Beach are public and equipped with fire rings, play equipment, rest rooms, showers, and a lifeguard all year. The southern part of the beach is reserved for swimming, the northern for surfing. The private La Jolla Beach and Tennis Club, with its 1930s Spanish architecture and striped beach tents reminiscent of F. Scott Fitzgerald's Riviera-based novel, *Tender Is the Night*, marks the south end of this stretch of beach.

Exploring the village should please you. The charm of La Jolla today owes much to its isolated setting on a natural peninsula bounded by Mount Soledad and the ocean, and to the efforts of its tradition-minded citizens. Residential-scale buildings, mature trees, brilliant tropical flowers, and the La Valencia Hotel tower give La Jolla the flavor of a classic resort town.

La Jolla is for strolling. Parking places are almost impossible to find; the layout of the streets is confusing; pedestrian traffic is erratic. Although the main street (Girard Avenue) has as wide a selection of shopping as you'll find anywhere in San Diego, the best walking is along the mile or so of Prospect Street from the cottage shops and plazas on the north to the museum on the south. Shops range in character from one specializing in understated tweedery to a Scandinavian import shop. The varied restaurants here often occupy old houses; several have a sea view. The popular old La Valencia Hotel offers meals indoors or out, along with a view from the tower. The La Jolla Museum of Contemporary Arts fits well into this community of many artists. It's open from 10 A.M. to 9 P.M. Tuesday through Thursday, 10 A.M. to 5 P.M. Friday through Sunday. There's a small entrance fee.

Mingei International Museum, in University Towne Centre, contains international folk art from pre-industrialized to contemporary times. The museum is open from 11 A.M. to 5 P.M. Tuesday through Thursday and on Saturday; from 11 A.M. to 9 P.M. on Friday; and Sunday afternoon.

Scripps Institution

La Jolla is world-famed as the center for research on the secrets of the sea. Located on the pier north of La Jolla Shores Beach is Scripps Institution of Oceanography, well known for its ocean study and now a part of the University of California at San Diego. The aquarium museum offers studies of tide motion, archeology, and beach lore. Its hours are from 9 A.M. to 5 P.M. daily. Admission is free; there's a small fee for parking. The pier is not open to the public.

The beach around Scripps Pier is a favorite for swimming, and you'll probably see considerable surfing action north of it.

The San Diego-La Jolla Underwater Park was established near Scripps to preserve the shoreline and underwater life of La Jolla Canyon.

Torrey Pines Mesa

The expanding edge of La Jolla is a former wilderness thick with groves of eucalyptus and unique stands of the rare Torrey Pines. Torrey Pines Road takes you from La Jolla up onto the mesa to join the old coast highway. Set in the thickest of the eucalyptus forests is the University of California at San Diego. Drive through the campus and visit the art museum at Revelle College.

The Salk Institute for Biological Studies, a surrealistic city of concrete, rises above the trees at the top of North Torrey Pines Road. Named for Dr. Jonas Salk, it was founded in the hope that scholars from different disciplines—including the arts—could move toward an understanding of life. The Institute's exterior has been called the most powerful architectural statement on the West Coast. Guaranteed to make you react, it creates a proper setting for the energetic study that takes place inside. Tours are offered Monday through Friday from 11 A.M. to 2 P.M. on the hour.

Next to the Institute is an active sail plane area where, on weekends, you can watch the pleasant sport of soaring—and often hang gliding—over the waves. A little farther north are two municipal golf courses. Even if you don't golf, you can have lunch at the restaurant (the only one on the mesa), with its grand view of the ocean. The complex also includes a comfortable motel.

Torrey Pines State Reserve protects some rare trees. The only natural grove of Torrey Pines in the world grows along the ocean here and on Santa Rosa Island 195 miles away. The rare pines in this beautiful, wind-shaped area are gnarled relics of a past age. The slanting trees were clinging to the eroded yellow sandstone cliffs when Cabrillo's ships first sighted California.

Occupying the whole northern tip of the mesa, the park is reached by North Torrey Pines Road. It is a good place for family hiking, having well-marked trails and picnic facilities. To hike along the ocean, use the north entrance to the park off U.S. 101. For beach hiking, consult a tide table to avoid being caught by rising waters.

Torrey Pines Reserve opens at 8 A.M. and closes at 10 P.M. from April to October; it closes at 5 during the winter. Admission to the reserve is free, but there is a parking charge. Most people find that merely driving through doesn't seem enough. The refreshing and fascinating change of scenery invites close-up exploration.

Coastal towns

Between Torrey Pines and Oceanside along the coast is strung a chain of small beach communities, interspersed with state and county beaches. These are some of the more interesting attractions:

Del Mar, a quiet, picturesque village, is best known for its horse-racing track (open from late July to mid-September).

Rancho Santa Fe (turn off I-5 at Via de la Valle) was originally a Spanish land grant. Douglas Fairbanks, Sr. founded Rancho Zorro in the 1920s, and Bing Crosby later owned the original ranch house. In and near the town are more eucalyptus trees than anywhere else in

DOLPHIN SPLASHES front-row visitors to Sea World (left), an aquatic playground on Mission Bay. Elegant Hotel del Coronado (below), a Victorian landmark, presents more formal face.

California—the result of an unsuccessful try by the Santa Fe Railway to use the wood for railway ties. The Rancho village has a small shopping area reminiscent of old-time La Jolla and a restaurant.

Encinitas, with its acres of flower fields, is a colorful sight when the flowers are in bloom. The largest poinsettia fields in the state turn nearby hills red in December. The "safest beach in California" is the city's claim.

Carlsbad built its reputation around the similarity of its mineral water to that of the original Karlsbad, Czechoslovakia, in what was then Bohemia. The Alt Karlsbad Hanse House (now a gift shop) is built over the spring. Nearby Twin Inns is a Victorian memento, having served country-fried chicken to happy diners since 1919 on the same blue willow pattern plates.

Oceanside, gateway to Camp Pendleton Marine base, has been a beach resort since the 1800s. The original fishing pier was operating in 1910; jutting into the sea for 1,900 feet, it attracts throngs of fisherfolk. At one end of the 4-mile beach are a boat harbor and a replica of a Cape Cod village.

Visitors are welcome to drive through Camp Pendleton. On the grounds you'll discover the former ranch house of Pio Pico, the last of California's Mexican governors.

Escondido, avocado capital of the world, is reached by following State Highway 78 inland from I-5 or by heading north on I-15 from San Diego.

The city's most famous attraction, the San Diego Wild Animal Park, is east of the city on San Pasqual Valley Road (State 78). Also along this road is the site of one of the least-known battles in U.S. history, and almost the only one fought in the conquest of California. A marker commemorates the 1846 battle between General Pico's native California troops and General Kearney's U.S. Army. The U.S. troops lost in what historians call the bloodiest battle of the Mexican War.

From Escondido, you can pick up State Highway 6, one approach to Palomar Observatory. It can also take you to pretty little Lake Wohlford for fishing, to the Bates Brothers Nut Farm (15954 Woods Valley Road) for a tour, and to groves where, in season, tree-ripened tangerines and Valencia oranges are sold from roadside stands at cut-rate prices.

Seven miles northwest of Escondido (off I-15—exit north on Mountain Meadow Road) is Lawrence Welk's theater-museum in the Village Center shopping arcade. At the nearby motel/restaurant, you might catch a band performance.

Temecula, 55 miles north of San Diego on I-15, is Southern California's newest wine-growing center.

WELCOME TO MEXICO

Although it's easy to visit Mexico, your trip will be even more enjoyable if you familiarize yourself with some information before you cross the border.

Tourist cards. You don't need a passport to visit Mexico, but if you go more than 75 miles into the interior (Ensenada and Mexicali are within this limit) or stay longer than 72 hours, you will need a tourist card. The cards are free from the Mexican Consulate and the Mexican Government Tourist Office in San Diego, but you must supply proof of your United States citizenship.

Car insurance. It is advisable to obtain auto insurance from a Mexican insurance company before you cross the border. American agents are not licensed to do business in Mexico, where an automobile accident is a criminal offense for which you can be detained until claims are adjusted. The Convention and Visitors Bureau in San Diego will provide a list of reputable Mexican insurance firms; some are located on your way to the border crossing. Short-term Mexican insurance is not expensive.

Driving. Traffic regulations similar to those in the United States are enforced. Speed limits are posted in kilometers (1 km = .62 miles), so be sure to make the reckoning. Road signs are generally in Spanish, but shapes and symbols are universally understood. Baja California has some new highways (including the road to its tip), but they are unfenced, so watch for livestock on the road. Major highways (1, 2, and 5) are well patrolled by Mexico's green emergency repair jeeps. Service is free, except for cost of parts. Gas stations are generally far apart; be sure to fill your gas tank at every opportunity.

Currency. Most Mexican stores will accept either pesos or dollars. You can exchange currency at banks, your hotel, or at currency exchange booths. The exchange fluctuates. Both Mexican and U.S. prices are indicated by dollar signs.

Customs. United States Customs permits each person to bring back $400 worth of goods without duty. Beyond that amount, you must itemize each purchase. Check the *Customs Hints* booklet, free from customs offices, for detailed information on declaring purchases over $400. California visitors may now bring back alcoholic beverages whether returning by commercial carrier or private car. The limit is one quart.

Rooms and meals. Good accommodations at reasonable prices and restaurants where you can eat with confidence are found in the Mexican towns discussed in this chapter. Besides Mexican restaurants, there are many North American, European, and Oriental establishments.

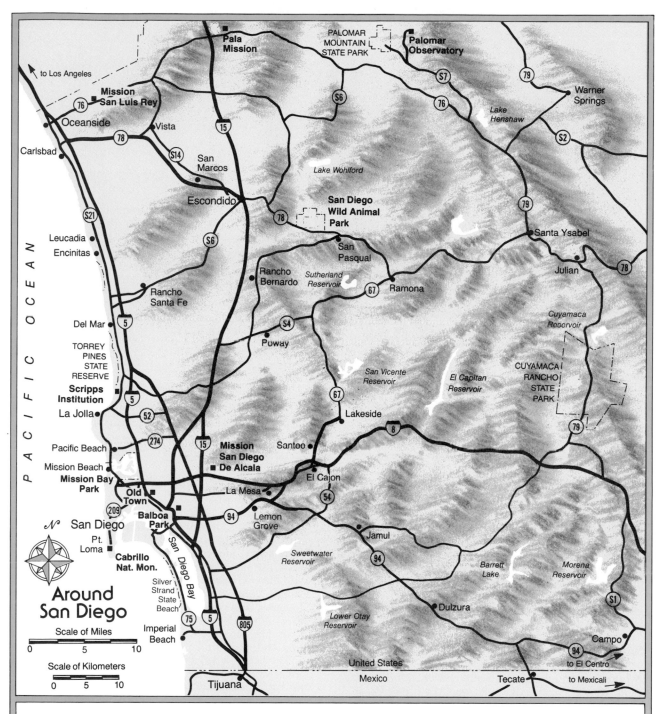

Major Points of Interest

Palomar Observatory — 12-story observatory and museum-exhibit hall; camping, picnicking

Pala Mission — Indian chapel in back country

Mission San Luis Rey — impressive "King of Missions"; picnic grounds, museum, public tours

Wild Animal Park — animals roam freely in spacious habitat; visitors view from monorail

Del Mar — "beside-the-sea" horse racing track

Torrey Pines — state reserve, rare pine groves alive when Cabrillo discovered California; active sail planing

Scripps Institution — public tours offered at museum for sea study; nearby underwater park

La Jolla — pearl of beach towns with intriguing shops, restaurants, caves

Tijuana — gateway to Mexico; shopping, jai alai, bullfights

Cuyamaca Rancho State Park — former Spanish ranch; Indian relics; hiking, riding

Julian — historic gold mining town; tours, festivals

AFRICAN ELEPHANTS take a morning walk. Moat separates their enclosure from San Diego Wild Animal Park's open space.

Most of the wineries that allow visitors line the Ranch California Road exit. Temecula is also home for the Frontier Historical Center (27999 Front Street), a museum focusing on the days of Buffalo Bill Cody and Wyatt Earp. Billed as "the world's largest Western history collection," it includes wax figures of some of the era's heroes and villains, a re-creation of Tombstone, and a display of more than 1,000 of the "firearms that won the West." The museum is open daily from June through November, closed Mondays the rest of the year.

San Diego Wild Animal Park

An innovation in American public zoos, the San Diego Wild Animal Park is also on State 78 near San Pasqual. The first zoo to give its breeding herd animals so much roaming room that it resembles their native habitat, it's already had some births, rare for animals in captivity. Developed in 1972 in chaparral terrain evocative of the dry upland plains of Africa, the park is home to some 2,200 animals—many of them rare and endangered species—who roam the park's 1,800 acres. This compares with 5,500 animals on the parent San Diego Zoo's 128 acres.

Visitors are kept mostly at a distance so as not to disturb the animals. A monorail train takes you through the park on a 5-mile drive that lasts a little less than an hour. One tip: Bring a pair of binoculars. The animals are most active and visible in late after-noon and early morning when the sun is mildest, the crowds thinnest.

The 1½-mile Kilimanjaro Hiking Trail offers spectacular vistas for animal observation and photography, plus picnicking sites. Nairobi Village, just inside the park entry, presents animals in a closer setting. You walk through a giant, free-flight, free-form aviary. You will also see babies in the animal nursery, lemurs on an island, flamingos in a lagoon, newborn animals, green iguanas, and lowland gorillas. And you can pet less exotic animals in a *kraal* (corral).

In addition, you'll find shops, outdoor eating facilities, and, in summer, live musical entertainment.

The park is open daily from 9 A.M.; closing hours vary from 8 P.M. in summer and on fall weekends to as early as 4 P.M. in winter. Summer visitors may stay until 10 P.M. One admission ticket includes animal shows, the monorail trip, and entrance to Nairobi Village.

To reach the park from San Diego, take Via Rancho Parkway exit from I-15 east onto San Pasqual Road, and follow the signs.

Rancho Bernardo

Red tile roofs are all you see of the town of Rancho Bernardo from I-15, south of Escondido, but it's worth turning onto the Rancho Bernardo exit just to visit the Mercado. Of all the enclaves of art and craft shops that have sprouted up in Southern California recently, this is one of the most handsome and lively.

Bold graphics and bright banners stand out against the two-story, tile-roofed buildings, faintly Mediterranean in inspiration. Grouped around courtyards at plaza level and on balconies are 40 shops, studios, and eating places. Artisans concentrate on creating pottery, jewelry, candles, and many other wares.

Visit daily, 10 A.M. to 6 P.M. Some craftsmen are always there; you'll see most on weekends.

The Back Country

Oceanside is a good jumping-off spot for a loop trip of the back country of San Diego County. A land of rural charm and historical intrigue, it offers rambling hills, meadows, rocky mountain peaks, and desert. Two or three days will go fast in the back country — it is full of Indian lore, past and present; California mission and gold mine history; pleasant ranches and farms; spectacular views; good hiking, riding, and camping. Not the least of its charms is that it offers the rare treat of unhurried country driving. Camp overnight in a forested state park, stop at a dude ranch in Warner Springs, or stay in the old Julian Hotel. For a circle trip of the area, follow State Highways 76 and 79 and U.S. Highway 80 between Oceanside and San Diego.

Mission San Luis Rey

Off State 76 just 5 miles east of Oceanside is one of the most impressive restorations in the mission chain, Mission San Luis Rey. Crowning a hill that dominates a beautiful valley, the "King of the Missions," founded in 1789, was the largest and most populous Indian mission of the Americas. Known for its artistic facade, the gracious and dignified mission (which at one time covered 6 acres) was built by a padre and Indians who had never before worked with tools.

The first pepper tree in California, which provided the padres with peppercorns to grind for seasoning, was brought from Peru in 1830 and still stands here. The trees were so widely planted that they are now called "California pepper."

On the always colorful grounds, you'll find picnic tables in a shady grove, an old cemetery, a small museum, and a gift shop. Now a seminary, Mission San Luis Rey is open to the public from 9 A.M. to 4 P.M. Monday through Saturday, and from 1:30 to 4:30 on Sunday.

Pala Mission

Located in the tranquil river valley a little farther east on State 76, San Antonio de Pala Mission, actually an *asistencia* (or branch) of Mission San Luis Rey, is the only chapel in the mission chain still used by a predominantly Indian congregation. This is the original building, built in 1815, with Indian frescoes still on the walls and an attractive separate campanile.

Behind Pala, the Tourmaline Queen Mountain echoes

days of lucrative gem mining that rivaled the activity in the gold rush town of Julian.

Palomar Observatory

Southeast of Pala, State 76 winds through Pauma Valley, site of the Palomar Observatory. The turn-off to Palomar is 5 miles beyond Rincon Springs, where the road rises abruptly through chaparral and rock-covered countryside and offers a winding but scenic ride.

High on Palomar Mountain are the great silver dome of the 12-story observatory, operated by the California Institute of Technology, and a museum-exhibit hall, where a tour will brief you on the workings of the large telescopes. The Hale, a 200-inch telescope weighing 500 tons, is viewed from a gallery. You may want to wear a sweater; the working interior of the dome must be kept at night-time temperatures, since even a few degrees of variation can cause distortions. The observatory is open daily from 9 A.M. to 5 P.M.

From the road up Palomar Mountain, you can turn west to Palomar Mountain State Park. This Sierralike country has many camp and picnic sites, good views, and trails to explore. You'll probably see the wild pigeons for which this area was named. As you drive in, ask the ranger for directions.

If your vehicle is heavily loaded, you should approach Palomar from Lake Henshaw, where the road is more gradual and less rough. The lake has boating and fishing. No matter which way you go up, you may want to descend this way to continue your loop trip.

You can spend some time at Warner Springs, a few miles off the loop on State 79. A ranch and golf resort, Warner Springs accommodates you in simple or luxurious adobes.

Santa Ysabel

The white-stuccoed chapel of Mission Santa Ysabel is on the site of the *asistencia* of the San Diego Mission, built in 1818. Rebuilt in the mission style about 1920, the church is still used. Surrounded by pleasant trees, a wishing well, a windmill, and picnic tables, the mission welcomes visitors

In the little town of Santa Ysabel, the old general store is claimed to date back to 1870. A good reason for stopping in this town is the Dudly Pratt Bakery, where nearly 50 varieties of bread are made. A little beyond here, on State 78, you can take a trip into the Anza-Borrego Desert State Park, headquartered in Borrego Springs. (This desert country is discussed on page 95.) A few miles farther along State 79 is the old gold rush town of Julian.

Julian

High in the pine and oak-covered hills, you'll find the mountain settlement of Julian, where a town started over a century ago and time stopped before the false-front buildings could go out of style.

A gold strike in 1869 turned Julian into a boom town, making it the second largest town in San Diego County. The end of the boom halted progress and settled the town

into a comfortable little agricultural community allowing supermarkets, super highways, and subdivisions to pass it by. Even today, you reach Julian on meandering, tree-lined country roads nearly empty of traffic and uncluttered by commercial development. Appaloosa ranches; cattle-speckled hillsides; apple, pear, and peach orchards; and fruit and homemade jam stands compose the scene.

Main Street in Julian retains its original false-front stores, wooden sidewalks, and the Julian Hotel (built in 1887). Here you'll also find homey restaurants, stores selling homemade pies from locally grown wares, and real sarsaparilla. You'll even find an adaptable parking lot offering space to "horseless carriages, stuttering bicycles, and mothers-in-law." Hardly changed, old homes still cling to the hillsides around town, and the old George Washington Mine, the first operated in the area, can still be reached from the end of Washington Street on a footpath. The mine entrance has been shored up, but you can still see ore cars on tracks running into the mine. You can also look into an assay office and a blacksmith shop nearby—both reconstructed.

Another mine in the area, the Eagle, is open for tours. To reach it, take C Street in the middle of town and follow the signs to the mine. It is open daily from 9 A.M. to 5 P.M. The short guided tour (there is a charge) includes an explanation of gold mining.

The Pioneer Museum, located where State 79 turns west for Santa Ysabel, is in an old masonry building once used as a brewery and a blacksmith shop. It is open from 10 A.M. to 4 P.M. on weekends and holidays. One of its articles of memorabilia is a mail pouch with parachute, dropped by the Coast Guard in 1938 to inaugurate Julian's first airmail delivery.

Cuyamaca Rancho State Park

An area of rugged mountain terrain and intermittent streams, Cuyamaca Rancho State Park lies about 40 miles from urban San Diego with views of the ocean to the west and the desert to the east. Its wilderness is graced by much bird and wildlife and wildflowers in all seasons. The name "Cuyamaca" is a Spanish version of the old Indian word for "the place where it rains."

Formerly a Spanish rancho in what had been isolated Indian country, the state park now features Caballos Campground, accommodating horseback riders; a nature trail at Wooded Hill; and an Indian exhibit containing relics of early Indian life. Some of the things depicted here, such as acorn gathering, are still practiced.

For those who like to ride and hike, there are over 75 miles of trails to explore. From the Paso Picacho Campground, you can climb to three peaks. On a clear day on top of Mount Cuyamaca, you can see from the Pacific Ocean to the Salton Sea and from Mexico to San Bernardino. Allow about 3 hours for the round trip.

For a leg-stretching return

For the return trip to San Diego you can follow either I-8 or take pokier, two-lane State Highway 94.

Off Interstate 8: Visit Santee Recreation Lakes in the small community of Santee. Here are six small reservoirs with islands reached by raft-ferry. The recreation area features small-boat channels, fishing, swimming, and picnicking.

Bird lovers will enjoy Silverwood Wildlife Sanctuary near Lakeside (a 167-acre reserve with trails, displays, and picnic spots). It's open Wednesdays and Sundays. From Lakeside, turn right on Maplewood and left on Ashwood, becoming Wildcat Canyon Road, for 5 miles.

Off State 94: Slow down at Boulevard or you'll miss the Wisteria Candy Cottage with homemade confections including 17 kinds of divinity, hand-dipped chocolates, nut brittles, fudge, and other temptations. The hours are 7 A.M. to 7 P.M. daily.

At both Lake Morena County Park (3 miles north of Cameron Corners) and Potrero County Park you can picnic or camp overnight.

Turn south at State Highway 188 for 2 miles to take a look at slow-paced Tecate just over the Mexican border.

Across the Border

Mexico is right next door when you're in San Diego—and most visitors find it an irresistible lure. Though Tijuana receives most of the traffic, there are two other border crossings—Tecate nearby and Mexicali beyond the mountains. It's only 2 hours from San Diego to Ensenada, south of Tijuana, on scenic Bahia Todos Santos; and San Felipe, on the Sea of Cortez, is only 127 miles south of Mexicali. For details on these and other Mexican cities, see the *Sunset Travel Guide to Mexico*.

After passing through the sleepy village of San Ysidro on I-5, you come to the dry Tijuana River bed and the gateway arch sweeping over 25 lanes of traffic that marks the end of California and the beginning of Baja California, Mexico. At the border (just 15 minutes from downtown San Diego), the bustling city of Tijuana brings you instantly to Mexico.

Tijuana

Tijuana (te-*wah*-nah) lays claim to the title of most visited city in the world—with some 30 million border crossings yearly. It's easy to see why the attraction is so strong. Many who come are weekenders attracted by horse and dog racing, the summer Sunday bullfights, or camping on the beach seaward of Tijuana. Many are active and curious shoppers seeking out the fine handicrafts, import stores, and colorful arcades of the shopping areas. And yet others come to experience a foreign culture, so accessible from the U.S. Realize that, as a border town, Tijuana is not typically Mexican.

To enjoy your visit more, it is best to know what to expect of this very diverse and busy city. The Tijuana Convention and Visitors Bureau has visitor information booths both at the border and at the Chamber of Commerce offices (Comercio at Avenida Madero).

Getting there. To get to Tijuana from San Diego, you can take the Greyhound bus (120 W. Broadway), the Mexicoach (Santa Fe Depot), or the popular Tijuana Trolley (see page 65) to the border.

You can also park a car on the U.S. side of the border and walk across, then take a Mexican taxi downtown or to the Cultural Center for a nominal fee. If you decide to drive across the border, be sure to stop at one of the Mexican insurance offices; American insurance is usually no good once you cross the border.

The new Tijuana. With a population of over a million, the city is growing in new directions. Paseo de los Heroes is the grand boulevard of the redevelopment zone, where the old bed of the Rio Tijuana has been transformed from a flood plain with squatters' huts into a channeled river bordered by landscaped avenues. Crown jewel of the new zone is the $35-million Tijuana Cultural Center, with an Omnitheater, performing arts center, and anthropological museum. At the center, you can shop, dine, or see a film on Mexico's sights and sounds splashed across a 75-foot screen (there's an admission charge). The center is open from 11 A.M. to 7 P.M. daily (until 8 P.M. weekends). The entrance fee is small.

Across from the cultural center lies Plaza Rio Tijuana, a modern, sprawling shopping center.

The old Tijuana. It's still there and still fun—and you'll notice change. Revolucion, the main street, was the first face-lift patient. Now there are more places to sit and watch the passing scene, plus fountains to sit beside and trees to sit under. A juxtaposition of old and new greets you at each block. Narrow old paseos and arcades bulge with goods from all over Mexico. A steady buzz of invitations to browse may turn up pleasant surprises.

Shopping. Tijuana's finds range from the richest Mexican folk art to the gaudiest of tourist gimcracks. Some of the best goods can be found at government-sponsored stores on Revolucion: Fonart (east side between calles 6 and 7) and State of Puebla (west side between calles 2 and 3). Also try Galeria Lucias (upstairs off an arcade between calles 5 and 6) and Bazar Las Palomas (rear of the same arcade). For your convenience, most prices are marked in dollars.

Sports are varied and different south of the border. The biggest crowd-attractor to Tijuana is Caliente Race Track, a couple of miles from downtown on Agua Caliente Boulevard. Its beautiful modern facilities include good restaurants and shops. Thoroughbreds race weekend afternoons the year around. In the evenings (except Tuesdays), the course is converted for greyhound racing.

Jai alai (hi-li), a colorful and often dangerous sport that is billed as the world's fastest ball game, is four centuries old. Traditionally played by the Basques in a show of grace, skill, and strength, jai alai offers thrills and pari-mutuel betting nightly except Thursday most of the year in the imposing Fronton Palacio on Revolucion at 7th Street.

Tijuana has two bullrings, both named and patterned after the famous ones in Mexico City. The downtown ring, El Toreo de Tijuana, is easily reached by way of Agua Caliente Boulevard. Plaza Monumental, 5 miles out of town near the ocean, is the second largest bullring in the world (the largest is in Mexico City). Whether or not you see a bullfight, it's a wonderful place to visit— enjoy beautiful landscaping, patios, toreros' chapel, and views of the Pacific Ocean. The classical art of bullfighting is celebrated Sunday afternoons from May through September.

Occasionally on Sundays, the local *charros* (cowboys) stage rodeos (or *charreadas*). There are several rodeo arenas; ask at the information booths in town when a rodeo is scheduled and where you can find it.

Tijuana to Ensenada

Outside Tijuana you find the ramshackle hillside huts of the Mexican poor. You'll also find industry, part of the new diversification of Tijuana, particularly eastward from Caliente Race Track on the Tecate Road, also known as Mexican Highway 2.

By following the Second Street extension to the ocean (or taking the direct route from the border), you encounter a change of scenery at Playas de Tijuana. Here you can pick up the scenic freeway, which takes you 65 miles south from Tijuana to the seacoast town of Ensenada. This four-lane, divided toll road in many places parallels the old Ensenada Libre (free) route, which takes you through rural Mexico but also slows you down. The 90-minute freeway drive takes you past spectacular cliffs and sea views.

Ensenada

With a pace much more relaxed than Tijuana's, Ensenada also has a much more inviting setting, curving gracefully around the bay of Todos Santos. Shoppers delight in the fact that Ensenada is a duty-free port. You'll also find several good restaurants; Hussong's Cantina is Baja California's famous watering hole.

Fishing is so excellent that Ensenada is known as the "Yellowtail Capital of the World." Pleasure boats abound in the protected harbor; cruise ships stop for a short stay. The world-famous Ensenada-Newport International Yacht Race, held during Mexico's Cinco de Mayo (May 5 independence celebration), attracts more than 500 participants.

Tecate

For a Mexican border town, Tecate is relatively quiet and uncommercial, but you will find it busy for a town its size, especially during festivals. It is about 30 miles east of Tijuana and 72 miles from Ensenada on good roads.

A famous beer that bears the town's name makes Tecate a popular refreshment stop. The brewery and Hidalgo Park are the town's main attractions. The city has a good restaurant (Los Candiles) and a small hotel (El Dorado). A few miles west of town along Highway 2 is Rancho La Puerta, a widely known health spa that attracts many Southern Californians.

Mexicali

Mexicali, the capital of Baja California, has a population of about 500,000, compared to Tijuana's million. Located in the center of a vast cotton-producing valley, it invites tourists to exchange dollars for goods at shops and restaurants clustered near the border between Madero and Reforma and Azueta and Altamirano.

Palm Springs

Most glittering of desert oases, Palm Springs introduces a land for sun worshippers. Beyond the pools, tennis courts, and golf courses lie rugged mountains (accessible by tram), palm-studded canyons, Coachella Valley's acres of dates, and inland Salton Sea. Great desert parks (Joshua Tree and Anza-Borrego) preserve terrain, and, along the Colorado River, Lake Havasu preserves reconstructed London Bridge.

Perhaps nowhere else do mountains and desert meet more abruptly than at Palm Springs, famed desert playground about 100 miles east of Los Angeles. To the west, the San Jacinto Mountains—often snow-draped in winter—drop sharply to the valley floor thousands of feet below. To the east, the sun—most important resource of the Southern California desert country—rises and shines all year, and the air is warm and dry.

Palm Springs, center of an expanding community of resorts, stands in desert that is mostly tamed. But close by is land rugged and open enough to urge your investigation of its tenacious plants, its shy animals, its rocks and sands, and its silent canyons. And the mountains, pine-covered and verdant in their upper reaches, offer spectacular views from the heights and some surprises in the easily accessible side canyons.

Nearby is Salton Sea, once a dry desert wasteland and now a recreation area popular for motor boating and water-skiing. Undeveloped desert canyons and unusual rock formations around the sea invite exploring.

Not far from the highly civilized resort areas surrounding Palm Springs and the activity of the Salton Sea are preserves of desert lands whose "stars" are the spiny ocotillos, sculptured Joshua trees, time-carved canyons, and wind-blown sands, all in the earth and sun colors of the desert.

Two great desert parks—Joshua Tree National Monument and Anza-Borrego Desert State Park—reveal the differences between the high and low desert.

The Colorado River, boundary between California and Arizona, is a boating mecca. Lake Havasu, formed by a dam on a once-wild river, is a water-world playground. On the Arizona side, in Lake Havasu City, is the London Bridge, reassembled from its original site on England's Thames River.

One of the great virtues of this vast land is that it seems far removed from California's more populous regions. Here, understated resorts provide bases for exploring, and campgrounds abound on empty stretches of sand, along the water's edge, or among pine-forested mountains.

Overview of "The Springs"

Palmiest desert resort in California or almost anywhere else, Palm Springs is known—perhaps too well—for the celebrities it attracts in winter. This oasis with one swimming pool for every 2½ registered voters is well equipped for those who like to live lavishly, but it offers more than that.

Palm Springs offers California's low desert climate at its best. Here, the steepest high mountain escarpment in the West (the 10,000-foot rise of the San Jacinto range) acts as a natural climate conditioner, throwing the whole town into shadow every afternoon, while the Coachella Valley to the east continues to shimmer in the sun. The mountains also give Palm Springs one more weather bonus: they act as a barrier against the ever-encroaching smog from the west.

Seen from the air, Palm Springs appears to be developed in a kind of checkerboard fashion—residences and commercial establishments in one giant square area, open desert in another. There's a good reason.

SAN JACINTO PEAKS *provide backdrop for desert golf course near Palm Springs. Winter oasis is dubbed "Golf Capital of the World."*

The city is divided into mile squares, every other one belonging to the Agua Caliente Indians, original settlers of the land. The land on which the Palm Springs Spa Hotel is located, as well as much other local real estate, is owned by the Agua Calientes.

If you drive up into verdant Palm Canyon, south of town, you'll enter the Indian reservation and pay a toll to proceed farther into Palm and other tributary canyons along the east side of the mountains.

Palm Springs is a wealthy community—but in a sense, its real wealth perhaps still belongs to its original owners.

Old-timers still think of Palm Springs as "the village." Some movie folk call it "The Springs." But more than just a resort, it is also a jumping-off point for desert adventure.

Something for Everyone

Visitors find in this desert city a wide range of activities. For those who like to swim, golf, play tennis, hike, picnic, ride horses, bicycle, bump through the sand on dune buggies, fly planes, watch polo or baseball, shop, bathe in hot-water spas, or relax in the sun, Palm Springs offers excellent facilities.

Golf

Known as the "Golf Capital of the World" (see below), Palm Springs has golf courses that stay green all year.

The entire community boasts almost three dozen courses. The Palm Springs Municipal Golf Course, one of the few public courses, is located at 1885 Golf Club Drive. Fairchild's Golf and Recreation Center (1001 S. El Cielo Road) features a nine-hole course, putting green, and night-lighted driving range and miniature golf course.

To play at private clubs, you usually must be a guest of a member, though a number of clubs offer reciprocal privileges to members of other private clubs. Some hotels provide guests with temporary cards.

Tennis

If you are interested in tennis, you'll be pleased to find 27 public courts. The Palm Springs Tennis Center (1300 East Baristo Road), with the feeling of a private club, allows you to make reservations before arriving. This municipal complex offers nine night-lighted courts, 11 automatic ball return practice lanes, a pro shop, and professional instruction. During the off-season (summer), courts are free.

Other public courts include those at Palm Springs High School (2248 E. Ramon Road), De Muth Park (4375 Mesquite Avenue), and Ruth Hardy Park (700 Tamarisk Road).

Surrounding resort towns—Cathedral City, Desert Hot Springs, Indian Wells, Indio, La Quinta, Palm Desert, and Rancho Mirage—actually contain most of the golf courses linked to Palm Springs. Many of the area's world-class tournaments are played at resorts and country clubs outside the city limits.

PALM SPRINGS — A GOLF CAPITAL

Golf is one of the main reasons people flock to the Palm Springs area. In 1951, the area's first championship course— the Thunderbird Country Club—was built in what is now the town of Rancho Mirage. It inaugurated a new era and made golf the prime influence on the character of Palm Springs.

Actually, the pilgrimage to Palm Springs began 30 years earlier. As visitor numbers increased, first class facilities became a major necessity. Those hotel facilities were built, but some people preferred to have their own homes in the desert. Thomas O'Donnell was one of them, and his love of golf resulted in the construction of a nine-hole course in his front yard. This golf course was really the first of its kind in the area.

Later promoters, realtors, and land developers saw the advantage of building and selling homes within range of a golf course. At that time courses were built around private homes, but soon they spread to hotels and then to country clubs with names like Eldorado, Marrakesh, Tamarisk, La Quinta, and others, as well as Thunderbird—all built to accommodate golf's popularity and to serve residents already living in the desert.

Palm Springs itself has everything from championship layouts to tricky three-pars and miniature golf. The desert communities as a whole have a greater concentration of golf courses in fewer square miles than anywhere else in the world—thus the nickname "golf capital of the world."

Many charity events—the Nabisco-Dinah Shore Invitational Golf Tournament, the Bob Hope Chrysler Golf Classic, and others—take place on courses in Rancho Mirage.

You get a list of the courses, public and private, from the Palm Springs Convention and Visitors Bureau (see page 87). One of the best public courses is lovely Palm Springs Municipal Golf Course, among the finest in the country. Palm Desert Country Club and Desert Crest Country Club (Desert Hot Springs) are two more courses that welcome visitors. Indio has three public courses, and you'll even find one at Salton Sea.

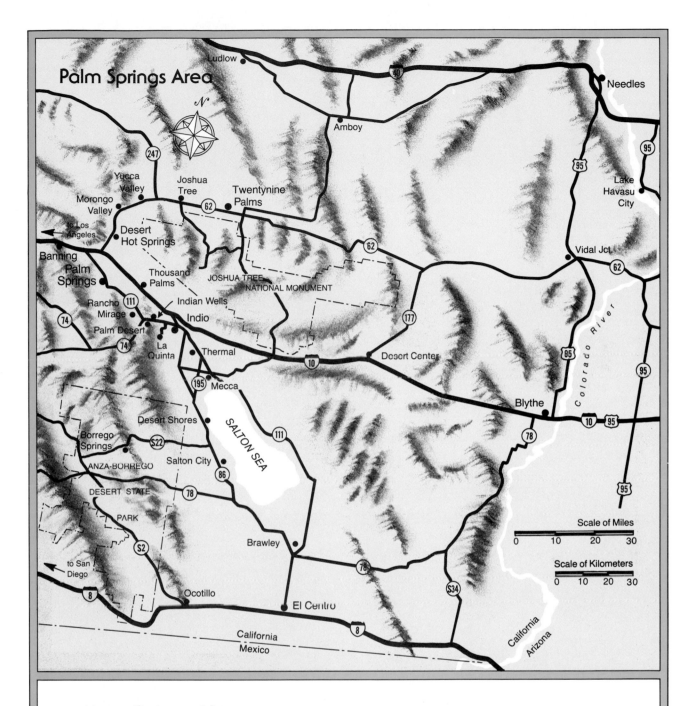

Palm Springs Area

Major Points of Interest

Twentynine Palms (Joshua Tree National Monument) — Visitor Center nature trail leads to palm forest

Anza-Borrego Desert State Park (Borrego Springs)—over ½ million acres of Colorado Desert wilderness; contains badlands and oases, wildlife and wildflowers, resort accommodations, and campsites

Date Gardens (Indio)—the "Date Capital of the U.S." Wander through date groves, watch a movie on the date palm's love life, have a date shake

Salton Sea — boating, fishing, camping. Float in below-sea-level salt-water lake, once inland sea

Lake Havasu (Colorado River)—beautiful lake offers water sports, camping, trailer park. See London Bridge, surrounding English village setting

Palm Springs—climb from desert floor to top of Mt. San Jacinto in 18 minutes on Aerial Tramway; tour celebrities' homes; view art exhibits in Desert Museum's striking setting; explore scenic Palm Canyon; swim, hike, play tennis or golf in one of country's top resorts

BRIEF BUT BREATHTAKING is ride that lifts visitors from desert heat of Palm Springs area to cool 8,500-foot mountain level.

Other sports

If you enjoy two-wheeled sightseeing and exercise, you can explore the city and foothills on any one of five separate bike trails. Local cycling shops rent bikes and carry trail maps. Riders will want to tour the nearby scenic canyons on horseback; contact Smoke Tree Stables at (619) 327-1372.

The California Angels, an American League baseball team, maintain spring training headquarters here. Visitors may attend spring practices and exhibition games, mostly in March, at the baseball stadium at East Ramon Road and South Sunrise Way.

Shopping and browsing

Shopping in Palm Springs is a popular diversion. In addition to several shopping centers, intriguing shops line Palm Canyon Drive. Many top national and California retail stores have branches here, providing opportunities for both window gazing and serious shopping. In this pace-setting community, new spring fashions are introduced in October before being put on the general market.

Palm Springs is also becoming known as an art center, with galleries and exhibits attracting many visitors each year. Most of the galleries are along the main downtown streets; the town also has an excellent museum (see page 88).

Your season in the sun

Palm Springs' magnet is its climate, especially from mid-October to mid-May. The days are generally sunny, warm, and cloudless, with dry air. Winter temperatures are comfortably warm—70° to 90°F. during the day; desert winter nights can dip to 25°, though 40° is a more usual minimum. In summer, daytime temperatures average in the 100°s, but the very low humidity keeps you relatively comfortable. Rainfall is scant. Most of the under-3-inch annual average falls in brief storms from November through April.

The Palm Springs "season" is from mid-December through April. During these months, particularly in January, February, and March, advance reservations are advisable. You'll find equally good weather (and fewer people) during the fall and spring seasons.

What to wear in Palm Springs? It's almost always "shirt sleeve" weather, with an accent on casual sports clothes. Men and women wear shorts downtown, but bathing suits are restricted to pool lounging. Women's sun dresses and pants outfits are popular, as are men's sport shirts and jackets.

Accommodations are many and varied. Hotels, motor inns, condominiums, and trailer parks (a number with landscaping, pools, and recreational facilities) are located in and around the city; room rates are competitive with those in other popular resort communities. Rates vary with the season (prices are lowest in summer). For specific information on accommodations and reservations, write to the Palm Springs Convention and Visitors Bureau, 255 N. El Cielo, Suite 315, Palm Springs, CA 92262; or call (619) 327-8411.

Exploring the City

As you approach Palm Springs from the northwest, the shadowy blue and dusty pink bulk of the layered San Jacinto Mountains provides an imposing backdrop of constantly changing colors and shadow patterns. Both contrasting and harmonizing with its surroundings, the city has assimilated the colors and textures of the desert.

Getting your bearings

Your introduction to Palm Springs is Palm Canyon Drive, lined with more than 3,000 palm trees along its 5-mile length. These trees aren't imports—they're native to the area. Illuminated at night, the beautiful palms are the only "street lamps" on this major thoroughfare.

From the moment you enter the city limits on State Highway 111, you notice the absence of billboards. In addition, you'll find few above-ground power lines or telephone poles, no large signs, no prices displayed, no neon or moving signs, and no high buildings. The uncluttered and unobtrusive character of the city is closely regulated.

Automotive navigation. The street grid makes it easy to find your way around Palm Springs. Palm Canyon Drive (a one-way route going south) is both the main arterial and the main shopping street. Indian Avenue, the secondary arterial a block east, runs one-way to the north through the central part of the city. At Tahquitz Way, the street numbering divides between north and south.

The older portions of Palm Springs are worth visiting for their lush garden plantings and handsome old trees. West Arenas Road leads you to one interesting district near the Palm Springs Tennis Club. In the north part of town, Via Las Palmas takes you west into a neighborhood of elegantly landscaped homes. Numerous movie stars and entertainers have homes in these areas of Palm Springs.

Tour opportunities. Gray Line, Celebrity Tours, and Palm Springs Safari all offer you the chance to see celebrity homes and other popular sights; balloon, helicopter, and plane rides are available for those who prefer a bird's-eye view of the city. You can explore the area on your own, of course: Palm Springs offers taxi, bus, and limousine service, as well as nine car rental agencies. Walking the flat area is easy.

Palm Springs at night

Downtown Palm Springs is relatively tranquil in the evening. There are numerous good restaurants, though many of the most popular eating places are southeast of Palm Springs toward Rancho Mirage.

With an emphasis on sports and sun activities, this is an early-to-bed community. During the season, several hotels and restaurants offer entertainment and dancing. If you search, you'll even find a disco. But unless you know some of the residents, you're not likely to get a peek at the social life of the city's glamourites.

A historical corner

A good place to begin your exploration of Palm Springs is at the corner of Tahquitz Way and Indian Avenue. Here is the popular Palm Springs Spa Hotel & Mineral Springs, an elaborate structure that houses the bubbling hot springs sacred to the Agua Caliente Indians. If you're not a guest at the spa, you can still enjoy these hot springs for a reasonable admission charge. You can take your pick of mineral baths, individual Roman "swirlpools," rock steam and infrared inhalation, needlepoint showers, massage, immersion in a 104°F. outdoor mineral pool, and an exercise gymnasium.

An 1853 government survey party noted that the Indians attributed special healing powers to the springs and considered them sacred. Today, the only reminder of this sacred shrine is a memorial plaque on the building—and, of course, the same "healing" waters.

Palm Springs Desert Museum

This fascinating museum and cultural center moved to its handsome quarters in 1976. It's located directly behind the Desert Fashion Plaza on Museum Drive, a block west of Palm Canyon Drive.

Two sunken sculpture gardens enhance its impressive exterior, and the 20-acre grounds include a sculpture court financed by Frank Sinatra. Inside you'll find a permanent fine arts collection, exhibits explaining the desert's natural history, and a 450-seat theater for the performing arts.

In the natural history galleries, two 50-foot dioramas of the desert by day and by night feature the common plant and animal inhabitants. Another diorama, 80 feet long, shows the desert at about 10 A.M. on a typical spring morning. In addition there are close to 1,300 Indian artifacts, including fine examples of basketry and rug making.

The museum is open Tuesday through Friday from 10 A.M. to 4 P.M., and weekends from 10 A.M. to 5 P.M.; it's closed in summer and on major holidays. You'll pay a moderate fee to view the building and grounds. Museum shops offer interesting gift items.

Living Desert

This 1200-acre park is just 15 miles southeast of Palm Springs, in the Colorado Desert town of Palm Desert. The park's focus is on local flora and fauna: plantings at the James Irvine Garden, one section of the reserve, include Joshua trees and 18 other species of high-desert succulent plants.

An ethnobotanical garden contains plants the Indians used for food, fiber, soap, and other purposes. Both gardens are described in a printed trail guide.

New to the reserve are the Pearl McManus Hall, an exhibit building featuring an "after sundown" room housing a variety of desert dwellers; the animal hospital; an aviary; and a bighorn sheep enclosure.

The Living Desert sanctuary is at 47-900 S. Portola Avenue, about 1½ miles south of State 111. It's open daily, 9 A.M. to 5 P.M., from September through May. Adults pay a nominal admission fee; there's no charge for visitors under 17 with an adult.

Moorten Botanical Garden

A stroll through this garden/wildlife sanctuary lets you take a look at many of the world's deserts. Founded in 1938, the private preserve has since collected 2,000 kinds of plants—flora typical of the arid regions of Africa, Central America, and North America. The collection is a diverse one; you'll see rare and unusual specimens, blossoming cacti, and some aptly named plant "personalities" (the "bearded grandfather" cactus, for example). The "cactusarium," a garden just for cacti, hosts botanical courses and research.

The 4-acre garden holds some surprisingly verdant spots; benches here provide a place for you to rest and watch the birds. At the garden's entrance, you can buy plants, rocks and minerals, and books on identifying and growing desert plants.

Located at 1701 S. Palm Canyon Drive, the garden is open daily from 9 A.M. to 5 P.M. Expect a small admission charge.

Miss Cornelia White's house

Built in 1894 from railroad ties, the small house near the corner of Indian Avenue and Tahquitz Way contains memorabilia of early Palm Springs, including the town's first telephone. Once the home of a pioneer woman, the house is maintained by the Palm Springs Historical Society and is open Tuesday through Saturday, as well as Sunday afternoon. Admission is free; donations are accepted.

Cabot's Old Indian Pueblo Museum

The desert has long attracted its share of eccentrics, and Cabot Yerxa was one. His unconventional home near Palm Springs stands testimony. Now a museum, the house with its unusual memorabilia is open to visitors.

In 1913, Yerxa homesteaded his land, but he didn't start the four-story house until 30 years later. Most of it was built within 5 years, but Yerxa added to it until his death in 1965. Working with recycled lumber, railroad ties, and handmade adobe bricks, he styled the house after the cliff dwellings of his Pueblo Indian friends. Odd-shaped pieces of glass he liked became parts of the 150 windows in 35 rooms.

Though he discovered hot and cold springs on his land, Yerxa was sparing with water. A bucketful was used first for cooking, then to wash dishes and clothes, later in a foot bath, and finally to water the flowers.

Scattered throughout the house are his odd mementos: an 8-foot stuffed brown bear; pictures of prospector Yerxa in Alaska with his friend Theodore Roosevelt; and an Indian medicine man's vestments, made of elk skin and human hair, given to him in 1929.

The museum at 67–616 E. Desert View Avenue in Desert Hot Springs (north of Palm Springs) is open daily except Tuesday. There's a slight admission charge, but the operator throws in a free guided tour.

Aerial tramway

When days get hot on the desert floor, Palm Springs residents and visitors have an instant escape route to

the high country of Mount San Jacinto, where the air is pine-scented and temperatures are 40 degrees cooler.

The tram trip up the mountain—beginning in the rugged Chino Canyon on the north edge of town—is refreshing, exciting, and beautiful any time of the year. You get an excellent view of the valley desert carpet, dotted with green palms and 7,000 blue swimming pools. Because of the awesome engineering challenges presented in its construction, the tramway, built in the early 1960s, has been called "the eighth engineering wonder of the world."

In a period of 2 years, 23,000 helicopter missions hauled men and materials to narrow ledges for construction of the towers. Today, the two 80-passenger trams move up and down one of the sheerest mountains in North America, over granite recesses deeper than the Grand Canyon.

The climb to the Mountain Station (8,516 feet) from the valley floor takes 14 minutes. This station is situated at the threshold of San Jacinto Wilderness State Park, where chattering jays and chipmunks attest that you are indeed in a different world. The top of Mount San Jacinto is a 6-mile hike from the tram station. Below sprawls the great desert expanse of the Coachella Valley, including the Salton Sea. On a very clear day the mountain ranges of Las Vegas are visible. At Mountain Station you can eat in the restaurant (open for lunch and dinner), shop in the gift store, and watch a free movie on the dramatic construction of the tram.

Behind Mountain Station, a concrete path leads down to Long Valley, where you can picnic in summer and play in the snow during the winter. During the summer, mules carry you from the top of the tram into the valley. Cross-country skiing is good from this point; ski equipment can be rented.

To reach the tramway base, turn off State 111 north of town and follow the signs. Gray Line offers a transportation service from Palm Springs. The Valley Station has a gift shop, snack bar, and a cocktail lounge. Be sure to take your tramway trip on a clear day; a desert haze will almost completely obscure the view.

The tram operates from 10 A.M. to 7:30 P.M. (from 8 A.M. on weekends) October through April; from May through Labor Day, it remains open until 8:30 P.M. After Labor Day, the tram is closed for annual maintenance for 4 to 6 weeks.

Into the Mountains

Though the tram is the most dramatic way to reach the upper level of the San Jacintos, you can enter this mountain recreation area by way of Banning (Interstate Highway 10 to State Highway 243) or the Riverside-Hemet route (Interstate 215 to State Highway 74 to State Highway 243). The latter is the Pines-to-Palms Highway, part of an enjoyable loop drive from mountains to desert.

Small in area but high on the horizon, the craggy ramparts of the San Jacintos support a cool, green, much-sought-after summer retreat between the hot wheat and orchard country of the San Jacinto Valley on the west and the hotter desert of the Coachella Valley on the east. The forested backbone slants up gradually from south to north until it breaks away suddenly at the tremendous north face of San Jacinto Peak—one of the world's most abrupt escarpments, rising from near sea level to 10,804 feet, face to face with Mount San Gorgonio (this area's highest mountain) across the San Gorgonio Pass.

Jumping-off place for exploring the upper San Jacintos by road or trail is the forest community of Idyllwild—a logical place to headquarter while you become acquainted with the region and decide where most of your interests lie. Available are hotels and motels, restaurants, camping supplies, and pack and saddle stock.

Mount San Jacinto State Park & Wilderness

This mountain park offers more than 50 miles of hiking trails. Only two state park campgrounds are accessible by automobile, but primitive camping is available in both state and federal wilderness areas. Whether you enter the wilderness on foot or horseback, you'll need a day-use permit. Apply in person at the Long Valley Ranger Station at the top of the tram or at the park or forest service offices in Idyllwild. Backpackers should get an overnight permit in advance. For maps and further information, call (714) 659-2607.

San Gorgonio Pass

If you take Interstate 10 east to Palm Springs, you pass Beaumont and Banning, lying in the divide between the San Bernardino and San Jacinto mountains. Side trips off the freeway in early spring reveal billowy colors of cherry and peach blossoms in nearby orchards and of apples up in Oak Glen. Later in the summer, you can pick your own fruit or get it from a roadside stand. Oak Glen apple stands offer homemade pies and cider.

Canyons east of the mountains

The scenic and historical canyons close to Palm Springs, for centuries the home of the Agua Caliente Indians, offer beauty and exploration for hikers, horse riders, bird watchers, botanists, and camera enthusiasts.

Tahquitz Canyon, containing a 60-foot waterfall, is the closest to town but is closed to the public at present. Its beauty was recorded for posterity in the original film version of *Lost Horizon*.

Palm Canyon cuts south from Palm Springs up into the mountains for more than 14 miles, dividing the San Jacinto from the Santa Rosa mountains. This valley was the traditional summer retreat of the Agua Caliente Indians, who still own this land of shady palm groves and cool streams.

To reach the canyon, drive south on Palm Canyon Drive (past the Canyon Hotel). Shortly after the road enters the Indian reservation, you'll come to a toll gate, open from 9 A.M. to 4 P.M. daily except during the period from May 15 to October 15, when the canyon is closed to the public because of extreme fire hazard.

During a "wet" year, the canyon may be closed for a slightly shorter time (June to September). Contact the Bureau of Indian Affairs, (619) 325-2086, for information. A small fee includes admission to Andreas Canyon. The last half-mile requires cautious driving.

You pass a number of interesting tributary canyons along the way, all containing fine stands of palms, many more than 1,000 years old. Proceeding south, the valley narrows, and you cut through the slot of Split Rock. Then the road climbs steeply to a level parking area called Hermit's Bench, where you'll find a souvenir shop, cold drinks, and rest rooms.

The steep but well-improved trail starts here, first dropping down into the canyon. Picnic tables are available, but there is no drinking water. The palms here reach an impressive height; for a short, pleasant outing, walk a mile or two along the trail winding beneath them. This is a popular trail for horseback riding.

Andreas Canyon's parking area is just over a half-mile off the main road in a grove of sycamores and cottonwoods. A clear stream runs the year around. You'll find picnic tables, rest rooms, and a wading pool (2 feet deep after a rain). The grounds are well cleared, shady, and pleasant, often crowded on weekends. Look for mortar holes gouged in large rocks near the parking lot; the Indians once used them for grinding meal. A trail follows the stream for about 4 miles along a climbing, winding route up to the head of the canyon.

Near the parking area stands a particularly impressive grove of native California fan palms (*Washingtonia filifera*), their skirts trimmed well above the ground to reduce fire hazard. These are survivors of ancient groves once widespread throughout the valley.

Murray Canyon, hidden between Andreas and Palm, has a stream flowing most of the year. From the Andreas parking area, you walk south to the canyon on a well-marked trail. Another trail leads up to a stand of fine palms. This large canyon is popular with the horsy set.

The Coachella Valley

Southeast of Palm Springs and the nearby resort areas is Coachella Valley, part of the Colorado Desert, which extends east to the Colorado River and south to the shores of the Gulf of California. The valley is endowed with a great variety of plant and animal life. There's a special fascination here in the transformation to rich farmland that has been wrought by 20th century irrigation. Average rainfall is under 2 inches a year, but artesian wells discovered around 1855 played an important role in the area's agricultural development. Many of the valley's 60,000 cultivated acres are below sea level.

From Palm Springs through Indio ("Date Capital of the United States") and south to the Salton Sea, 200,000 date palms annually yield 40 million pounds of dates of numerous varieties. You pass thick gardens of date palms along the highways. Dates and various date concoctions are sold at roadside stands on State 111 and 86; here's your chance to try a date milkshake. At Shields Date Gardens, 3½ miles west of Indio, watch a 25-minute film on how dates are grown. There is also a rose garden well worth viewing. The popular Indio National Date Festival (held in connection with the Riverside County Fair in mid-February) features an Arabian theme, with camel races (see page 93).

The most productive general farming in the valley is in the southeastern section, where the two largest cities, Indio and Coachella, are processing and shipping centers for a wide variety of agriculture. Not until you approach the Salton Sea does the desert take over again. Even here, development is underway, increasing the recreational facilities at this lake that is saltier than the oceans (see page 93).

South of the Salton Sea lies the Imperial Valley, greater in area than the Coachella Valley and acre-for-acre the most productive agricultural region in the world.

Lake Cahuilla, one of Riverside County's newest parks, makes a stopping spot for a picnic. If you bring a boat, you can also go fishing (license required). Swimming is a good way to cool off on a hot day. The park is open daily from 7 A.M. to sunset. There's a day-use fee plus an extra charge for fishing.

Joshua Tree National Monument

Though civilization is changing the character of the desert surrounding Joshua Tree, this area remains a rare desert sanctuary. The monument (lying at the edge of two great deserts—the low Colorado and the high Mojave) is a transition land of beautiful desert studded with dramatic trees and plants and covered with wildflowers in spring. It is less a playground than an area dedicated to the preservation of a characteristic desert scene and the wildlife it supports. In Joshua Tree you can drive, hike, climb, picnic, and camp.

The monument covers more than 850 square miles and is located east of Palm Springs, less than an hour's drive away. The Cottonwood Springs (or south) entrance is 25 miles east of Indio on Interstate 10; the north entrance on State Highway 62 can be reached through the towns of Joshua Tree and Twentynine Palms (the park headquarters).

The living desert

The distinctive plants and animals of this region are notable for their adaptation to the heat and aridity of the desert habitat.

The Joshua tree (*Yucca brevifolia*), most famous of the native plants, is actually a giant member of the lily family and one of the most spectacular plants of the southwestern deserts. Clusters of white blossoms, sometimes 14 inches long, appear at the ends of its angular branches; the plants have been known to attain a height of 40 feet.

Growing at 3,000 to 5,000-foot elevations in the central and western parts of the monument, the Joshua tree will bloom in March and April, except during unusually dry years. Legend has it the Mormons named the plant "Joshua tree" or "praying plant" because of its upstretched arms. At first, the newcomer might confuse it with the Mojave yucca (*Yucca schidigera*), more common at lower elevations and distinguished by much longer leaves and a shorter stature.

ALGERIAN DATE PALMS
(above) rise against distant
Santa Rosa Mountains in
Coachella Valley. Sunset
heightens drama of Joshua trees
(left) in national monument.

In addition to extensive stands of Joshua trees, the monument has the distinctive ocotillo, the feathery nolina, and many colorful kinds of cactus with large, showy blossoms. Stately California fan palms are found in several of the shady oases. One grove in Lost Palm Canyon contains more than 100 of these trees.

The spring wildflower show at Joshua Tree is dependent upon winter rains. Average annual rainfall here is 5 inches. In a normal year, the color show begins in lower elevations as early as March.

Wildlife in the monument resembles that of other desert regions, but it is more abundant here because of the higher altitudes and a cooler, more varied climate. As with plant life, adaptation is necessary to the animals' survival. The kangaroo rat with long tufted tail is often seen around campgrounds at night. This creature and other native rodents manufacture water in their own bodies and can survive a normal lifetime without a drink. The largest animal, the desert bighorn sheep, is impressive but rarely seen. You're most likely to spot a coyote or the lively, side-blotched lizard (little brown uta). Thirty-eight species of reptiles and amphibians and 249 kinds of birds have been reported in the monument.

History unfolds in the monument

Joshua Tree National Monument has a long history of human habitation. Artifacts discovered along an ancient river terrace in the Pinto Basin indicate the presence of primitive man in days when there was enough water to support a culture. Much later, Indians who mastered the art of desert survival settled at springs and waterholes and left traces of their campsites. Old mine shafts and mills on the hillsides attest to settlement around 1865 by gold prospectors—the first white men to arrive. The cattlemen who followed left small dams or "tanks" at natural rock basins to catch rainwater for their herds.

Visiting the Desert Queen Ranch (also called Keys Ranch) is like taking a time-capsule trip back almost a century. This little-known landmark in the monument is better preserved than many desert ghost towns.

Trips are scheduled from mid-February through Memorial Day and mid-October through mid-December. A schedule for the hour-long guided tour is available at the visitor center in Joshua Tree.

At the ranch you'll see bedrock mortars, signs of Indian habitation; an adobe barn dating from the 1880s, when the area was reputedly a cattle rustler's hangout; and a stamp mill from the Desert Queen Mine of the 1890s.

But the dominant presence is that of William Keys, a colorful character who homesteaded here just after World War I, raised a family, and died here in 1969. You'll visit his now-derelict ranch house, guest cabins, school teacher's cabin and tiny schoolhouse, dam, and orchard. All of these—even the family tombstones in a touching little burial plot on the premises—are examples of Bill Keys's own handiwork.

Scattered around the landscape is a veritable catalog of old-time appliances—cars, trucks, and farm gear—all reminders of the old days when the nearest town, Banning, was 50 miles away over road so rough it hardly merited the name.

Climate and accommodations

Because much of Joshua Tree is high desert, the weather is pleasant most of the year, particularly on winter days. The altitude ranges from 1,000 to 6,000 feet in the Little San Bernardino Mountains. Since most roads are at the 3,000 to 4,000-foot level and go as high as 5,185 feet at Salton View, the monument seldom gets too hot for comfort even in summer. Most visitors come from October through May. Remember that desert nights get cold.

Joshua Tree offers several good campsites. Be sure to bring your own fuel and water; gathering firewood in the monument is prohibited, and only the Cottonwood and Black Rock Canyon campsites and the headquarters at Twentynine Palms have running water. For information, write to Joshua Tree National Monument, 74485 National Monument Drive, Twentynine Palms, CA 92277; or call (619) 367-7511.

You'll find no lodging or eating facilities within the monument, but accommodations are available in and around the entrance towns.

Exploring Joshua Tree

Your visit can include several interesting stops and adventures on your way to—and within—this diversified monument. If you are traveling State 62 to the north entrance, look for interesting antique and junk shops. Big Morongo Canyon Wildlife Preserve, at Morongo Valley, has a stand of large cottonwoods and springs that create a natural oasis.

Yucca Valley, between the San Bernardino Mountains and Joshua Tree, is built among fantastic rock formations, thick stands of Joshua trees, and spring wildflowers. Shortly after entering town, you can turn off to Pioneertown, site of many Hollywood westerns. The Pioneer Pass Road continues to Big Bear Lake but is accessible only by four-wheel-drive vehicles. On a mountain overlooking the town, Desert Christ Park features large Biblical figures sculptured of white concrete.

Along Old Woman Springs Road in Landers (north of State 62) are trailer parks for recreational vehicles and horse riders. This road also takes you to Giant Rock Airport; here, in three rooms hewn from a mammoth desert boulder, UFO buffs gather to discuss "sightings." Still another Yucca Valley attraction is the Hi-Desert Nature Museum.

Twentynine Palms, the northeastern gateway and headquarters to the monument, was once a watering place for prospectors. Now it is an oasis for health seekers, retired persons, aspiring artists, and tourists.

An early visit to the visitor center and museum here will acquaint you with the fascinating land that you are about to explore. This building contains displays, desert artifacts, and maps and brochures. Ask the rangers for additional information. A self-guided nature trail leads through the nearby palm oasis.

Cottonwood Springs, at the south entrance (just north of I-10), is another visitor center site. A 4-mile trail takes you to Lost Palms, an oasis known for its bird life and wide variety of native palms.

Hidden Valley is a few miles in from the Joshua Tree entrance to the monument. Legend has it that the massive boulders and haphazard rocks here were once hideouts for cattle rustlers. Today, they shelter a campground and provide an intriguing jumble for agile explorers. To reach the valley from the parking lot, you can either climb through a narrow passageway under jumbled granite or take a surface trail. A 1½-mile nature trail winds through the valley.

Salton View, at the end of the paved road that runs south from Hidden Valley, is 5,185 feet high, giving you a panoramic view of the area stretching from Mexico and the Salton Sea (235 feet below sea level) to the San Jacinto and San Gorgonio mountains (over 10,000 feet above sea level). Nearby, the Lost Horse Mine area is rewarding for its display of desert plants and its view to Pleasant Valley.

To reach Lost Horse Mine, you follow a dirt side road to a trail. The walk (about 2 miles each way) is too long for a 1-day visitor to the monument, but the mine remnants are quite complete and interesting.

Squaw Tank, a self-guided motor nature trail, is marked by a sign from the main park road. You'll cover 18 miles of sweeping views, inactive mines, and a fine stand of barrel cactus. Remnants of early Indian habitation are found in this area. Nearby, the climb to the top of Ryan Mountain (5,401 feet) is a steep 1.5 miles but well worth the effort.

Old Dale and New Dale, in the eastern section of the monument, is basin and range country, often overlooked by visitors.

Nature trails are numerous. Other than those already mentioned, there are well-marked walking trails at Cholla Cactus Garden and Cap Rock, each keyed to explanatory booklets.

Arch Rock, about 300 yards east of White Tanks campground, is a remarkable span of granite you can walk under. Descriptive signs mark the way.

Salton Sea

Sandwiched between the rich farmlands and resort centers of the Imperial and Coachella valleys is one of California's most interesting stretches of desert—the below-sea-level depression that contains Salton Sea.

Once a dry desert wasteland, the sea was formed in 1905 when the Colorado River overstepped its bounds; billions of gallons of its flood waters were impounded in the basin. The sea remained at a nearly constant level until about 15 years ago. Then the water began rising steadily, overtaking deserted resort buildings and leaving them half-submerged in ghostly silence.

When and how to go. Salton Sea is a hot place in summer, but winter temperatures stay in the comfortable low 50s to high 80s. Water temperatures drop as low as 50°F. in midwinter and climb to as high as 90°F. in summer. The best months are November and December and February through April.

The sea is circled by good highways—State Highway 86 on the west, State 111 on the east. The highway between Anza-Borrego Desert State Park and Palm Springs passes along its southwest shore. Dusty side roads and rocky trails lead to hot mineral springs, Indian relics and petroglyphs, rock-hunting grounds, ancient shell deposits, colorful canyons, and sand dunes.

Where to stay. The 17,868-acre Salton Sea State Recreation Area, about 26 miles northeast of Indio on State 111, provides both primitive and improved campsites and picnic areas. Brochures describing the recreation area and its facilities are available; write to the Park Supervisor, Salton Sea State Recreation Area, P.O. Box 3166, North Shore, CA 92254 (or call (619) 393-3052).

Almost all campsites are available on a first-come, first-served basis. There's one exception (a 25-site area); call MISTIX at (800) 446-7275 to reserve a spot from October through May. You'll also find privately owned campgrounds near the recreation area.

CAMELS RACE IN INDIO

A highlight of Riverside County's National Date Festival at Indio in mid-February is the wild camel race. At best, camel racing is a precarious sport for riders and handlers and a hilarious spectacle for watchers.

Members of the International Order of Camel Jockeys (an organization of Nevada and California-based camel riders who promote this ancient sport) insist camels dislike each other, the rider, and handlers who help the rider mount.

Camels stomp, kick, bite, and spit. At the starting line (if the camel ever gets there), he's apt to buck, drag handlers in circles, run away, or lie down and refuse to participate at all. When the camel is on the run, the jockey must hang on and bounce precariously 6 or 7 feet above ground, holding his saddle (no stirrups) by skill, grit, and lots of luck. Betting is risky.

Both camel and elephant racing are listed as "intermission" events during the National Horse Show in the fairgrounds main arena (State Highway 111 and Arabia Street). Admission to the arena is moderate, and spectators attest to the popularity of the entertainment. Get there early for a seat as close as possible to the race route.

BLOOMING OCOTILLOS dot desert after torrential summer rains. Many are preserved in Anza-Borrego Desert State Park.

What's happening. Fishing, motor boating, and waterskiing are the major water attractions. Racers consider Salton Sea one of the fastest bodies of water in the world; because it's below sea level, internal combustion engines run more efficiently. Strong winds create waves up to 10 feet high at times; the park has a storm alert system.

Varner Harbor is the hub of most boating and fishing activities at the recreation area. The marina offers launching and boat-washing facilities.

Although the gradual leaching of minerals from the land has made the sea saltier, fish (originally introduced in the 1950s by the Department of Fish and Game) have adapted and survived. The breakwater is popular with croaker fishermen; corvina and pargo fishing is best done from your boat.

Salton Sea National Wildlife Refuge

The east shore highway takes you close to the water for several miles before swinging east about halfway down. The sea then drops from sight and you could easily miss one of its most fascinating aspects: the great bird gatherings on the south shore.

A short detour gives you a close look. State 111 turns south at Niland; after about 4 miles, turn west on Sinclair Road. In about 6½ miles (1 mile before the pavement ends), you reach the shore at Salton Sea National Wildlife Refuge. A short trail up a pile of gargantuan twisted rocks (appropriately named Rock Hill) leads you to a panorama point.

The setting is serene, but hardly quiet. When the geese are there in force, they bicker in an impressive din. Birds are attracted by the shallows and ponds and by marshes and fields beside the sea. In winter, some 150 species can usually be seen.

The refuge once extended far out into what is now the sea, but rising water reduced 32,000 above-water acres to only about 3,000.

The nearby desert

Because the desert around Salton Sea has not been developed to a large extent, it's still full of fascinating natural features.

Mecca Hills, a choice desert country just north of Salton Sea, has three canyons that are favorites of desert explorers—Painted Canyon, Box Canyon, and Hidden Spring Canyon. All are reached along State Highway 195 a few miles west of Mecca. The smoke tree (*Dalea spinosa*) and desert ironwood plant (*Olneya tesota*) found throughout these desert hills present a show of purple blossoms.

Rocks and formations abound in this desert region. About 7½ miles due west of Mecca, you'll find the Fish Traps, circular pits formed from piles of large travertine-covered boulders. Archeologists aren't certain why these pits were built, but their favorite theory seems to be that the stones were collected by Indians and piled in these circular forms to trap fish in ancient Lake Cahuilla, which covered the Salton Sink from about 900 to 1400 A.D.

Travertine Rock is a mound of enormous boulders located approximately 100 yards off State 86 about 6 miles south of its intersection with State 195. Once partially submerged by Lake Cahuilla, the mound is covered with a scaly, knobby limestone (actually not true travertine but a calcareous rock called tufa). A climb to the top (about 200 feet) reveals a full view of the Coachella Valley and its miles of farms plotted in geometric precision.

The country south of Travertine Rock along State 86 is happy hunting ground for amateur geologists and rock collectors. Each year desert rains sweep clean the broad shallow washes of the Santa Rosa Mountains and carry down brightly colored and oddly formed quartzites, flints, granites, schists, and sandstone. Look for them in washes around the south end of the sea—the farther from the highway the better.

Anza-Borrego Desert State Park

Anza-Borrego is a large desert. The area preserved within state park boundaries extends almost the entire length of San Diego County's eastern edge from Riverside County to the Mexican border. It ranges from 40 feet above sea level near the Salton Sea to 6,000 feet above on San Ysidro Mountain. You can't see it all in one visit. Covering over half a million acres, the desert comprises more than two-thirds of all the land in California's system of preserves.

The southern part of the present state park was originally a separate desert park named for Captain Juan Bautista de Anza, the Spanish explorer who pioneered this route to Alta California in 1774. Borrego State Park, taking its name from the Spanish word for "sheep," adjoined it on the north. In 1957 the two parks were combined.

Anza-Borrego is often pictured as a wrinkled wasteland of harshly eroded, nearly barren clay and gravel, possibly because its gullied badlands are its most extraordinary phenomenon. There is more to it than that: cool piny heights, springs and oozing *cienagas*, spectacular though brief waves of wildflowers in spring, and native fragrances of pervasive sage, subtle cottonwood, and even more subtle earth. Today's visitor can traverse a terrain nearly as wild and untouched as that found by early Spanish visitors. Many travelers consider November through May the best time of year to explore this desert—then it has a clean-washed, fresh look.

This state park is one of California's last untamed desert areas. The privately owned enclave of Borrego Valley in the northern part of the park is the only section to have been developed, and with development isolated to that region, Anza-Borrego can remain one of California's last frontiers. Like Palm Springs and Salton Sea, the valley taps underground sources for water. Nearby, 6,000 acres of former wasteland are cultivated for grapes, gladioli, citrus fruits, and grains. Along with its farms, subdivisions, shopping centers, golf courses, and airports, the area offers tourist accommodations.

Wildlife is worth watching for. Some desert bighorn sheep still live in remote areas of the north end of the park and in the Santa Rosa Mountains beyond. At points

farthest away from human activity, the natural desert is often a noisy place, with the humming of winged insects, the buzz of the cicada, the croaking of frogs in the springs and marshes, and the sounds of many birds.

About 600 species of plants are native to the park. Depending on altitude and exposure, desert flowers bloom profusely in March and April. Wildflowers range from tiny, pin-size blooms to clusters of red on the ocotillo, which punctuate the landscape after a rainstorm. The California fan palm groves and the stands of smoke trees are among the finest anywhere, but Anza-Borrego is most renowned for its low, fat-boled elephant trees (*Bursera microphylla*), fairly common in parts of Baja California but north of the border practically confined to the Anza-Borrego region.

Driving is not difficult. More than 600 miles of roads follow the scenic, weathered hills and flatland. Though a deftly handled automobile can do surprisingly well in the desert, there are many roads that require high clearance or even four-wheel-drive vehicles. Pickup campers can get to some remote places; jeeps are advisable for the really tough routes.

Rangers conduct family cars in caravans to many scenic destinations and can point out roadside geological features, sea fossils, wildlife, and some unusual plants.

Camping has a unique feature here. This is the only California state park in which you may camp anywhere you wish. The only rules are that you ride a horse or drive on existing roads (hikers are not restricted), that you not light fires on the ground, and that you leave things just as you found them. The nearest ranger will come to your rescue if you've camped off the beaten path and have failed to check in at a prearranged time the next day. Camping areas vary from highly developed (Borrego Springs) to less than the basic (your own site in a remote spot).

Desert camping is most popular from November through May, though there may be high winds or a few very cold nights during these months.

For a short visit to the park, it is best to select a relatively small area and explore it thoughtfully. Check at the visitor center for information. If you can spend several days, establish a preliminary headquarters near one of the ranger stations, where you can attend campfire programs, get latest information on backcountry driving conditions, and check out and back in for your own safety. Based on locations of active ranger stations, the most logical divisions of the park and some of their features are listed here:

Borrego Springs, a small resort community at the foot of San Ysandro Mountain a few miles north of State Highway 78, is the center of park activity. Park headquarters is Borrego Palm Canyon, 3 miles northwest of Borrego Springs. For a list of lodgings, write to the Chamber of Commerce, Borrego Springs, CA 92004. State 78 and County Road S2 are the major routes leading into the park. The Borrego-Salton Sea Road (County Road S22) parallels State 78 as a short cut from Borrego Springs to Palm Springs, Indio, and the Salton Sea.

Borrego Palm Canyon is the site of park headquarters and the most improved campground in the park. Its many conveniences include gas stoves, ramadas (sun shelters), showers, and trailer sites with hookups. Nearby are several points of interest: a 1½-mile, self-guided nature trail leading up to a canyon of palms; the most famous view point in the park, overlooking barren, spectacularly eroded Borrego Badlands; date groves; and a jeep road to Pumpkin Patch, a flat area covered with large, round concretions of unexplained origin.

Culp Valley is in high country, up to 4,500 feet. Here you'll find primitive camping on semiwooded land with many huge boulders. From here a dramatic view extends across Borrego Valley to the badlands. Culp Valley is a cool retreat from the summer heat of the lower desert.

Tamarisk Grove has an improved campground that faces the beautiful, flowery slopes of the North Pinyon Mountains and a remarkable natural concentration of cactus. Good auto exploring is possible on a primitive road along San Felipe Creek and Grapevine Canyon. Borrego Valley is a few minutes away by way of Yaqui Pass. Yaqui Well, a historic watering spot above Tamarisk Grove, has magnificent desert ironwood trees and a busy wildlife population.

Blair Valley can be reached on the Overland Stage Route, hacked through historic Box Canyon by the Mormon Battalion and still in use as County S2. A year-round "use" area, Blair Valley has improved campgrounds at Old Vallecito Stage Station and at Agua Caliente Springs.

Fish Creek comes into view along a dramatic motor route up Fish Creek Wash through Split Mountain to Sandstone Canyon, with a jeep trail continuing through Hapaha Flat to the Pinyon Mountains. Eerie mud hills and elephant trees are features of this area. Supplies and meals are available in Ocotillo Wells.

Bow Willow has many palm groves, especially in the Mountain Palm Springs area; about 300 *torotes* (a Spanish word for "elephant trees") in Torote Canyon; a smoke tree forest; the old Carrizo Stage Station site; many inviting roads, jeep trails, and foot trails; the Well of the Eight Echoes (some say only seven); and the Dos Cabezas area, with monumental rocks, lava flow, a mine, Mortero Palms, and the giddy, canyonside tracks of the San Diego and Arizona Eastern Railway.

The Colorado River

With its most renowned handiwork the Grand Canyon, the mighty Colorado carves through rugged terrain on the earth's surface, winding some 1,400 miles before reaching the sea. Once described as "too thick to drink and too thin to plow," the once-raging river (forming a natural boundary between California and Arizona) was used by early American Indians as a thoroughfare for canoe travel. Petroglyphs cut in rocks near Lake Havasu City are believed to be shoreline messages of these ancient river voyagers.

Important today as a major water supplier to the metropolitan areas on the Southern California coast, the Colorado River has been harnessed by dams and developed into a vacation and recreation area. Once traversed by paddle wheel steamers, the river is now dotted along its shoreline with campgrounds and marinas.

Most of the 265 miles of river from Hoover Dam in Nevada to the Mexican border are suitable for public recreation purposes. Along the lower Colorado River, Havasu Lake is the largest recreational development, increasingly popular each year.

This is "low desert" country where the summers are hot, and in July and August, boating, fishing, and water-skiing at the lakes are outstanding.

Around Needles

At the Arizona border, the town of Needles is at the junction of two major highways—Interstate 40 and U.S. 95. Established in 1869 as a steamboat landing and supply station on the Old Emigrant Trail, Needles today has many boating facilities. Good beaches line the river, and diversified fishing is possible in the Havasu National Wildlife Refuge. A marina and golf course add to the attractions. The nearby rock formations known as "The Needles" are visible from the highway crossing at Topock; they are a backdrop for the spectacular boat trip down through Topock Gorge to upper Lake Havasu.

Park Moabi is 11 miles southeast of Needles on I-40. The park surrounds a lagoon opening into the river, directly across from the wildlife refuge. Launching facilities, boat docking, and boat rentals (including houseboats) are available. Secluded, sun-bleached, sandy inlets invite camping, and fishing is good.

Topock Gorge to Lake Havasu is an easy weekend trip on a houseboat through spectacular multicolored canyons. Fishing is varied: deep trolling may produce striped bass or trout; catfish are plentiful for bait fishermen plumbing holes in warmer bays.

Though onshore camping is prohibited in many areas, houseboaters may anchor overnight in sheltered bays and backwaters. Park Moabi is the best place to rent a boat.

For information on other recreation activities and facilities along this section of the Colorado River, write to the Economic Development Department, County Civic Bldg.—West, 175 W. Fifth Street, San Bernardino, CA 92415; or call (714) 383-2913.

Lake Havasu

Construction of Parker Dam in 1938 not only tamed the lower Colorado River but also created a 45-mile-long fresh-water lake that, contrasting with the raging red river, was quiet and very blue. Named Havasu (an Indian word for "blue water"), this lake is lined with deep bays and picturesque coves. Set between the Chemehuevi, Mohave, and Whipple mountains, the beautiful lake has become a favorite destination for sports enthusiasts and the setting for an extensive recreational development—Lake Havasu City.

Three national championship water sports contests annually take place on Lake Havasu: the Desert Regatta for sailing craft in May, the National Invitational Ski Championships in midsummer, and the Outboard World Championships.

The London Bridge is the most conspicuous addition to the desert landscape around Lake Havasu. This historic span, moved block by block from its site on the Thames River, was reassembled across dry land. Then the mile-long channel now separating the airport island from the shore was excavated beneath it. After the bridge was sold by the city of London for almost $2½ million, it took an additional $5½ million to dismantle the 130,000 tons of granite, ship them 10,000 miles to Lake Havasu City, and reassemble them. The bridge looks at home in an English village setting, with pub, restaurant, and shops built around it. A London double-decker red bus is parked on the waterfront. In early October an annual week-long event celebrates the London Bridge Anniversary.

Lake Havasu City, 19 miles south of Interstate 40, is served daily by scheduled airlines from Phoenix and Las Vegas. Private planes dot the parking strips, and amphibians take off and land on the water. Hotels are located in the middle of the shopping center, overlooking the lake, and near the golf course. Facilities for campers and trailers are at Havasu Cove on the lakefront.

Lake Havasu State Park

A 13,000-acre preserve, this park has headquarters at Pittsburgh Point on the airport island. Check with rangers for information on camping around the lake. There is no shoreline road, but roads do penetrate to the shore at a few points for boat launching. At some points are resorts, boating facilities (including rentals), trailer parks, and camping spaces.

The park has wide, sandy beaches with picnic tables, fountains, barbecue pits, showers, and rest rooms. The blue green bay offers good water-skiing, limited only by your endurance, and safe swimming in exceptionally clear water.

Anglers usually catch their limit of bass, trout, crappie, bluegill, and channel fish. The clear, cold Colorado River waters connecting Lake Havasu and Lake Mohave to the north are noted for good bass and trout.

For additional information about the park, write to Lake Havasu State Park, 1350 W. McCulloch Boulevard, Lake Havasu City, AZ 86403.

The lower Colorado

The Imperial Dam, near Yuma, Arizona, mixes work and play. Here water is diverted to irrigate the lands of Southern California and Arizona. But the dam also raises the water level of the Colorado, widening the river for 30 miles upstream and providing good facilities for boaters, anglers, and water-skiers.

A good introduction to the stretch of Colorado between Blythe and Martinez Lake is the annual fall Colorado River Cruise. On this overnight family campout, each small flotilla of motorboats is accompanied by an experienced guide who allows plenty of time for exploring.

The launching begins on a Saturday morning at Blythe for the 6-hour trip to the night's camp at Martinez Lake; the return cruise the next day, going against the current, takes longer. For trip details and entry forms, write to the Blythe Chamber of Commerce, 201 S. Broadway, Blythe, CA 92225.

Santa Barbara

Spanish Santa Barbara offers an entree to surrounding beach communities, pastoral inland valleys, and off-the-road missions. North on El Camino Real, visit Danish Solvang, dig for Pismo clams, and begin a coast-hugging trip from Morro Bay to San Simeon, site of incredible Hearst Castle.

Santa Barbara is a city of obvious beauty and year-round allure. Spreading north from a wide and gently curving beach, the city lies in a sunny sheltered plain. Offshore to the south, the Channel Islands seem a protective barrier against the ocean beyond. And behind the city, the mountains of the Santa Ynez range form a rugged east-to-west backdrop. Yet its stunning setting is not the foremost thing you notice about Santa Barbara. Most likely you will be impressed by the signs of its historical perpetuation: the Spanish and mission architectures; adobes, old and new; tile roofs; bell towers; and the Spanish love of color.

Not all of Santa Barbara's urban charm is manmade—nature contributes a gentle lushness that contrasts with and enhances the traditional buildings. Like living picture frames around large-scale masterpieces, stately palms ring many buildings. Fir trees—decorated at Christmas—are planted along the streets, marking pedestrian crossings. Santa Barbara's cultural calendar is testimony to the city's love for plants and flowers—the International Orchid Show is held here every spring, and the Santa Barbara National Horse and Flower Show occurs annually in mid-July.

Visitors can choose from a varied schedule of events, ranging from popular Old Spanish Days in August, to the earlier Summer Sports Festival, and the Fishermen's Derby in spring.

Some of Santa Barbara's warmest, sunniest days are in autumn. Fishing holds up well into fall, and ocean temperatures remain warm enough for swimming into November. In September you find a significant change in accommodation prices; off-season rates are in effect until June.

Spaniards who settled here called it "La Tierra Adorada" (the beloved land); today's visitors find it hard not to share their enchantment.

This chapter also takes you into the inland hills, where you can drive country roads or camp beside a peaceful lake. Solvang, in the Santa Ynez Valley, is a paradise for those partial to Scandinavian culture and shopping possibilities. The Ojai Valley is lake and mountain country, home of the largest land birds in North America—the condors.

Stretch your trip up the coast to include Pismo Beach (clam capital), inland San Luis Obispo, Morro Bay with its prominent rock formations, and San Simeon, headquarters for touring "Hearst Castle," now a State Historic Monument.

An Architectural Heritage

The big earthquake of 1925 destroyed many of the city's post-Victorian structures, forced early demolition of others, and opened the way for Santa Barbara to express its Mediterranean consciousness in the course of rebuilding. An architectural review board has been approving or rejecting designs for business and public buildings ever since.

Spanish names were given (or restored) to streets in the heart of town, with the one significant exception of State Street, which did not revert to the Spanish tongue twister "Calle del Estado." Most of the reconstructed adobes are within a block or two of De la Guerra Plaza.

TILE ROOFS and palm trees, sprinkled throughout the city, lend Mediterranean touch to coastal Santa Barbara.

Downtown Santa Barbara

The 12-block downtown area (bounded by Victoria, Chapala, Ortega, and Santa Barbara streets) includes Pueblo Viejo (Old Town), a historic preserve and original core of the city that surrounded the Presidio. As you walk around, you'll find plaques and markers identifying early buildings. Only a few are open to visitors.

In downtown Santa Barbara you won't feel dwarfed by a Manhattanlike cluster of high-rises—the area is designed for pedestrians. Buildings, with few exceptions, are four stories or less, tightly controlled by a height ordinance that can't be varied unless approved by the voters. At the Santa Barbara Chamber of Commerce (1330 State Street), you can pick up a copy of the Red Tile Tour—a guide and map for a 24-mile scenic drive in and around the city. Park in any of the nine city lots shown on the downtown tour map; the first 90 minutes of parking are free.

State Street is perhaps the best place to begin the tour. Rebuilt as a plaza boulevard in 1969, it is the heart of downtown. In the 1960s, Santa Barbara's downtown was decaying. Competition from the new La Cumbre Plaza shopping center a few miles away was cutting off retail trade. New shops were opened downtown, and convenient parking brought back business. Though State Street is still a main artery, its wide, landscaped sidewalks shield pedestrians from traffic.

Wherever you begin your exploring, you'll find some interesting buildings and shops along your route. Here are some highlights of Old Town:

The Santa Barbara Museum of Art (corner of State and Anapamu streets next to the public library) is small, bright, airy, and—unlike other landmarks on the route—modern. Soft natural light enters the gallery through skylights, falling on Greek, Roman, and Egyptian sculptures and priceless glassware; an encircling gallery and adjacent halls contain impressive collections of Asian and American art from many periods. The museum is privately supported. It's open daily except Monday and holidays, from 11 A.M. to 5 P.M. (Sunday from noon to 5). Guided tours take place at 1:30 P.M. weekdays, 2 P.M. weekends.

The Santa Barbara County Court House buildings and grounds cover a square block bounded by Santa Barbara, Anacapa, Anapamu, and Figueroa streets. Built in 1929, the courthouse, with its great archway, wrought-iron balconies, gay mosaics, murals, red-tiled roof, romantic towers, and hand-carved doors, resembles a Spanish-Moorish castle. It's truly architecture on a grand scale. Above the entrance arch on Anacapa Street is an appropriate Roman motto in Spanish; the nearby English version reads, "God gave us the country. The skill of man hath built this town."

Built on the site of the first encampment in this area of peripatetic Portola and his men (1769), the courthouse and elaborate sunken gardens are the setting for pageants, concerts, and celebrations. Most notable is Old Spanish Days.

In the Assembly Room, huge, two-story murals colorfully depict Santa Barbara history, including the arrival of Juan Rodriguez Cabrillo in 1542, the founding of Mission Santa Barbara in 1786, and Colonel John Fremont's 1846 announcement heralding American rule in California.

The tower, El Mirador, provides an unequalled view of the city and courthouse grounds. Stairs lead to the top; an elevator also operates on weekdays.

Today, many courthouse functions take place in the new county administration building located nearby, but the courtrooms, law library, and some of the offices are still used. You can visit the courthouse on weekdays from 8 A.M. to 5 P.M. and weekends from 9 to 5. Free guided tours are given Friday at 10:30 A.M.

The Santa Barbara Historical Society Museum, at the corner of De la Guerra and Santa Barbara streets, houses many of the city's historical treasures. Representative of the old and new, the building is made of adobe bricks formed from soil at the site and is reinforced with modern steel.

One wing is devoted to the Mexican and Spanish periods of Santa Barbara's history and displays a carved statue of Saint Barbara from the Royal Presidio, fascinating old letters, early costumes, and relics of Richard Henry Dana's famous visits to the city, including a model of his brig, *Pilgrim*, and a portrait of its captain.

The museum, home of the Santa Barbara Historical Society, offers free admission. It is open afternoons except Monday; you can take a guided tour Wednesday and Sunday at 1:30 P.M.

Casa de Covarrubias and Historic Fremont Adobe are around the corner, at 715 Santa Barbara Street. The casa, built in 1817, hosted the last meeting of Congress under Mexican rule. Colonel Fremont made the adobe his headquarters after the American takeover in 1846.

The Rochin Adobe, at 820 Santa Barbara Street, is sheathed in clapboard as protection from the weather. Built of adobe salvaged from the Presidio ruins, it is a double house with two street entrances. Privately owned, it is not open to the public.

Lobero Theatre, at the corner of Anacapa and Canon Perdido, stands on the site of the city's first theater.

El Presidio de Santa Barbara State Historic Park (122 and 123 E. Canon Perdido) includes some of the city's oldest structures: the recently restored Padre's quarters, the Presidio chapel, El Cuartel, and La Caneda Adobe.

Founded in 1782, the Presidio was the fourth and last Spanish army post in California. El Cuartel—then soldiers' quarters—was built soon after the Presidio in the original quadrangle. Across the street from El Cuartel is La Caneda Adobe. This lovingly restored house contains both a private residence and the office for the Santa Barbara Trust for Historic Preservation.

The park, including exhibits and a museum shop in El Cuartel, is open weekdays from 9 A.M. to noon, and from 1 to 4 P.M.; weekend hours are noon to 4 P.M. The park is closed on major holidays.

The Hill-Carrillo Adobe (11 E. Carrillo Street) was built by Massachusetts-born Daniel Hill in 1826 for his Spanish bride. The most modern house of its day, it had wooden floors instead of the usual hard-baked clay. Now fully restored, it's open weekdays from 9 A.M. to 4 P.M.

(Continued on page 103)

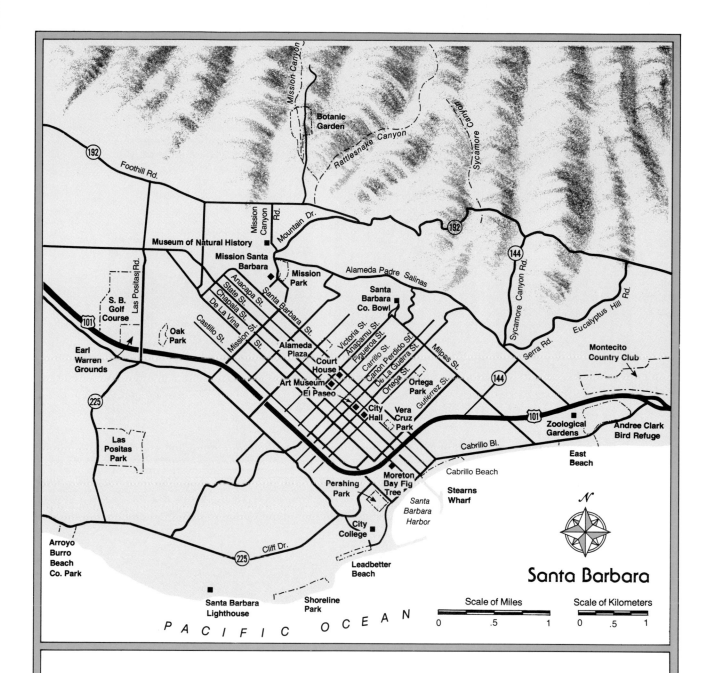

Major Points of Interest

Santa Barbara Court House (downtown) — Spanish-Moorish castle facade; historical murals; good city view from tower

El Paseo (downtown) — Mediterranean shopping arcade built in and around historic adobes; indoor and outdoor cafes

Mission Santa Barbara (Mission Canyon) — picturesque "Queen of Missions" still in continuous use by Franciscans

Museum of Natural History (just north of mission) — fascinating exhibits focusing on natural phenomena of the West

Santa Barbara Botanic Garden (1½ miles above mission) — indigenous California plants displayed in their natural settings

Moreton Bay Fig Tree (corner Chapala and Montecito streets)—one of the nation's largest trees, planted in 1877; branch spread of over 160 feet

Santa Barbara Zoological Gardens (overlooking waterfront) — children's park features zoo, playground, picnic area among landscaped grounds

Andree Clark Bird Refuge (waterfront) — preserve for geese, swans, migrant fowl; trails permit biking, hiking

SAVORING THE OUTDOORS
ranks as year-round activity in
Santa Barbara. Pedestrians stroll
downtown streets (left), eat at side-
walk restaurants (below), enjoy
splashes of color in El Paseo's
entryway (bottom).

. . . Continued from page 100

El Paseo (814 State Street), a picturesque shopping arcade reminiscent of old Spain, was built in and around the adobe home of the De la Guerra family. It was begun in 1819 by mission Indians, and a brick in the wall of the passageway bears the date of completion—1826. Casa de la Guerra, noted for its hospitality, was made famous in Dana's *Two Years Before the Mast* as the setting for a colorful Spanish wedding fiesta.

Some of the shops spill over into the Orena adobes next door. Here the antiques you see are for sale. Elsewhere in El Paseo you can find stores specializing in leather goods, candles, books, local pottery, and Mexican, Scandinavian, and Oriental imports. Art stores and galleries are particularly at home here. The El Paseo restaurant is a popular spot for full-scale lunch or dinner. For simpler daytime fare, the El Paseo Cafe offers an outdoor dining area.

Across the street is the plaza where the first City Council met in 1850 and where the first City Hall was located. During Fiesta Week, it becomes a colorful *mercado* (marketplace).

Mission Canyon

You can take many drives into the hills behind Santa Barbara, but one of the prettiest is Mission Canyon Road. It begins at the old mission and takes you north into the hills to the Museum of Natural History and Santa Barbara Botanic Garden. This "back country," a beautiful, semirural area on the slopes of the Santa Ynez Mountains, is separated from the city by 500-foot-high foothills known as "The Riviera."

The scenic drive along The Riviera on Alameda Padre Serra winds through a pleasant residential area (also location of the El Encanto Hotel), giving you a beautiful view of the city and the ocean. You can turn into some of the little canyons, but they're somewhat difficult to navigate. To return to town, take Gutierrez Street.

Mission Santa Barbara

Overlooking the city from a knoll at the end of Laguna Street sits the tenth in a long line of missions. Founded in 1786 by Father Fermin Lasuen, it is the only mission that has been continuously in the hands of the Franciscans.

Having a unique stone facade—the only California mission to display two similar towers—"the Queen of the Missions" is a popular subject for photographers. Design for the facade was copied from a Roman book on architecture written by Vitruvius in 27 B.C. (The book is still in the mission archives.) The strange mixture of classical and mission style was later retained when the face was rebuilt because of earthquake damage and wear.

The water system developed by the mission padres was so complete that part of it is still used by Santa Barbara's water company. You can see an Indian-built dam in the Botanic Garden.

Off the arcade corridor (the floor tiles were made in 1811) are three of the original rooms, one a primitive kitchen. The rooms and artifacts suggest some of the quality of mission life when the Franciscans were teaching the Indians not only religion and language but also agriculture and some 50 crafts.

Under huge pepper trees, the Moorish fountain flows into a stone laundry basin where Indian women once washed their clothes.

You can enter the old cemetery through a Roman archway with two real skulls and crossbones hanging above it, a common sight in Mexican churches.

The mission altar light has burned constantly since the mission was built. Still used daily as a parish church, the mission is open to the public from 9 A.M. to 5 P.M. Monday through Saturday, 1 to 5 P.M. on Sunday. The chapel, curio room, and library contain relics of the mission days. Self-guided tours cost 50 cents for adults and are free to children under 16.

Museum of Natural History

You'll find this museum just 2 blocks north of Mission Santa Barbara, at 2559 Puesta del Sol Road; it's set amid 2 acres of wooded ground. Displays cover a range of topics, but the focus is on natural phenomena of the West, including regional plant and animal life, geology, and prehistoric Indian culture. There are well-conceived exhibits, comprehensible even to young children; some perform mechanically at the push of a button.

Museum hours are 9 A.M. to 5 P.M. Monday through Saturday, 10 A.M. to 5 P.M. Sunday and holidays. Tours are offered on Sunday at 2 P.M. The museum is closed on major holidays. Call (805) 682-4711 for further information.

Nearby Gladwin Planetarium has closed circuit television, enabling several people to view the skies together through the large telescope. Call (805) 682-4334 for admission rates and program information.

Santa Barbara Botanic Garden

Indigenous California plants, from wildflowers to giant redwoods, grow in their natural settings on 65 acres in Mission Canyon, just 1½ miles above the mission.

Over 5 miles of trails wind through canyon, desert, channel island, arroyo, and redwood sections along historic Mission Creek, and past the old dam and aqueduct built in 1806 to supply water for the mission. The History Trail takes you back to the days when the local Indians had to support themselves from the land, using plants for food, drink, soap, medicine, and household needs. Self-guided, the trail begins and ends near the Information Office. Plan about an hour for a leisurely walk.

Spring and summer offer the most colorful tours of the garden. Flowering shrubs, poolside plants, and brilliant wildflowers blaze in the meadow section; the ceanothus (mountain lilac) flowers white and blue; and the desert section comes alive with blooming cacti, yuccas, and wildflowers.

The Botanic Garden, at 1212 Mission Canyon Road, is open all year from 8 A.M. to dusk. You can take a guided tour on Thursday at 10:30 A.M. Admission is free.

Another Santa Barbara park of interest to gardeners is Franceschi Park on Mission Ridge Road, high on the crest of The Riviera.

Attractions around Town

As you drive the scenic route around Santa Barbara you'll pass through the Montecito and Hope Ranch areas. These rank high among the country's most luxurious residential communities. Both areas have private country clubs and golf courses. North of the Hope Ranch section, campers will find an RV park; near the beach, in the Carpenteria area, is another camping facility with complete camper hookups.

Earl Warren Showgrounds

Horses and horse shows are very popular in Santa Barbara. Hardly a month goes by without an amateur local or regional horse show. The Earl Warren Showgrounds, Las Positas Road at U.S. 101, is home for Santa Barbara's National Horse and Flower Show, held annually in mid-July. This top-rated event combines equestrian excellence with entertainment and 22,000 feet of garden displays. Another popular event is the annual San Fernando Arabian Horse Association Show held Memorial Day weekend. This colorful activity is free for spectators.

Moreton Bay fig tree

The Moreton Bay fig, at the corner of Chapala and Montecito streets, is the largest tree of its kind in the nation. Native to Australia, it was planted by a little girl in 1877. Today, it's believed that 10,000 people could stand in its shade at noon. Measurements made in 1970 indicated a branch spread of 160 feet.

Fernald House and Trussel-Winchester Adobe

Multigabled, 14-room Fernald House (414 W. Montecito Street) is a Victorian mansion handsomely furnished and accessorized in fitting style. The lovely stairway and carvings throughout the house attest to yesteryear's craftsmanship. The adobe next door was built in 1854 with timbers from a wrecked ship and bricks. Both houses are owned and maintained by the Santa Barbara Historical Society. They're open on Sunday only, from 2 to 4 P.M.; there's a small admission fee.

Carriage house

The vintage surreys, hansoms, and buggies of the Carriage Museum look their best for the Old Spanish Days parade in August—their annual chance to show they're still street-worthy. Decorated to a turn, carriages carry dignitaries along the line of march.

The rest of the year the venerable vehicles are on display in the museum at 128 Castillo Street, a block inland from Cabrillo Boulevard. Look sharp for the building; it sits back from the street next to a field. You can visit the old-timers without charge any Sunday from 2 to 4 P.M., except the Sunday before the parade. The Sunday after the parade, the museum holds an open house from 1 to 4 P.M.

At the Waterfront

It is a surprise to many people that Santa Barbara has a southern exposure to the sea. In fact, the California coastline runs almost due west from Ventura to Point Conception, the magic dividing point for California's coast. South of Conception, the climate is Mediterranean; north of it, waters grow progressively cooler. Santa Barbara is as Mediterranean in her waters as in her architecture.

In spite of Navy missiles to port (Point Mugu) and Air Force missiles to starboard (Vandenberg Air Force Base on Point Conception), Santa Barbara boasts one of the most alluring stretches of developed coastline that you will find. Miles of wide, gently curving beaches are lined with palms. Swimmers, surfers, picnickers, scuba divers, fishermen, and grunion-hunters enjoy it all, except in a few places where oil rigs take over.

The main pier, Stearns Wharf, could be called an extension of State Street, the city's main thoroughfare. Rebuilt after a fire several years ago, it offers shops, restaurants, and good ocean views.

Cabrillo Boulevard, a palm-lined drive along the ocean, is especially popular with strollers and cyclists. To the west of the wharf, West Cabrillo Boulevard is lined with attractive motels, nearly all with swimming pools and many with balconies facing the yacht harbor. Nearby are a municipal swimming pool, a lovely shaded park, and—west of the yacht harbor and breakwater—another stretch of beach. The municipal pool, Los Banos del Mar, is open all year; there's also a wading pool.

The picturesque 92-acre yacht harbor, protected by a long breakwater, shelters the local fishing fleet, as well as hundreds of pleasure craft.

East of the wharf, the curving beach extends to the Andree Clark Bird Refuge at the end of East Cabrillo Boulevard.

Sunday art activity on the Santa Barbara waterfront is so lively that rows of canvases and sculpture stretch as far as a mile along East Cabrillo Boulevard. At this "Arts and Crafts Show" you'll find pottery, leather craft, metalwork, handmade clothing, and jewelry, in addition to paintings. Open only to local artists, the nonrestrictive, unjuried show is extremely popular.

Andree Clark Bird Refuge

A landscaped preserve along the beach protects geese, swans, and other fowl. There are trails for biking and benches where one can sit and photograph, or just observe tame birds. Bird feeding is discouraged.

Just east of the refuge, turn right on Channel Drive to see the lovely gardens of Marriott's Santa Barbara Biltmore Resort and the exclusive Montecito district.

Zoological Gardens

Situated on a hilltop on East Cabrillo Boulevard is a garden of play and adventure formerly known as Child's Estate. Overlooking the ocean and the refuge, this park has a charming garden zoo, playground, and picnic area.

It is being developed by the community of Santa Barbara, which also oversees the displays.

Most animals at the zoo meet youngsters at eye level. From lacy white strutting peacocks to ruffled little ducklings swimming with their mothers in pathside ponds, the animals seem at once natural and friendly. Their names are often presented in a childlike scrawl on signposts. From the zoo entrance, a 24-gauge miniature train takes you on a tour past the adjoining Andree Clark Bird Refuge and fresh-water lagoon.

Athletic and popular seals show off in a sealarium with viewing portholes for visitors of any height. At the Rancher's Pet Park, children delight in mingling with tame animals—small deer, domestic and African pygmy goats, cows, and pigs.

Besides Susi the Chimp, Herman the Llama, the alligator, owls, bobcats, and the rest of the community, the park also contains a wild west playground of rocky hideouts, a covered wagon and tepee, and a rest area for parents. The fountain, pergola, and picnic area are peaceful stops.

The zoo is open daily except Monday from 10 A.M. to 5 P.M. Admission is moderate; the train ride and parking are extra.

The beaches

Along the 70-mile stretch of coastline running due east between Point Conception and Ventura are a number of state and county parks centered around beaches characterized by a lack of strong winds and predominantly warm waters.

Jalama Beach, just north of Point Conception, is the most isolated and uninhabited of the area's beaches; no supplies are available. It is the only point of public access to the Point Conception fishing grounds. Rough surf prevents swimming or boating; however, the beach is reached by a very scenic road. Rock hunting is good here, and Jalama is probably the southernmost driftwood beach along the Pacific Coast.

Between Point Conception and Santa Barbara are five beach parks: Gaviota State Park (public fishing pier, boat rentals, swimming, campgrounds, trailer sites, picnic and camp fees); Refugio Beach (swimming, surf fishing, camping, picnic tables, picnic and camp fees); El Capitan Beach (campgrounds, trailer sites, boat rentals, boat launching ramp, picnic and camp fees); popular Goleta Beach (sheltered cove for boats, electric boat hoist, fishing pier, swimming, picnicking); and Arroyo Burro Beach (surf fishing, swimming, picnicking) at the outskirts of Santa Barbara.

The long beach area in Santa Barbara proper is open to the public, except for a few spots that are reserved for occupants of some oceanfront hotels.

Carpinteria State Beach, just off U.S. 101 at Carpinteria (campgrounds, fishing pier, boat launching ramp, food concession, picnic and camp fees), calls itself "the world's safest beach." A long, sandy slope extends into deep water with no riptides.

Emma Wood State Beach is about 3 miles north of Ventura (campgrounds, surf fishing, swimming). The last beach in this area is San Buenaventura State Beach, facing the city of Ventura. Ventura's beaches are wide, sandy, and inviting. Walkways line the main section of the city beach, offering fine ocean views.

Water sports

For many visitors, the activities centered around the ocean are the main attraction of Santa Barbara.

Surfing and snorkeling are good a few miles north or south along the shore from Santa Barbara. You will find clear water for snorkeling and reefs that push the mild, incoming swells up into respectable, long-lasting, diagonal waves that are good for surfing. Some of the best water is at Arroyo Burro and Leadbetter beaches, both west of the breakwater; they're rough but inviting.

Boating centers around the yacht harbor. A concrete launching ramp (fee required, $1 in quarters) and a large parking area for boat trailers at the foot of Bath Street are provided. You can rent motor boats or sailboats in any of several classes.

Water-skiing takeoff area is the beach immediately to the east (lee side) of Stearns Wharf. After launching your boat at the yacht harbor ramp, you usually do your skiing between the wharf and East Beach. You can stay inside the natural breakwater formed by offshore kelp beds if the water is too choppy outside.

Offshore fishing is about as productive here as anywhere else along the California coast. Party boats usually head for Santa Cruz, largest of the Channel Islands, and anchor in a relatively sheltered zone. At a day's end, with ordinary luck, you should have more than enough rockfish.

Some charter boats are available at the yacht harbor for pursuit of albacore, big-game tuna, marlin, and sailfish. But for a day or a half-day of less ambitious deep-sea angling at minimum cost, you can go to Sea Landing at the foot of Bath Street and Cabrillo Boulevard. Here you will find a harbor and an offshore excursion boat. All equipment you will need and a temporary California fishing license are available.

No license is necessary for pier fishing. Still-fishing with shrimp for bait may produce a nice haul of tasty perch.

The Channel Islands

Lying south of Santa Barbara across the Santa Barbara Channel are the Channel Islands. A clear day will reward you with a glimpse of them from the mainland; otherwise, only their mountainous outlines are hazily prominent in the mist.

The islands are in fact the tops of submerged mountains—possibly the continuation of the Santa Monica range. To ensure the preservation of rare indigenous wildlife, five of the Channel Islands were designated a national park (the nation's 40th) in 1980. The waters surrounding the park were subsequently declared a national marine sanctuary.

The residents of "America's Galapagos" include cormorants, sea lions, and California brown pelicans; trail systems and boat tours give you the chance to observe these and other fauna and flora. Plant enthusiasts won't be disappointed with the island's unique trees, shrubs, and wildflowers. The vivid blooms of the giant coreopsis steal the show in late winter, visible from the mainland and far out to sea as splashes of brilliant yellow.

Park headquarters and the visitor center are at 1901 Spinnaker Drive in Ventura harbor; hours are 8 A.M. to 5 P.M. daily except major holidays. Call (805) 644-8262 for information, including specifics on transportation and primitive camping. Reservations for transportation arrangements are strongly encouraged. Prepare for the islands' variable weather by dressing in layers; rubber-soled shoes improve boat footing.

Around Santa Barbara

The leisurely atmosphere and relatively slow pace you find in Santa Barbara also extend into much of the surrounding countryside. Even when U.S. 101 and the ocean beaches are crowded with vacationers, just a few minutes away you can enjoy peaceful back-country driving or lakeside camping. In this inland area, rolling hills and soft meadows dominate the landscape, and quiet little communities fit the slow tempo.

Goleta Valley

One quick and easy trip is to the beautiful modern campus of the University of California at Santa Barbara, located 10 miles west of town near Goleta. Follow U.S. 101 west; signs direct you to the seaside campus. Biking is a popular activity in Goleta, and you can easily find a bicycle to rent. Bike trails are marked; an easy ride will take you past many historic landmarks, the Santa Barbara airport, the marshland of Goleta Slough, along the beach, and through the college, despite signs to the contrary; ask at the gate for instructions.

Stow House, heart of a once vast ranch, was built in 1872. This gracious country home, outbuildings, and gardens are now maintained by the Goleta Valley Historical Society. Wide verandas and gingerbread detailing adorn the outside; inside, the rooms are furnished with period antiques, including a square grand piano, a portable piano that folds up to trunk-size, and (in a child's room) an old-fashioned doll house. You can wander through the parklike gardens, a carriage house, and a bunkhouse containing a collection of Chumash Indian artifacts. From U.S. 101, take the Los Carneros Road exit and drive north toward the mountains for 3 blocks. The house is open most weekends from 2 to 4 P.M.

Stow Grove Park, on La Patera Road, was formerly a part of the Stow Ranch. Now the 13-acre park has picnic tables and a barbecue area in a grove of redwood trees, unusual for Southern California.

Dos Pueblos Orchid Company is one of the world's largest growers of cymbidium orchids. It is located off U.S. 101 at Ranchos Dos Pueblos (15 miles north of the airport). Visitors are welcome from 8:30 A.M. to 4 P.M. Sunday through Thursday.

Hope Ranch Park, just northwest of Santa Barbara (take La Cumbre exit from U.S. 101), is reached by another pleasant drive through a luxury residential development that was formerly a great ranch.

Ojai Valley

For a pleasant lake and mountain loop trip from Santa Barbara to Ventura, or as a byway en route to Los Angeles, the Ojai Valley has much to offer. The moon-shaped valley is well insulated by its altitude and by the Topa and Sulphur mountains against the fog, wind, and smog that sometimes bother the nearby coast. Some say that Ojai (pronounced O-high) is the Indian word for "The Nest," a name given the valley because of its protected location. Coming from Santa Barbara, leave U.S. 101 at Casitas Pass Road (which joins State Highway 150 to the valley) for a drive through land dotted with orchards, streams, and ranches. Among California valleys, Ojai ranks high as a year-round resort.

Lake Casitas, west of Ojai, is a favorite spot for camping, boating, and fishing (swimming and water-skiing are prohibited). These activities are located at the upper end of the reservoir where boat rentals are available at the landing. You can fish or explore the many inlets and coves while you enjoy the shelter and scenery of the surrounding mountains. Campsites are numerous and spacious, though few are tree shaded; trailers are permitted. Day-use and overnight camping fees are small.

An observation point at Lake Casitas Dam on the southeast end of the lake is reached from State Highway 33 or Santa Ana Road on Casitas Vista Road.

Ojai has changed very little over the years. It manages to preserve a pleasant atmosphere of the early Spanish days in some of its buildings and maintains a certain easy manner in its way of life. A shopping arcade with a facade of arches and the post office bell tower distinguish the main street. Civic Center Park in the heart of town is the hub of the community's active life. Cultural activities, arts and crafts, and special events are nurtured in Ojai. The Ojai Musical Festival in May is the highlight of the year. A colorful Folk Dance Festival is staged every other year. Ojai Artists' Art Sunday is an extremely popular outdoor event. The inns, motels, and fine restaurants of this quiet town are inviting. Resort facilities of the Ojai Valley Inn include an 18-hole golf course. Ojai is also a leading tennis center.

Many miles of wild and rugged mountain terrain stretch beyond this serene little valley, noted for its air of contagious leisureliness. For automobile explorers, there are creeks, campsites, and places to picnic. North on State 33, Wheeler Gorge at 1,000 feet is the largest and most popular of public camping parks. You'll pass scenic Matilija Dam. Farther north is a back road to Piedra Blanca, a spectacular outcrop of large, white sandstone rocks. On State 150 going east, several pretty little canyons—Bear, Sisar, Wilsie, and Horn—nip into the mountains, and side roads follow their streams for only a few miles. At Dennison Park, barbecue pits and tables are shaded by tall oaks. Here is perhaps as nice a place as you can find for a picnic with a view.

Ventura & the Santa Clara Valley

Bypassed by the freeway, Ventura is well worth a stop. It offers miles of beaches and a great pier for fishing, and it is the cast-off spot for sightseeing trips to the Channel Islands. From October to March, the Monarch butterflies winter around Ventura, coloring the sky orange.

SOLVANG'S *Danish architecture (left) and Lompoc's colorful flower fields (below) invite motorists to drive back roads around Santa Barbara.*

Ventura also provides a base for exploring the Ojai Valley and the Santa Clara Valley. It's an easy day's drive to wander through the back country.

Ventura. The Visitors and Convention Bureau (785 S. Seward Avenue) publishes "mini-tours" of the area with good maps and points of interest. Plazas, plantings, and a new downtown museum make this a good place to start a walking tour. The handsome Ventura County Historical Museum at 100 E. Main Street houses Chumash Indian and Spanish relics, plus displays on the surrounding oil wells and agriculture. Hours are 10 A.M. to 5 P.M., Tuesday through Sunday.

City Hall is also part of the tour. Built in 1912, it's a Roman-Doric wedding cake of a building, waiting for the reception to begin. You can explore its cavernous interior weekdays from 8 A.M. to 5 P.M. Visible from the freeway, the courthouse is 1 block off Main Street at the end of California Street.

The 2-hour walking tour also includes Mission San Buenaventura, which appears a modest, graceful lady-in-waiting to the Queen of Missions in Santa Barbara. Next door, archeologists are digging for mission artifacts, and a pleasant little park centers around the restored mission aqueduct and filtration house.

Two historic adobes are the Ortega Adobe downtown and the Olivas Adobe on Olivas Park Drive (en route to the harbor).

Picnickers head for tree-shaded Plaza Park at Santa Clara and Chestnut streets, or the beach promenade at the south end of California Street. (The promenade and Surfer's Point Park at its west end are good places for vicarious surfing.)

Down at the harbor you'll find sportfishing boats, restaurants, and the Channel Islands National Park headquarters. From here you can take the regularly scheduled excursions to Anacapa Island.

Oxnard. South of Ventura on State Highway 1, Oxnard began life around the turn of the century as a sugar beet processing center. Little trace of the farming community remains. Today, Oxnard has a strong U.S. Naval stamp because of the installations that dominate so much of the shore south of Ventura at Port Hueneme and Point Mugu. Though inland from the sea, Oxnard has easy access to beaches. Closest is McGrath State Beach, 7 miles south on Channel Islands Boulevard. At Port Hueneme, in Building 99 at the Naval Construction Battalion Center, you can visit the Seabee Museum, which houses numerous cultural artifacts from the countries where Seabees serve. The free museum is open from 8 A.M. to 4:30 P.M. weekdays, from 9 A.M. on Saturday, and on Sunday afternoons.

At Channel Islands Harbor, charter companies operate cruise and fishing boats and also offer regularly scheduled cruises to the Channel Islands. A free public boat launching ramp lies at Victoria Avenue, just south of Channel Islands Boulevard. Colorful Fisherman's Wharf invites browsers, shoppers, and diners to the water's edge.

Santa Paula. In the Santa Clara Valley, at the junction of State Highways 150 and 126, this little town is the shipping center for the valley. Here, lemons and oil compete for space. The valley had one of California's earliest oil booms, a fact memorialized in the California Oil Museum (Tenth and Main streets).

TOURING A NEW WINE COUNTRY

Pack a picnic and meander through the state's newest major premium wine district, just off U.S. Highway 101 within Santa Barbara and San Luis Obispo counties. The district extends about 100 miles south from San Miguel (site of a mission and some of the earliest vineyards) to the Santa Ynez Valley (location of Solvang and two more missions, Santa Ines and La Purisima Concepcion). Some 50 vineyards stretch across almost 10,000 acres. Use the list below to get started; you're sure to make your own discoveries along the way. For further details, see the *Sunset* book *Guide to California's Wine Country*.

You can start your tour going either north or south. The best towns in which to assemble picnic supplies are Santa Barbara, Solvang, and San Luis Obispo.

• Santa Barbara Winery (202 Anacapa Street, Santa Barbara)—open 10 A.M. to 5 P.M. daily.
• Santa Ynez Valley Winery (343 N. Refugio Road, Santa Ynez)— daily tours and tasting, 10 A.M.

to 4 P.M., groups by appointment. Telephone (805) 688-8381.
• J. Carey Cellars (3 miles north of Solvang on State 246 at 1711 Alamo Pintado Road)—open for tours and tasting daily, 10 A.M. to 4 P.M.
• Firestone Vineyard (Zaca Station Road north of Los Olivos)—10 A.M. to 4 P.M. daily except Sunday; tours, tasting, sales room.
• Zaca Mesa Winery (9 miles northeast of Buellton, on Zaca Station/Foxen Canyon Roads) —guided tours and tasting daily from 10 A.M. to 4 P.M.
• York Mountain Winery (State Highway 46 from Morro Bay to Paso Robles)—10 A.M. to 5 P.M. daily; restored century-old winery with artifacts.
• Hoffman Mountain Ranch (tasting room at 24th Street exit in Paso Robles); winery visits by appointment; ask at tasting room, open daily 11 A.M. to 6 P.M.
• Estrella River Winery (7 miles east of Paso Robles on State 46)—open daily from 10 A.M. to 5 P.M. Gift shop and picnic sites available.

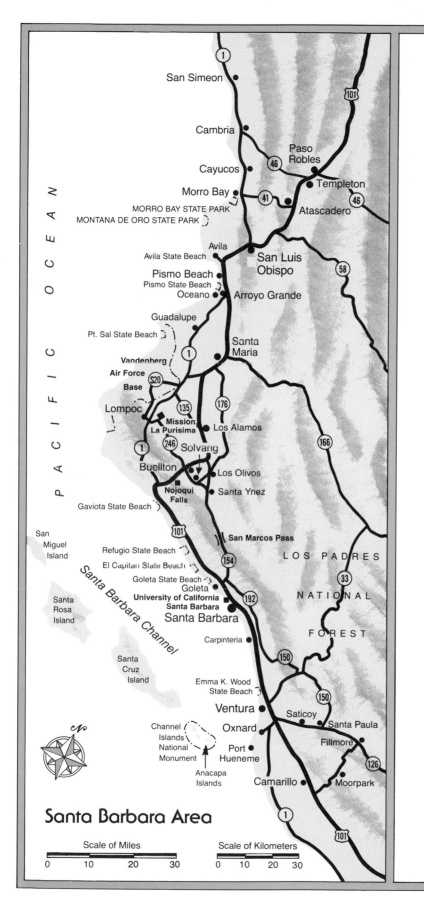

Major Points of Interest

Hearst Castle (San Simeon)—famous mountaintop mansion now historic monument; guided tours of buildings

Paso Robles—gateway town to the wine country of San Luis Obispo-Santa Barbara counties. Take a walk back through time at Mission San Miguel Arcangel

Morro Bay—atmospheric seaside resort-fishing town dominated by Morro Rock; sportfishing and clamming popular here

San Luis Obispo—great place to look at an old California city; Path of History walk past mission, adobes, Ah Louis store

Pismo Beach—California's largest expanse of sand dunes; camping available in nearby Oceano; clamming

Lompoc—site where over half of the world's flower seeds are produced. Tour Vandenberg Air Force Base and the museum of Chumash Indian artifacts

Mission La Purisima (west of Buellton)—restored mission, now historic park; original crafts displays; large gardens

Solvang (Santa Ynez Valley)—Danish village complete with windmills. Don't miss bakeries; visit Mission Santa Ines, wineries

Nojoqui Falls (near Solvang)—lovely 164-foot cascade. Enjoy a picnic or hike in the county park named after these graceful falls

University of California at Santa Barbara (Goleta Valley)—seaside campus 10 miles west of Santa Barbara. Visit Storke Tower's magnificent carillon

Ojai Valley—pastoral back country drives through ranches and resorts; Lake Casitas provides fishing, boating, camping; town of Ojai offers music and arts festivals

Ventura—beach city with mission and original adobes; starting point for boat trips to Channel Islands and into Santa Clara Valley; home of condors, citrus, oil wells. Visit California Oil Museum in Santa Paula

Oxnard—access to beaches (closest one is McGrath State Beach). View Seabee Museum in Port Hueneme's Naval Construction Battalion Center

Channel Islands (offshore)—take a boat trip to islands (Anacapa and Santa Barbara) from Oxnard and Ventura; now national park

BOATS ROCK at anchor as afternoon fog slowly dissipates over hills around Morro Bay harbor.

Condor country. Fillmore, east on State 126, is the entrance point into the Sespe Wildlife Area of Los Padres National Forest, traditional home for North America's largest land bird, the condor. Called "thunderbird" by the Indians, this endangered species once could be seen soaring effortlessly over the valley. But man has invaded the condor's domain—and since these birds lay only one egg every 2 years and may abandon their young at the approach of humans, their numbers have diminished rapidly. In hopes of preventing the condor's extinction, the government has set out to capture the birds and transport them to a controlled environment.

Santa Ynez Valley

Snuggled between the Santa Ynez and San Rafael mountains in back of Santa Barbara is the Santa Ynez Valley, a land of rich green hills and multicolored flower fields, of cattle and horse ranges, and of stagecoach towns and missions. Ideal wine-growing conditions have turned the area into the "Napa Valley of the South." Tours and tasting are available at many of the valley wineries.

Since its discovery by the Portola expedition in 1769, this valley has been known as cattle country. Modern ranchers were preceded by Indians, padres, and Mexican rancheros. Today, large ranchos from Spanish land grants retain their names, if not their original size, and the *Rancheros Visitadores* (by invitation) symbolically perpetuate the old Spanish custom of helping neighboring ranches at roundup time. Each May this dedicated group of horsemen starts off on a 4-day ride.

At the western end of this unspoiled pastoral valley, where its river meets the sea, you can see the rising missiles at Vandenberg Air Force Base. Plan a loop trip through the Santa Ynez Valley from Santa Barbara along State Highways 154 and 246 to U.S. 101 for a pleasant day.

Time really hasn't stood still along State 154, but the back roads wander among the hills in gentle contrast to the rush and noise of U.S. 101. Climbing through historic San Marcos Pass, once the stagecoach route north, you'll have a panoramic view out over the foothills to the ocean.

Lake Cachuma. About 11 miles beyond the San Marcos Summit, you'll come to the entrance of Lake Cachuma Recreation Area. This 9,000-acre county park centers around Lake Cachuma, a reservoir created when a dam was built across the Santa Ynez River in 1953.

California live oaks and native white oaks shade the grassy camping and trailer spaces. There are fire pits, tables, and shower and laundry facilities. A store, filling station, snack bar, and post office are inside the entry gate.

In winter when the water cools, the lake is stocked with fingerling rainbow trout and Kamloops trout from British Columbia. As on most Southern California lakes, angling slows down during the heat of summer. Cool spring and fall months provide the best fishing. Tackle and boat rentals are available.

No swimming or water-skiing is allowed here because the lake supplies drinking water for Santa Barbara. But three swimming pools are open from April through October.

Lake Cachuma Recreation Area is open all year, 24 hours a day, and a ranger is on duty most of the time. There is a daily admission and parking fee, plus an overnight camping fee. Crowded in the summer, the park takes no camping reservations, so plan to arrive early and make a day of it.

The little valley towns. On a short loop trip from Santa Ynez to Los Olivos and Solvang, you'll see a picturesque area affected only slightly by California's growth.

Santa Ynez, at one time the valley's busiest community, is now slower paced. Residents have deliberately retained the high-front buildings and Old West atmosphere, even adding a "Western Town" complex. The white-steepled church at the corner of Tivola and Lincoln streets, built in 1897, is one of the oldest church edifices in the valley. On Sagunto Street you can visit an historical museum (open weekend afternoons).

Los Olivos was known as a stage stop for the famous Butterfield Stage Lines. Today, the old stagecoach inn, Mattei's Tavern, built in 1886, is a State Historic Landmark.

Ballard, established in 1880, was the first settlement in the valley. You'll still see some of the old homes and the Little Red Schoolhouse founded in 1883. A beautiful drive in the foothills from here is out Alamo Pintado Road.

Solvang. "Sunny valley" is the translation of the Danish name Solvang. In this town that reflects its Scandinavian heritage, windmills are prominent features, and the old-world appearance of homes and businesses comes from thatched, aged copper or steep tile roofs with traditional storks perched on top, stained-glass windows, and high dormers. More recent additions of gas lights and cobblestone walks set the scene for residents walking in *traeskos* (wooden shoes).

At first glance the town suggests a quaint environment manufactured for tourists. Then you discover it possesses the chief element of a true Danish commu-

nity—real Danes and their descendants. The village was established in 1911 next to Mission Santa Ines as a place to educate immigrants from Denmark. It acquired its Danish facade (over its Spanish architecture) only after visitors began to discover it as a cultural enclave and source of European foods and goods.

For 2 days in mid-September, colorful Danish Days bring out costumes in Solvang; you'll see the Danish flag flying everywhere.

Mission Santa Ines, another of the old missions still in use, is located a short distance east of the main business district. Founded in 1804, it is one of the best restored of all the missions. You can tour the museum, church, and cemetery daily.

Shopping in Solvang leans heavily toward imports from Denmark and other northern European countries, with an emphasis on gourmet and delicatessen foods, traditional and contemporary housewares, toys, apparel (especially shoes), and things that can be classified only as gifts. These days you will also find imports from other parts of the world.

But the shops that really made Solvang famous are the bakeries, many of which serve pastries and coffee. If you visit some of the bakeries in the morning when activity is light, you may be able to watch the preparation and baking processes. Shops open by midmorning but close up tight at 5 P.M.

Atterdag Road is worth seeking out. There you will find Bethania Church, patterned after a typical rural Danish church. Inside you'll see an interesting, hand-carved wooden pulpit. A scale model of a fully rigged ship hangs from the ceiling, facing the altar—a common tradition in Scandinavian churches. Farther along on Atterdag Road near the Solvang Lutheran Home is a famous chiming wind harp.

Buellton. Three miles west of Solvang is Buellton, a hospital town with the curious distinction of being the "home of split pea soup" (a specialty of Andersen's Restaurant). At the crossroads of U.S. 101 and State 246, Buellton is the gateway to the valley for freeway drivers, only minutes from points of interest in all directions.

Look for La Purisima Concepcion Mission nestled in a valley 15 miles west of Buellton. If you can visit just one mission, especially with children, this should be it. Carefully restored in the 1930s, it's the site of a colorful fiesta every May.

Lompoc. Long, rainless summers in the Lompoc Valley help to produce over half of the flower seeds grown in the world. One of spring and summer's most beautiful spectacles occurs here beginning in May when several thousand acres of flowers bloom, turning the landscape into a rainbow of color. Hues of row after row of sweet peas, poppies, calendulas, nasturtiums, and larkspurs compete for your attention into September.

Fields are not open for public browsing because the flowers are grown commercially for seed, but you can see most of them from the road. Maps showing field locations are available from the Chamber of Commerce at 119 E. Cypress Street. The annual Flower Festival in late June includes a flower show, blossom parade, and a guided tour of the fields.

In the museum at Cypress and H streets, you can see an extensive exhibit of Chumash Indian artifacts. The museum is open weekend afternoons; admission is free.

Nojoqui Falls. One of the most graceful waterfalls in all California is the highlight of the scenic drive along U.S. 101 between the coast and Solvang. You leave the freeway about 5 miles north of Gaviota Pass on a road marked "To Nojoqui Falls County Park." The 2-mile drive traverses choice countryside of green fields and native oaks. From the north, go to Solvang and then turn south on Alisal Road. It's 6.5 miles.

From the parking lot, a short walk on a woodsy path along a clear creek brings you to the waterfall, which is usually at its best in late winter and early spring—it generally dries up in summer.

Up the Coast

Following El Camino Real (U.S. 101) northward adds even more memorable dimensions to your travel in Southern California. It's easy to see the Spanish and Indian influence on this part of California—between Los Angeles and San Francisco—when the map spells out such musical names as Guadalupe, Santa Maria, Oceano, Nipomo, Arroyo Grande, San Luis Obispo, Morro Bay, Cayucos, and Cambria. You'll drive through valleys, pastures, and (on side trips) along the ocean-front.

Sleepy Nipomo (off U.S. 101) in its heyday was considerably larger than now-bustling Santa Maria. Today most of the original buildings are gone, having fallen victim to fire or removal to the larger town. One exception is the Dana house, once home for the famous Dana family, original settlers in the area.

The freeway by-passes most of the historical and recreational spots. To see these, it's better to take to the back roads. Following State Highway 166 west from Santa Maria to Guadalupe (on State 1), you pass through more large flower seed farms. Countryside tours take place from May to September.

Pismo Beach and nearby coast

State 1 is the back entrance to the home of the Pismo clam. The broad, surf-swept arc of the bay provides an ideal environment for clams. But unfortunately for these creatures, the shore is too accessible to clam-loving humans. As a result, the greater part of the beds has been made a preserve. Only the north end of the state park, north of Oceano, is now open to digging. But that is still the main reason visitors come to these pleasant towns and their wide and level beaches.

Adventure-seeking dune buggy riders also congregate in the area, particularly on the July 4th and Labor Day weekends. Most people bring their own vehicles; you can rent a ride at one of several spots along the beach.

Pismo State Beach, which has some 6 miles of shoreline, runs south from the town of Pismo Beach through Oceano and on into the north end of one of California's best and largest expanses of sand dunes. Shifting sands often overrun the camping area, but the dunes make the park special. Here you can picnic, hike, climb, or slither up and down the slopes.

Public automobile entrances give access to the beach. One is from Oceano, a once-aspiring seaside resort of the Victorian era. A couple of gingerbread houses

remain—one set incongruously amidst a mobile home park.

At the north end of the park, in the town of Pismo Beach, is a pier. Fish can be caught from it, and so can party boats for deep sea fishing. You will also find the necessary equipment and information for clam digging; there's good activity in the winter.

Avila Beach nestles within the north arc of San Luis Obispo Bay. Along the beach front is a small park, organized for active recreation. Water along the shore in this cove is warm, always above 60°F. and frequently into the low 70° range, ideal for ocean swimming. Facilities include a fishing pier, picnic tables, fire rings, charter boats, launching ramp, and rental concession for salty gear.

San Luis Bay Inn, with golf course and tennis courts, is set among scenic hill country. It's a lovely drive from U.S. 101 to Avila Beach; a freeway exit leads to the country road that runs to the beach.

San Luis Obispo

Cradled in a small valley with the Santa Lucia Mountains forming a gentle backdrop, San Luis Obispo is the county seat and center of a vast grain, livestock, poultry, and dairy region. The city grew up around Mission San Luis Obispo de Tolosa, established in 1772.

California State Polytechnic University, which has the largest undergraduate agricultural division in the West, is situated on rolling hills overlooking the city. Its Spanish-style and contemporary buildings spread over a 2,850-acre campus, attractively landscaped with tropical and semitropical plants and trees, some of them rare.

State 1 and U.S. 101 separate in San Luis Obispo, and from this point you can explore the Santa Lucia Mountains or follow the coastline north to Morro Bay and fabulous San Simeon.

Exploring the town. From the visitor's point of view, perhaps the best thing to happen to San Luis Obispo was to have a freeway relieve the city of downtown highway traffic. If you're just passing through town, your most lasting impression will be the "pink palace" (Madonna Inn), southwest of the main business district. It's worth a stop just to see the lobby; overnighters have a choice of rooms varying from the Safari Room to the Cave Suite. It's wise to reserve in advance, as the hotel is usually fully booked.

If you detour into the city, though, you'll discover one of the most surprising showcases of California history on the coast. Starting with the Spanish era, nearly every period and contributing culture, including the Chinese, is represented in the architecture. Many of the nostalgic remnants are lived in or nicely adapted to present-day use.

San Luis is livelier than you might expect a museum town to be. Exploring is made more meaningful by a *Path of History*. You walk (or drive) a route marked by a line painted in the street. With no short cuts, the walk is a little more than 2 miles and takes about 1½ hours. A free brochure, available at the County Museum (corner of Broad and Monterey streets) or from the Chamber of Commerce (1039 Chorro Street), describes about 20 stops on the way.

Among the high points are Mission San Luis Obispo, the San Luis Obispo County Historical Museum (696 Monterey Street), and the 1874 Ah Louis store (800 Palm Street). The store still sells herbs and general merchandise; in times past, it also served as bank and post office for numerous Chinese railroad workers.

In contrast to the old Dallidet Adobe and gardens, on Pacific and Santa Rosa streets is the still-modern building (now a medical clinic) designed by Frank Lloyd Wright. Keep an eye out for other discoveries along the route.

Mission San Luis Obispo. The city grew around this church—the first mission built with a tile roof. Located at Chorro and Monterey streets, the restored building is today both a parish church and a historical museum. Cal Poly students designed the attractively landscaped plaza between the mission and the creek. Footbridges cross the creek to shops and restaurants.

Following State 1 north

The attractive seaside resort-fishing town of Morro Bay spreads along the eastern shore of the estuary that gives it its name. Some travelers think of Morro Bay only as a stopover point, but this recreation area, 12 miles west of San Luis Obispo on State 1, is well worth the consideration of vacation planners or weekend sightseers. Motels and seafood restaurants ring the waterfront; a steam-wheeler paddles around the harbor for 1½-hour cruises.

The one prominent landmark that attracts your attention as Morro Bay comes into sight is high, rounded Morro Rock, looming 576 feet above the ocean just offshore from town. Unfortunately, distracting smoke stacks share the scene just inshore from the great rock. The crown-shaped rock was named by the explorer Juan Cabrillo in 1542. You can drive over a causeway from the beach area north of town to the rock.

Fishing and clamming are good. Shore fishing from piers, the causeway, and the rock coast brings in perch and flounder. (You don't need a license for bay fishing from piers, breakwaters, or jetties.)

Sportfishing boats are numerous, taking parties out to deeper waters where prospects are better.

Clamming is very popular; the shore north of Morro Rock and south to Oceano promises good catches of Pismo clams (the limit is 10; you'll need a license).

One all-year feature of Morro Bay is the Clam Taxi, which operates between the Morro Bay Marina at Fourth Street and the peninsula section of Morro Bay State Park. The water taxi takes clammers, fishermen, and assorted beachcombers across the bay to a landing area on the peninsula. From the landing area, it's about a quarter-mile hike across the dunes to the ocean beach, where you'll find the best clamming, surf fishing, and shell, rock, and driftwood collecting.

Morro Bay State Park, a mile south of town, spreads over some 1,500 acres that slope down to the bay. Spacious and verdant, it is an inviting place for camping and picnicking. You can play golf on an 18-hole course or rent a boat at the boat harbor.

Stop at the attractive Natural History Museum for a wonderful panoramic view of the bay and Morro Rock. The museum has fascinating displays and movies featuring wildlife and area history.

Montana de Oro State Park is largely undeveloped. This 5,600-acre hiker's park faces the ocean south of Morro Bay. Made up largely of rugged cliffs and headlands, it also contains little coves with relatively secluded sandy beaches. Hikers can explore Valencia Peak and other 1,500-foot-high hills that overlook nearly 100 miles of coastline from Point Sal in the south to Piedras Blancas in the north. Spring wildflowers abound; the predominantly yellow color inspired the park's name—Montana de Oro means "mountain of gold."

About 50 campsites are located near the old Rancho Montana de Oro headquarters beside Islay Creek.

Harmony, population 18, is 6 miles south of Cambria off State 1. The former dairy town has gone from grazing to glazing—now it houses a pottery shop, design studio, music box shop, antique store in a false-front building, wine cellar, restaurant, and wedding chapel.

San Simeon: a kingdom by the sea

For William Randolph Hearst to have called his San Simeon estate "the ranch" is an understatement if ever there was one. Here you'll find a strangely eclectic but glamorous collection of mansions, terraced gardens, pools, fine art objects, exotic trees, bunkhouses, garages, and shacks crowning a spur of the Santa Lucia Mountains about 45 miles northwest of San Luis Obispo. The large central structure, *La Casa Grande*, looks more like a Spanish cathedral than a castle, but its imposing ridgetop position on "Enchanted Hill" has given it the aspect of a castle when viewed from afar.

Hearst Castle today is a State Historic Monument. Only the central cluster of impressive buildings and the immediately surrounding grounds have been deeded to California. The rest of the vast ranch—the cattle range (of which the castle served as a kind of baronial headquarters), the houses and barns, the airport, and most of the village of San Simeon—remains a single private holding. Hearst properties in the area once totaled 275,000 acres.

Tours of the estate reveal many delights: a classic Neptune pool, a walk-in fireplace, Cardinal Richelieu's bed. Unlike most parks and museums, the castle is not open for families to wander through at will. Visitors take only the conducted tours, which often require reservations.

You can choose from four different tours of the castle and grounds. Tour 1 takes in the gardens, a guest house, and the main floor of the mansion. Tour 2 covers the mansion's upper level, including bedrooms and personal libraries. On Tour 3, you'll see bedrooms, sitting rooms, bathrooms, and works of art. Tour 4, offered from April through mid-October, shows you the wine cellar, hidden terrace, underground vaults, and bowling alley. Each tour lasts about 2 hours and requires considerable walking and climbing. You'll need 2 consecutive days to take all four tours.

It's wise to make reservations in advance at Ticketron offices in large cities. At the castle, tickets are sold on a first-come, first-served basis. Tour prices are moderate, and there's a separate charge for each tour. Ticketron charges a reservation fee. For monument information, phone (805) 927-4621.

Southern Sierra

In and around the southern tip of the Sierra Nevada lie some of nature's most varied attractions: giant sequoias in Sequoia and Kings Canyon National Parks; the state's highest peak; ancient bristlecone pines and Southern California's winter playground in Owens Valley; the rumpled hills and dry salt flats of awesome Death Valley; mining towns of yesterday in vast Mojave Desert; blanketing fields of wildflowers in Antelope Valley; and one of the largest towns in San Joaquin Valley, the nation's agricultural center.

Sequoia and Kings Canyon National Parks dominate the southern part of the Sierra Nevada. These large parks contain several thousand acres of the most massive trees on earth, the giant sequoias (*Sequoiadendron giganteum*). Mount Whitney's 14,495-foot peak rises from magnificent granite mountains on the eastern edge of Sequoia National Park. The rugged back country of both parks offers unsurpassed mountain scenery and a hiker's domain of spectacular peaks and canyons, threaded with an intricate trail system that includes the southern end of the famed John Muir Trail.

Owens Valley, to the east of the Sierra, offers some of the best access into the mountains. Here visitors find ghostly remains of mining communities, a 4,000-year-old forest, and an opulent display of wildflowers.

To the east also lies legendary Death Valley, distinguished from other desert valleys by its great size, low altitude, diverse topography, and colorful history.

In contrast, the Central Valley, lying to the west of the towering mountain range, is a broad agricultural belt and the setting for several of John Steinbeck's novels.

South and east of the Sierra lies the vast Mojave Desert. For many, this desert holds a special magnetism, drawing them back again and again. It lures them on to explore rugged hills and rocky canyons, thrills them with its sunsets and wildflowers, and shares the secrets of its shy creatures and hidden oases. The best time to explore the Mojave is between February and May, after the winter rains but before the intense heat of summer. In spring, the desert blushes with thousands of square miles of wildflowers. No seed was ever planted here by man; this is nature's garden, haphazard in arrangement, tended only by sun, rain, and wind. The wildflower capital of the Mojave is Antelope Valley.

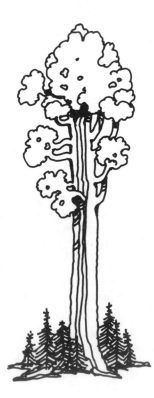

Sequoia & Kings Canyon National Parks

Giant trees, awesome canyons, cascading streams, and sparkling lakes greet visitors to these spectacular mountain parks. Much of their natural beauty can be explored by road or trail. Self-guided nature trails and naturalist-conducted walks allow everyone to sample some of California's most unspoiled mountain country.

These all-year parks offer a variety of activities. Summer is the time for hikers and backpackers. You can hire saddle horses at several corrals and join guided parties for exploring the back country. Fishing is good for brook, brown, rainbow, and golden trout—you'll need a California license, available in both parks. Winter activities include Nordic and downhill skiing and sledding; snow enthusiasts head for Wolverton Ski Bowl, Lodgepole, Grant Grove, and Giant Forest.

How to get there? Sequoia and Kings Canyon, joined end to end along the Sierra ridge and administered by the same park headquarters at Ash Mountain, can be reached from the west by two main highways: State Highway 180 from Fresno, which leads through the Grant Grove section of Kings Canyon National Park,

SNOW ADDS FROSTING to awesome giants of Sequoia National Park. Visitors view General Sherman Tree, world's largest.

penetrating the canyon of the South Fork of Kings River for a short distance; and State Highway 198 from Visalia, which enters Sequoia National Park at Ash Mountain.

At one time, the park concessioner operated a bus between the parks and Fresno, meeting planes, trains, and buses. At present, there is no public transportation from nearby cities.

Several companies operate 1 and 2-night sightseeing tours by motorcoach from Fresno. Prices include meals and lodging.

Where to stay? At Sequoia and Kings Canyon, rustic cabins in perfect harmony with towering sequoias coexist with more modern accommodations. Campgrounds are numerous, well equipped, and located in strategic and beautiful spots throughout both parks. Some allow trailers (there are no hookups). Lodgepole and a few lower-elevation sites are open all year.

Reservations for all park campgrounds except Lodgepole are on a first-come, first-served basis; make Lodgepole reservations through Ticketron.

Giant Forest Lodge in Sequoia has one or two-room cabins scattered among the Big Trees, and an excellent dining room. Daily rates are about $65 for two for deluxe accommodations. Some units are open the year around; others are available from mid-May to mid-October. You can rent housekeeping and sleeping cabins reasonably during the summer.

Grant Grove Lodge in Kings Canyon offers rates comparable to those of Giant Forest Lodge. Bearpaw Meadow Camp offers tent-camping with dining facilities and hot showers from the end of June until Labor Day. Farther north, Cedar Grove Camp has a limited number of canvas-top cabins.

You should make advance reservations (a deposit is required) for lodges and cabins. Write to Reservations Manager, Sequoia & Kings Canyon Guest Services, Sequoia National Park, CA 93262. For year-round information and reservations, call (209) 561-3314.

For additional information on the parks, including a detailed map of the back country, hiking trails, and campgrounds, write to Sequoia and Kings Canyon National Parks, Three Rivers, CA 93271; or call (209) 565-3341.

Sequoia spectacles

The first national park in California and the second in the entire national park system, Sequoia National Park was established to protect its groves of giant sequoias, found here in greater abundance than anywhere else in California—their only native habitat.

A visit to the park on the Generals Highway (State 198) is a journey not easily forgotten. This beautiful road connecting the two parks was completed in 1934. A hint of the care taken to preserve the natural scene around it is Tunnel Rock, a great boulder left in place to span the road. As you twist among the sequoias, look for other interesting spots along the 16 miles from Ash Mountain to Giant Forest.

At Hospital Rock, 6 miles inside the park, Indians lived in the shelter of another huge boulder. Legend has it that the sick were brought here for healing. Later, pioneers took refuge under it. Intriguing reminders of the Indian camp are rock paintings and mortar holes in the flat rocks. Exhibits in a nearby shelter tell the story.

The best fishing reached by road in Sequoia is along the Kaweah River's Middle Fork. You'll find turnouts for scenic vistas along this route above the river. An easy footpath takes you down from Hospital Rock.

Lodgepole is the site of Sequoia Park's visitor center and campground. Once in Giant Forest, these facilities were recently relocated to reduce damage to tree roots. Giant Forest still offers lodging and stores—but these, too, will eventually be moved to Lodgepole, leaving Giant Forest old-fashioned and unhurried.

The General Sherman Tree, the world's largest tree (though not the tallest), is 102 feet in base circumference and 36½ feet thick, with a height of 275 feet; 140 feet above ground level extends a limb 6.8 feet in diameter.

Near the General Sherman Tree is the beginning of Congress Trail, a 2-mile loop that will take you to some of the more famous and spectacular of the trees: the

---

BIG, BAD BODIE

"Goodbye, God, I'm going to Bodie," was the conclusion to one little girl's prayer when her family moved to what was then one of the wildest mining camps in the West. Her dismay was not unfounded—there was allegedly at least one murder a day in "big, bad Bodie." Sixty-five saloons once operated there, and the girls along Maiden Lane and Virgin Alley were sometimes rewarded with gold nuggets from the big mines.

Now a State Historic Park maintained in a condition of "arrested decay," Bodie is a true ghost town. Weeds grow freely around the dozens of old weathered buildings, and no attempt has

been made to restore the buildings to their original grandeur. A few rangers and their families are the town's only residents.

Its edges curled by time, the old wooden boardwalk rises and falls along Main Street past the venerable Miners' Union Hall, the Odd Fellows Hall, and the brick post office. Other points of interest are the tiny Methodist church, the Cain home, the jail, and several "boot hills."

To reach Bodie, take U.S. 395 to a junction 7 miles south of Bridgeport (north of Mono Lake); turn east on a dirt road that winds through barren hills for 13 miles. Bring your own lunch; there are no stores or overnight facilities.

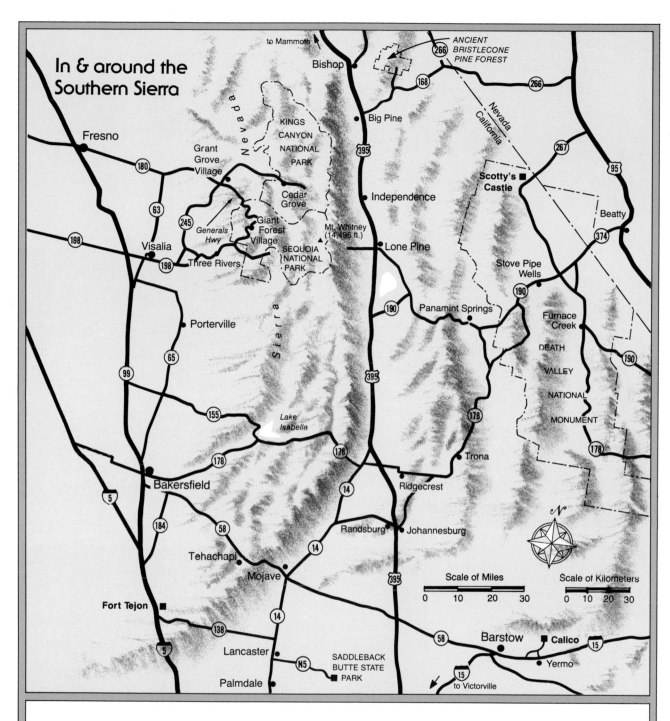

In & around the Southern Sierra

Points of Interest

Sequoia-Kings Canyon National Parks — home of giant sequoias, mighty Mt. Whitney

Pioneer Village (Bakersfield) — 12-acre collection of furnished historic buildings

Fort Tejon (Lebec) — military post once housed First Dragoons and Camel Corps; restored as park

Mammoth Country (east of Sierra Nevada)—Southland winter sports area; summer fishing at June Lake; seismic wonders in Owens Valley. View Devil's Postpile, Mono Lake moonscape

Bristlecone Pines (White Mountains) — ancient forest of world's oldest living trees

Death Valley — dramatic desert landscape, old mining relics, Borax Museum, Scotty's Castle tour, Rhyolite house of bottles

Antelope Valley — spring wildflower wonderland around Lancaster. Tour Tropico gold camp

Calico (near Barstow) — silver mining town now regional park; mine tours, train rides, "boot hill"

DEATH VALLEY'S BADLANDS (above) are deeply etched by wind and occasional cloudbursts. Century-old charcoal kilns (right), remnants of Death Valley mining days, line up in Wildrose Canyon.

Senate, House, and Founder's groves, as well as the President, McKinley, and Chief Sequoyah trees. Posted at the beginning of the trail are guide booklets explaining the numbered stakes along the way.

The high country, for nine months of the year, is quiet, inhabited only by wildlife; this road-free domain is a playground for hikers and backpackers. The main traffic arterial is the John Muir Trail, which begins in Yosemite Valley and runs south for 225 miles to Whitney Portal.

To control the number of people in the wilderness area of the parks, backpackers are put on a permit system. Though some permits are issued on a first-come, first-served basis, it is wise to write in advance, giving the dates of your trip, your route, the number of people in your party, and whether you plan to hike or use horses. Send your request to Ranger, Sequoia and Kings Canyon National Parks, Three Rivers, CA 93271, or call (209) 565-3341.

Bearpaw Meadow provides a good sampling of the Sequoia back country in a short period; no camping permit is required here. The trip to this camp is 11 miles one way by trail from Crescent Meadow. Perching on the edge of a tremendous overlook at the base of the Great Western Divide, the camp offers comforts and good food, in addition to a spectacular view. Side trails through bold mountains lead to good stream and lake fishing. The camp, with tent accommodations and ranger station, is generally open from June through September. For information on fees and reservations, call Sequoia & Kings Canyon Guest Services, (209) 561-3314, well in advance of your trip.

Kings Canyon attractions

Kings Canyon has the distinction of being one of the oldest and newest national parks. When established in 1940, it absorbed tiny General Grant National Park— now known as the General Grant Grove—a sanctuary set up after Sequoia was created in 1890.

The park is actually two entirely separate areas with the west side containing the only two developed sections—the General Grant Grove and Kings Canyon regions. Densely forested, it is usually comfortably cool (the elevation varies from 4,600 to 6,600 feet). A rugged mass of spectacular peaks and canyons comprises the largest area of the park.

General Grant Grove is the destination of most visitors to the area since, along with all the park facilities, it contains the famed General Grant Tree. The second largest tree in the world, the Grant Tree has a base circumference of 108 feet (actually 6 feet larger than the General Sherman Tree) but it has a smaller total volume. Both of these trees were standing in the Bronze Age more than 3,000 years ago. Because General Grant is the nation's official Christmas tree, each Yule season an impressive ceremony is held here.

Informative campfire programs are given every summer night in the amphitheater. In the village you'll find posted schedules of daily ranger-conducted trips, full of facts and park lore.

Kings Canyon and Cedar Grove are reached from a 30-mile highway that drops 2,000 feet before attaining its destination. From parking overlooks on wide sweeping curves, you can gaze into the canyons of the Middle and South forks of the Kings River and beyond to the bewildering maze of jagged peaks that constitute the greater portion of Kings Canyon National Park. These breathtaking views are the best hints you will get of the country beyond. About 10 miles before Cedar Grove is Boyden Cave, 450 to 600 feet underground, which you can tour in an hour.

Cedar Grove has a store, coffee shop, ranger station, and a few cabins. A variety of conducted trips led by ranger naturalists are offered here, as are nightly illustrated campfire programs.

East of the Sierra

The full impact of the Sierra Nevada is rarely appreciated until you see its abrupt east side—the face it turns toward the desert. This eastern side of the Sierra, to the west and north of Death Valley and east of Sequoia and Kings Canyon, offers myriad attractions for vacationers: high desert country, spectacular mountains, uncrowded trails, good fishing, ghost mining towns, wildflowers, mineral deposits—most accessible by good roads. In winter, these mountains offer excellent skiing.

One important route, U.S. Highway 395, leads north and south through the whole section, linking a chain of little towns. From this arterial highway you can go east into Death Valley or west a short distance into the towering mountains.

People may wonder why Inyo and Mono counties are considered part of Southern California when even the largest towns are 300 to 400 miles from Los Angeles. Mainly, it is because they are tied more closely with Los Angeles than with San Francisco, both economically and recreationally. Residents, too, are most oriented to the Southland.

Owens Valley

The bending and cracking of the earth's surface that created the Sierra Nevada and the parallel ranges of the White, Panamint, and Inyo mountains also sank a long, deep trough between them—Owens Valley, a place of hot springs, craters, lava flows, and earthquake faults.

Owens Valley's first inhabitants were the ancestors of the Paiute Indians; then came ranchers and farmers. Today the tourists who pass through the valley have become its most important industry.

Lone Pine is one of the points on U.S. 395 where you can turn off to the famed hiking trails of Sequoia and Kings Canyon. Going west on Whitney Portal Road, you pass through the picturesque Alabama Hills, named by Confederate sympathizers. Ringed by these knobby hills is Movie Flat, a favorite location for TV and movie westerns. One road to Movie Flat turns south from Whitney Portal Road (the same road also takes you to Tuttle Creek Campground).

Independence, the turnoff for the Kearsarge Pass entrance to the Sierra high country, is also the home of the excellent Eastern California Museum. Located at Center and Grant streets, the museum houses natural and local history displays and Indian artifacts. The museum is open daily all year; hours differ depending on the season.

One block north of Center Street on U.S. 395 is the Commander's House, the only extant structure of Camp Independence, established in 1862 to protect early Owens Valley residents from Indian attacks. It is open Wednesday through Saturday from 10 A.M. to 5 P.M.

About a mile west of the highway north of town is the interesting Mount Whitney Fish Hatchery, built of native stone in 1917.

Ancient bristlecone pines (some more than 4,000 years old) have been stunted and twisted by the harsh forces of nature so that they resemble upright pieces of driftwood decorated with green needles. The trees grow in a 28,000-acre area of Inyo National Forest; to reach them, turn east on State Highway 168 to Westgard Pass, just north of Big Pine. A winding but well-marked road takes you north to the Schulman Memorial Grove.

At the grove (open June through October), you'll find a ranger station, information center, picnic area, and starting points to Pine Alpha and Methusela groves. Travel with warm clothing, water, and a full gas tank—there are no services after Big Pine.

Bishop, with a population of over 3,000, is the bustling metropolis of the Owens Valley. Known as the world's mule capital, the city stages a colorful Mule Days celebration on Memorial Day weekend. Its Chamber of Commerce, at 125 E. Line Street, has useful travel literature for points of interest in this area. The 50-mile Petroglyph Loop Trip described in one of the chamber's folders is especially worthwhile.

At Laws, the rhythm of puffing steam engines, clanging bells, and freight platform bustle has long been stilled, but more people come to see this old Owens Valley railroad station now than ever came during its prime. The Laws Railroad Museum and Historical Exhibit has interesting daily tours of period houses and buildings (weather permitting). Located 5 miles out of Bishop and ½ mile off U.S. 6, it offers a good break from a long drive. From March through November, displays are open from 10 A.M. to 4 P.M. every day (weekends only the rest of the year).

Mammoth Country

Though Mammoth Mountain is only 30 air miles from Yosemite National Park and east of San Francisco, it serves as a Southern California playground. There's a geographical reason for this. Part of the isolated eastern crest of the Sierra Nevada, Mammoth is easily reached from the south over U.S. 395 (though the drive takes about 7 hours), but it is cut off from the west except in late summer when the mountain passes are open.

This diverse area offers excellent winter-skiing above 10,000 feet and all-year trout fishing and great inner-tubing in the 28-mile stretch of the Owens River from Pleasant Valley Reservoir to Tinemaha Reservoir.

In the intermediate elevations from Mammoth Mountain to Owens Valley are abandoned mills and mines to explore, volcanic remains to discover, and picnic spots.

Visitors to Mammoth will find a variety of lakes and creeks. Most are fishermen's retreats; others are good for swimming, boating, and viewing. Turn east off U.S. 395 on the road to the fish hatchery to reach Hot Creek. The hot springs, a 25-foot-wide natural pool, are about 4 feet deep and have practically no current. High in mineral content, the water is unusually buoyant; it can also be *very* hot. If you get too warm, paddle away from the springs into the cool eddies of the creek.

Mammoth Lakes, an area dotted with more than 30 lakes in a 9,000-foot basin, can be reached by a paved side road that cuts off U.S. 395 at Casa Diablo Hot Springs and meanders to the shore of Lake Mary, heart of the region. Five of the lakes, popular with anglers for many years, may be reached by good roads. Mountain lodges offer woodsy comfort, log fires, and hearty meals. U.S. Forest Service campgrounds are usually crowded in midsummer but are virtually deserted after the end of September. Summer aerial tram gondola rides on Mammoth Mountain are spectacular. Boats may be rented at Lake Mary and Twin Lakes, and packers offer pack and saddle animals and guides.

Mammoth Mountain skiing rivals the best in the state and certainly is the best in spring, when at 10,000 feet there is still powder snow.

The lodge at Mammoth Mountain is 4 miles from the town of Mammoth Lakes. The ski lifts serve slopes to challenge any skier; for the sightseer there's a panoramic chair ride. Snow touring is popular—on skis, snowshoes, or dog sleds. Accommodations range from dormitories to chalets. For information on housing or package ski trips, write Mammoth Lakes Resort Association, P.O. Box 48, Mammoth Lakes, CA 93546; or write June Mountain and June Lake Reservation and Information Service, P.O. Box 216, June Lake, CA 93529.

Death Valley

Legendary Death Valley is distinguished from other desert valleys by its great size, low altitude, diverse desert, and colorful history.

Now a national monument, it is unique among deserts for its great extremes, one of these being its summer heat. Its record high of 134°F. was set in 1913. Up the enclosing slopes, it may not be hot at all, but down on the flats it can stay about 100° all night long.

Another of the valley's extremes is its low elevation. An area of about 14 square miles is more than 280 feet below sea level. In the salt beds west and northwest of Badwater, two places 3 miles apart and 282 feet below sea level are the lowest points in the Western Hemisphere. Nearby Telescope Peak is 11,049 feet *above* sea level, another example of the dramatic extremes to be found in this valley.

Throughout the valley you'll see evidence of human occupation, as well as geologic history. Indian petroglyphs appear in more than 200 sites. Many places carry names of pioneers and prospectors of the gold rush days. The valley, probably first referred to as Death Valley in January 1850, did not really deserve its name. Though the pioneer parties crossing the area suffered extreme hardships, only one '49er died in Death Valley (but not from heat or thirst), and a party of nine others also may have perished there. Death Valley's record of human lives lost, measured against that of the rest of the Western desert, is reassuringly low.

Natural features

All of the great divisions and nearly all of the subdivisions of geologic time are represented in the land formations of Death Valley. Fossils of prehistoric mammals discovered here show that the arid salt flats, gravel desert, and harsh peaks were once a fertile plain. As the climate became drier, ancient lakes evaporated into salt flat deposits and mud playas. Wind reduced granite to sand and blew it into dunes. Since the wind blows from all directions, the dunes remain intact.

Plants and animals

The popular belief that nothing lives or grows in Death Valley is discounted by the common animal and plant life that has tenaciously adapted to the burning heat and dryness. Almost all of the perennial plants have deep or far-spreading roots and special adaptations of leaves and stems to help tap and conserve vital water. Over 600 species of plants and trees flourish at all elevations in the monument, and 22 species—including the Panamint daisy, Death Valley sage, and rattleweed—exist only here. Bristlecone pines, thousands of years old, grow at 10,000-foot elevations on Telescope Peak.

On a favorable spring day, when the unexpected brilliance of myriad wildflowers mantle the dark, alluvial slopes and narrow canyon washes, the name Death Valley seems inappropriate.

Visitors to Death Valley see few animals, for most emerge only at night in search of food. A great variety of natural life exists in a 2-mile area between Telescope Peak and Badwater, where the desert animals can find plants to feed on. Only the plantless central salt flats are barren of animal life. Even fish live in this desert. Descended from Ice Age ancestors, the rare pupfish or "desert sardine" thrives in Salt Creek, Saratoga Springs, and Devil's Hole and is an astonishing example of super-rapid evolutionary adaptation to changing environmental conditions.

Planning a visit

Though visitors in summer may remember the blazing sun and intense heat, in other seasons they will find a mild climate. Tourist facilities are in full operation from November to mid-April. In summer, a list of Hot Weather Hints, distributed in the monument, will help make your visit safe and pleasant.

State Highway 136 from Lone Pine to Towne's Pass is the most spectacular and most improved route from the west into the valley. State Highway 178 from the south to Wildrose picnic area is another popular approach.

State Highway 127 from the southeast joins State 190 at Amargosa (Death Valley Junction). En route to the junction, the highway passes Tecopa Hot Springs, a unique watering hole where visitors partake of the baths free of charge. The curative springs once belonged

to Indians whose ancestors brought their lame and sick to bathe. When they gave up the hot springs to the white settlers, it was with the stipulation that the good water be left free to all comers. And so it has remained.

Clusters of trailers around the bathhouses make the little settlement visible for miles. For information on desert camping, write to the Park Superintendent, P.O. Box 158, Tecopa, CA 92389.

Amargosa Opera House, at Death Valley Junction, has weekend performances from September through May. Reservations are necessary. In the opera house you'll be joined by an "audience" in a realistic, wall-size mural depicting 260 members of a Spanish court, ranging from bawdy commoners to sedate nobles. The painter of the mural is also the dancer in the one-woman ballet, Marta Becket. In the 1½-hour performance, you'll see both classical ballet and dance characterizations such as a dancing doll and a peasant girl.

For performance reservations, write Manager, Amargosa Opera House, Death Valley Junction, CA 92328; or call the operator and ask for Death Valley Junction toll station #8.

Tours of Death Valley are popular; check with a travel agent for specific information. Las Vegas, Nevada, is the closest air terminal. For light planes, paved landing strips are located at Furnace Creek and Stove Pipe Wells.

Where to stay in Death Valley

Lodging is not really a problem except during Easter and Thanksgiving weekends and the weekend of the Death Valley '49ers Annual Encampment in early November.

Furnace Creek Inn is a luxurious resort hotel with resort prices that include meals. The inn has a swimming pool, tennis courts, stables; and an 18-hole golf course. Furnace Creek Ranch, a mile down the road, also has resort facilities on a more modest scale. Lodging is a choice between simple cabins or newer, motel-style accommodations. The inn is open from mid-October to mid-May; the ranch stays open throughout the year. For information and reservations, write directly to the Furnace Creek Inn and Ranch Resort, P.O. Box 1, Death Valley, CA 92328. Write well in advance if you're thinking of going to the desert for a holiday season.

Stove Pipe Wells Hotel, actually about 6 miles from the site of old Stovepipe Wells, is a motel-style resort, open November through April. The postal address is Death Valley, CA 92328.

Campgrounds provide scenic backdrops, ranging from whispering sand dunes to sweeping mountain views. Of nine monument campgrounds, the three most improved are in the valley: near the visitor center are Texas Spring and Furnace Creek (open all year but very hot in summer); Mesquite Spring is south of Scotty's Castle.

Other campgrounds include Thorndike and Mahogany Flats; both provide fireplaces and tables, but bring your own water. The campgrounds at higher elevations are open in summer; at year-round Emigrant Junction you'll enjoy good mountain and valley views. All campgrounds require that you furnish your own firewood; at some, the water must be boiled.

In the frequented parts of the valley, camping is strictly confined to established campgrounds. But back-country campers are permitted to use outlying locations as long as they don't disturb or litter the ground, or burn the plants.

Located at 3,500 feet on the west side of the Panamint Range outside of Death Valley proper is the Wildrose picnic area, providing a nice change of pace from the campgrounds. A day-use facility only, Wildrose has tables and fireplaces. The area is open the year around.

There's life in Death Valley

At first glance, Death Valley seems little different from the desert you have driven through to reach it. But as closeup follows closeup and you make your way to both labeled phenomena and some secret finds of your own, you perceive new dimensions. The mountain face—apparently unbreached when seen from afar—is really slotted with fascinating labyrinths that lead you on and on. The featureless salt flat is a vast maze of miniature crystalline alps. The sand ridges in the distance are mountains in their own right—but mountains that yield underfoot and restore themselves to an unmarked pristine state with every fresh breeze. The unnatural splotch on the far hillside is a waste pile marking an abandoned mine, with tunnels, shafts, headframes, and railroad beds still more or less intact.

Death Valley can be explored on more than 500 miles of improved roadways. Additional miles of primitive roads wind through the back country.

Furnace Creek, because of an excellent and dependable water supply from nearby springs, has always been a center of activity. To plan your stay, stop by the all-year visitor center or call (619) 786-2331. You can buy maps and useful publications and tour a museum of local geology, plants, and wildlife.

The Borax Museum nearby exhibits an outdoor assembly of implements once used in the extraction and refining of borax and other minerals. It's a parking lot of the past: exhibited are stagecoach and buggy, buckboard and wagon, railroad handcar and locomotive. A homemade mining machine and hand-operated stamp mill are also on the grounds. You'll find smaller displays inside the oldest building left in the valley, an 1883 mining office-bunkhouse from nearby Twenty Mule Team Canyon. The great 20-mule-team wagons, nearly as sound as when they were maintaining their remarkable schedules 80 years ago, are 2 miles farther north, marking the site of the Harmony Borax Works, a restored processing plant.

Zabriskie Point, southeast of Furnace Creek on State 190, is an area of 5 to 10-million-year-old lake beds that are especially dramatic at sunrise.

Artist's Drive, off the main road south of Furnace Creek, takes you through a rainbow canyon colored by oxidation. The even more intense color of Artist's Palette is splashed on a hillside halfway through the canyon.

Badwater, a few miles farther south, is known as the lowest point in the Western Hemisphere (282 feet below sea level). Often crusted over, the salt pools at close range reveal weird formations of rugged rock salt.

Dante's View, on the crest of the Black Mountains, is one of the most spectacular scenic overlooks in the United States, rising 5,775 feet directly above Badwater.

Charcoal kilns, resembling giant stone beehives, blend into the hillside of the Panamint Mountains. They appear as good as new after nearly a century of existence. These kilns reduced pines and junipers to charcoal for the Modoc Mine smelter, 25 miles west. To reach the kilns from the Wildrose Ranger Station, follow the road to upper Wildrose Canyon.

Skidoo was the one boom town near Death Valley that really did pan out. At the end of its 2-year existence, it was ahead by $3 million.

Rhyolite, Nevada, a ghost town, is just outside the monument on State Highway 58. Here a $130,000 railroad station without a railroad houses a museum and store. The Rhyolite Bottle House, with walls built of 51,000 beer bottles set in adobe, is still occupied by a Rhyolite citizen who sells desert glass and curios. Once a spirited boom town around the turn of the century, Rhyolite thrived for only 5 years.

Titus Canyon is reached by a one-way dirt road that must be entered from State 58 on the east. This 25-mile trip through the wineglass-shaped canyon with changing colors and soaring walls is a memorable experience.

Scotty's Castle is the incredible desert mansion built by Death Valley Scotty (Walter Scott) and his millionaire friend Albert M. Johnson. Located in the extreme northern part of the monument, the Spanish-Moorish mansion, lavishly furnished, cost $2 million and took about 10 years to build. Scotty's flamboyant escapades are a part of the Death Valley folklore; the castle remains as a testimony to his natural showmanship and eccentric personality. Hourly tours are conducted daily from 9 A.M. to 5 P.M.; there is an admission charge. You can visit the grounds and picnic area without charge from 7 A.M. to 7 P.M. daily.

Colorful Ubehebe Crater, a half-mile wide and 800 feet deep, was created 3,000 years ago by a volcanic explosion. It's not far from Scotty's Castle.

The Racetrack, 27 miles south of the crater, is a mud playa, occasionally subject to high velocity winds that are responsible for the "mystery of the moving rocks." When wet, the Racetrack is so slippery that the wind can move great boulders across it.

The Mojave Desert

Parts of the Mojave have never been fully explored. Much of it is rugged terrain, fit only for the seasoned desert traveler and a well-equipped car. Though any car can handle most of the trips mentioned here, some are best made in a four-wheel-drive vehicle.

Some parts of the desert are being closed to recreational vehicles under a Bureau of Land Management plan. (The BLM manages the East Mojave National

BRILLIANT COLOR enlivens desert when spring wildflowers bloom in Antelope Valley.

Scenic Area, almost 1½ million acres of desert.) Within the off-limits areas are fragile Indian pictographs and the habitats of endangered species. Before camping off main roads, be sure you're not in such a restricted area.

Desert driving precautions

The rules for safe automobile exploration of the desert are few, but they are mandatory:

Don't turn off main roads without inquiring locally about conditions of side roads. Above all, don't hesitate to turn back if travel becomes difficult; back roads are likely to become worse, not better.

Remember that you often gain necessary traction in sand by deflating your rear tires to about half normal pressure (take along an air pump so you can reinflate tires when you're back on hard surface). Be sure in advance that your engine's cooling system is in good working order. Always carry adequate supplies of water, gasoline, and oil. Don't count on desert springs as water sources—they are often dry. If stranded in the desert during the summer, don't leave the shade of your car.

Maps

Up-to-date, detailed maps are necessary to any back-road exploring. You can usually get good ones from counties, the U.S. Forest Service, state monuments and parks, and the U.S. Geological Survey. The Bureau of Land Management, the agency in charge of much of California's desert country, has section maps that indicate private or government-owned lands within the desert. For a free map, write to the BLM, 1695 Spruce Street, Riverside, CA 92507.

In the northern Mojave

The vast northwestern Mojave Desert is a land of great contrasts. To the west rise the high, imposing peaks of the Sierra Nevada; yet throughout this desert can be seen the low, crystalline sinks of primeval lakes. Human history is recorded in ancient Indian drawings on the rocks and in old mines and mining towns left by 19th century prospectors. Today, man is making his mark here with secluded military establishments and missile sites. At Brown, off U.S. 395 on State 58 north of Edwards Air Force Base, is the world's largest open-pit borax mine. Still active, the great pit yields snow-white hills of processed borax.

Randsburg, a gold town but not a ghost town, is hidden from U.S. 395, which passes through its neighbor, Johannesburg. From a distance Randsburg still resembles old photographs of early mining communities. Houses, some built with wood from dynamite boxes, stand weather-beaten and full of memories. The town has lived through three booms: gold (it had one of the richest mines in Southern California), tungsten, and silver. The Desert Museum (open weekends and holidays) has miners' and Indian artifacts and objects from the famed Yellow Aster Mine. Nearby Koehn Dry Lake, resembling a snowstorm on the desert, is the site of still another kind of mining—salt mining.

At China Lake, in the Coso Mountains, you can see the most extraordinary concentration of prehistoric rock pictures in North America. The site in Renegade Canyon, within the China Lake Naval Weapons Center firing range, is now a National Historic Landmark. The Navy and the Maturango Museum, a geological treasure trove located on the center, team up to conduct day-long caravans to the pictographs. There is no definite schedule for the tours; if you would like to join one, write to the museum at Box 5514, China Lake, CA 93556.

To reach the museum, leave U.S. 395 or State Highway 14 at the Ridgecrest-China Lake exit and drive to the end of the road, where you'll come upon the Naval center's main gate. The museum is open only on weekends from 2 to 5 P.M.; admission to the museum is free. You will need a pass from the main gate.

Little Lake, just off U.S. 395 about 20 miles north of the road to China Lake, is worth a stop for a look at some notable Indian pictographs. You can see some of the rock drawings from the lakeshore, but others are best sighted from a rowboat (for rent at the boathouse at the north end of the lake). The greatest concentration of drawings is found on the basalt cliffs on the west shore and at the southeast end of the lake.

The fee for overnight camping includes bank-fishing privileges. All campsites have tables, fireplaces, and water.

To reach Fossil Falls, turn east from U.S. 395 onto Cinder Road, almost 3 miles north of Little Lake. Turn southwest at the first intersection, left at the next intersection, and drive to the end of the road. It's a short hike to the falls on a marked trail. The falls were formed by ancient lava flows from the Coso Mountains.

Trona Pinnacles make a logical side trip from the popular Wildrose Canyon route into Death Valley; you can see them at a distance.

Rising from the desert floor south of the crystalline Searles Lake, the spires are believed to have been built up by algae from an ancient sea.

The northern approach to the Pinnacles is very primitive but gets you there in the least amount of time. If there have been very recent rains, a safer approach is on the rough but all-weather road from the south that runs more or less parallel to the Trona railroad tracks.

A leisurely lunch stop among the formations will give you time for a brief exploration. You could easily spend a day investigating the area. You can camp overnight on the east side of the Pinnacles in the shadow of some of the tallest spires.

In and around Barstow

An old mining center, Barstow lies at the junction of two main Interstate Highways: Interstate 15, a heavily traveled freeway between Los Angeles and Las Vegas, and Interstate 40, which heads southeast for the Colorado River and the California-Arizona border. Along both routes you'll discover some spots to explore, but to do so you may have to get off the fast interstate, and drive once-famous U.S. Highway 66.

Barstow is a good base for exploring the surrounding countryside. You can venture into canyons, climb mountains, hunt gemstones, or follow trails leading to historic landmarks and old waterholes.

The Mojave Valley Museum (open daily) has a variety

BASQUES IN BAKERSFIELD

Basques began arriving in the Central Valley almost a century ago. Originally from the French side of the Pyrenees Mountains (separating France and Spain), they came as sheepherders, ranging up and down vast empty stretches of land with their flocks. This lonely occupation is today almost a disappearing way of life, though a few Basques (now mostly Spanish) come into the area on a work-contract basis.

Bakersfield became home to many who gave up sheepherding to start other occupations, including opening Basque restaurants. You can enjoy a Basque meal at several restaurants. Most are located in east Bakersfield around Summer and East 21st streets (now called International Village): Noriega's, Pyrenees, Maitia's, and Woolgrowers Cafe. Chateau Basque is at Union and 1st streets; Chalet Basque is on Oak Street near State Highway 99.

Noriega's serves boarding-house style. Everyone eats together at 6:30 P.M., and there's no choice of menu. All the restaurants feature some traditional side dishes (including stew and tongue) in addition to your entree. Lamb is a specialty; try "mountain oysters" in the spring.

If you want to assemble the makings for a picnic, buy your French bread at Bakersfield's long-established Pyrenees Bakery, 717 E. 21st Street.

Late summer finds Basques and friends gathering for a special mass, picnic, and festival, including dances from their original homeland. (See photos of some of the fun on page 126.) Though these activities are not generally open to the public, for information write to the Basque Club, % Highmoor Street, Bakersfield, CA 93308.

---

of desert artifacts, mining exhibits, and a small Indian collection. For information on wildflowers, make this your first stop in Barstow; conducted tours are held during spring. The museum is located in Dana Park.

Southeast of Barstow, an area has been set aside for driving the ubiquitous dune buggies and motorcycles—so they won't overrun the entire desert.

Calico, founded in 1881 as the result of one of the West's richest silver strikes, is experiencing a new boom: an influx of tourists instead of prospectors. The town was named for the multicolored mountains that lie behind it. The original residents were proud of the local saloon (Lil's), hotel, mercantile store, bank, railroad station, and schoolhouse—but especially of the high-producing Maggie Mine. Today you can explore its tunnels, ride the Calico-Odessa Railway, take a cable tram ride, and visit the buildings that are probably a bit more orderly and better scrubbed than before, but still colorful. There's a fee for parking as well as a slight charge for the tram ride from the parking area to town. Some attractions in town also charge fees.

Calico was restored and opened to the public by Walter Knott of Knott's Berry Farm, whose uncle grub staked the original Calico Hills prospectors. Later, the area was deeded to San Bernardino County, which now manages it as a regional park with emphasis on its mining history. For information on Calico's spring festival in May and Calico Days in October, call (619) 254-2122.

A campground in the area allows you to spend the night in the "Old West." In addition, there are motels in nearby Yermo and Barstow. Calico is 9 miles east of Barstow (3½ miles west of Yermo) off I-15.

Apple Valley

Situated east of the Mojave River and north of the San Bernardino foothills, Apple Valley has the clean dry air, beauty, warmth, and solitude of the desert. Once a sanctuary for early Indians, Apple Valley is now a resort community with golf courses, guest ranches, swimming pools, and fishing lakes. The resort also offers an airport favored by sailplane pilots, riding stables, and a thoroughbred breeding farm where you can observe horses in training. Ranch clothes are in order here. Barbecues are reached by hay wagons, and Western entertainment centers around a crackling campfire.

The Apple Valley Inn—center of most visitor activity in town—offers accommodations in detached cottages. Inside the inn, you'll find game trophies, antique rugs, and old portraits. The Roy Rogers Museum, formerly on the grounds, was moved to Victorville some time ago to form the nucleus of a new entertainment center—Western World, a 300-acre complex reached by taking the Palmdale offramp from I-15.

Apple Valley is located southeast of Victorville on State Highway 18, which continues east through Lucerne Valley (also offering enjoyable guest ranches) on its way to Big Bear Lake. An unusual rock formation in Lucerne Valley is Hercules Fingers, a granite boulder 60 feet high. Drive out Camp Rock Road to the second power company road; turn east for approximately 3 miles; small bamboo sticks mark the road.

Mojave Narrows Park is near here. This great oasis, halfway between San Bernardino and Barstow, is one of Southern California's least-known parks.

Along a 2-mile stretch where the underground Mojave River rises to the surface, the park is an inviting expanse of green meadows, cottonwoods, willow thickets, and year-round water in river channels, creeks, bogs, ponds, and two small lakes. Birds and small animals visit from the desert, and beavers build dams here.

The park is open daily; there is a modest car entry fee. To get there, take the Bear Valley cutoff from I-15 east to Ridge Crest Road and then go north to the entrance.

BASQUE FESTIVAL marks late summer in Bakersfield. Drinking from a bota (above) and whirling through native dance (right) are watchable arts.

Antelope Valley

This corner of the Mojave Desert slopes gradually upward to the west as it narrows between the rolling foothills of the converging Tehachapi and San Gabriel mountains. The pastoral aspect of much of Antelope Valley sets it somewhat apart from the rest of the Mojave. Without its Joshua trees, it would not look like desert. Yet it is a part of the Great Basin, 2,000 to 3,000 feet above sea level, where cold winters, hot summers, and harsh winds discourage human settlement. Plants from the desert, from the Central Valley, and from coastal hills grow in Antelope Valley, making it a beautiful and popular destination in the spring. Even in other seasons there is much to observe. Antelope Valley's largest town, Lancaster, has fine motels and restaurants and is a convenient base for exploring open

country a few miles to the west and east. Accommodations are also available in Palmdale, Mojave, Tehachapi, Lebec, and Gorman.

You get more than just a scenic view of the valley if you pull off State 14 (heading north) at the lookout point a few miles south of Palmdale. You can also see the valley's geologic features that have been formed by California's dominant rift zone, the San Andreas Fault. A plaque at the lookout shows the location of the fault line, extending west of Palmdale across the valley to its highest elevation at Big Pines Summit (6,862 feet).

Wildflower viewing is often at its best in Antelope Valley. Sometimes the show is shimmering and brilliant, but it is always unpredictable.

The Jane S. Pinheiro Interpretative Center (located in the Antelope Valley California Poppy Reserve) features exhibits of local wildlife and plants, most notably California's state flower, the poppy. The center is open all year, but perhaps the best time to visit is during the spring floral fireworks display. Call the center, (805) 724-1180, or the Lancaster Chamber of Commerce, (805) 948-4518, to find out when and where wildflowers are blooming. To reach the center, take State 14 northeast to Avenue I in Lancaster; then go west on Avenue I for 13½ miles. The center is on your right.

One suggested loop trip centers around State 14. Drive north from Lancaster to Rosamond and west to visit Burton's Tropico Gold Mine and Museum. Continue 3 miles west to almost-deserted Willow Springs (just off the highway), a former stage and freight station and, in the early 1900s, a health resort. Head north to Backus Road; turn right past the headframe of the Cactus Mine.

Saddleback Butte State Park is 17 miles east of Lancaster on Avenue J. At the park's northwest corner, a small headquarters building, a parking lot, and some picnic tables are all the civilized embellishments you will find. Beyond is a splendid, sunny, 2-mile sweep of yucca-studded desert, culminating in alluring Saddleback Butte. Ask the ranger where to find the large waxy wildflowers known as desert candles.

Burton's Tropico Gold Mine and Museum lies 4 miles west of Rosamond, not far from Mojave, at the edge of a big forest of Joshua trees.

The mine yielded one of the most successful strikes in the Southland. In its shadowy interior, you'll see gold ore and miners' gear; proceed through a stope (the sloping cavity left after a vein is mined) to view the 900-foot-deep shaft, in operation until 1956. A tour guide explains common mining methods and procedures as you follow the vein out to the "glory hole," an open pit created by steam-shovel mining.

In the buildings, you'll see displays of mining equipment, a collection of rocks and gems, and relics such as period clothing and old newspapers. A safe guards the collection of gold nuggets.

To reach the mine, drive 11 miles north of Lancaster on State 14 to Rosamond Boulevard, then go west about 5 miles to Tropico Mojave Road and follow the signs uphill. The mine and museum displays are open for touring all year long, from 10 A.M. to 4:30 P.M. Thursday through Sunday. Expect a modest admission charge. For further information about the mine and museum, call (805) 256-2644.

San Joaquin Valley

Encompassing the southern half of California's great Central Valley, the San Joaquin Valley ranks high among the nation's producers of food, fuel, and fiber. Sunshine, fertile soil, a long growing season, and plentiful water from surrounding mountains create ideal growth conditions for cotton, citrus fruits, grapes, nuts, and a wide variety of other fruits and vegetables. The valley is also the state's top oil-producing region; it's not uncommon to see an oil well pumping in the midst of an expansive vineyard or potato field.

Sunshine and the vast reservoir system that feeds the valley's large-scale irrigation system attract an increasing number of newcomers and visitors. Major air, rail, and bus lines link the larger valley cities to metropolitan areas. Interstate Highway 5, an expressway along the sparsely populated western edge of the valley, and State Highway 99, cutting through the valley's center, offer easy north/south access. State highways 58 and 178 are major east/west routes.

Years ago, to enter the southern half of California's Central Valley from Los Angeles you followed the "Grapevine," a twisting road with all the thrills of an amusement park ride, on the Ridge Route over the Tehachapis and down into the outer limits of Bakersfield. No longer an obstacle course, today's road is a smooth freeway that gives no indication of the troubles experienced in building a wagon route over this same pass.

Valley cities are "gateways" to national parks and the high country of the Sierra Nevada. During peak seasons, they make attractive bases for all-day trips into the nearby mountains.

Bakersfield

Situated on the south bank of the Kern River in the southern end of the San Joaquin Valley is Bakersfield—county seat for Kern County and a junction of major highways through Southern California.

One of the Southland's fastest growing cities, Bakersfield is a center for agriculture, petroleum, tourism, and related industries. Both residents and visitors enjoy the city's numerous parks, playgrounds, golf courses, tennis clubs, and riding academies. The nearby Kern River provides a natural setting for fishing, hiking, camping, picnicking, and horseback riding.

The city is a popular location for state and national equestrian contests and for competitions in auto and boat drag racing, tennis, swimming, and white-water rafting.

Kern County Museum's Pioneer Village, a 12-acre indoor-outdoor museum, makes frontier history come alive. Outdoors, about 40 historic structures (originals and restorations) are laid out as a model town of the 1870–1910 period.

Indoors, the main museum houses fossils from the nearby McKittrick oil field area, a diorama of birds and mammals, Indian relics, and the most unusual curiosity—a dog-powered butter churn. The museum at 3801 Chester Avenue and the village are open weekdays from 8 A.M. to 5 P.M., weekends and holidays from 10 A.M. to 5 P.M. Admission to the museum is free; there's a slight charge for the outdoor displays.

Fort Tejon, an old military post established by the U.S. Army in 1854, is handily situated for today's travelers, just off the freeway near Lebec (30 miles south of Bakersfield). Fort Tejon once quartered the Army's most unusual unit—the First Dragoons and Camel Corps.

Abandoned in 1864, the post was restored as a State Historic Park. It's open daily the year around. You can picnic on the grounds in the shade of some lovely old trees. On the third Sunday of each month from May through October, a "Civil War" skirmish takes place at 10 A.M., 11 A.M., and 2 P.M.

Index

C O M B I N E D   I N D E X

A comprehensive index to both volumes appears
on the following pages. This is in addition to
the individual book indexes which appear on
page 128 of each title.

Northern California

*Morning light filters through redwoods at
Richardson Grove State Park*

Southern California

*Gondola carries passengers through watery world
of Naples, near Long Beach*

San Francisco cable car

Carson Mansion, Eureka

CHAD SLATTERY

Wilshire Boulevard, L.A.'s Miracle Mile

COMBINED INDEX